First World War
and Army of Occupation
War Diary
France, Belgium and Germany

18 DIVISION
Divisional Troops
30 Mobile Veterinary Section,
Divisional Train (150, 151, 152, 153, Companies A.S.C.),
Divisional Salvage Company
and Divisional Anti-Gas School
23 July 1915 - 11 November 1918

WO95/2032

The Naval & Military Press Ltd
www.nmarchive.com
Published in association with The National Archives

Published by

The Naval & Military Press Ltd

Unit 10 Ridgewood Industrial Park,

Uckfield, East Sussex,

TN22 5QE England

Tel: +44 (0) 1825 749494

www.naval-military-press.com

www.nmarchive.com

This diary has been reprinted in facsimile from the original. Any imperfections are inevitably reproduced and the quality may fall short of modern type and cartographic standards.

Contents

Document type	Place/Title	Date From	Date To
Heading	WO95/2032 18th Division Divisional Troops 30 Mobile Veterinary Section Jul 1915-Jan 1919		
Heading	18th Division 30th Mob Vety Secn Jly 1915 Jan 1919		
Miscellaneous	War Diary 30th Mobile Vet Sec.		
Heading	18th Division 30th Mobile Vet. Sect. Vol I Jly Aug & Sept 15 Jan 19		
War Diary	Codford	27/07/1915	27/07/1915
War Diary	Havre	28/07/1915	28/07/1915
War Diary	Flesselles	29/07/1915	29/07/1915
War Diary	Frechincourt	08/08/1915	23/08/1915
War Diary	Ville-Sur Ancre	23/08/1915	17/09/1915
War Diary	Mericourt L'Abbe	18/09/1915	30/09/1915
Heading	18th Division 30th Mobile Vet. Sect. Vol. 2 Oct 15		
War Diary	Mericourt L'Abbe	01/10/1915	27/10/1915
Heading	18th Division 30th Mob. Vet. Sect Vol. 3 Nov 15		
War Diary	Mericourt L'Abbe	01/11/1915	29/11/1915
Heading	30th Mobile Vet. Section Dec Vols 4		
War Diary	Mericourt L'Abbe	01/12/1915	31/12/1915
Heading	30th Mob Vet Sec 18th Div Vol. 5.6.		
War Diary	Mericourt L'Abbe	01/01/1916	04/02/1916
War Diary	Ribemont	05/02/1916	26/02/1916
Heading	XVIII 30 M Vet S Vol 7		
War Diary	Ribemont	01/03/1916	04/03/1916
War Diary	Montigny	06/03/1916	19/03/1916
War Diary	Ribemont	20/03/1916	31/03/1916
War Diary	Sailly Laurette	04/04/1916	03/05/1916
War Diary	Picquigny	05/05/1916	08/06/1916
War Diary	St. Pierre A Gouy	10/06/1916	22/06/1916
War Diary	Sailly E. Sec	23/06/1916	30/06/1916
Heading	18 Vol II 30th Mobile Veterinary Section		
War Diary	Sailly-Le Sec.	01/07/1916	01/07/1916
War Diary	With Advanced Collecting Station	02/07/1916	04/07/1916
War Diary	Bois de Tailles	06/07/1916	21/07/1916
War Diary	Allonville	21/07/1916	21/07/1916
War Diary	Longpre Les Corps Saints	22/07/1916	23/07/1916
War Diary	Lynde	24/07/1916	28/07/1916
War Diary	Fletre	29/07/1916	31/07/1916
Heading	30 M.V.S. Vol 12		
War Diary	Fletre	04/08/1916	04/08/1916
War Diary	Sequemeau	05/08/1916	25/08/1916
War Diary	Le Quesnel	26/08/1916	04/09/1916
War Diary	Rebreuviette	09/09/1916	09/09/1916
War Diary	Le Marais Sec	10/09/1916	10/09/1916
War Diary	Acheux	11/09/1916	24/09/1916
War Diary	Hedauville	25/09/1916	05/10/1916
War Diary	Outre Bois	06/10/1916	15/10/1916
War Diary	Hem. ToutenCourt	16/10/1916	16/10/1916
War Diary	Albert	17/10/1916	23/11/1916
War Diary	L'Heure	25/11/1916	30/11/1916
Miscellaneous	18th Division G	09/01/1917	09/01/1917

War Diary	L'Heure	03/12/1916	11/12/1916
War Diary	Hautvillers	13/12/1916	21/12/1916
War Diary	Abbeville Precinct	21/12/1916	11/01/1917
War Diary	Yvrench	11/01/1917	11/01/1917
War Diary	Bernaville	12/01/1917	12/01/1917
War Diary	Marieux	14/01/1917	14/01/1917
War Diary	Martinsart	16/01/1917	23/03/1917
War Diary	Pont de Metz (by Amiens)	25/03/1917	25/03/1917
War Diary	Morbecque	31/03/1917	24/04/1917
War Diary	Pernes	26/04/1917	26/04/1917
War Diary	Habarcq	27/04/1917	27/04/1917
War Diary	Agny	28/04/1917	16/05/1917
War Diary	Bois Leux Au Mont	17/05/1917	17/06/1917
War Diary	Couin	18/06/1917	04/07/1917
War Diary	Hopoutre	05/07/1917	15/08/1917
War Diary	Lederzeele	16/08/1917	04/09/1917
War Diary	Esquelbecq	05/09/1917	22/09/1917
War Diary	Sh 27 F28b 1.4	23/09/1917	30/09/1917
War Diary	Sh 27 F28b 1.4 Between Poperinghe & Proven	02/10/1917	10/10/1917
War Diary	Sh. 28 A22 C 6.0	11/10/1917	30/10/1917
War Diary	Sh. 28 A14 b 8.3	30/10/1917	31/10/1917
War Diary	Sh. 28 Belgium A 14 b 8.3	04/11/1917	09/11/1917
War Diary	Sh 28. Belgium A14 b 8.8	10/11/1917	18/12/1917
War Diary	Proven	18/12/1917	31/12/1917
War Diary	Sh 28 A 2 d 9.9	03/01/1918	29/01/1918
War Diary	Proven	30/01/1918	08/02/1918
War Diary	Salency France Sh Yoe 1/40,000 J18a	09/02/1918	15/02/1918
War Diary	Grandru	16/02/1918	24/03/1918
War Diary	Dive-Le-Franc	24/03/1918	24/03/1918
War Diary	Pimprez	25/03/1918	25/03/1918
War Diary	Carlpont	26/03/1918	26/03/1918
War Diary	Audignicourt	27/03/1918	27/03/1918
War Diary	Choisy	29/03/1918	29/03/1918
War Diary	Arsy	30/03/1918	30/03/1918
War Diary	La Neuville En Hez	31/03/1918	31/03/1918
Miscellaneous	A Form Messages And Signals.		
War Diary	Auchy La Montagne	01/04/1918	01/04/1918
War Diary	Loeuilly	02/04/1918	02/04/1918
War Diary	Saleux	03/04/1918	30/04/1918
War Diary	Crouy	05/05/1918	05/05/1918
War Diary	Montigny	06/05/1918	13/07/1918
War Diary	Breilly	15/07/1918	31/07/1918
War Diary	St. Gratien	07/08/1918	12/08/1918
War Diary	Montigny	12/08/1918	24/08/1918
War Diary	Warloy	24/08/1918	26/08/1918
War Diary	Albert	26/08/1918	31/08/1918
War Diary	Mametz Wood Sh S4D X 23 b 2.9	01/09/1918	16/09/1918
War Diary	Moislains	16/09/1918	01/10/1918
War Diary	Montauban	01/10/1918	01/10/1918
War Diary	Montigny	02/10/1918	14/10/1918
War Diary	Combles	17/10/1918	17/10/1918
War Diary	Ronssoy	18/10/1918	18/10/1918
War Diary	Serain	19/10/1918	19/10/1918
War Diary	Maretz	20/10/1918	23/10/1918
War Diary	Le Cateau	24/10/1918	31/10/1918

Miscellaneous	19 Vol 38 War Diary of 39 Mile War Month of November 1918	30/11/1918	30/11/1918
War Diary	Trefcon	01/11/1918	06/11/1918
War Diary	Bantouxelle	07/11/1918	07/11/1918
War Diary	Arleux	08/11/1918	08/11/1918
War Diary	Pont-A Marcq.	09/11/1918	09/11/1918
War Diary	Gaufrain Ramecroix	10/11/1918	10/11/1918
War Diary	Villers St Amand	11/11/1918	11/11/1918
War Diary	Maffle	12/11/1918	12/11/1918
War Diary	Callannelle	13/11/1918	17/11/1918
War Diary	Neufvilles	18/11/1918	18/11/1918
War Diary	Eccausinnes	19/11/1918	21/11/1918
War Diary	St Gery	22/11/1918	22/11/1918
War Diary	Franc Waret	23/11/1918	24/11/1918
War Diary	Oteppe	25/11/1918	27/11/1918
War Diary	Tilff	29/11/1918	29/11/1918
War Diary	Dohlain	30/11/1918	30/11/1918
War Diary	Le Cateau	01/11/1918	13/11/1918
War Diary	Serain	13/11/1918	16/12/1918
War Diary	Ligny-En Cambresis	17/12/1918	29/01/1919
Heading	WO95/2032 18 Division Divisional Troops Divisional Train (150,151,152,153, Companies A.S.C.) Jul 1915-Apr 1919		
Heading	18th Division 18th Divisional Train ASC 1915 Jly-1919 Apl (150-153 Coys ASC)		
Miscellaneous	War Diary 18th Div. Train		
Heading	18th. Division 18th Divisional Train Vol I July 1915		
War Diary	Codford	23/07/1915	24/07/1915
War Diary	Havre	25/07/1915	26/07/1915
War Diary	Flesselles	27/07/1915	31/07/1915
Heading	18th Division 18th Div L. Train Vol. 2 August 15		
War Diary	Flesselles	01/08/1915	07/08/1915
War Diary	Montigny	08/08/1915	19/08/1915
War Diary	Heilly	20/08/1915	31/08/1915
Miscellaneous			
War Diary	Flesselles	01/08/1915	07/08/1915
War Diary	Montigny	08/08/1915	19/08/1915
War Diary	Heilly	20/08/1915	31/08/1915
Heading	18th Division 18th Divl Train Vol III Sept. 15		
War Diary	Heilly	01/09/1915	16/09/1915
War Diary	Heilly	01/09/1915	30/09/1915
Heading	18th Division 18th Divl. Train Vol 4 Oct 15		
War Diary	Heilly	01/10/1915	31/10/1915
Heading	18th Divl. Train Vol 5 Nov 15		
War Diary	Heilly	01/11/1915	30/11/1915
Heading	18th Divl. Train Vol. 6 Dec 15		
War Diary	Heilly	01/12/1915	31/12/1915
Heading	18th Divl. Train Vol. 7 Jan 16		
War Diary	Heilly	01/01/1916	31/01/1916
Heading	18th Div L. Train Vol 8		
War Diary	Heilly	01/02/1916	04/02/1916
War Diary	Ribemont	05/02/1916	29/02/1916
Heading	18th Div Train Vol 9		
War Diary	Ribemont	01/03/1916	08/03/1916
War Diary	Montigny	09/03/1916	19/03/1916
War Diary	Etinehem	20/03/1916	04/05/1916

War Diary	Cavillon	05/05/1916	22/06/1916
War Diary	Chipilly	23/06/1916	30/06/1916
Heading	18th Divisional Train Vol. 13		
Miscellaneous	Head Quarters 18th Division	03/08/1916	03/08/1916
War Diary	Chipilly	01/07/1916	02/07/1916
War Diary	Sailly-Le-Sec.	03/07/1916	20/07/1916
War Diary	Hallen-Court	21/07/1916	23/07/1916
War Diary	Renescure	24/07/1916	31/07/1916
Miscellaneous	A Form. Messages And Signals.		
Heading	18th Division Train A.S.C Vol 14		
War Diary	Renescure	01/08/1916	01/08/1916
War Diary	Croix Du Bac	02/08/1916	23/08/1916
War Diary	Bailleul	24/08/1916	24/08/1916
War Diary	Roellecourt	25/08/1916	08/09/1916
War Diary	Doullens	09/09/1916	10/09/1916
War Diary	Acheux	11/09/1916	25/09/1916
War Diary	Hedauville	25/09/1916	05/10/1916
War Diary	Bernaville	06/10/1916	15/10/1916
War Diary	Albert	16/10/1916	31/10/1916
War Diary	Beauval	01/10/1916	31/10/1916
War Diary	Albert	01/11/1916	21/11/1916
War Diary	Contay	22/11/1916	22/11/1916
War Diary	Doullens	23/11/1916	23/11/1916
War Diary	Bernaville	24/11/1916	24/11/1916
War Diary	Yvrench	25/11/1916	27/11/1916
War Diary	Buigny St Maclou	28/11/1916	10/01/1917
War Diary	Yvrench	11/01/1917	11/01/1917
War Diary	Bernaville	12/01/1917	13/01/1917
War Diary	Marieux	14/01/1917	15/01/1917
War Diary	Bouzincourt	16/01/1917	24/03/1917
War Diary	Steenbecque	25/03/1917	25/04/1917
War Diary	Pernes	26/04/1917	28/04/1917
War Diary	Achicourt	29/04/1917	11/05/1917
War Diary	Arras	12/05/1917	15/05/1917
War Diary	Bois Leux St. Marc	16/05/1917	17/06/1917
War Diary	Couin	18/06/1917	03/07/1917
War Diary	Steenvoorde	04/07/1917	06/07/1917
War Diary	Bussebom G 22 d 1.7	07/07/1917	08/07/1917
War Diary	G 22 d 1.7.	09/07/1917	30/07/1917
War Diary	Reninghelst	31/07/1917	03/08/1917
War Diary	Canal Reserve Area	04/08/1917	12/08/1917
War Diary	Reninghelst	13/08/1917	14/08/1917
War Diary	Lederzeele	15/08/1917	17/08/1917
War Diary	Answer for O/C. Train Trench	17/08/1917	22/08/1917
War Diary	Lederzeele	23/08/1917	02/09/1917
War Diary	Esquelbecq	03/09/1917	23/09/1917
War Diary	Poperinghe	24/09/1917	07/10/1917
War Diary	Peselhoek	08/10/1917	24/10/1917
War Diary	Proven Road	25/10/1917	25/10/1917
War Diary	Poperinghe	26/10/1917	31/10/1917
War Diary	Proven	01/11/1917	04/11/1917
War Diary	I. Camp	05/11/1917	21/11/1917
War Diary	Elverdinghe	22/11/1917	23/12/1917
War Diary	Roussbrugge	24/12/1917	03/01/1918
War Diary	Elverdinghe	04/01/1918	29/01/1918
War Diary	Rousbrugge	30/01/1918	09/02/1918

War Diary	Noyon	10/02/1918	16/02/1918
War Diary	Baboeuf	17/02/1918	28/02/1918
War Diary	Villequier Aumont	01/03/1918	21/03/1918
War Diary	Baboeuf	22/03/1918	23/03/1918
War Diary	Dive-Le-Franc	24/03/1918	24/03/1918
War Diary	Pimprez	25/03/1918	25/03/1918
War Diary	Carlepont	26/03/1918	26/03/1918
War Diary	Adingli-Court	27/03/1918	28/03/1918
War Diary	Choisy	29/03/1918	29/03/1918
War Diary	Arsy	30/03/1918	30/03/1918
War Diary	Laneuvelle	31/03/1918	31/03/1918
War Diary	Auchy La-Montagne	01/04/1918	01/04/1918
War Diary	Loeuilly	02/04/1918	02/04/1918
War Diary	Saleux	03/04/1918	13/04/1918
War Diary	Saleux Area	14/04/1918	25/04/1918
War Diary	Saleux	26/04/1918	27/04/1918
War Diary	Riencourt	28/04/1918	04/05/1918
War Diary	Bavelincourt	05/05/1918	23/05/1918
War Diary	Molliens Au Bois	24/05/1918	23/06/1918
War Diary	Field	23/06/1918	23/06/1918
War Diary	Molliens-au-Bois	24/06/1918	13/07/1918
War Diary	Cavillon	14/07/1918	31/07/1918
War Diary	Querrieu	01/08/1918	06/08/1918
War Diary	St Gratien	07/08/1918	13/08/1918
War Diary	Contay	14/08/1918	24/08/1918
War Diary	Ribemont	25/08/1918	31/08/1918
Miscellaneous	Head Quarters. "A" 18th Division.	07/10/1918	07/10/1918
War Diary	Albert 62 Sheet X-29.d Central	01/09/1918	15/09/1918
War Diary	Moslains	16/09/1918	30/09/1918
War Diary	Montigny	01/10/1918	16/10/1918
War Diary	Ronssoy Wood	17/10/1918	18/10/1918
War Diary	Serain	19/10/1918	19/10/1918
War Diary	Maretz	20/10/1918	22/10/1918
War Diary	Le Cateau	23/10/1918	12/11/1918
War Diary	Serain	13/11/1918	30/11/1918
Miscellaneous	Head Quarters "A" 18th Division	10/01/1919	10/01/1919
War Diary	Serain	01/12/1918	16/12/1918
War Diary	Ligny	17/12/1918	31/12/1918
War Diary	Field	01/01/1919	27/01/1919
War Diary	Ligny en Cambresis	01/02/1919	28/02/1919
Miscellaneous	Head Quarters. "A" 18th Division.	08/05/1919	08/05/1919
War Diary	Ligny en Cambresis	01/04/1919	30/04/1919
Heading	WO95/2032 18th Division Divisional Troops. Divisional Salvage Company Jul 1916-June 1917		
Heading	18th Division Salvage Coy. Jly 1916-Jun 1917		
Miscellaneous	War Diary Salvage Coy		
Miscellaneous	War Diary 18th Div Salvage Coy		
War Diary	Elinchem	01/07/1916	01/07/1916
War Diary	Grovetown & Carnoy	02/07/1916	02/07/1916
War Diary	Carnoy	03/07/1916	11/07/1916
War Diary	Grovetown	13/07/1916	24/07/1916
War Diary	Hallencourt Renescure	24/07/1916	31/07/1916
Miscellaneous	War Diary of Salvage Co 18th Division		
Miscellaneous			
Heading	War Diary August. Salvage Co. 18th Division		
War Diary		01/08/1916	29/08/1916

Heading	1916 October War Diary Salvage Coy.		
War Diary	Pioneer Road	01/10/1916	18/10/1916
War Diary	Albert	22/10/1916	22/10/1916
War Diary	Ovillers	25/10/1916	31/10/1916
Heading	War Diary 18th Div Salvage Coy November 1916		
War Diary	Albert	01/11/1916	23/11/1916
War Diary	Acaeux	23/11/1916	23/11/1916
War Diary	Abbeville	24/11/1916	24/11/1916
War Diary	Buigny	25/11/1916	03/01/1917
War Diary	Havre	04/01/1917	05/01/1917
War Diary	Buigny	07/01/1917	09/01/1917
War Diary	Marieux	10/01/1917	11/01/1917
War Diary	Bouzincourt	12/01/1917	13/01/1917
War Diary	Aveluy	14/01/1917	31/01/1917
Heading	War Diary Salvage Coy. 18 Div February 1917 Vol 8		
War Diary	Aveluy	03/02/1917	27/03/1917
War Diary	Steenbecque	30/03/1917	31/03/1917
Heading	April War Diary Salvage Coy 18th Division		
War Diary	Steenbecque	01/04/1917	26/04/1917
War Diary	Pernes	27/04/1917	27/04/1917
War Diary	Achicourt	28/04/1917	28/04/1917
War Diary	Neuville Vitasse	30/04/1917	30/04/1917
Heading	Salvage Coy War Diary May 1917		
War Diary	Neuville Vitasse	01/05/1917	11/05/1917
War Diary	Mercatel	15/05/1917	18/05/1917
War Diary	Boisleux St Marc	24/05/1917	29/05/1917
Heading	War Diary June		
War Diary	Boisleux St Marc	01/06/1917	24/06/1917
Heading	WO95/2032 18th Division Divisional Troops Divisional Anti-Gas School Jul 1916-Nov 1918		
Heading	18th Division Divl Anti Gas School Jly 1916-Nov 1918		
Heading	War Diary July 1916 Vol 18 18th Div Anti-Gas School Vol I		
Miscellaneous	18th Division	13/07/1916	13/07/1916
War Diary	Bray	01/07/1917	02/07/1917
War Diary	Grovetown	03/07/1917	21/07/1917
War Diary	Hallencourt	22/07/1917	24/07/1917
War Diary	Renescure	25/07/1917	31/07/1917
Miscellaneous	Anti-Gas School 18th Division Vol 2		
Heading	War Diary For August 1916		
War Diary	Thieshouk	01/08/1917	02/08/1917
War Diary	Meteren	03/08/1917	04/08/1917
War Diary	Croix Du Bac	04/08/1917	23/08/1917
War Diary	Bailleul	24/08/1917	25/08/1917
War Diary	Roellecourt	26/08/1917	30/08/1917
Heading	War Diary For September 1916 Vol 3		
War Diary	Roellecourt	01/09/1917	08/09/1917
War Diary	Doullens	09/09/1917	10/09/1917
War Diary	Acheux	11/09/1917	12/09/1917
War Diary	Lealvillers	13/09/1917	13/09/1917
War Diary	Arqueves	14/09/1917	14/09/1917
War Diary	Puchevillers	15/09/1917	15/09/1917
War Diary	Acheux	16/09/1917	24/09/1917
War Diary	Hedauville	25/09/1917	30/09/1917
Heading	War Diary Vol. IV For October, 1916		
War Diary	Hedauville	01/10/1917	04/10/1917

War Diary	Bernaville	07/10/1917	14/10/1917
War Diary	Albert	16/10/1917	31/10/1917
Heading	18th Divisional Gas School War Diary. Vol. V November. 1916		
War Diary	Albert	01/11/1917	21/11/1917
War Diary	Buigny St Maclou	22/11/1917	30/11/1917
Heading	18 Div. Gas School War Diary December. 1916 Vol. VI		
War Diary	Buigny St Maclou	01/12/1917	31/12/1917
Heading	War Diary 18th Div. Gas School January 1917 Vol 7		
War Diary	Buigny St Maclou	01/01/1917	16/01/1917
War Diary	Hedauville	17/01/1917	31/01/1917
Heading	War Diary February, 1917 Vol. 8		
War Diary	Hedauville	01/02/1917	21/02/1917
War Diary	Bouzincourt	22/02/1917	28/02/1917
Heading	18th Divisional Anti Gas School War Diary Vol IX For March 1917		
War Diary	Bouzincourt	01/03/1917	26/03/1917
War Diary	Steenbecque	27/03/1917	31/03/1917
Heading	War Diary April, 1917 Vol. X.		
War Diary	Steenbecque	01/04/1917	26/04/1917
Heading	18th Divisional Anti-Gas School War Diary Vol. XI May 1917		
War Diary	Agny	01/05/1917	31/05/1917
Heading	War Diary of 18th Divl. Anti-Gas School Vol. XII. June 1917		
War Diary	Agny	01/06/1917	17/06/1917
War Diary	Couin	17/06/1917	30/06/1917
Heading	War Diary For July Vol. XIII		
War Diary	Couin	01/07/1917	04/07/1917
War Diary	Steenvoorde	06/07/1917	07/07/1917
War Diary	Reninghelst	10/07/1917	31/07/1917
Heading	War Diary For August 1917. Vol 14		
War Diary	Reninghelst	01/08/1917	15/08/1917
War Diary	Lederzeele	15/08/1917	30/08/1917
Heading	War Diary For September Vol 15.		
War Diary	Lederzeele	01/09/1917	03/09/1917
War Diary	Esquelbecq	04/09/1917	24/09/1917
War Diary	Poperinghe	25/09/1917	30/09/1917
Heading	War Diary For October 1917 Vol. XVI.		
War Diary	Poperinghe	01/10/1917	10/10/1917
War Diary	Border Camp	11/10/1917	25/10/1917
War Diary	Poperinghe	25/10/1917	29/10/1917
War Diary	Proven	30/10/1917	30/10/1917
Heading	War Diary For November. 1917. Vol. XVII		
War Diary	Proven	01/11/1917	04/11/1917
War Diary	J Camp	05/11/1917	10/11/1917
War Diary	Elverdinghe Chateau	11/11/1917	30/11/1917
Heading	War Diary For December 17. Vol. XVIII		
War Diary	Elverdinghe Chateau	01/12/1917	16/12/1917
War Diary	Rousbrugge	18/12/1917	31/12/1917
Heading	War Diary For January 1918. Vol. XIX.		
War Diary	Rousbrugge	01/01/1918	03/01/1918
War Diary	Elverdinghe Chateau	08/01/1918	30/01/1918
War Diary	Rousbrugge	31/01/1918	05/02/1918
War Diary	Rousbrugge Salency	08/02/1918	17/02/1918

War Diary	Baboeuf	18/02/1918	27/02/1918
War Diary	Rouez	28/02/1918	01/03/1918
War Diary	Villequier Aumont	01/03/1918	21/03/1918
War Diary	Ugny-Le-Gay	23/03/1918	23/03/1918
War Diary	Baboeuf	24/03/1918	25/03/1918
War Diary	Estrees-St Denis	28/03/1918	28/03/1918
War Diary	Villers Cotterets	28/03/1918	01/04/1918
War Diary	Saleux	04/04/1918	04/04/1918
War Diary	Amiens	12/04/1918	12/04/1918
War Diary	St Fuscien	14/04/1918	24/04/1918
War Diary	Cavillon	27/04/1918	04/05/1918
War Diary	Bavelincourt	05/05/1918	02/06/1918
War Diary	Contay	03/06/1918	12/07/1918
War Diary	Cavillon	13/07/1918	01/08/1918
War Diary	St Gratien	02/08/1918	12/08/1918
War Diary	Cautley	12/08/1918	25/08/1918
War Diary	Wortley Baillon	26/08/1918	29/08/1918
War Diary	Ribemont S/A	30/08/1918	31/08/1918
War Diary	Bernafay Wood	05/09/1918	16/09/1918
War Diary	Lieramont	17/08/1918	24/08/1918
War Diary	Combles	25/08/1918	27/08/1918
War Diary	Lieramont	28/08/1918	30/08/1918
War Diary	Beaucourt	01/10/1918	16/10/1918
War Diary	Le Cateau	22/10/1918	11/11/1918

(1)

WO 95/2032

18 Division

Divisional Troops

30 Mobile Veterinary Section

Jul. 1915 - Jan 1919

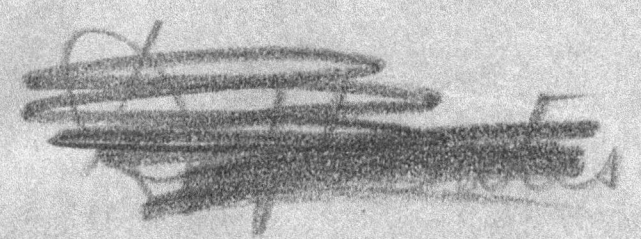

18TH DIVISION

30TH MOB VETY SECN

JLY 1915-JAN 1919

[redacted]

War Diary

30th Mobile Vet. Sec.

18th Division

121/7/53

30th Mobile Vet: Sect:

Vol: I

Jly Aug & Sept. 15

Jan '19

Instructions regarding War Diaries and Intelligence Summaries are contained in F. S. Regs., Part II. and the Staff Manual respectively. Title Pages will be prepared in manuscript.

WAR DIARY

~~or~~

~~INTELLIGENCE SUMMARY~~

(Erase heading not required.)

Army Form C. 2118

Place	Date	Hour	Summary of Events and Information	Remarks and references to Appendices
CODFORD	27.7.15		Entrained at WYLYE ~~Station~~ departing at 4.30 am. Detrained Southampton 8.45 am, & embarked on Anglo California sailing at 5 pm.	
HAVRE	28.7.15		Disembarked at HAVRE at noon. Entrained at Gare le Marchandises 6 pm. departing at 10 pm.	
FLESSELLES	29.7.15		Detrained AMIENS 8.30 am marched to FLESSELLES arriving 4.45 pm, & went into billets	
FRECHINCOURT	8.8.15		In accordance with instructions received marched to FRECHINCOURT & took up billet there.	
	9.8.15		Trucked ten horses at MERICOURT-RIBEMONT for No 5 Vety Hospl ABBEVILLE this being the first batch of sick horses despatched since arrival in the country	
	10.8.15		O.C. (Capt W.N. ROWSTON) received instructions to report at War Office to take over as ADVS in 5th Army	
	12.8.15		O.C. handed over to Lt ROWBOTHAM & left for England	
	13.8.15		Lt Rowbotham made a tour by motor car inspecting horses left with natives in former Divisional Area with a view to collection.	
	14.8.15		Lt. E.E. Jelbart AVC arrived & took over from Lt Rowbotham & collected four horses left with inhabitants.	
	15.8.15		Made a long tour collecting seven horses left with inhabitants. Horses were far apart & from FRECHINCOURT – the round took 11 hours.	
	18.8.15		Despatch nine sick horses from MERICOURT ~~[illegible]~~ RIBEMONT to No5 Vety Hospl Abbeville	
	22.8.15		Pte. EJ GRINDLAY. SE 6521 evacuated to Hospital to be operated upon for varicose veins	E.E.J.

1875 Wt. W593/826 1,000,000 4/15 J.B.C. & A. A.D.S.S./Forms/C. 2118.

Instructions regarding War Diaries and Intelligence Summaries are contained in F. S. Regs., Part II. and the Staff Manual respectively. Title Pages will be prepared in manuscript.

WAR DIARY
or
~~INTELLIGENCE SUMMARY~~
(Erase heading not required.)

Army Form C. 2118.

Place	Date	Hour	Summary of Events and Information	Remarks and references to Appendices
FRECHINCOURT	23/8/15		Owing to Division moving forward, influx of cases admitted to Section, some for evacuation to Hospital, but several suitable for treatment here & return to unit	
VILLE-SUR ANCRE		6 pm	Having received instructions — Section marched to VILLE-SUR-ANCRE and went into billets. Five horses unable to travel left in charge of Maire of FRECHINCOURT	
	24.8.15		Informed by A.D.V.S. that on present distribution of areas it will be necessary that I take vety charge - in addition to the Mobile Section - of all the horses in the Ville sur ANCRE and TREUX areas. comprising one Fd ambulance, Divisional Cavalry, two batteries RFA. and three Brigade Ammun: Cols R.F.A. but that this would probably only be a temporary arrangement.	
	27.8.15		Went to FRECHINCOURT to see horses left behind - decided that two should be destroyed & having heard of a Boucher Chevaline in CORBIE sent Interpreter to make arrangements with him.	
	28.8.15		Went to Corbie & saw these two horses destroyed in the Public abattoir. - destroyed humanely by a blow on the head from a hammer & then bled. Informed that there is rigid inspection first of ~~animal~~ horse alive & then of carcase by a veterinarian particularly with view of detecting glanders. The horses were taken to Corbie in a "float" and the price obtained was Francs 100 each — an advance of 200 % on price obtainable last spring in Bethune. BETHUNE.	

[signature]

1875 Wt. W593/826 1,000,000 4/15 J.B.C. & A. A.D.S.S./Forms/C. 2118.

Army Form C. 2118.

Instructions regarding War Diaries and Intelligence Summaries are contained in F. S. Regs., Part II. and the Staff Manual respectively. Title Pages will be prepared in manuscript.

WAR DIARY
or
~~INTELLIGENCE SUMMARY~~
(Erase heading not required.)

Place	Date	Hour	Summary of Events and Information	Remarks and references to Appendices
VILLE-SUR-ANCRE	31.8.15		Despatched 16 horses from MERICOURT-RIBEMONT to ABBEVILLE S. L. Gilbert Lt AVC OC No 30 Mobile Vety Section 18th Division	

1875 Wt. W593/826 1,000,000 4/15 J.B.C. & A. A.D.S.S./Forms/C. 2118.

Instructions regarding War Diaries and Intelligence Summaries are contained in F. S. Regs., Part II. and the Staff Manual respectively. Title Pages will be prepared in manuscript.

WAR DIARY
or
~~INTELLIGENCE SUMMARY~~
(Erase heading not required.)

Army Form C. 2118.

Place	Date	Hour	Summary of Events and Information	Remarks and references to Appendices
VILLE-SUR ANCRE	1.9.15		In the present state of affairs when there is no long trekking to be done & the line is stationary, it is found that a considerable amount of the men's time & labour is taken up with the horses belonging to the Section. This is particularly felt when the number of sick horses is large – as is frequent, for many cases are such that a fortnight's treatment in the Section fits them for duty again & this can be done when there is little prospect of moving. But of course, there will no doubt come a time when the establishment of horses will be fully ~~not fit~~ required & to be ever ready is essential.	
	8.9.15		Went to DAOURS & collected a horse which had had azoturia – Thereafter went to FRECHINCOURT & MONTIGNY in regard to horses which had been left there. These horses had been attended to well by the inhabitants & their recovery was largely due to this. In chatting with the native M. DOUCHET at FRECHINCOURT I gathered that the maximum amount of Fr 1.75 was insufficient, in the present circumstances, to pay for fodder for a horse. He told me this not, I think, with the view of trying to better himself, for I found he was anything but of a grasping nature.	
	9.9.15		Went to CORBIE to see 2 horses sold to butcher destroyed.	
	10.9.15		Sent 19 horses to No 5 Vety Hospl ABBEVILLE	
	11.9.15		Sgt A.T.E. SPILSTED No SE 1915 reported for duty with Section.	
	12.9.15		Pte. W. TAYLOR S.E. 3463 reported for duty with section. – making it one overstrength	

[illegible signature]

1875 Wt. W593/826 1,000,000 4/15 J.B.C. & A. A.D.S.S./Forms/C. 2118.

Army Form C. 2118.

Instructions regarding War Diaries and Intelligence Summaries are contained in F. S. Regs., Part II. and the Staff Manual respectively. Title Pages will be prepared in manuscript.

WAR DIARY
or
~~INTELLIGENCE SUMMARY~~
(Erase heading not required.)

Place	Date	Hour	Summary of Events and Information	Remarks and references to Appendices
VILLE-SUR ANCRE	13·9·15		In view of the fact that under existing arrangements the N.C.O's are on guard every third night (~~& when one~~ has gone to ABBEVILLE with horses, every other night) appointed two Acting Supernumerary Lance Corporals. viz:– {Chas E. PAYNE No 6486. & {Wm M FOX - 6812	
	16·9·15		Sent 18 horses to No 5 Veterinary Hospital.	
	17·9·15		According to instructions proceeded to MERICOURT met the billeting officer & selected a billet to take up tomorrow	
			It having appeared from Div Routine Orders that under the distribution of the reduced number of Interpreters, the Section would be deprived of its Interpreter, & that there was no provision at all for the services of one – wrote ADVS on 15th inst pointing this out & representing that the work of the Section will be considerably hampered if the Interpreter is withdrawn even if it be given the services of another along with other units, – Received intimation from Division through ADVS ~~that~~ it would be impossible to allot one Interpreter for use of Section only ~~but that~~ the section could demand the services of Interpreter allotted to Divl mounted Troops & other units. Interpreter M DUMAS withdrawn of this date	
MERICOURT L'ABBÉ	18·9·15		Section moved to MERICOURT L'ABBÉ being now less than half mile from railhead and a mile & a half from Divisional H.Q. which promises to be much more convenient.	
			Went to Corbie to see that two horses sold to Butcher were destroyed.	
			[signature]	

1875 Wt. W593/826 1,000,000 4/15 J.B.C. & A. A.D.S.S./Forms/C. 2118.

Instructions regarding War Diaries and Intelligence Summaries are contained in F. S. Regs., Part II. and the Staff Manual respectively. Title Pages will be prepared in manuscript.

WAR DIARY
or
INTELLIGENCE ~~SUMMARY~~

(Erase heading not required.)

Army Form C. 2118.

Place	Date	Hour	Summary of Events and Information	Remarks and references to Appendices
MERICOURT L'ABBE	24.9.15		Sent 43 sick horses to No 5 Veterinary Hospital	
			Sgt P. J. Harvie No 1668 having applied & been recommended for an Infantry Commission proceeded today to report to ~~the~~ O.C. 28th London Regt at G.H.Q. for a fortnights service there before taking Cadets Course.	
	27.9.15		Liaison Officer having informed A.D.V.S. that he was now able to send an Interpreter to the Section Mons. PETIN arrived.	
	28.9.15		Sent 15 horses to No 5 Vety Hospl	
	30.9.15		D.D.V.S. (3rd Army) Lt Col. AXE called when passing but did not stay long	
			During the month I have been able to hire from a farmer a float capable of carrying two medium sized horses at once. This has been found to be very convenient & to considerably lessen the work of the O.C in circumstances like the present for instead of having disabled horses in different & far off parts, he can immediately on hearing of a case unable to travel send the float & have it brought to the section. It is also advantageous from the economic point of view, for instead of horses being left to the tender care of a native & seen only at intervals by a V.O. they may be at the Section continually under his supervision & regularly dressed. Further, possession of a float enables one to send to Hospital many cases - suitable for operation which would otherwise have to be destroyed. It is a point worthy of	

1875 Wt. W593/826 1,000,000 4/15 J.B.C. & A. A.D.S.S./Forms/C. 2118.

Instructions regarding War Diaries and Intelligence Summaries are contained in F. S. Regs., Part II. and the Staff Manual respectively. Title Pages will be prepared in manuscript.

WAR DIARY
or
INTELLIGENCE SUMMARY
(Erase heading not required.)

Army Form C. 2118.

Place	Date	Hour	Summary of Events and Information	Remarks and references to Appendices
MERICOURT L'ABBÉ	30-9-15		consideration (doubtless for not the first time) whether a float ought not to form part of the equipment of a Section – even in place of one of the G.S. Limber Waggons. Probably however, such an arrangement would only be found practicable when the line is stationary or moving only slowly. At other times the float might be cumbersome as a baggage cart + insufficient as an ambulance.	
			There has been a comparatively large number of horses evacuated to Hospital this month. Quite a large proportion of these have been cases of debility which it has been thought should be sent back in view of the approach of winter. The number of other cases has been swelled by the desire that the Division should not be hampered by sick horses in view of expected developments in the military situation.	
			Referring to Mobilisation Store Table A.F. G 1098-89 Augt 1915 Section 2 K. it is found ~~that~~ the number of Heel Ropes allowed (six) ~~is~~ inadequate & that one for each Section horse + an allowance for sick horses would be advantageous.	
			L E Jelbart Capt AVC O/c 30 Mobile Vety Section 18th Division	

1875 Wt. W593/826 1,000,000 4/15 J.B.C. & A. A.D.S.S./Forms/C. 2118.

18th Division

121/7593

L

30th Mobile Vet: Sect:
Vol: 2

Oct 15

AUD

Nil

Cu.

Instructions regarding War Diaries and Intelligence Summaries are contained in F. S. Regs., Part II. and the Staff Manual respectively. Title Pages will be prepared in manuscript.

WAR DIARY of 30 Mobile Veterinary Section

~~or~~

~~INTELLIGENCE SUMMARY~~

~~(Erase heading not required.)~~

Army Form C. 2118

Place	Date	Hour	Summary of Events and Information	Remarks and references to Appendices
MERICOURT L'ABBÉ	1-10/15		Evacuated 12 horses to No 5 Veterinary Hospital.	
"	7-10/15		" 24 " " " " "	
"	11-10/15		" 18 " " " " "	
"	16 10/15		No 464 Sgt ~~...~~ S.Y. BRADY reported for duty with Section	
"	20 10/15		Evacuated 20 horses to No 5 Veterinary Hospital.	
"	22 10/15		No 5640 Pte W.B. OWEN - Section Shoeing Smith admitted to Hospl	
"	24 10/15		No SE.1915 Sgt A.T.E. SPILSTED to England on 8 days leave	
"	25 10/15		No SE. 497 Sgt T. THORNLEY " "	
"	27 10/15		Evacuated 18 horses (including 2 Remount cases) to No 5 Veterinary Hospl	
			E.E. Jelbart Capt A.V.C.	
			O/C No 30 Mobile Veterinary Section	
			18th Division	

1875 Wt. W593/826 1,000,000 4/15 J.B.C. & A. A.D.S.S./Forms/C. 2118.

18th Division

30th Mob: Vet: Sect:
Vol: 3

121/7624

L

Nov 15

[illegible]

Instructions regarding War Diaries and Intelligence Summaries are contained in F. S. Regs., Part II. and the Staff Manual respectively. Title Pages will be prepared in manuscript.

WAR DIARY
~~or~~
~~INTELLIGENCE SUMMARY~~ of 30 Mobile Veterinary Section 18 Divn

(Erase heading not required.)

Army Form C. 2118

Place	Date	Hour	Summary of Events and Information	Remarks and references to Appendices
MERI-COURT L'ABBE	1 11/15		Evacuated to No. 9 Veterinary Hospital 9 sick + 2 remount cases	
	"		No. SE. 1915 Sgt E. SPILSTED rejoined from leave	
	"		No SE 6683 Pte. J. HARRIS admitted to Hospital	
	2.11.15		No. SE 497 Cpl J. THORNLEY rejoined from leave	
	8. 11/15		Visited DAOURS to see 3 horses left behind by 22nd Divl Train collected one of them. – put other two in more suitable places.	
	9 11/15		No. 3463 Pte W. TAYLOR + No. 6763 Pte W.C. DRURY 8 days leave to England	
	11 11/15		Evacuated to No. 5 Veterinary Hospital 16 sick horses	
	16 11/15		Re-visited DAOURS + collected the two horses seen on 8th inst.	
	"		No. SE 5884 Pte A. THROWER admitted to Hospital	
	17 11/15		Ptes TAYLOR + DRURY return from leave	
	18 11/15		Evacuated to No. 5 Veterinary Hospital 23 sick horses	
	20 11/15		No. 5622 Shoeing Smith W. CROWTHER joined for duty	
	22 11/15		Visited PONT NOYELLES to collect a sick horse but found he had been sent to another mobile Section.	
	23 11/15		Visited ALLONVILLE and collected a horse left there	

1875 Wt. W593/826 1,000,000 4/15 J.B.C. & A. A.D.S.S./Forms/C. 2118.

Army Form C. 2118

WAR DIARY
or
~~INTELLIGENCE SUMMARY~~
(Erase heading not required.)

Instructions regarding War Diaries and Intelligence Summaries are contained in F. S. Regs., Part II. and the Staff Manual respectively. Title Pages will be prepared in manuscript.

Place	Date	Hour	Summary of Events and Information	Remarks and references to Appendices
MERI-COURT L'ABBE	25/11/15		Evacuated 13 sick horses to No 5 Veterinary Hospital	
	26/11/15		Village bombed by hostile aircraft but there were no casualties in the Section	
	29/11/15		Evacuated to No 5 Veterinary Hospital 10 sick + 3 remount cases.	
			E E Jelbart Capt AVC o/c 30 Mobile Veterinary Section 18th Division	

1875 Wt. W593/826 1,000,000 4/15 J.B.C. & A. A.D.S.S./Forms/C.

30th Mobile Vet: Section.

Dec

Fols 40

10

Army Form C. 2118

Instructions regarding War Diaries and Intelligence Summaries are contained in F. S. Regs., Part II. and the Staff Manual respectively. Title Pages will be prepared in manuscript.

WAR DIARY

~~or~~

~~INTELLIGENCE SUMMARY~~

(Erase heading not required.)

Place	Date	Hour	Summary of Events and Information	Remarks and references to Appendices
MERI-COURT L'ABBE	1 12/15		O.C. and No. 10434 Pte A.W. OLIVER to England on leave. Major L.M. VERNEY A.V.C. answering for O.C.	
	8 12/15		No. 2336 Pte J. MARTIN reported for duty	
	10 12/15		Evacuated 11 horses to Hospital	
	10 12/15		O.C. + Pte Oliver rejoined from leave (12th) Cpl THORNLEY. T. promoted Sgt from 1.12.15 (L.C. Order 42 d. 12.12.15)	
	17 12/15		No 6814 Pte F. ELGAR to England on leave	
	18 12/15		Evacuated 11 horses to Hospital	
	19 12/15		No 1915 ~~A~~ Sgt A.T.E. SPILSTED to No 6 Vety Hospl (L.C. Order 43 d. 15.12.15)	
	27 12/15		Pte ELGAR rejoined from leave. Evacuated 26 horses to Abbeville	
	28 12/15		Visited LA HOUSSOYE + collected sick horse left there by 53rd Division	
	31 12/15		Soldat A. PETIN (Interpreter) left on 6 days leave.	

E.E. Jelbart Capt A.V.C
O/c 30 Mobile Vety Section
18th Division

30th Mob. Vet Sec
18th Div.

Vol. 5.6.

Instructions regarding War Diaries and Intelligence Summaries are contained in F. S. Regs., Part II. and the Staff Manual respectively. Title Pages will be prepared in manuscript.

WAR DIARY of 30 Mobile Vety Section

or

~~INTELLIGENCE SUMMARY~~

(Erase heading not required.)

Army Form C. 2118

Place	Date	Hour	Summary of Events and Information	Remarks and references to Appendices
MERICOURT, L'ABBE	1.1.16		No 6107 Cpl W. Brown to England on 8 days leave	
	2.1.16		19 horses evacuated to ABBEVILLE	
	4.1.16		12 — do — — do —	
	8.1.16		Bombs dropped by hostile aircraft – one bomb dropping in Section yard but failed to explode	
	–		Soldat A. PETIN (~~Interpreter~~) rejoined from leave	
	11.1.16		No 6107 Cpl. W Brown rejoined from leave	
	12.1.16		No 7294 Pte W Brown to England on 8 days leave	
	13.1.16		22 horses evacuated to ABBEVILLE	
	14.1.16		Collected horse left at VAUX-SUR-SOMME by Reserve Park of another Division	
	15.1.16		Float presented to Corps by R.S.P.C.A. arrived from No 5 Vety Hospl. In place however of 2 sets of harness left with limber only one set issued with float.	
	17.1.16		Section visited by a number of Officers of this Division who are making a tour of the Division for information in regard to reorganisation	
	18.1.16		Evacuated 20 Horses to ABBEVILLE	
	21.1.16		No 7294 Pte W Brown rejoined from leave	
	22.1.16		No 5921 Cpl J. DOYLE to England on 8 days leave	

1875 Wt. W593/826 1,000,000 4/15 J.B.C. & A. A.D.S.S./Forms/C. 2118.

Instructions regarding War Diaries and Intelligence Summaries are contained in F. S. Regs., Part II. and the Staff Manual respectively. Title Pages will be prepared in manuscript.

WAR DIARY
or
INTELLIGENCE SUMMARY
(Erase heading not required.)

Army Form C. 2118

Place	Date	Hour	Summary of Events and Information	Remarks and references to Appendices
MERI-COURT L'ABBE	29.1.16		Evacuated 24 sick horses & 12 remount cases to ABBEVILLE	
	31.1.16		No. 5921 Cpl J. DOYLE rejoins from leave	
	-		Evacuated 32 horses to ABBEVILLE	
			G. L. Gelbart Capt AVC o/c 30 Mobile Vety Section 18th Division	

1875 Wt. W593/826 1,000,000 4/15 J.B.C. & A. A.D.S.S./Forms/C. 2118.

Army Form C. 2118

Instructions regarding War Diaries and Intelligence Summaries are contained in F. S. Regs., Part II. and the Staff Manual respectively. Title Pages will be prepared in manuscript.

WAR DIARY
or
~~INTELLIGENCE~~ SUMMARY of 30 Mobile Veterinary Section

(Erase heading not required.)

Place	Date	Hour	Summary of Events and Information	Remarks and references to Appendices
MERICOURT L'ABBÉ	2.2.16		No 2338 Pte J. MARTIN to England – 8 days leave	
	4.2.16		Evacuated 13 sick horses to No 22 Veterinary Hospital	
RIBEMONT	5.2.16		Section moved to RIBEMONT	
–	8.2.16		Evacuated 17 sick + 11 Remount cases to No 22 Veterinary Hospital	
	11.2.16		No 2338. Pte J. MARTIN rejoined from leave	
	14.2.16		Evacuated 16 sick horses to No 22 Veterinary Hospital	
	17.2.16		No 7138 Pte A. Hyde to England – 8 days leave	
	19.2.16		Evacuated 11 sick horses to No 22 Veterinary Hospital	
	22.2.16		Evacuated 12 sick + 1 remount case to —do—	
	26.2.16		No 7138 Pte A Hyde rejoined from leave	
			E. L. Gelbart Capt AVC O/c 30 MVS 18th Div	

1875 Wt. W593/826 1,000,000 4/15 J.B.C. & A. A.D.S.S./Forms/C. 2118.

XVIII

30 m vets

Vol 7

Instructions regarding War Diaries and Intelligence Summaries are contained in F. S. Regs., Part II. and the Staff Manual respectively. Title Pages will be prepared in manuscript.

WAR DIARY of 30 Mobile Vety Section 18 Division

or

~~INTELLIGENCE SUMMARY~~

(Erase heading not required.)

Army Form C. 2118

Place	Date	Hour	Summary of Events and Information	Remarks and references to Appendices
RIBEMONT	1·3·16		No 9403 Pte J. D. HUGHES reports for duty from No 14 Vety Hospl.	
			Evacuated 29 sick horses to ABBEVILLE.	
	2·3·16		Section Interpreter Soldat A. PETIN withdrawn from Section	
	4·3·16		Evacuated 31 horses to ABBEVILLE	
MONTIGNY	6·3·16		Section moved to place marginally noted	
	9·3·16		No 4353 Pte A.E. SEABOURNE – 8 days special leave to England 10 to 17 3/16	
	13·3·16		Evacuated 18 horses to abbeville	
	19·3·16		Evacuated 10 horses to abbeville	
RIBEMONT	20·3·16		Section returned to Ribemont	
	22·3·16		No 4353 Pte A.E. SEABOURNE rejoined from leave	
	29·3·16		Evacuated 24 horses to ABBEVILLE	
	31·3·16		Section moved to SAILLY-LAURETTE	

E. E. Jelbart Capt AVC
O/c 30 MVS
18 Divn

1875 Wt. W593/826 1,000,000 4/15 J.B.C. & A. A.D.S.S./Forms/C. 2118.

XVIII

Instructions regarding War Diaries and Intelligence Summaries are contained in F. S. Regs., Part II. and the Staff Manual respectively. Title Pages will be prepared in manuscript.

WAR DIARY ~~or~~ of 30 Mobile Vety Section
~~INTELLIGENCE SUMMARY~~
(Erase heading not required.)

Army Form C. 2118

30 MVS
Vol 8

Place	Date	Hour	Summary of Events and Information	Remarks and references to Appendices
SAILLY-LAURETTE	4 4/16		35 sick horses evacuated to No. 22 Veterinary Hospital	
	7 4/16		No. 9403 Pte. J. D. Hughes ten days leave to England (8 to 17 4/16)	
	8 4/16		31 sick horses evacuated to No. 22 Veterinary Hospital	
	12 4/16		25 - do - - do - - do -	
	19 4/16		38 - do - do - do.	
			No. 9403 Pte J. D. Hughes rejoined from leave	
	20 4/16		No. 6451 Pte G. Axhorn eight days special leave (21 to 28 4/16)	
	23 4/16		40 sick horses (+ 1 foal) evacuated to No. 22 Veterinary Hospital	
	28 4/16		20 - do - — do -	
	29 4/16		No. 6451 Pte. G. Axhorn rejoined from leave. During the month the number of horses evacuated to Hospital has been abnormally high viz - 189. This is accounted for by the number evacuated for attached troops, - 87 - being 54 for 30 Divn + 33 for Corps + Army Troops	

[illegible] Capt AVC
O/c 30 M.V.S.

1875 Wt. W593/826 1,000,000 4/15 J.B.C. & A. A.D.S.S./Forms/C. 2118.

XVIII VOL 9

Army Form C. 2118

Instructions regarding War Diaries and Intelligence Summaries are contained in F. S. Regs., Part II. and the Staff Manual respectively. Title Pages will be prepared in manuscript.

WAR DIARY
~~or~~
~~INTELLIGENCE SUMMARY~~ of 30 Mobile Veterinary Section.

(Erase heading not required.)

Place	Date	Hour	Summary of Events and Information	Remarks and references to Appendices
SAILLY LAURETTE	3.5.16		Evacuated 15 sick horses to No 22 Veterinary Hospital.	
PICQUIGNY	5.5.16		Section moved to PICQUIGNY	
	9.5.16		No 5622 S.S. W. CROWTHER ten days leave to England	
	14.5.16		O.C (Capt E.E. JELBART) ten days leave to England - Major L.M. VERNEY - answering for him	
	16.5.16		Evacuated 8 Sick horses to No 22 Veterinary Hospital	
	20.5.16		No 5622 S.S. W CROWTHER returned from leave	
	23.5.16		Evacuated 14 Sick horses to No 22 Veterinary Hospital	
	25.5.16		O.C. rejoined from leave	
	26.5.16		Evacuated 16 horses to No 22 Veterinary Hospital	
	30.5.16		No 64186 A/L/Cpl C. PAYNE to England on ten days leave	
			Evacuated 13 horses to No 22 Veterinary Hospital.	

E.E. Jelbart, Capt A.V.C
O/C 30 Mobile Veterinary Section
18 Division

1875 Wt. W593/826 1,000,000 4/15 J.B.C. & A. A.D.S.S./Forms/C. 2118.

Instructions regarding War Diaries and Intelligence Summaries are contained in F. S. Regs., Part II. and the Staff Manual respectively. Title Pages will be prepared in manuscript.

WAR DIARY
or
~~INTELLIGENCE SUMMARY~~ of 30 Mobile Veterinary Section
18 Division

(Erase heading not required.)

XVIV

Army Form C. 2118

June

Vol 10

Place	Date	Hour	Summary of Events and Information	Remarks and references to Appendices
PICQUIGNY	8 6/16		Evacuated 15 sick horses to Hospital	
ST. PIÈRRE À GOUY	10 6/16		Section moved to Convent LEGARD, St PIÈRRE À GOUY	
			No. 6486 L/Cpl C. PAYNE rejoined from leave	
	13 6/16		Evacuated 10 horses to Hospital	
	14 6/16		No. 5004 Pte N. McCALLUM 7 days leave to England	
	15 6/16		No. T/2 13580 Dr A. LEEMING ASC. 7 days special leave to England	
	18 6/16		Evacuated 10 horses to Hospital	
	22 6/16		do 8 - -	
	-	-	Pte McCallum rejoined from leave	
SAILLY le-SEC	23 6/16		Section marched to SAILLY-LE-SEC	
	25 6/16		Dr LEEMING rejoined from leave	
	-		Established an advanced collecting station in Bois de TAILLES (France - Sheet ALBERT 1/40,000 K 23-a)	
	27 6/16		Evacuated 17 horses to Hospital	
	29 6/16		Evacuated 8 horses to Hospital	
	30 6/16		Evacuated 13 horses to Hospital	

1875 Wt. W593/826 1,000,000 4/15 J.B.C. & A. A.D.S.S./Forms/C. 2118.

Instructions regarding War Diaries and Intelligence Summaries are contained in F. S. Regs., Part II. and the Staff Manual respectively. Title Pages will be prepared in manuscript.

WAR DIARY ~~or~~ ~~INTELLIGENCE SUMMARY~~ of 30 Mobile Vety Section 18 Divn

(Erase heading not required.)

Army Form C. 2118

Place	Date	Hour	Summary of Events and Information	Remarks and references to Appendices
			With reference to the increase of mange at the front, it is suggested for consideration, that cases of sarcoptic mange discharged from Hospital cured, should be given an additional two months of quarantine. To allow these cases to eat their heads off during this time would of course be foolish; but if it could be arranged that certain units on the L. of C. (or even at the front) should take <u>all</u> these cases & work them for two months, and then after careful inspection, pass them on to Remounts for distribution broadcast, I think it would be advantageous	
			E E Jelbart Capt AVC O/c 30 Mobile Veterinary Section 18 Division	

1875 Wt. W593/826 1,000,000 4/15 J.B.C. & A. A.D.S.S./Forms/C. 2118.

18/Vol 11

30TH MOBILE VETERINARY SECTION.

Instructions regarding War Diaries and Intelligence Summaries are contained in F. S. Regs., Part II. and the Staff Manual respectively. Title Pages will be prepared in manuscript.

WAR DIARY ~~or INTELLIGENCE SUMMARY~~ of 30 Mobile Vety Section 18 Divn

(Erase heading not required.)

Army Form C. 2118

Place	Date	Hour	Summary of Events and Information	Remarks and references to Appendices
SAILLY-LE SEC.	1·7·16		One Mange case evacuated to Hospital.	
with advanced	2·7·16		Evacuated 8 sick horses to Hospital	
collecting Station	4·7·16		do 9 do	
BOIS de TAILLES				
	6·7·16		do 8 do	
	8·7·16		do 13 do	
	10·7·16		do 8 do	
	11·7·16		do 3 mange cases to Hospital	
	12·7·16		do 15 sick horses to Hospital	
	13·7·16		do 14 sick horses and 3 remount cases to Hospital	
	15·7·16		do 14 " to Hospital	
	17·7·16		do 20 " "	
	18·7·16		do 9 " "	
	19·7·16		do 14 " "	
	20·7·16		do 33 " "	
	21·7·16		do. 4 " "	
ALLONVILLE	..		Section marched and bivouaced for night at ALLONVILLE.	

1875 Wt. W593/826 1,000,000 4/15 J.B.C. & A. A.D.S.S./Forms/C. 2118.

Instructions regarding War Diaries and Intelligence Summaries are contained in F. S. Regs., Part II. and the Staff Manual respectively. Title Pages will be prepared in manuscript.

Army Form C. 2118

WAR DIARY ~~or~~ of 30 Mobile Vety Section

~~INTELLIGENCE SUMMARY~~ 18 Divn

(*Erase heading not required.*)

Place	Date	Hour	Summary of Events and Information	Remarks and references to Appendices
LONGPRÉ LES CORPS SAINTS	22·7·16		Section marched from ALLONVILLE to LONGPRÉ LES CORPS SAINTS	
	23·7·16		Evacuated 5 sick horses to ABBEVILLE (22 Vety Hospl) by road	
	23·7·16		Section marched to PONT REMY + entrained at midnight 23/24	
LYNDE	24·7·16		Section detrained 10 AM 24/7/16 at St. OMER and marched to LYNDE.	
	26·7·16		No 13920 Pte A J. ARNOLD reports for duty from No 2 Vety Hospital	
	27·7·16		No 2338 Pte J. MARTIN despatched for duty to No 2 Vety Hospital (transfer arranged)	
	28·7·16		Evacuated 12 sick horses to No 23 Vety Hospl	
			No 5004 Pte N. McCALLUM admitted sick to 56 Fd ambce	
FLÈTRE	29·7·16		Section marched to ~~F~~ FLETRE.	
	31·7·16		~~Intimation~~ received that No 5004 Pte N. McCALLUM has been evacuated sick to C.C.S.	
			In view of the uncertainty of getting trucks for sick horses (owing to trans:port of troops and prisoners) and the possible irregularity in time of trains running one had previously formed the idea that it would be a great convenience to M.V.Ss if there were at Railhead a Veterinary Depot which would receive cases from M.V.Ss entrain them + provide attendants for the journey. No 12 M.V.S (with a very obliging O.C) being situated at Railhead along with a party of men from the base to act as attendants with the trucks amounted practically to a Veterinary Depot and was found to be a great convenience.	
			E.E. Gelbart? Capt AVC O/C 30 M.V.S. 18 Divn	

1875 Wt. W593/826 1,000,000 4/15 J.B.C. & A. A.D.S.S./Forms/C. 2118.

Vol 12

30 MVS

Instructions regarding War Diaries and Intelligence Summaries are contained in F. S. Regs., Part II. and the Staff Manual respectively. Title Pages will be prepared in manuscript.

WAR DIARY ~~or~~ ~~INTELLIGENCE SUMMARY~~

(*Erase heading not required.*)

of 30 Mobile Veterinary Section
18 Division

Army Form C. 2118

Place	Date	Hour	Summary of Events and Information	...ks and references to Appendices
FLETRE	4 8/16		Evacuated 40 sick horses to No 23 Vety Hospl by road.	
SEQUE-MEAU	5 8/16		Section marched to SEQUEMEAU. O.C. detailed as Officer in charge of loading sick horses on barge at Bac St MAUR for transport to No 23 Vety Hospl	
	8 8/16		Evacuated 4 sick horses to 23 Vety Hospl by barge.	
	11 8/16.		Evacuated 10 -do- by train from WIPPENHOEK.	
			Evacuated 2 -do- by barge	
	12 8/16		No S.E. 6284 Pte SIMMONDS. W. reports for duty.	
	15 8/16		Evacuated 4 sick horses by barge	
	17 8/16		Evacuated 29 -do- by road to No 23 Vety Hospl	
	18 8/16		Evacuated 6 -do- by barge	
	21 8/16		Evacuated 21 -do- by road	
	22 8/16		Evacuated 8 -do- by barge	
	23 8/16		No 44 M.V.S. arrived to take over + shared billet for two days	
	24 8/16		Evacuated 14 sick horses to Hospital by barge and 21 by road	
	25 8/16		Section marched to BAILLEUL entrained - leaving 9.10 pm.	
LE QUESNEL	26 8/16		Detrained DIEVAL 1 A.M. + marched to LE QUESNEL	

[illegible] Capt AVC
O/C 30 M.V.S

1875 Wt. W593/826 1,000,000 4/15 J.B.C. & A. A.D.S.S./Forms/C. 2118.

Instructions regarding War Diaries and Intelligence Summaries are contained in F. S. Regs., Part II. and the Staff Manual respectively. Title Pages will be prepared in manuscript.

WAR DIARY of 30 Mobile Veterinary Section
or
~~INTELLIGENCE SUMMARY~~
(Erase heading not required.)

Army Form C. 2118

Vol 13

78/24 H
9/10/16

Place	Date	Hour	Summary of Events and Information	Remarks and references to Appendices
LE QUESNEL	4 9/16		Evacuated 19 sick horses to No 22 Vety Hospl.	
REBREUVIETTE	9 9/16		Section marched to REBREUVIETTE according to Divl March table	
LE MARAIS SEC.	10 9/16		Section marched to LE MARAIS SEC — do —	
ACHEUX	11 9/16		Section marched to ACHEUX — do —	
	14 9/16		No SE 5921 P/A/Cpl J. DOYLE sent to 3rd Infy Bde Guards Divn to be Vety Sgt. on instructions received from O/C AVC Records 3rd Echelon.	
	15 9/16		Evacuated 8 sick horses to Hospl (No 22) in charge of L/Cpl C. PAYNE who thereafter reported to No 5 Vety Hospl & received instruction in sharpening Clipping Machine knives.	
	22 9/16		Evacuated 23 horses to No 22 Vety Hospl.	
	23 9/16		Evacuated 29 horses to — do —	
	24 9/16		No SE 5084 Pte A.W.H. THROWER joined for duty from No 6 Vety Hospl.	
HEDAUVILLE	25 9/16		Section marched to HEDAUVILLE & bivouaced	
	27 9/16		Evacuated 17 sick horses to No 22 Vety Hospl.	
	28 9/16		Evacuated 16 sick horses to — do —	
	29 9/16		Evacuated 24 sick horses to — do —	

E. Gilbart Capt AVC
O/c 30 Mobile Vety Section

1875 Wt. W593/826 1,000,000 4/15 J.B.C. & A. A.D.S.S./Forms/C. 2118.

Instructions regarding War Diaries and Intelligence Summaries are contained in F. S. Regs., Part II. and the Staff Manual respectively. Title Pages will be prepared in manuscript.

WAR DIARY of 30 Mobile Veterinary Section 18 Div^n ~~or INTELLIGENCE SUMMARY~~

(Erase heading not required.)

Army Form C. 2118

Vol ~~[illegible]~~ Sh. 1. Vol 14

Place	Date	Hour	Summary of Events and Information	Remarks and references to Appendices
HEDAUVILLE	1 10/16		Evacuated 20 sick horses to No 22 Veterinary Hospital	
	2 10/16		" 8 " " " 22 " "	
	3 10/16		" 31 ~~27~~ " " " 22 " "	
	5 10/16		" 18 " " " 22 " "	
OUTREBOIS	6 10/16		Section marched to OUTREBOIS & took up billet at LE QUESNEL FARM.	
	10 10/16		No 6284 Pte W. SIMMONDS ten days leave to England	
	13 10/16		- 8400 a/L/Cpl A. AMESBURY -do-	
	14 10/16		- 6746 Pte T. SLOAN ——— -do-	
			Evacuated 16 horses to No 22 Veterinary Hospital	
	15 10/16		No 6693 Pte E. Odds ten days leave to England	
HEM.			Section marched to HEM.	
TOUTENCOURT	16 10/16		" " " TOUTENCOURT	
ALBERT	17 10/16		" " " ALBERT and bivouacced in the Brickfields there	
	19 10/16		No 6501 Pte T.W.G. Taylor + No 5084 Pte ~~A.W.~~ H. THROWER ten days leave to England	
	20 10/16		Evacuated 8 sick horses to No 4 Veterinary Hospital	
			~~No 6284 Pte W. Simmonds rejoined from leave~~	
	21			

Instructions regarding War Diaries and Intelligence Summaries are contained in F. S. Regs., Part II. and the Staff Manual respectively. Title Pages will be prepared in manuscript.

WAR DIARY of 30 Mobile Veterinary Section 18 Divn
or
~~INTELLIGENCE SUMMARY~~
(Erase heading not required.)

Army Form C. 2118

Vol XV Sh. 2.

Place	Date	Hour	Summary of Events and Information	Remarks and references to Appendices
ALBERT	21 10/16		No 6486 u/a/Cpl C.E. PAYNE appointed P/a/Cpl with effect from 14 9/16 Authy LCO. No 57 d 15 10/16	
	24 10/16		Evacuated 8 sick horses to No 4 Veterinary Hospital	
			No 6284 Pte W. Simmonds rejoined from leave	
	26 10/16		Evacuated 16 horses to No 4 Veterinary Hospital	
	27 10/16		" 8 " " " 4 " "	
	28 10/16		" 24 " " " 4 " "	
			No 8400 a/L/Cpl A. AMESBURY rejoined from leave.	
			No 6746 Pte T. SLOAN ——— " " "	
	29 10/16		Evacuated 24 sick horses to No 4 Veterinary Hospl.	
			No 7294 Pte W. Brown reported sick & admitted to Field Ambulance	
	30 10/16		No 6693 Pte E. Oddo rejoined from leave	
			Evacuated 8 sick horses to No 4 Veterinary Hospl.	
	31 10/16		" 55 " " " " 4 " "	

E. E. Gelbart Capt AVC
O/c 30 Mobile Veterinary Section
18 Division

1875 Wt. W593/826 1,000,000 4/15 J.B.C. & A. A.D.S.S./Forms/C. 2118.

Army Form C. 2118.

Instructions regarding War Diaries and Intelligence Summaries are contained in F. S. Regs., Part II. and the Staff Manual respectively. Title Pages will be prepared in manuscript.

WAR DIARY or ~~INTELLIGENCE~~ SUMMARY of 30 Mobile Vety Section

(Erase heading not required.)

Vol ~~XVI~~ Sh 1 Vol 15

Place	Date	Hour	Summary of Events and Information	Remarks and references to Appendices
ALBERT	2/11/16		Evacuated 26 sick horses to No 7 Veterinary Hospital	
	3/11/16		— do — 8 — do — — do —	
	4/11/16		— do — 8 — do — — do —	
	5/11/16		No SE 7294 Pte. W Brown reported evacuated	
	6/11/16		Evacuated 31 sick horses to No 7 Veterinary Hospital.	
			No S.E 6501 Pte T.W.G. TAYLOR + No S.E 5084 Pte A.W.H. THROWER rejoined from leave	
	7/11/16		Evacuated 8 sick horses to No 7 Veterinary Hospital	
			The following N.C.O + 5 men reported from base (through No 31. mobile Veterinary Section) to give assistance temporarily:— SE 925 Cpl BURGE. A: SE 15367 Pte PORRILL C.: SE 22676 Pte. WALES. R: S.E. 4032 Pte BATEMAN, G: S.E 20543 FARLY, A: S.E 1996 Pte GILLIES, D.	
	9/11/16		Evacuated 39 sick cases to No 7 Veterinary Hospital	
			No S.E. 10434 Pte A.W. OLIVER admitted II Corps Rest Station.	
	10/11/16		T/2/13580 Dr LEEMING A. (A.S.C driver attached) admitted to Hospital	

2449 Wt. W14957/M90 750,000 1/16 J.B.C. & A. Forms/C.2118/12.

Army Form C. 2118.

Instructions regarding War Diaries and Intelligence Summaries are contained in F. S. Regs., Part II. and the Staff Manual respectively. Title Pages will be prepared in manuscript.

WAR DIARY or ~~INTELLIGENCE~~ SUMMARY

of 30 Mobile Vety Section
18 D...

(Erase heading not required.)

Vol XVI Sh. 2

Place	Date	Hour	Summary of Events and Information	Remarks and references to Appendices
LBERT	10/11/16		32 sick Cases evacuated to No 4 Vety Hospl	
	11/11/16		16 — do — — do —	
	12/11/16		23 — do — — do —	
	13/11/16		8 — do — — do —	
			No SE 13920 Pte A. J. ARNOLD despatched to England, – having been selected for attendance at a Cadet Unit.	
	14/11/16		14 sick Cases evacuated to No 4 Vety Hospl	
	15/11/16		15 — do — — do —	
	19/11/16		24 — do — — do —	
			No SE 6284 Pte W. SIMMONDS evacuated to Hospital sick	
	20/11/16		14 sick cases evacuated to No 4 Vety Hospl	
	21/11/16		22 — do — — do —	
	22/11/16		SE 10434 Pte A.W. OLIVER rejoined from Rest Station	
			Section marched to CANDAS.	
	23/11/16		Section marched to ~~& went into billets~~ at L'HEURE. (3 Kilometres N.E. of ABBEVILLE.)	

2449 Wt. W14957/M90 750,000 1/16 J.B.C. & A. Forms/C.2118/12.

Army Form C. 2118.

Instructions regarding War Diaries and Intelligence Summaries are contained in F. S. Regs., Part II. and the Staff Manual respectively. Title Pages will be prepared in manuscript.

WAR DIARY

or

~~INTELLIGENCE SUMMARY~~

(Erase heading not required.)

of 30 Mobile Vety Section 18 Divn

Vol ~~XVI~~ Sh 3

Place	Date	Hour	Summary of Events and Information	Remarks and references to Appendices
LIHEURE	25/11/16		No SE 6812 a/L/Cpl W. M. FOX to England on leave 27/11/16 to 6/12/16	
	27/11/16		No S.E. 2665 Pte P. C. WOODRUFF reports for duty with Section.	
	29/11/16		No SE 15924 Pte A. E. GOVER and SE 2088 Pte W. H. WHEELER — do —	
"	30/11/16		1 sick horse evacuated by road to No. 22 Vety Hospl	

E. E. Gelbart Capt AVC
O/c 30 mobile Vety Section

2449 Wt. W14957/M90 750,000 1/16 J.B.C. & A. Forms/C.2118/12.

18th Division "G."

Herewith War Diary of this Unit for December Volume XVII Sheets 1 & 2.

Kindly acknowledge receipt.

E.E. Gilbert Capt. A.V.C.

9-1-17. O.C. 30 Mobile Vety Section

HEAD QUARTERS
No. ...
9 JAN 1917
18TH DIVISION

Army Form C. 2118.

Instructions regarding War Diaries and Intelligence Summaries are contained in F. S. Regs., Part II. and the Staff Manual respectively. Title Pages will be prepared in manuscript.

WAR DIARY
or
~~INTELLIGENCE SUMMARY~~ of 30 Mobile Veterinary Section 18 Div.

(Erase heading not required.)

Vol ~~XVII~~ sh. 1. Vol 16

Place	Date	Hour	Summary of Events and Information	Remarks and references to Appendices
L'HEURE	3/12/16		Capt E.E. JELBART A.V.C. granted ten days leave to England. – Capt W.R. MACDOUGALL A.V.C. placed temporarily in charge of unit.	
	4/12/16		Evacuated 11 sick cases to No. 22 Veterinary Hospl.	
	6/12/16		No SE 10443 Pte W.G. WRIGHT ten days leave to England	
	7/12/16		Evacuated 6 sick cases to No 22 Veterinary Hospl	
	9/12/16		" 8 " " " — do –	
	11/12/16		" 21 " " " — do –	
			No SE 6812 A/L/Cpl W. M. FOX rejoined from leave	
HAUT-VILLERS	13/12/16		Section marched to FERME de LA HALLE, HAUTVILLERS.	
	14/12/16		Capt E.E. JELBART rejoined from leave	
	15/12/16		Evacuated 12 sick cases to No 22 Veterinary Hospl	
	16/12/16		" 20 " " " " "	
	17/12/16		" 2 " " " " "	
	18			HEAD QUARTERS No. .... 9 JAN. 1917 18TH DIVISION

Instructions regarding War Diaries and Intelligence Summaries are contained in F. S. Regs., Part II. and the Staff Manual respectively. Title Pages will be prepared in manuscript.

WAR DIARY or ~~INTELLIGENCE~~ SUMMARY of 30 Mobile Vety Section 18 D.W.

(Erase heading not required.)

Army Form C. 2118.

Vol XVII Sl. 2

Place	Date	Hour	Summary of Events and Information	Remarks and references to Appendices
HAUT-VILLERS	18 12/16		No SE 10443 Pte W. G. WRIGHT rejoined from leave.	
			Evacuated 41 sick cases to No 22 Veterinary Hospl.	
	19 12/16		" 21 " " " " " "	
	20 12/16		" 16 " " " " " "	
	21 12/16		" 10 " " " " " "	
ABBEVILLE PRECINCT			Section marched to BRICKFIELD. 2 K.Ms N. of ABBEVILLE on MONTREUIL Road	
			No SE. 18789 Pte W.A. HATTERSLEY reports for duty from No 1 Convalescent Horse Depot	
			No SE 4950 Pte F. WALKER reports for duty from No 8 Veterinary Hospl	
	23 12/16		Evacuated 12 sick cases to No 22 Veterinary Hospl.	
			No T2 13200 attached Driver W. ORR ASC 10 days leave to England	
	24 12/16		Evacuated 21 sick cases to No 22 Veterinary Hospl.	
	25 12/16		" 3 " " " " " "	
	28 12/16		" 7 " " " " " "	
	30 12/16		" 14 " " " " " "	
	31 12/16		" 5 " " " " " "	
			[illegible] Capt AVC Oc 30 Mobile Vety Section	

2449 Wt. W14957/M90 750,000 1/16 J.B.C. & A. Forms/C.2118/12.

Instructions regarding War Diaries and Intelligence Summaries are contained in F. S. Regs., Part II. and the Staff Manual respectively. Title Pages will be prepared in manuscript.

WAR DIARY of 30 Mobile Vety Section
or
~~INTELLIGENCE SUMMARY~~
(~~Erase heading not required.~~)

Vol XVIII

Army Form C. 2118.

Vol 17
Sh 1.

Place	Date	Hour	Summary of Events and Information	Remarks and references to Appendices
ABBEVILLE PRECINCT	1/1/17		Evacuated 14 horses and 3 mules to No 22 Veterinary Hospital	
			No T/12657 Dr SHORT. F. A.S.C. reports for duty.	
	2/1/17		Evacuated 10 horses and 2 mules to No 22 Veterinary Hospital.	
	4/1/17		No T/2 13200 Dr W. ORR rejoined from leave	
			One Corporal + 4 men of this Unit sent to join M.V.S. of 61st Division to assist while 18 Div RA attached to 61 Div.	
	7/1/17		Evacuated 7 horses and 1 mule to No 22 Vety Hospl	
	8/1/17		No 7308 Pte HALL A.T. AVC 10 days leave to England.	
	9/1/17		Evacuated 13 horses and 2 mules to No 22 Vety Hospl	
	10/1/17		" 4 " " " "	
			No 7138 Pte HYDE A. despatched to No 11 M.V.S. for duty. Authy DDVS 4th Army 125/3/17 d. 6.1.17.	
	11/1/17		Evacuated one horse to No 22 Vety Hospl.	
YVRENCH			Section marched to YVRENCH	
BERNAVILLE	12/1/17		do " BERNAVILLE	
MARIEUX	14/1/17		do " MARIEUX	
MARTINSART	16/1/17		do MARTINSART + took over billet vacated by M.V.S. 61st Div together with 31 sick horses left by them. The Cpl + 4 men temporarily attached to MVS.	

Army Form C. 2118.

Instructions regarding War Diaries and Intelligence Summaries are contained in F. S. Regs., Part II. and the Staff Manual respectively. Title Pages will be prepared in manuscript.

WAR DIARY ~~or~~ ~~INTELLIGENCE SUMMARY~~ of 30 Mobile Vety Section

(Erase heading not required.)

Vol XVIII Sh 2

Place	Date	Hour	Summary of Events and Information	Remarks and references to Appendices
MARTINSART	16/1/17		61st Divn rejoined this unit and 1 L/Cpl and 4 men of M.V.S 61st Divn. joined this unit temporarily whilst 61st Div. R.A. attached 18 Divn.	
	17/1/17		Evacuated 12 horses + 6 mules to No 7 Veterinary Hospl	
	18/1/17		" 14 " + 2 " to "	
			No 464 Sgt BRADY S.V. 10 days leave to England	
	22/1/17		No 7308 Pte HALL A.T. rejoined from leave	
	23/1/17		No T2/024169 Dr PIDDINGTON T. ASC 10 days leave to England	
			No T2/10042 Dr LOVERING A. reported for duty and No T/2 13200 Dr W. ORR. transferred to No 151 Co. ASC	
	24/1/17		Evacuated 62 sick cases to No 22 Vety Hospl	
	25/1/17		" 8 " to 7 "	
			During the month it has been found necessary to destroy in the Section an unusually large of number of horses – the total being 53. most of these have been cases of debility which were thought unsuitable for transference to Hospital.	
			G.L. Gelbart Capt AVC O/C 30 Mobile Veterinary Section 18 Division	

2449 Wt. W14957/M90 750,000 1/16 J.B.C. & A. Forms/C.2118/12.

Army Form C. 2118.

Instructions regarding War Diaries and Intelligence Summaries are contained in F. S. Regs., Part II. and the Staff Manual respectively. Title Pages will be prepared in manuscript.

WAR DIARY
or
~~INTELLIGENCE SUMMARY~~
(*Erase heading not required.*)

30 Mobile Veterinary Section
Vol XIX Sh. 1.

Vol 18

Place	Date	Hour	Summary of Events and Information	Remarks and references to Appendices
MARTIN: SART	8/2/17		No. S.E. 497 Sgt THORNLEY T. ten days leave to England 9-19/2/17	
	12/2/17		Evacuated 32 Mange cases to No. 22 Veterinary Hospital	
	13/2/17		No S.E. 2088 Pte WHEELER W. H. ten days special leave to England 14-24/2/17	
	14/2/17		Evacuated 31 sick cases to No. 22 Vety Hospl.	
	"		No S.E. 794 Sgt WHITTINGTON. G reported for duty from 31st D.A.C.	
	16/2/17		Evacuated 31 sick cases to No. 22 Vety Hospl.	
	19/2/17		" 29 —do— " —do—	
	"		No. S.E. 706 Sgt LITTLEWOOD H. reported for duty from No 4 Vety Hospl.	
	21/2/17		Evacuated 28 sick cases to No. 22 Vety Hospl.	
	23/2/17		—"— 29 —do— " —do—	
	25/2/17		No S.E. 497 Sgt THORNLEY T. rejoined from leave	
	26/2/17		Evacuated 34 sick cases to No. 22 Vety Hospl.	
	27/2/17		No S.E. 2088 Pte WHEELER W.H. rejoined from leave	

2449 Wt. W14957/M90 750,000 1/16 J.B.C. & A. Forms/C.2118/12.

Army Form C. 2118.

WAR DIARY
or
INTELLIGENCE SUMMARY
(*Erase heading not required.*)

30 Mobile Veterinary Section
Vol XIX Sh 2.

Instructions regarding War Diaries and Intelligence Summaries are contained in F. S. Regs., Part II. and the Staff Manual respectively. Title Pages will be prepared in manuscript.

Place	Date	Hour	Summary of Events and Information	Remarks and references to Appendices
MARTIN-SART	28/2/17		Evacuated 34 sick cases to No 22 Vety. Hospl.	
			With reference to the question of the number of horses in a M.V.S. it is thought that the number of riding horses might quite well be reduced during the present system of trench warfare. At the same time I should like to draw attention to the insufficiency of the transport and to suggest that another limber or G.S. wagon be supplied. Recent experience on the ground opposite the enemy withdrawal has shown that the float cannot, on account of the state of the roads, be relied on as a baggage cart.	
			E.E. [illegible] Capt AVC I/C 30 M.V.S.	

2449 Wt. W14957/M90 750,000 1/16 J.B.C. & A. Forms/C.2118/12.

Instructions regarding War Diaries and Intelligence Summaries are contained in F. S. Regs., Part II. and the Staff Manual respectively. Title Pages will be prepared in manuscript.

WAR DIARY

~~or~~

~~INTELLIGENCE SUMMARY~~

(Erase heading not required.)

Army Form C. 2118.

of 30 Mobile Veterinary Section

Vol XX Sh. 1.

18th Div.

Vol. 19

Place	Date	Hour	Summary of Events and Information	Remarks and references to Appendices
MARTINSART	2 3/17		Evacuated 24 sick cases to No 22 Veterinary Hospital.	
	5 3/17		" 28 — do — — do —	
	7 3/17		" 4 — do — — do —	
	9 3/17		" 17 — do — — do —	
	10 3/17		No S.E 1060 Pte LEWIS F. reported for duty from No 9 Vety Hospl.	
	12 3/17		Evacuated 23 sick & 2 ~~remount cases~~ to No 22 Veterinary Hospl.	
			Established an Advanced Dressing & Collecting Post at St Pierre Division in view of expected developments.	
	14 3/17		Evacuated 17 sick cases to No 22 Veterinary Hospital	
	16 3/17		" 38 — do — — do —	
			No S.E. 794 Sgt WHITTINGTON Geo. sent to A/82 Bty RFA for duty	
	19 3/17		Evacuated 64 sick cases to No 22 Veterinary Hospital	
	21 3/17		" 42 — do — — do —	
	23 3/17		" 58 — do — — do —	

Instructions regarding War Diaries and Intelligence Summaries are contained in F. S. Regs., Part II. and the Staff Manual respectively. Title Pages will be prepared in manuscript.

WAR DIARY ~~or INTELLIGENCE SUMMARY~~ of 30 Mobile Veterinary Section

(Erase heading not required.)

Army Form C. 2118.

Vol XX Sh. 2.

Place	Date	Hour	Summary of Events and Information	Remarks and references to Appendices
PONT de METZ (by AMIENS)	25 3/17		Section marched from MARTINSART under orders to entrain at BACOUEL at 10AM. 26 3/17. Halted night 25/26 at PONT de METZ by AMIENS. Ascertained trains running late – remained at Pont de Metz until 7a.m. 27th when section marched to BACOUEL Station, & entrained. Detrained 11a.m. 28th at	
MORBECQUE			BERGUETTE (between AIRE & LILLERS) and marched to MORBECQUE (3 Kms. S. of HAZEBROUCK.)	
	31 3/17		No S.E. 1060 Pte LEWIS F. sent to No 2 Veterinary Hospital. (Authy D.D.V.S. Fifth Army 576/3/17 d 23.3.17)	
			G. E. Gilbert Capt AVC O/C 30 Mobile Vety Section 18 Division	

2449 Wt. W14957/M90 750,000 1/16 J.B.C. & A. Forms/C.2118/12.

Army Form C. 2118.

Instructions regarding War Diaries and Intelligence Summaries are contained in F. S. Regs., Part II. and the Staff Manual respectively. Title Pages will be prepared in manuscript.

WAR DIARY
or
INTELLIGENCE SUMMARY

(Erase heading not required.)

of 30 Mobile Veterinary Section

Vol XXI

Vol ~~17~~ 20

18

HEAD QUARTERS No 10 MAY 1917 18TH DIVISION

Place	Date	Hour	Summary of Events and Information	Remarks and references to Appendices
MORBECQUE	5.4.17		Evacuated 23 sick cases to No 23 Veterinary Hospl. by Road	
	6.4.17		No T3/10042 Dr LOVERING A. A.S.C. ten days leave to England 6. to 16.4.17	
	8.4.17		Evacuated 40 sick cases to No 23 Veterinary Hospital by Road	
	11.4.17		" 43 — do — — do —	
	16.4.17		" 38 — do — — do —	
	19.4.17		" 44 — do — — do — (including 4 by motor float)	
	20.4.17		No T3/10042 Dr Lovering A. A.S.C. rejoined from leave	
	21.4.17		Evacuated 25 sick cases to No 23 Veterinary Hospl. by Road	
	24.4.17		" 16 — do — — do —	
PERNES	26.4.17		Section marched to PERNES	
HABARCQ	27.4.17		— do — HABARCQ	
AGNY	28.4.17		— do — AGNY and took over camp of 40 M.V.S (S. of ARRAS - 2 KILOM.)	

E. S. Jelbart Capt AVC
O/c 30 M.V.S.
18 Division

2449 Wt. W14957/M90 750,000 1/16 J.B.C. & A. Forms/C.2118/12.

Army Form C. 2118.

*Instructions regarding War Diaries and Intelligence Summaries are contained in F. S. Regs., Part II. and the Staff Manual respectively. Title Pages will be prepared in manuscript.

HEAD QUARTERS JUN. 1917 18TH DIVISION

WAR DIARY
or
~~INTELLIGENCE SUMMARY~~
(Erase heading not required.)

of 30 Mobile Veterinary Section

Vol XXII

Vol 21

Place	Date	Hour	Summary of Events and Information	Remarks and references to Appendices
AGNY	1/5/17		Evacuated 28 sick cases to No 22 Veterinary Hospital	
	2.5.17		Established advanced Collecting Post of 1 N.C.O. + 1 man at SUCRERIE, NEUVILLE VITASSE	
	5.5.17		One Cpl + three men sent to VII Corps Mobile Vety Detachment for duty:— No 6107 Cpl Brown W; No 6814 Pte ELGAR F.; No 9403 Pte HUGHES, J.D.; and No 3463 Pte TAYLOR W;	
	8.5.17		Evacuated 32 sick cases to No 22 Veterinary Hospital	
	11.5.17		— " — 21 — do — — do —	
	14.5.17		" 7 — do — — do —	
	16.5.17		" 10 — do — — do —	
BOISLEUX AU MONT	17.5.17		Section marched to BOISLEUX AU MONT	
	20.5.17		No T/12657 Driver SHORT F. ten days leave to England 21 to 31 5/17	
	21.5.17		Evacuated 11 sick cases to No 7 Veterinary Hospital	
	22.5.17		Sgt + 6 men of 40 M.V.S. left to rejoin their unit on marching out of Divisional artillery	
	23.5.17		22 sick cases evacuated to No 7 Veterinary Hospital	
	26.5.17		No 3463 Pte TAYLOR W. 10 days leave to England 27.5.17 to 6.6.17	
			12 sick cases evacuated to No 7 Veterinary Hospital	
	28.5.17		11 — do — — do — — do —	

2449 Wt. W14957/M90 750,000 1/16 J.B.C. & A. Forms/C.2118/12.

Army Form C. 2118.

WAR DIARY
or
INTELLIGENCE SUMMARY of 30 Mobile Vety Section

(Erase heading not required.)

Vol XXII Sh. 2

Instructions regarding War Diaries and Intelligence Summaries are contained in F. S. Regs., Part II. and the Staff Manual respectively. Title Pages will be prepared in manuscript.

Place	Date	Hour	Summary of Events and Information	Remarks and references to Appendices
BOISLEUX AU MONT	30 5/17		Evacuated 22 cases to No 4 Veterinary Hospital	
			E.E. Jelbart Capt AVC o/c 30 M.V.S.	

2449 Wt. W14957/M90 750,000 1/16 J.B.C. & A. Forms/C.2118/12.

Instructions regarding War Diaries and Intelligence Summaries are contained in F. S. Regs., Part II. and the Staff Manual respectively. Title Pages will be prepared in manuscript.

WAR DIARY
or
~~INTELLIGENCE SUMMARY~~
(Erase heading not required.)

of 30 Mobile Veterinary Section

Vol ~~XXIII~~ Sh 1 Vol 22

Army Form C. 2118.

Place	Date	Hour	Summary of Events and Information	Remarks and references to Appendices
BOISLEUX au MONT	2 6/17		Evacuated 14 sick cases to No 4 Veterinary Hospl	
	6 6/17		— " — 23 — " — ——— " —	
	7 6/17		No T/12657 Driver Short F (A.S.C.) rejoined from leave	
	9 6/17		No 6763 Pte DRURY W.C ten days leave to England 10 to 20 6/17	
			No 6814. Pte ELGAR F. rejoined from VII Corps Mobile Vety Detachment.	
	11 6/17		No 6814 Pte ELGAR F. despatched to No 2 Vety Hospital with view of joining Inland Water Transport Section R.E. (Authy D.A.G. to 18 Divn No C.R. No 42410/41/A d. 3.6.1917)	
			No T/12657 Dr SHORT. F A.S.C. evacuated sick	
			Evacuated 22 sick cases to No 4 Veterinary Hospital	
	12 6/17		No 3463. Pte TAYLOR W. rejoined from leave	
	13 6/17		Evacuated 9 sick cases to No 4 Veterinary Hospital	
	15 6/17		No 6107 Cpl BROWN W. appointed P/A/Sgt. as from 15.6.17. (Authy L C.O. No 65)	
	17 6/17		Transferred 4 sick cases to No 33 M.V.S.	
COUIN.	18 6/17		Section marched to COUIN.	
	19 6/17		No 7308 a/L/Cpl HALL A.T. sent to VII Corps Mob Vety Detachment in relief of P/A/Sgt BROWN W.	

Army Form C. 2118.

Instructions regarding War Diaries and Intelligence Summaries are contained in F. S. Regs., Part II. and the Staff Manual respectively. Title Pages will be prepared in manuscript.

WAR DIARY or ~~INTELLIGENCE SUMMARY~~ of 30 Mobile Veterinary Section

(Erase heading not required.)

Vol XXIII Sh 2.

Place	Date	Hour	Summary of Events and Information	Remarks and references to Appendices
COUIN.	20/6/17		No 6107 P/A/Sgt BROWN. W. despatched for duty to No 24 Vety Hospl (Authy O/s i/c AVC Base Records No T/8/436/17 d. 15/6/17	
	22/6/17		Capt E.E. JELBART AVC. ten days leave to England 23/6/17 to 3/7/17 — Capt P. J. AUSTIN answering for him	
	23/6/17		No 6763 Pte DRURY W.C rejoined from leave.	
			No 24845 Pte BROWN T. reported for duty from No 2 Vety Hospl	
	30/6/17		Evacuated 4 sick cases to No 22 Vety Hospl	
			E E Jelbart Capt AVC i/c 30 M. V. S	

2449 Wt. W14957/M90 750,000 1/16 J.B.C. & A. Forms/C.2118/12.

17

Instructions regarding War Diaries and Intelligence Summaries are contained in F. S. Regs., Part II. and the Staff Manual respectively. Title pages will be prepared in manuscript.

WAR DIARY
or
~~INTELLIGENCE SUMMARY.~~

(Erase heading not required.)

of 30 Mobile Vety Section

Vol XXIV Sh. 1

Vol 23

Army Form C. 2118.

Place	Date	Hour	Summary of Events and Information	Remarks and references to Appendices
COUIN	1/7/17		Advance billetting party of 1 Cpl + 1 man proceeded to new area	
	4/7/17		Section marched to DOULLENS and entrained there – departing 2-30 pm. Detrained BOESCHEPE 10 pm and marched to Sh. 27 L 24 C.3.9. (near HOPOUTRE Siding.	
HOPOUTRE	5/7/17		No 2665 Pte WOODRUFF P.C. ten days leave to England 6 to 16/7/17	
	5/7/17		Capt E.E. JELBART AVC rejoined from leave	
	8/7/17		No T4 263533 Driver SMITH W.H. ASC reported for duty from Base	
	9/7/17		No 116 Pte CLINTON. R. AVC reported for duty from No 1 Veterinary Hospital	
	10/7/17		Established Advanced Collecting Post in DICKEBUSCH Sh 28 H33. B2.5.	
			Evacuated 9 sick horses to No 23 Veterinary Hospital by road.	
	14/7/17		On instructions of ADVS II Corps the following 4 O.R. sent to II Corps Mobile Veterinary Detachment for temporary duty (1) No SE 7308 A/L/Cpl. HALL A.T.; (2) No SE 6763 Pte DRURY W.C. (3) No S.E. 7353 Pte SEABOURNE A.E. + (4) No SE 2088 Pte WHEELER W.H.:	
	15/7/17		No 641 Sgt Cook J. reported for duty from No 8. Veterinary Hospital	
	16/7/17		24 Sick Cases evacuated to II Corps Mob. Vet. Detachment	
			No 15924 Pte GOVER A.E. sent to II Corps M.V.D. in relief of No 7353 Pte SEABOURNE A.E. who is selected for leave.	

(A7092) Wt W12839/M1293 750,000 1/17. D. D. & L., Ltd. Forms/C.2118/14.

1

Instructions regarding War Diaries and Intelligence Summaries are contained in F. S. Regs., Part II. and the Staff Manual respectively. Title pages will be prepared in manuscript.

WAR DIARY ~~or~~ ~~INTELLIGENCE~~ ~~SUMMARY~~. of 30 Mobile Veterinary Section

(Erase heading not required.)

Army ~~Form~~ C. 2118.

Vol. XXIV Sh. 2.

Place	Date	Hour	Summary of Events and Information	Remarks and references to Appendices
HOPOUTRE	17/7/17		No 4353 Pte SEABOURNE A.E. 10 days leave to England 18 to 28/7/17	
			No 2665 Pte. WOODRUFF P.C rejoined from leave.	
	18/7/17		No SSR/556 P/A/Staff/Sgt WARSOP J.W. reported for duty from No 12 Veterinary Hospital.	
	21/7/17		No T4/122471 Driver NEVARD. J. reported for duty from Base	
	23/7/17		No T2/10042 Dr LOVERING. A. transferred to 150 Co A.S.C.	
			Evacuated 28 sick cases to II Corps Mobile Veterinary Detachment	
	24/7/17		" 15 — do — — do —	
	28/7/17		" 8 — do — — do —	
			No 9403 Pte HUGHES J.D. 10 days leave to England 29/7/17 to 8/8/17	
	29/7/17		Capt P. J. AUSTIN A.V.C. rejoined from leave	
	31/7/17		Evacuated 14 sick cases to II Corps Mobile Veterinary Detachment	

E. E. Gelbart Capt AVC
O/C 30 M.V.S.
18 Divn

(A7092). Wt. W12839/M1293. 750,000. 1/17. D. D. & L., Ltd. Forms/C.2118/14.

Instructions regarding War Diaries and Intelligence Summaries are contained in F. S. Regs., Part II. and the Staff Manual respectively. Title pages will be prepared in manuscript.

WAR DIARY ~~or INTELLIGENCE SUMMARY.~~ of 30 Mobile Veterinary Section

(Erase heading not required.)

Army Form C. 2118.

Vol XXV Sh. 1

WO 24

Place	Date	Hour	Summary of Events and Information	Remarks and references to Appendices
HOPOUTRE	1/8/17		Capt P. J. AUSTIN AVC proceeded to No 9 Vety Hospl for duty	
			No 7353 Pte SEABOURNE A.E. rejoined from leave to England	
	2/8/17		Evacuated 5 sick cases to II Corps Mob. Vety Detachment	
	4/8/17		" 23 — do — — do —	
	8/8/17		" 24 — do — to No 23 Vety Hospl by road	
	10/8/17		" 25 — do — to II Corps M.V.D.	
	–		" 24 — do — to No 23 Vety Hospl by road	
	–		No 9403 Pte HUGHES J.D. rejoined from leave to England	
	12/8/17		Evacuated 30 sick cases to No 23 Vety Hospl by road	
	13/8/17		" 10 — do — to II Corps M.V.D.	
	14/8/17		" 49 — do — to — do —	
	15/8/17		" 12 — do — to — do —	
	–		" 24 — do — to No 23 Vety Hospl by road	
LEDERZEELE	16/8/17		Section marched to LE CINQ RUES, LEDERZEELE & took up billet (Sheet 27 1/40,000 G 20 d 5.0.)	
	18/8/17		No 6486 a/L/Cpl Payne C.F. No 3463 Pte Taylor W, and No 9403 Pte Hughes J.D. despatched to M V S 56 Divn for temporary duty while 18 Divnl R.A. administered by 56 Division	

(A7092). Wt W12839/M1293 750,000 1/17. D. D. & L., Ltd. Forms/C.2118/14.

Army Form C. 2118.

Instructions regarding War Diaries and Intelligence Summaries are contained in F. S. Regs., Part II. and the Staff Manual respectively. Title pages will be prepared in manuscript.

WAR DIARY ~~or~~ ~~INTELLIGENCE SUMMARY.~~ of 30 Mobile Veterinary Section

(*Erase heading not required.*)

Vol XXV Sh. 2

Place	Date	Hour	Summary of Events and Information	Remarks and references to Appendices
LEDERZEELE	18/8/17		No 6451 Pte AXHORN. G. W. 10 days leave to England 20 to 30 8/17	
	31 8/17		Evacuated 7 sick cases to No 23 Veterinary Hospl by road.	
			G. E. Gilbart Capt AVC o/c 30 M.V.S. 18 Divn	

(A7092). Wt W12839/M1293 75,000. 1/17. D. D. & L., Ltd. Forms/C.2118/14.

16

Instructions regarding War Diaries and Intelligence Summaries are contained in F. S. Regs., Part II. and the Staff Manual respectively. Title pages will be prepared in manuscript.

WAR DIARY ~~or INTELLIGENCE SUMMARY.~~ of 30 Mobile Veterinary Section

(Erase heading not required.)

Army Form C. 2118.

Vol XXVI Sheet 1.

Vol 25

Place	Date	Hour	Summary of Events and Information	Remarks and references to Appendices
LEDERZEELE	1/9/17		No 6511 Pte AXHORN G.W. rejoined from leave	
	3 9/17		No 6486 A/L/Cpl PAYNE C.F. No 3463 Pte TAYLOR W. + No 9403 Pte HUGHES J.D. rejoined from temporary duty with 56 + 23 Division M.V.Ss	
	4 9/17		Evacuated 5 sick cases to No 23 Veterinary Hospital by road.	
ESQUELBECQ			Section marched to ESQUELBECQ + took up billet in Route de BERGUES	
	5 9/17		No 6463 Pte DRURY W.C. rejoined from duty with II Corps M.V.D.	
	8 9/17		Evacuated 18 sick cases to No 23 Veterinary Hospital by road	
	12 9/17		— do — 20 — do — — do —	
	15 9/17		No 15924 Pte GOVER A.E. ten days leave to England 15 to 25 9/17	
	18 9/17		Evacuated 15 sick cases to No 23 Veterinary Hospital by road.	
	20 9/17		— do — 1 — do — — do — — (in float)	
	21 9/17		— do — 1 — do — — do — — (— do —)	
	22 9/17		— do — 4 — do — — do — —	
Sh 27 F28 b1.4	23 9/17		Section moved to Camp at F28 b1.4. Sh. 27 1/40,000 Belgium + France	
	24 9/17		No 5622 S.S. CROWTHER W. ten days leave to England 24 9/17 to 4 10/17	
			No 15924 Pte GOVER A.E. rejoined from leave.	
			No 6486 A/L/Cpl PAYNE C.F. No 3463 Pte TAYLOR W.; No 9403 Pte HUGHES J.D. and No 2665 Pte WOODRUFF P.C. sent XIV + XVIII Corps joint M.V.D for duty	

(A7092). Wt W12539/M1293. 750,000. 1/17. D. D. & L., Ltd. Forms/C.2118/14.

Instructions regarding War Diaries and Intelligence Summaries are contained in F. S. Regs., Part II. and the Staff Manual respectively. Title pages will be prepared in manuscript.

WAR DIARY ~~or INTELLIGENCE SUMMARY.~~ of 30 Mobile Veterinary Section Vol XXVI Sheet 2.

(~~Erase heading not required.~~)

Army Form C. 2118.

Place	Date	Hour	Summary of Events and Information	Remarks and references to Appendices
Sh. 27 F28b1.4	28 9/17		Evacuated 17 sick cases to XVIII + XIV Corps joint M.V.D.	
	30 9/17		— do — 6 — do — — do —	
			G. E. Gilbert Capt AVC O/C 30 Mobile Vet. Section 18 Division	

(A7092). Wt. W12839/M1293. 75,000. 1/17. D. D. & L., Ltd. Forms/C.2118/14.

16

Instructions regarding War Diaries and Intelligence Summaries are contained in F. S. Regs., Part II. and the Staff Manual respectively. Title pages will be prepared in manuscript.

WAR DIARY of 30 Mobile Veterinary Section

~~or~~

~~INTELLIGENCE SUMMARY.~~

(Erase heading not required.)

Vol XXVII Sh 1

Army Form C. 2118.

Vol 26

Place	Date	Hour	Summary of Events and Information	Remarks and references to Appendices
Sh 27 F28 b1.4	2/10/17		Evacuated 26 sick cases to Corps M.V.D.	
(between POPERINGHE + PROVEN.	3/10/17		— " — 10 — " — " —	
	5/10/17		No SSR 556 Staff Sgt WARSOP J.W. 10 days leave to England 6 to 16/10/17	
	6/10/17		Evacuated 10 sick cases to Corps M.V.D.	
	9/10/17		— " — 13 — " — " —	
	10/10/17		— " — 5 — " — " —	
			No 5622 S.S. CROWTHER W. rejoined from leave	
Sh 28 A22 C6.0	11/10/17		Evacuated 3 sick cases to Corps M.V.D.	
			Section marched to Sh 28 A22 C6.0. (between POPERINGHE & ELVERDINGHE) & took over billet & 31 sick cases from No 22 M.V.S.	
			No T.T. 03066 Pte RUTHERFORD T. and No 25541 Pte LACY W.R. reported for duty from No 4 Vety Hospl. Established advanced Dressing Post at C15 C8.6 Sh 28	
	12/10/17		Evacuated 2 sick cases to Corps M.V.D. by float	
	13/10/17		— " — 43 — " — " —	
	14/10/17		— " — 24 — " — " —	
	15/10/17		No 8400 P.A Cpl Amesbury A. and No 10443 P/A/Cpl WRIGHT W.G despatched to No 2 Vety Hospl. for duty (Authy Base Vety Records T/9/734/17, 4/10/17)	
	"		Withdrew Advanced Dressing Post	

(A7092). Wt. W12839/M1293 750,000 1/17. D. D. & L., Ltd. Forms/C.2118/14.

Instructions regarding War Diaries and Intelligence Summaries are contained in F. S. Regs., Part II. and the Staff Manual respectively. Title pages will be prepared in manuscript.

WAR DIARY
or
~~INTELLIGENCE SUMMARY.~~
(Erase heading not required.)

of 30 Mobile Veterinary Station

Army Form C. 2118.

Vol XXVII Sh 2

Place	Date	Hour	Summary of Events and Information	Remarks and references to Appendices
Sh. 28 A 22 C 6 0.	16 10/17		No 6486 Pte PAYNE C.E. and No 4308 Pte HALL A.T. appointed U/A/Cpls	
			No 6486 U/A/Cpl PAYNE C.E. 10 days leave to England 16 to 26 10/17	
	17 10/17		No SSR 556 Staff Sgt WARSOP J.W. rejoined from leave	
	20 10/17		Evacuated 22 sick cases to Corps M.V.D.	
	21 10/17		—"— 46 —"— —"—	
	26 10/17		—"— 58 —"— —"—	
	27 10/17		—"— 33 —"— —"—	
	28 10/17		—"— 13 —"— —"—	
	30 10/17		No 78489 Pte HATTERSLEY W.A. 10 days leave to England 31 10/17 to 9 11/17	
Sh. 28 A 14 b 8 3.			Section marched to location marked & took over camp recently occupied by 44 M.V.S. together with 200 sick cases for evacuation. The Section then formed along with 45 M.V.S. Corps Veterinary Casualty Clearing Station	
	31 10/17		Evacuated 200 sick cases to ~~Corps~~ No 13 Vety Hospl.	

(A7092). Wt W12839/M1293 750,000. 1/17. D. D. & L., Ltd. Forms/C.2118/14.

Instructions regarding War Diaries and Intelligence Summaries are contained in F. S. Regs., Part II. and the Staff Manual respectively. Title pages will be prepared in manuscript.

Army Form C. 2118.

WAR DIARY
or
~~INTELLIGENCE~~ SUMMARY.
(Erase heading not required.)

of 30 Mobile Veterinary Section Vol XXVII Sh 3

Place	Date	Hour	Summary of Events and Information	Remarks and references to Appendices
Sh 28 A 14 b 8.3			It has become increasingly apparent that many horses are evacuated to the Base Hosps which might be successfully treated without being sent so far. Except in times of pressure every endeavour is made to treat in M.V.S. any case which will probably be fit in ten days if it has become impossible to treat it in the Unit lines. But when casualties are severe the strain on the establishment & accommodation of M.V.S prevent even this being done. Moreover, when a Division is about to move, all horses not immediately fit, are as a rule sent to M.V.S; but M.V.S is then also about to move so that it can do nothing but evacuate them. Over and above the cases which would probably be fit in ten days there are a large number which would be fit in 3 weeks. The time from horses leaving their units until their arrival at Base Treating Hospitals, and from their discharge fit until their return to work at the front, must be considerable, and it is suggested for	

(A7092). Wt W12839/M1293 75,0.0. 1/17. D. D. & L., Ltd. Forms/C.2118/14.

Instructions regarding War Diaries and Intelligence Summaries are contained in F. S. Regs., Part II. and the Staff Manual respectively. Title pages will be prepared in manuscript.

WAR DIARY

or

~~INTELLIGENCE SUMMARY.~~

(*Erase heading not required.*)

of 30 Mobile Veterinary Section

Army Form C. 2118.

Vol XXVII Sh 4

Place	Date	Hour	Summary of Events and Information	Remarks and references to Appendices
			for consideration whether an advance Hospital for selected cases would not be practicable. If it were close enough it would save considerable transportation as well as horse working time.	
			Units similar to M.V.S. but local & not Mobile, and with suitable standings and security of tenure would meet the case to some extent.	
			E. S. Gelbart Capt AVC O/c 30 Mobile Vety Section 18 Divn	

(A7092) Wt W12839/M1293 75,0.0. 1/17. D. D. & L., Ltd. Forms/C.2118/14.

17

18/44 A
-6 DEC. 1917
18TH DIVISION

Instructions regarding War Diaries and Intelligence Summaries are contained in F. S. Regs., Part II. and the Staff Manual respectively. Title pages will be prepared in manuscript.

WAR DIARY or INTELLIGENCE SUMMARY.

of 30 Mobile Veterinary Section

Vol 28. Sh 1.

Army Form C. 2118.

(Erase heading not required.)

Vol 27

Place	Date	Hour	Summary of Events and Information	Remarks and references to Appendices
Sh 28 Belgium A14 ~~6.8.~~ b8-3.	4/11/17		Evacuated 88 sick cases to No 13 Veterinary Hospital	
	5/11/17		" 195 " " "	
	7/11/17		" 154 " " "	
	9/11/17		" 271 " " "	
Sh 28. Belgium A14 b8.8	10/11/17		Section took over Camp at A14 b8.8. Sh 28 from 45 M.V.S.	
			Established Advanced Dressing Post at Sh 28 B20 a 5.3 in relief of 29 M.V.S	
			No SE4950 Pte WALKER F. fourteen days leave to England	
	12/11/17		Evacuated 81 sick cases to No 4 Veterinary Hospital	
	13/11/17		No 78789 Pte HATTERSLEY W.A. rejoined from leave	
			No 6746 Pte SLOAN T. fourteen days leave to England	
	19/11/17		Evacuated 96 sick cases to No 4 Veterinary Hospital	
	22/11/17		Advanced Dressing Post withdrawn	
	23/11/17		Evacuated 32 sick cases to No 13 Veterinary Hospital	
	24/11/17		No 4950 Pte Walker F. rejoined from leave	
	28/11/17		No 6693 Pte Oddo F. fourteen days leave to England	
			Evacuated 63 sick cases to No 13 Veterinary Hospital	

(A7092) Wt. W12839/M1293 75,000. 1/17. D. D. & L., Ltd. Forms/C.2118/14.

Instructions regarding War Diaries and Intelligence Summaries are contained in F. S. Regs., Part II. and the Staff Manual respectively. Title pages will be prepared in manuscript.

WAR DIARY
or
INTELLIGENCE SUMMARY.
(Erase heading not required.)

of 30 Mobile Vety Section Army Form C. 2118.
Vol 28 Sh 2.

Place	Date	Hour	Summary of Events and Information	Remarks and references to Appendices
			In the earlier part of the month 30 M.V.S. along with 45 M.V.S. + a party from the Base acted as Vety C.C.S. to 19th Corps. Casualties were very heavy at the time and there was much movement of troops, and accordingly the number of horses handled by C.C.S. was very large. From 10.11.17 however Divisional M.V.S. entrained their own cases with the exception of float cases. As regards float cases 30 M.V.S. acted as Corps Vety C.C.S. but otherwise merely as a divisional M.V.S. I think this arrangement is preferable to having a Corps Vety C.C.S. formed out of Divl. M.V.S.	
			E.E. Gilbert Capt AVC O/c 30 M.V.S 18 Division	

(A7092) Wt W12839/M1293 75,0.0. 1/17. D. D. & L., Ltd. Forms/C.2118/14.

Instructions regarding War Diaries and Intelligence Summaries are contained in F. S. Regs., Part II. and the Staff Manual respectively. Title pages will be prepared in manuscript.

WAR DIARY ~~or~~ ~~INTELLIGENCE SUMMARY.~~ of 30 Mobile Veterinary Section

(Erase heading not required.)

Army Form C. 2118.

Vol 29. Sh 1

Vol 28

Place	Date	Hour	Summary of Events and Information	Remarks and references to Appendices
Sh 28 Belgium A14 B.88.	1 12/17		No 6746 Pte Sloan T. rejoined from leave	
	2 12/17		No 6501 Pte Taylor T.W.G. 14 days leave to England 2 to 16 12/17	
	2 12/17		Evacuated 57 sick cases to No 13 Veterinary Hospl.	
	6 12/17		Lt Bisset N. AVC joined for temporary duty	
			Capt JELBART F.E. 14 days leave to England 7 to 21 12/17	
			No 4097 Sgt Thornley T. transferred to No 2 Vety Hospl. for duty Authy (ADMS 3/68 12.12.17)	
			Evacuated 47 sick cases to No 13 Vety Hospl.	
	8 12/17		No 30874 Pte THROWER A.W.H. 14 days leave to England 9 to 23 12/17	
	10 12/17		Evacuated 30 sick cases to No 13 Vety Hospl.	
	11 12/17		No 6812 Pte Fox N.M. 14 days leave to England 11 to 25 12/17	
	14 12/17		No 6693 Pte Odds E. rejoined from leave	
	14 12/17		No 6501 Pte Taylor T.W.G. rejoined from leave	
			Evacuated 75 sick cases to No 13 Veterinary Hospl.	
	18 12/17		No 7308 A/Cpl HALL A.T. 14 days leave to England 18 12/17 to 1 1/18	
			No 26844 Pte Harding J. No 30868 Pte Cantle S. and No 22872 Pte Gregory E. reported for duty from No 23 Veterinary Hospl.	

D. D. & L., London, E.C. (A7883) Wt. W809/M1672 350,000 4/17 Sch. 52a Forms/C/2118/14

Instructions regarding War Diaries and Intelligence Summaries are contained in F. S. Regs., Part II. and the Staff Manual respectively. Title pages will be prepared in manuscript.

WAR DIARY of 30 Mobile Veterinary Section

or

INTELLIGENCE SUMMARY.

(Erase heading not required.)

Army Form C. 2118.

Vol 29 Sh 2

Place	Date	Hour	Summary of Events and Information	Remarks and references to Appendices
PROVEN	18 12/17		XIX Corps Vet C.C.S. handed over to 2/1 N. Lancs M.V.S. and Section marched to PROVEN.	
	19 12/17		No 6501 Pte TAYLOR T.W.G.; No 24848 Pte BROWN T. and No 7592A Pte GROVER A.E. despatched to No 2 Vety Hospl Authy OC AVC Base Records No 74/165A/17 d 12.12.17.	
	23 12/17		Capt JELBART E.E. returned from leave & Lt Brosset N. rejoined his unit	
			No 393 Sgt PALMER W.G. reported for duty from No 12 Vety Hospl	
	26 12/17		Evacuated 18 sick cases to No 13 Vety Hospl	
			No 706 Sgt LITTLEWOOD H. 14 days leave to England 27/12/17 to 10/1/18	
			No 5084 Pte THROWER A.W.H. returned from leave	
	28 12/17		No 6812 Pte FOX W.M. returned from leave	
	31 12/17		Evacuated 20 sick cases to No 13 Vety Hospl	
			E.E. Jelbart Capt AVC O/c 30 M.V.S. 18 Divn	

D. D. & L., London, E.C.
(A7883) Wt. W803/M1672 350,000 4/17 Sch. 52a Forms/C/2118/14

14

Instructions regarding War Diaries and Intelligence Summaries are contained in F. S. Regs., Part II, and the Staff Manual respectively. Title pages will be prepared in manuscript.

WAR DIARY or INTELLIGENCE SUMMARY.
(Erase heading not required.)

of 30 Mobile Veterinary Section

Vol XXX Sh. 1

Army Form C. 2118.

VA 29

Place	Date	Hour	Summary of Events and Information	Remarks and references to Appendices
Sh 28 A2 d 9.9.	3 1/18		Section marched to Sh 28 A2 d 9.9 and took over XIX Corps Vety. C.C.S from M.V.S of 2/1 W Lancs 57th Division	
	6 1/18		No 11852 Pte Smith T.E. AVC reported for duty from No 2 Vety Hospl.	
	7 1/18		Evacuated 46 sick cases to No 13 Vety Hospl. Base train conducting party of 6 other ranks attached to Corps V.C.C.S returned to Base	
	8 1/18		No 35479 Pte Gerrard E reported for duty from No 2 Veterinary Hospl.	
	10 1/18		No 3463 Pte Taylor W. AVC despatched to No 2 Vety Hospl. authy (14/1654/14 of AVC Records d. 28.12.17)	
	11 1/18		No 406 Sgt Littlewood H. rejoined from leave	
	14 1/18		Evacuated 41 sick cases to No 4 Vety Hospl.	
	21 1/18		— " — 49 — " — — " —	
			No 3463 Pte Taylor W. and No 24848 Pte Brown T. reported for duty from No 2 Vety Hospl.	
	28 1/18		Evacuated 37 Sickcases to No 13 Vety Hospl.	
			No 35479 Pte Gerrard E and No 11852 Pte Smith T.E. despatched to No 2 Vety Hospl. for duty (authy No 2 Vety Hospl. D/54/18 d 19.1.18)	
	29 1/18		No 2088 Pte Wheeler W.H. 14 days leave to England 29 1/18 to 12 2/18	

D. D. & L., London, E.C. (A7883) Wt. W809/M1672 350,000 4/17 Sch. 52a Forms/C/2118/14

Army Form C. 2118.

Instructions regarding War Diaries and Intelligence Summaries are contained in F. S. Regs., Part II. and the Staff Manual respectively. Title pages will be prepared in manuscript.

WAR DIARY of 30 Mobile Veterinary Section

or

~~INTELLIGENCE SUMMARY.~~

(Erase heading not required.)

Vol ~~XXX~~ Sh 2.

Place	Date	Hour	Summary of Events and Information	Remarks and references to Appendices
PROVEN	30/1/18		Section marched to PROVEN Sh 27 E12 d 3.9.	
			E.E. Gilbert Capt AVC	
			O/c 30 M.V.S	
			18 Divn.	

D. D. & L., London, E.C.
(A7883) Wt. W809/M1672 350,000 4/17 Sch. 52a Forms/C/2118/14

11

Instructions regarding War Diaries and Intelligence Summaries are contained in F. S. Regs., Part II. and the Staff Manual respectively. Title pages will be prepared in manuscript.

WAR DIARY
or
INTELLIGENCE SUMMARY.
(Erase heading not required.)

of 30 Mobile Veterinary Section
18 Division

Army Form C. 2118.

Place	Date	Hour	Summary of Events and Information	Remarks and references to Appendices
PROVEN.	6 2/18		Transferred 8 sick cases to No 42 Mobile Vety Section	Vol 30
	7 2/18		—"— 6 —"— —"— —"—	
	8 2/18		Section entrained at PROVEN 2 pm.	
SALENCY France Sh. 70E 1/40000 J18a	9 2/18		Section detrained at NOYON 9-30 a.m. and marched to SALENCY	
	11 2/18		No 22765 Pte DODDS T. reported for duty from No. 2 Veterinary Hospl.	
	12 2/18		No T4/122777 Driver NEVARD J A.S.C. 14 days leave to England 14–28 2/18	
	13 2/18		No 24828 Pte BROWN T. AVC 14 days leave to England 15 2/18 to 1 3/18	
	15 2/18		No 6486 U/A/Cpl PAYNE C.E. despatched to No 2 Vety Hospl for training as Sgt AVC to field unit. (Authy Base Records No T10/40/18 of 7 2/18	
GRANDRU	16 2/18		Section marched to GRANDRU Sh. 70E K3a and took up billets with the view of preparing a camp to be used as a Corps Vety C.C.S.	
			No 2088 Pte WHEELER W.H. rejoined from leave to England.	
	19 2/18		Evacuated 16 sick cases to No 7 Vety Hospl. (Railhead APPILLY)	
	22 2/18		—"— 8 —"— —"— —"—	
	26 2/18		—"— 26 —"— —"— —"—	

S.A. Jellart Capt AVC
O/c 30 M.V.S
18 Division

(A7092). Wt W12839/M1293 750,000. 1/17. D. D. & L., Ltd. Forms/C.2118/14.

Jan 5/4 27 18

Instructions regarding War Diaries and Intelligence Summaries are contained in F. S. Regs., Part II. and the Staff Manual respectively. Title pages will be prepared in manuscript.

4837 8 APR 1918

WAR DIARY or INTELLIGENCE SUMMARY.

(Erase heading not required.)

of 30 Mobile Veterinary Section

Army Form C. 2118.

Vol XXXII Sh 1

Vol 31

Place	Date	Hour	Summary of Events and Information	Remarks and references to Appendices
GRANDRU	1 3/18		Evacuated 9 sick cases to No 7 Veterinary Hospital	
			No 6763 Pte DRURY W.C admitted to Hospital	
	2 3/18		No T4/122771 Dr NEYARD J. ASC rejoined from 14 days leave to England 14 – 28 2/18	
	3 3/18		No 22872 Pte GREGORY E. 14 days leave to England 5 to 19 3/18	
			No 24265 Pte BROWN T. rejoined from 14 days leave to England 15 2/18 – 1 3/18	
	6 3/18		Took over 2 acres of land & commenced preparation of same for cultivation of vegetables	
	8 3/18		Evacuated 9 sick cases to No 7 Veterinary Hospl.	
			No 6512 Pte FOX W M admitted to Hospital.	
	12 3/18		Evacuated 12 sick cases to No 7 Veterinary Hospl.	
	13 3/18		No 26977 Pte LITTLEJOHN S.W. AVC joined from III Corps H.Q. for duty of flaying dead horses in the Division	
	15 3/18		Evacuated 8 sick cases to No 7 Veterinary Hospl.	
	20 3/18		No 26977 Pte LITTLEJOHN S.W. despatched to Divl Salvage Co for duty there	
			Since arrival at Grandru the Section has been engaged in the preparation of Standings, watering facilities &c &c for a Vety Casualty Evacuation Station	

Instructions regarding War Diaries and Intelligence Summaries are contained in F. S. Regs., Part II. and the Staff Manual respectively. Title pages will be prepared in manuscript.

WAR DIARY
or
~~INTELLIGENCE SUMMARY.~~
(Erase heading not required.)

of 30 Mobile Vety Section

Army Form C. 2118.

Vol XXXII Sh 2

Place	Date	Hour	Summary of Events and Information	Remarks and references to Appendices
GRANDRU			Station for III Corps. A great deal of work of the nature of clearing buildings, disinfection and whitewashing, carting of rubble &c. for standings & roads has been done and good accommodation for 120 horses under cover provided. The work has now been completed with the exception of the construction of a Horse Dip.	
			Further, two acres of land have also been prepared ready for seed for cultivation of vegetables.	
	22/3/18		No 22872 Pte GREGORY E. rejoined from 14 days leave 5 to 19/3/18	
	24/3/18		Evacuated 27 sick cases to No 7 Veterinary Hospl from NOYON.	
		1.20pm	In view of retirement of our troops & approach of enemy, Section marched & halted at SALENCY & on receipt of instructions from Divn marched to DIVE-LE-FRANC. En route Section was joined by the following O.R. who had been sent from No 14 Vety Hospl to assist at III Corps V.C.E.S. :- No 598 Sgt McGLORY J.; No 2375 Cpl BYATT. W.J.; 13909 Pte. Alexander T. No 19614 Pte Atkins T.L. No 20056 Pte Ashford A.S.; No 20028 Pte Burrows A.J.; No 23547 Pte COURAGE L. No 27914 Pte CHARGE T.; No 9054 Pte GILBEY S. No 21824 Pte HANCOCK T.R.	
			No	

D. D. & L., London, E.C.
(A7883) Wt. W809/M1672 350,000 4/17 Sch. 52a Forms/C/2118/14

Instructions regarding War Diaries and Intelligence Summaries are contained in F. S. Regs., Part II. and the Staff Manual respectively. Title pages will be prepared in manuscript.

WAR DIARY
or
~~INTELLIGENCE~~ SUMMARY.
(Erase heading not required.)

of 30 Mobile Veterinary Section

Army Form C. 2118.

Vol XXXII sh. 3.

Place	Date	Hour	Summary of Events and Information	Remarks and references to Appendices
DIVE-LE-FRANC			No. 22540 Pte Jackson J. G. No. 22457 Pte Johnson W. No. 28501 Pte Paton W. No. 13953 Pte Smith J. H.	
PIMPREZ	25 3/18		Section marched to PIMPREZ	
CARLPONT	26 3/18		" " CARLPONT	
AUDIGNICOURT	27 3/18		" " AUDIGNICOURT	
CHOISY	29 3/18		" " CHOISY	
ARSY	30 3/18		" " ARSY	
LA NEUVILLE EN HEZ	31 3/18		" " LA NEUVILLE-EN-HEZ	
			During the march the Horse Ambulance a float has been the cause of considerable anxiety. It is built so that the clearance between the axle and the ground is very little and as a consequence it can travel with safety only on the best roads & can be pulled in only on very good ground, which makes the selection of horse lines very difficult. It is suggested that a float for active service should have at least 18 inches of clearance and that the wheels should be 4 or 5 inches broad. It is thought there would be no difficulty in loading horses into a float so constructed.	
			G. E. Gelbart Capt AVC O/C 30 Mobile Vety Section 18 Divn	

D. D. & L., London, E.C.
(A7883) Wt. W809/M1672 350,000 4/17 Sch. 52a Forms/C/2118/14

Army Form C. 2121
(in pads of 100).

"A" Form
MESSAGES AND SIGNALS.

No. of Message................

Prefix............Code..............m.	Words. Charge.	This message is on a/c of:	Recd. at..........m.
Office of Origin and Service Instructions.	Sent	..........................Service.	Date..............
	At..............m.		From..............
	To..................		
	By..................	(Signature of "Franking Officer.")	By..................

D.A.G. 11 JUN 1918 WAR OFFICE

TO War Diaries and Record Department
DAG GHQ 3rd Echelon

Sender's Number.	Day of Month.	In reply to Number.	AAA
* Q 507	4		

Herewith war Diary for the following unit of this Division for April 1918

30th MVS

From 18 Div H
Place
Time

The above may be forwarded as now corrected. (Z)

Censor. Signature of Addressor or person authorised to telegraph in his name. [illegible] Capt for Major DAAG

* This line should be erased if not required.

(18965.) Wt. W12952/M1294. 187,500 Pads. 1/17 McC. & Co., Ltd. (E. 818.)

18

Instructions regarding War Diaries and Intelligence Summaries are contained in F. S. Regs., Part II, and the Staff Manual respectively. Title pages will be prepared in manuscript.

WAR DIARY or INTELLIGENCE SUMMARY.

(Erase heading not required.)

of 30 Mobile Veterinary Section

Vol XXXIII Sh 1

Army Form C. 2118.

Place	Date	Hour	Summary of Events and Information	Remarks and references to Appendices
AUCHY LA MONTAGNE	1 4/18		Section marched from LANEUVILLE EN HEZ to AUCHY LA MONTAGNE	
LOEUILLY	2 4/18		— " — to LOEUILLY	
SALEUX	3 4/18		" to SALEUX	
	4 4/18		Advanced Collecting Post of 1 Cpl + 2 men established at BOVES under I/O 18 Divl Train	
	5 4/18		Evacuated 13 horses to No 7 Veterinary Hospl by Rail from SALEUX	
	6 4/18		" 12 " 6 " "	
			No 26977 Pte LITTLEJOHN AVC rejoined from 18th Divl HQ. as Horse Skinner.	
	7 4/18		Evacuated 16 sick cases to No 6 Vety Hospl	
	9 4/18		" 14 " " 14 "	
	10 4/18		" 2 " " 14 "	
			Six O.R from 8th Suffolks joined for temporary assistance to M.V.S	
	11 4/18		Took over Standings + 16 sick cases from "A" Canadian Cav. M.V.S	
	12 4/18		Saleux Railhead being closed - evacuated 41 sick cases by road to 4th Army Vety Evacuation Station at PICQUIGNY.	
	13 4/18		Evacuated 34 sick cases to 4th Army V.E.S.	

D. D. & L., London, E.C. (A7883) Wt. W803/M1672 350,000 4/17 Sch. 52a Forms/C/2118/14

Instructions regarding War Diaries and Intelligence Summaries are contained in F. S. Regs., Part II. and the Staff Manual respectively. Title pages will be prepared in manuscript.

WAR DIARY
or
INTELLIGENCE SUMMARY.
(Erase heading not required.)

30 Mobile Vety Section
Vol. XXXIII Sh 2

Army Form C. 2118.

Place	Date	Hour	Summary of Events and Information	Remarks and references to Appendices
SALEUX	13/4/18		Advanced Collecting Post withdrawn from BOVES	
	14/4/18		Evacuated 15 Sick Cases to 4th Army V.E.S	
	15/4/18		" 16 " " "	
	16/4/18		" 1 " (float case)	
			Following 5 O.R reported from No 8 Vety Hospl for temporary assistance.	
			No 26417 Pte McFarlane C.; 20432 Pte Illingworth O.; 26624 Pte	
			ETCHELLS L.; 20441 Pte WHEAL J.; 32944 Pte PAYNE F. all AVC	
	17/4/18		Evacuated 19 sick cases to ~~No~~ 4th Army V.E.S.	
	18/4/18		" 12 " "	
			Following 2 men reported for duty from No 2 Vety Hospl (permanent) { No 6621 Pte HACON T. 22046 Pte COOPER J.	
	19/4/18		D.V.S, A.D.V.S III Corps & D.A.D.V.S. 18 Dn visited Section - O.C unfortunately out	
	20/4/18		Evacuated 15 sick cases to 4th Army V. E. S.	
			Advanced Collecting Post (1 Cpl + 2 men) established at ST. FUSCIEN.	
	22/4/18		Evacuated 12 sick cases to No 15 Vety Hospl	
	23/4/18		" 14 " " "	
	24/4/18		" 22 " " "	

D. D. & L., London, E.C. (A7883) Wt. W809/M1672 350,000 4/17 Sch. 52a Forms/C/2118/14

Instructions regarding War Diaries and Intelligence Summaries are contained in F. S. Regs., Part II, and the Staff Manual respectively. Title pages will be prepared in manuscript.

WAR DIARY *or* INTELLIGENCE SUMMARY.

(*Erase heading not required.*)

of 30 Mobile Vety Section
Vol XXXIII Sh. 3.

Army Form C. 2118.

Place	Date	Hour	Summary of Events and Information	Remarks and references to Appendices
SALEUX	26 4/18		Evacuated 14 sick cases to No 14 Vety Hospl	
	28 4/18		" 24 " to 4th Army V.E.S at Picquigny	
	30 4/18		" 18 " to "	
			I was not in command of 30 M V S when it was mobilised	
			Capt W. N. ROWSTON was. I understand the Section joined 18th	
			Division at CODFORD early in May 1915. and embarked for France on 27 7/15	
			R.S. Gilbert Capt AVC	
			O/c 30 M.V.S 18 Divn	

D. D. & L., London, E.C.
(A7883) Wt. W809/M1672 350,000 4/17 Sch. 52a Forms/C/2118/14

27

18

Instructions regarding War Diaries and Intelligence Summaries are contained in F. S. Regs., Part II, and the Staff Manual respectively. Title pages will be prepared in manuscript.

WAR DIARY ~~or INTELLIGENCE SUMMARY.~~ of 30 Mobile Vety Section

(*Erase heading not required.*)

Army Form C. 2118.

Sheet I Vol XXXI

Vol 33

Place	Date	Hour	Summary of Events and Information	Remarks and references to Appendices
CROUY	5.5.18		Capt Colton took over command of the section Capt Gilbert being evacuated sick. Section marched to MONTIGNY. Evacuated 19 horses to 4th Army V.E.S. 2 O.R. A.V.C 30868 Pt Castle S & 22046 Pt Cooper sent to No 3 V.E.S. for duty	
MONTIGNY	6.5.18		D.A.D.V.S. joined the Section	
	8.5.18		Evacuated 2 French horses to No 7 V.E.S.	
	9.5.18		Evacuated 5 horses to No 7 V.E.S	
	10.5.18		Evacuated 12 horses to No 7 V.E.S Pt ODDS awarded 10 F.P. No 1 (Drunkeness)	
	11.5.18		Evacuated 11 horses to No 7 V.E.S	
	12.5.18		Evacuated 17 horses to No 7 V.E.S.	
	14.5.18		Evacuated 8 horses to No 7 V.E.S	
	15.5.18		Pt Rutherford admitted to hospital	
	16.5.18		Evacuated 9 horses to No 7 V.E.S 6763 Pt Drury W.C. despatched to No 2 Vety hospital for P.B. duty Authority A.D.M.S 18th Div. Pt Littlejohn admitted to 56 F.A	
	17.5.18		24265 Pt DODDS 22875 Pt GREGORY 6671 Pt HACON sent to No 7 V.E.S for duty Authority A.D.V.S. III Corps 25/13.	
	18.5.18		Evacuated 9 Horses to No 7 V.E.S	
	21.5.18		Evacuated 8 Horses to No 7 V.E.S	
	22.5.18		— — 6 — — —	
	23.5.18		Evacuated Col Walter Wright V.C. Chargers to No 13 Vety Hospt by Motor Ambulance	
	24.5.18		Evacuated 3 horses to No 7 V.E.S	

Instructions regarding War Diaries and Intelligence Summaries are contained in F. S. Regs., Part II. and the Staff Manual respectively. Title pages will be prepared in manuscript.

WAR DIARY of No 30 Mobile Vety Section
or
~~INTELLIGENCE SUMMARY.~~
(Erase heading not required.)

Sheet II

Army Form C. 2118.

Vol XXXV

Place	Date	Hour	Summary of Events and Information	Remarks and references to Appendices
MONTIGNY	25-5-18		DADVS + 3 OR left Section + rejoined 18th Div H.Q	
	27-5-18		Evacuated 7 horses to No 7 VES	
	28-5-18		A.D.V.S III Corps visited Section	
	29-5-18		Evacuated 8 horses to 7 VES 3463 A TAYLOR transferred to 7 VES for duty authority	
			ADVS III Corps T471 d 28-5-18	
	31-5-18		Evacuated 12 horses to No 7 VES	

Vaughton Capt AVC
OC 30 MVS

D. D. & L., London, E.C.
(A7883) Wt. W809/M1672 350,000 4/17 Sch. 52a Forms/C/2118/14

27 18

Instructions regarding War Diaries and Intelligence Summaries are contained in F. S. Regs., Part II, and the Staff Manual respectively. Title pages will be prepared in manuscript.

WAR DIARY
or
~~INTELLIGENCE SUMMARY.~~
(Erase heading not required.)

of 30th Mobile Veterinary Section Army Form C. 2118.

Sheet I Vol ~~XXXVI~~ Vol 34

Place	Date	Hour	Summary of Events and Information	Remarks and references to Appendices
MONTIGNY	1/6/18		Sgt Worsop transferred to No 2 Vety Hospital for duty (authority Officer i/c Base records No 2/1466/4.	
	2/6/18		Evacuated 3 mules to No 7 V.E.S. One by float	
	4/6/18		Evacuated 13 animals to No 7 V.E.S	
	5/6/18		Pt Lacey W.R proceeded on 14 days leave to England	
	7/6/18		Evacuated 10 horses & 2 mules to No 7 V.E.S	
	8/6/18		" 5 " 2 " " "	
	11/6/18		" 5 " "	
	12/6/18		" 5 " 1 " "	
	14/6/18		" 8 " "	
	15/6/18		Pt Smith W.H. (ASC) proceeded on leave to England.	
	17/6/18		Evacuated 5 horse & 5 mules to No 7 V.E.S	
	18/6/18		14709 Pt Gibson T reported for duty from No 2 Vety Hospital	
	19/6/18		Evacuated 5 horses & 1 mule to No 7 V.E.S	
	21/6/18		7308 Cpl Hall A.T. Evacuated sick to 52nd Fld Amb. (Fracture rib)	

(A7883) Wt. W809/M1672 350,000 4/17 D. D. & L., London, E.C. Sch. 52a Forms/C/2118/14

Instructions regarding War Diaries and Intelligence Summaries are contained in F. S. Regs., Part II, and the Staff Manual respectively. Title pages will be prepared in manuscript.

WAR DIARY of 30th Mobile Vety Section
or
~~INTELLIGENCE~~ SUMMARY. Sheet II Vol XXXVI
(*Erase heading not required.*)

Army Form C. 2118.

Place	Date	Hour	Summary of Events and Information	Remarks and references to Appendices
MONTIGNY	23/6/18		Evacuated 6 horses to No 7 V.E.S. 22212 Pt Dobson J. attached as skinner from III Corps	
	24/6/18		Pt Lacey W.R. returned from leave	
	28/6/18		Evacuated 3 horses & 1 mule to No 7 V.E.S	
	28/6/18		14011 Pt Bailey B. 8th Suffolk Regt (attached) evacuated sick with P.U.O	
	29/6/18		24868 Pt Brown T & 6693 Pt Odds E of 30 M.V.S. & S/S Cpl S.15984 of 8th Suffolks evacuated to 54 Field Amb with Influenza	
	30/6/18		Evacuated 3 horses & 3 mules to No 7 V.E.S. 12645 Pt Semley J of 8th Suffolks evacuated to 54 Fld Amb with Influenza	

Sam Hatton Capt AVC
O.C. 30 M.V.S.

D. D. & L., London, E.C.
(A7883) Wt. W809/M1672 350,000 4/17 Sch. 52a Forms/C/2118/14

27 18

Instructions regarding War Diaries and Intelligence Summaries are contained in F. S. Regs., Part II, and the Staff Manual respectively. Title pages will be prepared in manuscript.

WAR DIARY of 30 Mobile Vety Section or ~~INTELLIGENCE SUMMARY~~. Vol XXXVII Sheet I.

(Erase heading not required.)

Army Form C. 2118.

VF 35

Place	Date	Hour	Summary of Events and Information	Remarks and references to Appendices
MONTIGNY	2/7/18		1 Horse evacuated by float to No 7 V.E.S	
	3/7/18		4 Horses + 4 mules evacuated to No 7 V.E.S by road No 6693 Pt ODDS. E discharged from hospital returned to this unit	
	4/7/18		P/S Last discharged from hospital returned to this unit. 2 horses destroyed. Capt. Cotton proceeded on leave to the United Kingdom. Capt Williams took over charge of Section	
	5/7/18		Pt SMITH W.H. returned from leave. Pt SCRUBY discharged from Hospital	
	6/7/18		Pt BAILEY discharged from hospital	
	8/7/18		10 horses evacuated to No 7 V.E.S. Pt Brown T discharged from hospital	
	9/7/18		1 Surplus mule received to No 3 Sect D.A.C	
	10/7/18		6 horses evacuated to No 7 V.E.S	
	12/7/18		2 horses + 2 mules evacuated to No 7 V.E.S	
	13/7/18		Handed over 3 sick horses to 42nd London M.V.S marched to Breilly No 30474 Pt IXER. T.H. reported for duty from No 2 Vety Hospital	

D. D. & L., London, E.C. (A7883) Wt. W803/M1672 350,000 4/17 Sch. 52a Forms/C/2118/14

Army Form C. 2118.

Instructions regarding War Diaries and Intelligence Summaries are contained in F. S. Regs., Part II, and the Staff Manual respectively. Title pages will be prepared in manuscript.

WAR DIARY of 30 Mobile Vety Section
or
~~INTELLIGENCE~~ SUMMARY.
(*Erase heading not required.*)

Sheet II

Place	Date	Hour	Summary of Events and Information	Remarks and references to Appendices
BREILLY	15 7/18		Reissued 1 surplus rider to 18th D H Q	
	16 7/18		Evacuated 4 horses & 1 mule to 19 V E S	
	17 7/18		1 LD reissued to C/82. 1 horse destroyed	
	20 7/18		5 Horses, 1 mule & 2 hides evacuated to No 19 V E S	
	22 7/18		5 horses evacuated to No 19 V E S Capt Cotton returned from leave	
	24 7/18		4 horses & 2 mules to No 19 V E S	
	28 7/18		2 horses & 3 mules evacuated to 19 V E S	
	30 7/18		4 horses & 3 mules evacuated to 19 V E S	
	31 7/18		Marched to St GRATIEN & took over from 5 Aust M V S	

D. D. & L., London, E.C.
(A7883) Wt. W809/M1672 350,000 4/17 Sch. 52a Forms/C/2118/14

27

Instructions regarding War Diaries and Intelligence Summaries are contained in F. S. Regs., Part II, and the Staff Manual respectively. Title pages will be prepared in manuscript.

WAR DIARY ~~or~~ ~~INTELLIGENCE SUMMARY.~~ of 30 Mobile Veterinary Section

(Erase heading not required.)

Army Form C. 2118.

18

Vol XXXVIII Sh 1.

Vol 36

Place	Date	Hour	Summary of Events and Information	Remarks and references to Appendices
ST. GRATIEN	7/8/18		Established advanced Veterinary Post at HEILLY (1 N.C.O. + 2 men)	
			Evacuated 8 sick cases to No 4 V.E.S	
	9/8/18		— " — 13 — " — — " —	
	10/8/18		— " — 2 — " — — " —	
	11/8/18		— " — 4 — " — — " —	
	12/8/18		— " — 6 — " — — " —	
MONTIGNY			Section marched to MONTIGNY + took over Camp from 1/2 London M.V.S.	
	16/8/18		Capt E.F. JELBART A.V.C. reported for duty from No 2 Vety Hospl.	
			Evacuated 11 sick cases to No 3 V.E.S.	
	17/8/18		Capt E.F. JELBART took over Command of Section and Capt S.J. COTTON A.V.C. evacuated to Base sick	
	18/8/18		No 116 ~~Cpl~~ Cpl CLINTON R. granted 14 days leave to U.K. 20/8/18 to 3/9/18	
	21/8/18		Evacuated 24 sick cases to No 3 V.E.S.	
			No 22212 Pte DOBSON J. AVC Trained Skinner despatched to No 3 V.E.S for duty. Authy ADVS III Corps	

D. D. & L., London, E.C. (A7883) Wt. W809/M1672 350,000 4/17 Sch. 52a Forms/C/2118/14

Instructions regarding War Diaries and Intelligence Summaries are contained in F. S. Regs., Part II. and the Staff Manual respectively. Title pages will be prepared in manuscript.

WAR DIARY of 30 Mobile Veterinary Section
or
~~INTELLIGENCE SUMMARY.~~
(Erase heading not required.)

Army Form C. 2118.

Vol XXXVIII Sh. 2

Place	Date	Hour	Summary of Events and Information	Remarks and references to Appendices
	22/8/18		Established Advanced Veterinary Post at WARLOY (1 NCO + 2 men)	
MONTIGNY	23/8/18		Evacuated 23 sick cases to No 3 V.E.S.	
	24/8/18		— " — 6 — " — — " —	
WARLOY			Section marched to WARLOY	
	25/8/18		No 2665 Pte Woodruff P.C. AVC 14 days leave to U.K. 26/8/18 to 9/9/18	
	26/8/18		Evacuated 6 sick cases to No 3 V.E.S.	
ALBERT			Section moved to camp west of BELLE VUE FARM ALBERT Sh. 62D E10 d 4.6.	
	28/8/18		Evacuated 2 float cases to No 3 V.E.S.	
	29/8/18		No 14645 Pte SCRUBY J. Suffolk Regt granted 14 days leave to UK 30/8/18 to 13/9/18	
			Evacuated 29 sick cases to No 3 V.E.S.	
	30/8/18		— " — 14 — " — — " —	
	31/8/18		— " — 4 — " — — " —	
			Section marched to western edge of MAMETZ Wood + took up camp Sh. 57D X 23 b 2.9.	
			E G Gilbert Capt AVC	
			of 30 M.V.S.	
			18 Division	

D. D. & L., London, E.C.
(A7883) Wt. W809/M1672 350,000 4/17 Sch. 52a Forms/C/2118/14

5

Instructions regarding War Diaries and Intelligence Summaries are contained in F. S. Regs., Part II, and the Staff Manual respectively. Title pages will be prepared in manuscript.

WAR DIARY or INTELLIGENCE SUMMARY.

(Erase heading not required.)

of 30 Mobile Veterinary Section

Vol XXXIX Sh 1

Vol 38

Army Form C. 2118.

Place	Date	Hour	Summary of Events and Information	Remarks and references to Appendices
MAMETZ WOOD	1 9/18		No 15984 S.S. LAST S.J. (Suffolk Regt) 14 days leave to England 2-16 9/18	
S.A.54.D X23 b 2.9	2 9/18		Evacuated 13 sick cases to No 3 Veterinary Evacuating Station	
	3 9/18		Established Advanced Post of 1 NCO + 2 men at TRONES WOOD	
	4 9/18		Evacuated 11 sick cases to No 3 V.E.S.	
	6 9/18		— " — 13 — " — — " —	
			No 116 Cpl CLINTON R. rejoined from leave	
	8 9/18		No 7353 Pte SEABOURNE A.F. 14 days leave to England 9 to 23 9/18	
	9 9/18		Evacuated 10 sick cases to No 3 V.E.S.	
	11 9/18		No 2665 Pte Woodruff P.C. rejoined from leave	
	12 9/18		Evacuated 4 sick cases to No 3 V.E.S.	
	13 9/18		No 3413 Sgt PALMER W.G. 14 days leave to England 14-28 9/18	
	16 9/18		Evacuated 4 sick cases to No 3 V.E.S.	
MOISLAINS			Section marched to MOISLAINS and took up camp near old Brickwork at Sh 62c C23 d 6.6. Post at Trones Wood withdrawn	
			No 74645 Pte SCRUBY J. rejoined from leave	
	19 9/18		No 15984 S.S. LAST S.J. rejoined from leave	

D. D. & L., London, E.C. (A7883) Wt. W809/M1672 350,000 4/17 Sch. 52a Forms/C/2118/14

Instructions regarding War Diaries and Intelligence Summaries are contained in F. S. Regs., Part II. and the Staff Manual respectively. Title pages will be prepared in manuscript.

WAR DIARY of 30 Mobile Veterinary Section

or

~~INTELLIGENCE SUMMARY.~~

(Erase heading not required.)

Army Form C. 2118.

Vol ~~XXXIX~~ Sh 2

Place	Date	Hour	Summary of Events and Information	Remarks and references to Appendices
MOISLAINS	22/9/18		Evacuated 39 sick cases to No 3 V.E.S.	
	23/9/18		— " — 5 — " — — " —	
	25/9/18		— " — 11 — " — — " —	
	26/9/18		No 7353 Pte SEABOURNE A.E. rejoined from leave.	
	27/9/18		No T4/122771 Driver NEVARD J. special leave to England 28/9/18 - 12/10/18	
			Established Advance Post of 1 NCO + 2 men at NURLU.	
	28/9/18		Evacuated 12 sick cases to No 3 V.E.S.	
	30/9/18		" 13 — " — — " —	
			No 373 Sgt PALMER W.G. rejoined from leave	
			No 13971 Pte LEECH. B.J. (Suffolk Regt) leave to England 1-15/10/18	
			E.G. Jelbart Capt AVC	
			O/C 30 M.V.S.	
			18 Divn	

D. D. & L., London, E.C.
(A7883) Wt. W809/M1672 350,000 4/17 Sch. 52a Forms/C/2118/14

4

Instructions regarding War Diaries and Intelligence Summaries are contained in F. S. Regs., Part II, and the Staff Manual respectively. Title pages will be prepared in manuscript.

"A" BRANCH, HEADQUARTERS, 78758 Date 10/11/18

WAR DIARY ~~or INTELLIGENCE~~ SUMMARY.

of 30 Mobile Veterinary Section

(Erase heading not required.)

Army Form C. 2118. 18

Vol XL Sh 1.

Vol 39

Place	Date	Hour	Summary of Events and Information	Remarks and references to Appendices
MOISLAINS	1/10/18		Evacuated 9 sick cases to No 3 V.E.S.	
MONTAUBAN			Section marched to MONTAUBAN and staged the night	
MONTIGNY	2 10/18		Section marched to MONTIGNY (sur L'HALLUE) & took up former camp	
	5 10/18		No 116 Cpl CLINTON R. AVC despatched to No 2 Vety Hospl for training as Sgt for Field Unit (Authy O/c AVC Base Records T/10/152/18 d. 25 9/18)	
			The following granted 14 days leave to U.K. (1) No 6451 Pte AXHORN G.W. & (2) No 9403 Pte HUGHES J.D. — leave of both 6th to 20th Octr 1918	
	9 10/18		No 5622 S.S. CROWTHER W. AVC & No 14609 L/Cpl CARD W (Suffolks) granted 14 days leave to U.K. 10 to 24 10/18	
	12 10/18		Evacuated 13 sick cases by Rail to No 4 Vety Hospl	
	14 10/18		No 706 Sgt LITTLEWOOD H. AVC 14 days special leave to U.K. 15 to 29 10/18	
COMBLES	17 10/18		Section marched to COMBLES and staged the night	
RONSSOY	18 10/18		Section marched to RONSSOY (Sh 62 c F21)	
SERAIN	19 10/18		Section marched to SERAIN (Sh 57 B. U 14)	
MARETZ	20 10/18		Section marched to MARETZ (Sh 57 B U 6) & took over camp from 1/1 E. LANCS M.V.S.	

D. D. & L., London, E.C. (A7883) Wt. W803/M1672 350,000 4/17 Sch. 52a Forms/C/2118/14

Instructions regarding War Diaries and Intelligence Summaries are contained in F. S. Regs., Part II. and the Staff Manual respectively. Title pages will be prepared in manuscript.

WAR DIARY of 30 Mobile Veterinary Section

~~or~~

~~INTELLIGENCE SUMMARY.~~

(Erase heading not required.)

Army Form C. 2118.

Vol XL Sh. 2.

Place	Date	Hour	Summary of Events and Information	Remarks and references to Appendices
MARETZ	21/10/18		No 13971 Pte LEECH B.J. (Suffolks) rejoined from leave	
	23/10/18		Evacuated 8 sick cases to No 13 V.E.S.	
			No 6451 Pte AKHORN G.W. rejoined from leave	
LE CATEAU	24/10/18		Section marched to LE CATEAU. Before marching 6 sick cases transferred to M.V.S 50th Divn adjoining - to be handed over to 13 V.E.S who took over 30 M.V.S camp at MARETZ next day	
	26/10/18		Evacuated 24 sick cases to No 13 V.E.S.	
	27/10/18		— " — 6 — " — " — " — " —	
			No 5622 S.S. CROWTHER W and No 14609 L/cpl CARD. W. (Suffolks) rejoined from leave	
			No 2517 Pte MORVILLE J. reported for duty from No 2 Vety Hospl	
	28/10/18		Evacuated 23 sick cases to No 13 V.E.S.	
	29/10/18		— " — 26 — " — — " —	
	30/10/18		— " — 41 — " — — " —	
	31/10/18		— " — 23 — " — — " —	
			No 706 Sgt LITTLEWOOD H. rejoined from leave.	

D. D. & L., London, E.C. (A7883) Wt. W803/M1672 350,000 4/17 Sch. 52a Forms/C/2118/14

Instructions regarding War Diaries and Intelligence Summaries are contained in F. S. Regs., Part II. and the Staff Manual respectively. Title pages will be prepared in manuscript.

WAR DIARY of 30 Mobile Vety Section

or

~~INTELLIGENCE~~ SUMMARY. Vol XL Sh 3

(*Erase heading not required.*)

Army Form C. 2118.

Place	Date	Hour	Summary of Events and Information	Remarks and references to Appendices
LE CATEAU	31/10/18		No 30474 Pte IXER T.H. granted 14 days leave to UK 2 to 16/4/18.	
			Since arrival in LE CATEAU the Section has evacuated a considerable number of animals — these were mostly belonging to other formations than 18th Division and were to a great extent cases of gunshot wounds although there were a number of debility cases. A few cases of stomatitis said to be due to eating grass in gas shelled areas were seen.	
			E. E. Jelbart Capt AVC O/C 30 M.V.S. 18 Divn	

D. D. & L., London, E.C. (A7883) Wt. W809/M1672 350,000 4/17 Sch. 52a Forms/C/2118/14

19 Vol 38

No. 39
MOBILE VETERINARY
SECTION.

No.
Date.

War Diary of
39 M.V.S.
For month of November
1918

Rupert L. L. Hart
T/Capt AVC
OC 39 MVS

30/11/18

(1)

Instructions regarding War Diaries and Intelligence Summaries are contained in F. S. Regs., Part II. and the Staff Manual respectively. Title pages will be prepared in manuscript.

WAR DIARY
or
INTELLIGENCE SUMMARY.
(Erase heading not required.)

Army Form C. 2118.

No. 34 MOBILE VETERINARY SECTION. VOL 38. 30/11/18

V R 39

Place	Date	Hour	Summary of Events and Information	Remarks and references to Appendices
TREFCON	1/11/18		Adm 15 Hussars – 3 8 Hussars – 1 9 C.F.A. – 1 Evac by Rail to 7 Vety Hospl 8 horses	
	2/11/18		Adm 19 Hussars – 1 Destroyed 1 horse hide sent to Hospl	
	4/11/18		Adm 15 – Found 1	
	5/11/18		Evacuated 18 horses to 7 V Hospl	
	6/11/18		Left TREFCON 9 am arrived BANTOUXELLE 3 30 pm (Destroyed 1 horse	
BANTOUXELLE	7/11/18		Left BANTOUXELLE 11 am arrived ARLEUX 5 pm Adm 9 M.G.S. 1 8 Hussars – 6 Destroyed 1 horse 8 Hussars	
ARLEUX	8/11/18		Left ARLEUX 9 am arrived PONT-A-MARCQ 4 30 pm Adm 5 Horses 19th Hussars (Evacuated to 18 V.E.S. – 17 horses	
PONT-A-MARCQ	9/11/18		Left Pont-a-Marcq 8 30 am arrived GAUFRAIN RAMECROIX 6 30 pm	
GAUFRAIN RAMECROIX	10/11/18		Left joined "B" Echelon at Ramecroix Adm 29 horses Destroyed 1 Evacuated to 3 V.E.S. – 28 horses & 1 Hide	
VILLERS ST AMAND	11/11/18		Left Ramecroix at 6 30 pm arrived VILLERS ST AMAND 12 midnight Armistice signed 11 am. Left Villers St Amand Chateau 5 pm arrived Maffle 9 pm Evacuated to No 1 M.V.S. – 26 horses	

R. L. Hart

D. D. & L., London, E.C. (10340) Wt W3300/P713 750,000 5/15 E 2688 Forms/C2118/16

Instructions regarding War Diaries and Intelligence Summaries are contained in F. S. Regs., Part II. and the Staff Manual respectively. Title pages will be prepared in manuscript.

11

WAR DIARY
or
INTELLIGENCE SUMMARY.
(*Erase heading not required.*)

Army Form C. 2118.

Place	Date	Hour	Summary of Events and Information	Remarks and references to Appendices
VILL MAFFLE	12/11/18		Left Maffle 8 am arrived Callennelle 4 pm	
CALLANNELLE	13/11/18		Adm 39 horses	
	14/11/18		Adm 17 horses.	
	15/11/18		Evacuated 56 horses to 3 V.E.S	
	16/11/18		Adm 30 horses also 11 Cast horses by D.D.R. Evac to 3 V.E.S. 6 horses.	
	17/11/18		Evac to 3 V.E.S. Tournai 25 horses & 11 Cast horses	
			Left Callannelle 7.30 pm arrived Neufvilles 11 pm	
NEUFVILLES	18/11/18		Left Neufvilles, 8.30 am arrived Eccausinnes 3.30 pm	
ECCAUSINNES	19/11/18		Adm 9th Cav Bde N.I.-1 15 Huss-3	
	20/11/18		Evac to Canadian V.E.S. 4 by road 1 by float. Pte Jerome W.A. Admitted - 12 horses Granted 14 days leave to U.K.	
	21/11/18		Evac to Canadian V.E.S. - 13 horses. Left Eccausinnes 8 am arrived St Gery 5 pm	
ST GERY	22/11/18		Left St Gery 7.30 am arrived FRANC-WARET 4.30 pm	

R.H. Hart

111

Army Form C. 2118.

Instructions regarding War Diaries and Intelligence Summaries are contained in F. S. Regs., Part II. and the Staff Manual respectively. Title Pages will be prepared in manuscript.

WAR DIARY
or
INTELLIGENCE SUMMARY

(Erase heading not required.)

No. 30 MOBILE VETERINARY SECTION.
No. Vol 38
Date 30/11/18

Place	Date	Hour	Summary of Events and Information	Remarks and references to Appendices
FRANC WARET	23/11/18		Adm 9th M.G.S. - 2 8 Hussars - 4 · 15 Hussars - 8.	
	24/11/18		Left Franc Waret 8.30 am arrived OTEPPE 1.30 pm	
OTEPPE	25/11/18		Adm 15 Hussars - 1 19 Hussars - 2 (Cast to Butchery) 2 horses Transaction thro No 1 M.V.S	
	26/11/18		5533 Sgt. Davies C.R. A.V.C adm to Hospl	
	27/11/18		Left Oteppe 8 am arrived Tilff. 4 pm	
TILFF	29/11/18		Left Tilff at 8.30 am arrived DOHLAIN 4 pm	
DOHLAIN	30/11/18		Rested 1 day.	

Rupert R. R. Hart
T/Capt AVC
O.C. 39 M.V.S

7/2

Instructions regarding War Diaries and Intelligence Summaries are contained in F. S. Regs., Part II. and the Staff Manual respectively. Title pages will be prepared in manuscript.

HEAD QUARTERS No 78/60 10 DEC. 1918 DIVISION

WAR DIARY or ~~INTELLIGENCE SUMMARY.~~

(Erase heading not required.)

30 Mobile Vety Section

Army Form C. 2118.

18

Vol XLI Sh 1

98 40

Place	Date	Hour	Summary of Events and Information	Remarks and references to Appendices
LE CATEAU	1/11/18		Capt BUIE J reported for duty and took over command from Capt E.F. JELBART AVC whilst the latter was acting DADVS 18 DW vice MAJOR L.M. VERNEY transferred for temporary duty to American Expeditionary Force.	
			Evacuated 23 sick cases to No 13 Vety Evacuating Station	
			No 2088 Pte WHEELER W.H. AVC admitted to Hospital	
	2/11/18		No 2665 " WOODRUFF P.C. AVC — do —	
			Evacuated 20 sick cases to No 13 V.E.S.	
	3/11/18		— " — 28 — " — — " —	
			No 26844 a/cpl HARDING J. AVC No 18789 Pte HATTERSLEY W.A. AVC and No 40423 Dr. BARNETT B.A. RFA granted leave to UK from 5 to 19.11.18	
	4/11/18		Evacuated 8 sick cases to No 13 V.E.S.	
	6/11/18		— " — 21 — " — — " —	
	7/11/18		— " — 1 — " — — " —	
	8/11/18		— " — 14 — " — — " —	

D. D. & L., London, E.C. (A7883) Wt. W803/M1672 350,000 4/17 Sch. 52a Forms/C/2118/14

Instructions regarding War Diaries and Intelligence Summaries are contained in F. S. Regs., Part II. and the Staff Manual respectively. Title pages will be prepared in manuscript.

WAR DIARY
or
~~INTELLIGENCE SUMMARY.~~
(*Erase heading not required.*)

of 30 Mobile Vety Section
Vol XLI

Army Form C. 2118.

Sh 2

Place	Date	Hour	Summary of Events and Information	Remarks and references to Appendices
LE CATEAU	9/11/18		Evacuated 12 sick cases to No 13 V.E.S.	
	10/11/18		— " — 20 — " — — " —	
	11/11/18		— " — 32 — " — — " —	
	12/11/18		— " — 14 — " — — " —	
			No 9403 Pte HUGHES. J.D rejoined from leave to U.K. having also been in Hospital	
	13/11/18		Evacuated 3 sick cases to No 13 V.E.S.	
SERAIN.			Section marched to SERAIN and took up billets there.	
	15/11/18		Evacuated 7 sick cases to No 13 V.E.S.	
	22/11/18		No 4950 Cpl WALKER F. granted leave to U.K. 24/11/18 to 8/12/18	
			Evacuated 6 sick cases to No 13 V.E.S.	
	23/11/18		No 6746 Pte SLOAN. T. granted leave to UK. from 25/11/18 to 9/12/18	
	24/11/18		No 6693 Pte ODDS E granted leave to UK from 26/11/18 to 10/12/18	
			No 26844 A/Cpl HARDING J AVC No 18789 Pte HATTERSLEY W.A AVC and No 40423 Dvr BARNETT BA. RFA rejoined from leave	
	26/11/18		Evacuated 2 sick cases to No 13 V.E.S.	

D. D. & L., London, E.C.
(A7883) Wt. W809/M1672 350,000 4/17 Sch. 52a Forms/C/2118/14

Instructions regarding War Diaries and Intelligence Summaries are contained in F. S. Regs., Part II. and the Staff Manual respectively. Title pages will be prepared in manuscript.

WAR DIARY *or* INTELLIGENCE SUMMARY. of 30 Mobile Vety Section

(Erase heading not required.)

Army Form C. 2118.

Vol XLI Sh 3

Place	Date	Hour	Summary of Events and Information	Remarks and references to Appendices
SERAIN.	28th/18		No 16647 Shoeing Smith JACKSON. W. J. reported for duty from No 93 Vety Hospl	
	30th/18		No 5622 S.S. CROWTHER W. despatched to No 23 Vety Hospl – authy O.i/c AVC base Records T/12/4/29/18	
			The pressure with evacuation cases experienced at the end of last month continued until Armistice day on 11th Nov. The cases were mostly from other formations than 18th Division and were largely gunshot casualties with a sprinkling of debility cases.	
			E. C. Gelbart(?) Capt AVC O/c 30 MVS 18 Div	

D. D. & L., London, E.C. (A7883) Wt. W809/M1672 350,000 4/17 Sch. 52a. Forms/C/2118/14

19 18

Instructions regarding War Diaries and Intelligence Summaries are contained in F. S. Regs., Part II. and the Staff Manual respectively. Title pages will be prepared in manuscript.

WAR DIARY of 30 Mobile Veterinary Section
or
~~INTELLIGENCE SUMMARY.~~
(Erase heading not required.)

Army Form C. 2118.

Vol XLII Sh. 1

VS 41

Place	Date	Hour	Summary of Events and Information	Remarks and references to Appendices
SERAIN	3 12/18		Evacuated 6 sick cases to 13 V.E.S	
	4 12/18		— " — 1 — " — — " —	
			Capt E.F. JELBART AVC took over command from Capt J Buie	
	6 12/18		Evacuated 4 sick cases and one remount case to 13 V.E.S.	
	7 12/18		— " — 1 — " — and 2 — " — — " —	
			No 5749 Pte DEIGHTON A. No 11690 Pte BASTEN. C. and No 33371 Pte THOMPSON F reported for duty from No 2 Veterinary Hospl	
	11 12/18		Evacuated 5 sick cases to No 13 V.E.S.	
	12 12/18		No 4950 Cpl WALKER F and No 6693 Pte ODDS E rejoined from leave	
	13 12/18		No 6746 Pte SLOAN T rejoined from leave	
	14 12/18		No 14709 Pte GIBSON T granted leave to UK from 16 12/18 to 30 12/18	
			Evacuated 2 sick cases to No 13 V.E.S.	
	16 12/18		— " — 14 — " — — " —	
LIGNY-EN-CAMBRESIS	17 12/18		Section marched to LIGNY-EN-CAMBRESIS + took up Billet	
	19 12/18		Evacuated 3 sick cases to No 13 V.E.S.	
	20 12/18		No 11690 Pte BASTEN.C granted 14 days leave to UK 22 12/18 to 5 1/19.	

Instructions regarding War Diaries and Intelligence Summaries are contained in F. S. Regs., Part II. and the Staff Manual respectively. Title pages will be prepared in manuscript.

WAR DIARY of 30 Mobile Veterinary Section
or
~~INTELLIGENCE SUMMARY.~~
(Erase heading not required.)

Army Form C. 2118.

Vol XLII Ch. 2

Place	Date	Hour	Summary of Events and Information	Remarks and references to Appendices
LIGNY-EN CAMBRESIS	22/12/18		Evacuated 8 sick cases to No 13 V. E. S.	
			No 3773 Sgt PALMER W.G. granted leave in France 22 to 31/12/18	
	28/12/18		No 5749 Pte DEIGHTON A. – 14 days leave to UK 30/12/18 to 13/1/19	
"			Evacuated 4 horses + 1 mule to 13 V E S	
	29/12/18		— " — 4 sick cases to — do —	
	31/12/18		— " — 12 animals to 13 V E S for sale + casting.	

G. E. Gilbert Capt AVC
O/C 30 Mobile Veterinary Section
18 Division

D. D. & L., London, E.C.
(A7883) Wt. W809/M1672 350,000 4/17 Sch. 52a Forms/C/2118/14

18/ 31

Instructions regarding War Diaries and Intelligence Summaries are contained in F. S. Regs., Part II, and the Staff Manual respectively. Title pages will be prepared in manuscript.

WAR DIARY or INTELLIGENCE SUMMARY.

(Erase heading not required.)

of 30 Mobile Veterinary Section 18 Division

Army Form C. 2118.

Vol XLII Sh 1

Vol 42

Place	Date	Hour	Summary of Events and Information	Remarks and references to Appendices
LIGNY EN CAMBRESIS	2/1/19		Evacuated 5 sick cases to No XIII V.E.S.	
	3/1/19		No 74709 Pte GIBSON T. rejoined from leave	
	8/1/19		Evacuated 6 sick cases to No XIII V.E.S.	
	10/1/19		No 11690 Pte BASTEN C. rejoined from leave	
	14/1/19		Evacuated 3 sick cases + 5 cases for sale to No 13 V.E.S.	
	15/1/19		No 16647 S.S JACKSON W. J. granted 14 days leave to U.K. 17 to 31/1/19	
	16/1/19		Evacuated 3 cases to 13 V.E.S.	
	17/1/19		— " — 4 — " — " — " —	
	18/1/19		— " — 8 — " — " — " —	
	19/1/19		— " — 11 — " — " — " —	
	20/1/19		Capt F E J ELBART granted 14 days leave to U.K. Capt J. BUIE taking over command in his absence	
	22/1/19		Evacuated 4 sick cases to 13 V.E.S.	
	24/1/19		— " — 4 — " — " —	
	27/1/19		A.D.V.S 13th Corps together with D.A.D.V.S Divn inspected Section	
	28/1/19		Evacuated 2 cases to 13 V.E.S	

D. D. & L., London, E.C. (A7883) Wt. W803/M1672 350,000 4/17 Sch. 52a Forms/C/2118/14

Instructions regarding War Diaries and Intelligence Summaries are contained in F. S. Regs., Part II, and the Staff Manual respectively. Title pages will be prepared in manuscript.

WAR DIARY
or
~~INTELLIGENCE SUMMARY.~~
(Erase heading not required.)

of No 30 Mobile Veterinary Section

Vol XLII Sh 2

Army Form C. 2118.

Place	Date	Hour	Summary of Events and Information	Remarks and references to Appendices
LIGNY-EN CAMBRESIS	1/19		Evacuated 3 cases to 13 V.E.S	
			There is little to note of interest this month. A number of horses have been admitted to M.V.S. & re-issued within the Division. Our time has also been well occupied on Veterinary Boards for classification of horses with view to demobilisation.	
			E. J. [illegible] Capt RAVC O/C 30 M.V.S. 18 Division	

D. D. & L., London, E.C.
(A7883) Wt. W809/M1672 350,000 4/17 Sch. 52a Forms/C/2118/14

WO 95/2032

(2)

18 Division

Divisional Troops

Divisional Train (150, 151, 152, 153
Companies A.S.C.)

Jul 1915 - Apr. 1919

18TH DIVISION

18TH DIVISIONAL TRAIN ASC

1915 JLY — 1919 APL

~~NOV 1915 — APL 1919~~

(150 – 153 COYS ASC)

War Diary

18th Div.l Train

L

18th Division

121/6250

18th Divisional Train

Vol: I

July 1915

Army Form C. 2118

Instructions regarding War Diaries and Intelligence Summaries are contained in F. S. Regs., Part II. and the Staff Manual respectively. Title Pages will be prepared in manuscript.

WAR DIARY
or
INTELLIGENCE SUMMARY
(Erase heading not required.)

Place	Date	Hour	Summary of Events and Information	Remarks and references to Appendices
Codford	23/7/15		Received revised programme of entrainment for XVIII Div.	
			Supply Units & 150 Coy + HQ Train to entrain at CODFORD on 24th inst	
			151 Coy to entrain at WYLLIE on 24th inst.	
			152 Coy " " " CODFORD on 25th "	
			153 Coy " " " CODFORD on 26th "	
			Spent time left before entraining in completing mobilization of Train.	
			Exchanged all unfit horses with 18th Reserve Pk, but AOD were unable to supply all the stores which were still owing to Coys on A.F.G. 1098.	
			All Supply & Baggage Section wagons sent to Units tonight. Supply wagons loaded.	
CODFORD	24/7/15		HQ entrained with 150 Coy for SOUTHAMPTON. 151 Coy & Supply Details ~~[illegible]~~ entrained earlier. Formations were split up by Embarkation Staff at Ships side. This is to be avoided as it causes a good deal of confusion altering returns & arrangements.	
			HQ & 150 Coy crossed in SS "KEPHREN" O/C Troops - Lt Col CHATTERTON. A.S.C.	
			Ships Adjt - Capt JESSIMAN.	
			Escorted by T. B. flotilla.	
HAVRE	25-7-15		Supply Details } all landed & proceeded to No 5 Camp.	
			150 Coy & HQ }	
			151 Coy } a few spare wagon parts &c drawn from A.O.D. HAVRE.	
			151 Coy entrained for LONGEAU at 10.30 pm.	

1875 Wt. W593/826 1,000,000 4/15 J.B.C. & A. A.D.S.S./Forms/C. 2118.

JH

Instructions regarding War Diaries and Intelligence Summaries are contained in F. S. Regs., Part II. and the Staff Manual respectively. Title Pages will be prepared in manuscript.

WAR DIARY
or
INTELLIGENCE SUMMARY
(Erase heading not required.)

Army Form C. 2118

Place	Date	Hour	Summary of Events and Information	Remarks and references to Appendices
HAVRE	26 7/15		150 Coy entrained for LONGEAU. O/C Train, Adjutant, & SO Div Troops & 2 Regtl Officers to FLESSELLE by motor car via Advanced Base at ABBEVILLE. Arrived at FLESSELLE 8.30 pm.	130 miles
			Wired Base Commandant ABBEVILLE that the road from FLIXCOURT to VIGNACOURT & FLESSELLE is suitable for motor transport.	
			Reported to A.Q.M.G. XVIII Division. 151 Coy arrived at MOULLEN-au-BOIS.	
FLESSELLE	27 7/15		Supply details left HAVRE to day for CALAIS.	
			150 Coy marched in from LONGEAU at 8.30 am & bivouacs in an orchard near Ry Station.	
			Established Train Office next to the church.	
			152 Coy due at TALMAS to night.	
			To DOULLENS & BEAUQUESNE with 330 re hay. Can get about 90 tons ex rail & by purchase. 84/- per ton approx.	
FLESSELLE	28 7/15		153 Coy due today at COISY.	
			Owing to certain units not having entrained with proper amount of rations, & not having complied with the order to preserve the one day food & grain in their Supply Section wagons, some little difficulty is experienced in adjusting supplies required from Supply Column.	
			Distribution of Troops as follows:— All have not arrived yet.	

Instructions regarding War Diaries and Intelligence Summaries are contained in F. S. Regs., Part II. and the Staff Manual respectively. Title Pages will be prepared in manuscript.

WAR DIARY
or
INTELLIGENCE SUMMARY

(Erase heading not required.)

Army Form C. 2118

3

Place	Date	Hour	Summary of Events and Information	Remarks and references to Appendices
FLESSELLE	28/7/15 Cont.		**HdQrs Area** Div H.Q. XVIII Div. HQ & No 1 Sec. Signal Coy HQ RE M.M.G. Batty Cyclists HQ & HQ Coy. Div Train R. Sussex Pioneer Bn 30th Mobile Vet Sec. HQ Sanitary Sec. Workshop ASC } FLESSELLES. 85 How Bde RFA – YAVX-EN-AMIENOIS. 1 Sqdn Yeomanry – WARGNIES. **54th Bde Group** HQ 54 Bde & Sig Sec. 83rd Bde RFA 15th Siege Batty (10th Corps) } NAOURS. 12th Middx R 7th Bedfords 6th Northants 11th R Fusrs 80th Fd Coy. RE 54th Fd Ambulance. 152 Coy. Div Train } – TALMAS. **55th Bde Group** HQ. 55th Inf Bde & Sig Sec. 7th Queens 7th Buffs. 8th E Surreys } BERTANGLES. 84th Bde RFA 92nd Fd Coy RE 55th Fd Ambce 153 Coy Div Train. } COISY. **53rd Bde Group** HQ. 53rd Bde & Sig Sec. 8th Norfolk R. 151 Coy. Div Train } Mollens Au Bois. 82nd Bde RFA – MIRVAUX. 10th Essex R. 6th R Berks } – RUBENPRÈS. 56th Fd Ambulance 79th Fd Coy } SEPTENVILLE 8th Suffolks – PIERREGOT 3rd Army Casualty Clearing Stn. 10th Corps Amn Pk } VILLARS. 7th W Kents – VILLARS Supply Column – RAMPONNET.	JP

1875 Wt. W593/826 1,000,000 4/15 J.B.C. & A. A.D.S.S./Forms/C. 2118.

Instructions regarding War Diaries and Intelligence Summaries are contained in F. S. Regs., Part II. and the Staff Manual respectively. Title Pages will be prepared in manuscript.

WAR DIARY
or
INTELLIGENCE SUMMARY
(Erase heading not required.)

Army Form C. 2118

4

Place	Date	Hour	Summary of Events and Information	Remarks and references to Appendices
29 7/15 FLESSELLES			Received a complete Ry Train with supplies for the Division for the first time. (at Amiens).	
			Supply situation at 4 pm to day:-	
			Supply Column full at RAMPONNET & will dump tomorrow in Group Areas at 6.30 am	
			Supply Section wagons also full & will issue tonight for consumption on 30th inst.	
			Of 152 Coy reported his arrival last night. } Train now present.	
			Of 153 " " " " today. }	
			83rd Bde RFA	
			1 Batty 82nd Bde } left today for MIRCOURT. Rationed up to 30th inclusive.	
FLESSELLES. 30 7/15.			1 " How Bde } Are attached to 51st Div from 31st inclusive.	
			Instructions to SSO to collect SO's requirements daily & to be at AMIENS rail head daily at 8 am to superintend loading of Supply Column by "groups"	
			Regtl Offrs are buying vegetables at AMIENS, & are apt to be in competition with each other & also with French authorities. In future these Officers will all meet at rail head at 8 am & will arrange their purchases on the spot. Supply Column can supply 2 lorries to carry vegetables to Refilling Points.	[initials]

1875 Wt. W593/826 1,000,000 4/15 J.B.C. & A. A.D.S.S./Forms/C. 2118.

Instructions regarding War Diaries and Intelligence Summaries are contained in F. S. Regs., Part II. and the Staff Manual respectively. Title Pages will be prepared in manuscript.

WAR DIARY
or
INTELLIGENCE SUMMARY
(Erase heading not required.)

Army Form C. 2118

Place	Date	Hour	Summary of Events and Information	Remarks and references to Appendices
FLESSELLES	31/7/15		Nothing of importance to day.	

1875 Wt. W593/826 1,000,000 4/15 J.B.C. & A. A.D.S.S./Forms/C. 2118.

18th Division

121/7594

18th Div: Train

Vol: 2

August 15

Instructions regarding War Diaries and Intelligence Summaries are contained in F. S. Regs., Part II. and the Staff Manual respectively. Title Pages will be prepared in manuscript.

WAR DIARY
or
INTELLIGENCE SUMMARY
(Erase heading not required.)

Army Form C. 2118

R/96

Place	Date	Hour	Summary of Events and Information	Remarks and references to Appendices
FLESSELLES	1/8/15		Completing supply & transport arrangements for move of foll. troops:— 53rd Inf Bde 79th Coy RE Bearer Div. 56th Fd Amb.ce 1 Coy R Sussex Pioneers } These march on 2nd & 3rd Aug to join the 51st Div. 84th Bde RFA 1 Batty 85th How. Bde RFA } leave on 2nd Aug to join 5th Division. If Pioneer Bns are to be employed by Coys it will necessitate a reorganization of their Train transport. Present system does not permit of Coys being separated.	H.
FLESSELLES	2/8/15		Railhead fixed at MERICOURT from 3rd Aug inclusive. 18th Div Supply Column to fill at 10 am.	H.
FLESSELLES	3/8/15		Excellent accommodation for filling S. Col lorries at MERICOURT Station. In order to issue fresher bread & meat to troops. Ry train on 5th inst will bring no bread & meat — this will arrive on 6th & be issued to Supply Secn on 6th for consumption on 7th inst.	H.

1875 Wt. W593/826 1,000,000 4/15 J.B.C. & A. A.D.S.S./Forms/C. 2118.

Instructions regarding War Diaries and Intelligence Summaries are contained in F. S. Regs., Part II. and the Staff Manual respectively. Title Pages will be prepared in manuscript.

WAR DIARY
or
INTELLIGENCE SUMMARY
(Erase heading not required.)

Army Form C. 2118

2

Place	Date	Hour	Summary of Events and Information	Remarks and references to Appendices
FLESSELLES	4 8/15		Demanded horses to replace casualties as under.	
			150 Coy (HQ Coy) — Dead 1; Left at Havre HD 1; HD unfit 5; R, unfit 1	
			153 Coy — Dead 2	
			Total 3 – 1 – 5 – 1	
			Reqd 10 horses. Reqd to evacuate 6 horses.	
			Of the 5 unfit, 2 were issued immediately prior to embarkation & are too small for all work. All these casualties in my opinion are due to :– (1) Vet authorities at S'hampton taking away our fit horses & replacing by others less fit. (2) Leaving Train Tpt with Units. Nearly all the casualties are among Baggage Section of RA units. Have asked for permission to withdraw all Baggage Secn transport.	H.
FLESSLES	5 8/15		Orders received for 54th & 55th Inf Bdes & remaining Div Troops to march to new area about St GRATIEN – BONNAY. Baggage section to march with Units. Supply Secn to march by groups, & not split up.	H.

1875 Wt. W593/826 1,000,000 4/15 J.B.C. & A. A.D.S.S./Forms/C. 2118.

Army Form C. 2118

3

WAR DIARY
or
INTELLIGENCE SUMMARY
(Erase heading not required.)

Instructions regarding War Diaries and Intelligence Summaries are contained in F. S. Regs., Part II. and the Staff Manual respectively. Title Pages will be prepared in manuscript.

Place	Date	Hour	Summary of Events and Information	Remarks and references to Appendices
FLESSELLES	6/8/15		55th Inf Bde, Bearer Div 55th Amb'ce, 153 Coy. Train } To area LA NEUVILLE - BONNAY - LA HOUSSAYE. to-day 5.30pm.	~~Refilling Programme~~ See Appendix I (since cancelled)
			Marched with Supply Section loaded for consumption on 7th inst, & will refill at FRANVILLERS at 5pm for consumption on 8th	
			HQ. & HQ Coy Train move to MONTIGNY & BEHENCOURT tomorrow, respectively. Div Troops also move to new area tomorrow followed by 54th Inf Bde on 8th inst.	
			Refilling programme Aug 6th - 9th attached.	H.
FLESSELLES	7/8/15		Previous March table & Refilling programme cancelled.	
			82nd Bde RFA marched today to BUSSY les DAOURS. Remainder of Division follow tomorrow. Fresh Refilling programme attached. Appendix I	Refilling Programme App. I
			H.	
MONTIGNY	8/8/15		Left FLESSELLES today. HQ Train established at Ms Du BOIS. MONTIGNY.	
			Complaint received from Supply Section 51st Div Train that 18th Div Train horses attached to them are unfit for work. 13 HD complained of chiefly too small & suffering from debility & defects. Propose to inspect these horses with V.O. tomorrow.	
			We had 38 seasoned LD horses taken away at CODFORD & got many others lighter still in exchange. In addition we had to embark with about 100 Remounts which	

1875 Wt. W593/826 1,000,000 4/15 J.B.C. & A. A.D.S.S./Forms/C. 2118.

Army Form C. 2118

4

Instructions regarding War Diaries and Intelligence Summaries are contained in F. S. Regs., Part II. and the Staff Manual respectively. Title Pages will be prepared in manuscript.

WAR DIARY
or
INTELLIGENCE SUMMARY
(Erase heading not required.)

Place	Date	Hour	Summary of Events and Information	Remarks and references to Appendices
MONTIGNY	8/8/15		had done no work. It is quite conceivable that some of these horses have broken down.	H.
MONTIGNY	9/8/16		To VADENCOURT & saw 9 out of 13 horses complained of by O/c 51st Div Train, remainder were out at work. The horses seen are poor & have been badly used, they were certainly not in their present condition when issued to RFA on 23rd July. They have the appearance of being over worked & under fed & watered. Have reported to 18 Div H.Q. These horses have been away from the Train since we left England. RFA are responsible for their present condition. HQ Coy Train to day to FRECHENCOURT.	H
MONTIGNY	10/8/15		G.O.C. informed G.O.C. R.A. that RA horses must be used to horse Train Vehicles with RA Units until the 13 horses referred to above are declared fit for work by V.O.	
			Location of Train to day. H Q at MONTIGNY HQ Coy " FRECHENCOURT 151 Coy " VADENCOURT 152 Coy " PONT NOYELLES. 153 Coy " VILLE sur ANCRE	
			Again ask DADOS to hasten wither pads. Several cases of wither galls caused by lack of wither pads & breechings. Whenever a wagon is backed the weight is brought on to the neck of the horse. Flies are awful & help to cause the trouble.	H.
			Communication is bad, it would help if Train Coy H^d Qrs could be linked up with Bde H.Q.	

1875 Wt. W593/826 1,000,000 4/15 J.B.C. & A. A.D.S.S./Forms/C. 2118.

Instructions regarding War Diaries and Intelligence Summaries are contained in F. S. Regs., Part II. and the Staff Manual respectively. Title Pages will be prepared in manuscript.

WAR DIARY
or
INTELLIGENCE SUMMARY
(Erase heading not required.)

Army Form C. 2118

5

Place	Date	Hour	Summary of Events and Information	Remarks and references to Appendices
MONTIGNY	11 8/15		Present system of drawing Bread & Meat from Railhead and issuing same day to troops for following days consumption is unsatisfactory. Troops find difficulty in cutting up & cooking the meat owing to its hard condition.	
			Moreover, so far as 18th Div is concerned it means that Refilling takes place late, (about 4 pm). The troops have insufficient time to cut up & pack rations for carrying to trenches (in sacks). Trench rations are usually sent out about 8 pm. Also, the late refilling is hard on the Train horses, & for that reason alone should, I think, be avoided if possible.	
			Under the old system whereby the Supply Column loaded at Railhead for the "day after tomorrows consumption" the Refilling was done early, the horses did not suffer, & the troops got their rations in good time.	
			No complaints were made regarding staleness of bread & meat.	H
MONTIGNY	12 8/15.		50 zinc wither plates received by 150 Coy, should help to reduce wither galls.	
			Ordered 151 Coy to come in from Vadencourt to BUSSY LES DAOURS on 17th inst	
			53 Inf Bde commences moving in tomorrow to area VECQUEMONT - DAOURS.	
			They will be attached to 54th Bde Group for rations until SO 53rd Bde comes in on 17th. 51st Div will continue to ration the 18th Div troops left in their area.	H

1875 Wt. W593/826 1,000,000 4/15 J.B.C. & A. A.D.S.S./Forms/C. 2118.

Army Form C. 2118

Instructions regarding War Diaries and Intelligence Summaries are contained in F. S. Regs., Part II. and the Staff Manual respectively. Title Pages will be prepared in manuscript.

WAR DIARY
or
INTELLIGENCE SUMMARY
(Erase heading not required.)

Place	Date	Hour	Summary of Events and Information	Remarks and references to Appendices
MONTIGNY	13 8/15		Lieut BROOKE with supply & baggage wagons of R Fus[rs] & Northants Regt moved to SUZANNES. H.Q. of 162 Coy Train will follow on 17th & billet at MORLANCOURT. 54th Inf Bde Units in 5th Div Area are being rationed by SO 66th Inf Bde until 17th inst when SO & RO 54th Bde will resume charge.	H.
MONTIGNY	14 8/15		Saw OC 5th Div Train & he concurs with above arrangements. Communications are very bad, "Signals" are too slow & push bicycle orderlies inadequate – 2 Motor cycles are badly wanted for HQ Train. To SUZANNE – Saw 54th Bde Tpt Offr re method of replacement of animals.	H
MONTIGNY	15 8/15		Nil.	
MONTIGNY	16 8/15		OC 5th Div Train reports 6 horses with 84th & 85th Bdes RFA require replacing, Wired him I would send him 4 HD which form part of 7 now on rail from DIEPPE, the remaining 3 are wanted for 83rd RFA Bde with 51st Div. OC 51st Div Train has evacuated 6 HD to date, 3 of 83rd Bde & 3 of A/82 Bde, but the latter move to day to BUSSY & must carry on with Battery horses. Recd "warning" from DHQ " 55th Inf Bde will move into billets CORBIE, -BONNAY- NEUVILLE on night of 18/19 – M'sex & Bedfords to 5th Div same night. [54th Bde]	H

1875 Wt. W593/826 1,000,000 4/15 J.B.C. & A. A.D.S.S./Forms/C. 2118.

Instructions regarding War Diaries and Intelligence Summaries are contained in F. S. Regs., Part II. and the Staff Manual respectively. Title Pages will be prepared in manuscript.

WAR DIARY
or
INTELLIGENCE SUMMARY
(Erase heading not required.)

Army Form C. 2118

7

Place	Date	Hour	Summary of Events and Information	Remarks and references to Appendices
MONTIGNY	16/8/15		Inspected 7 HD horses of 150 Coy. (HQ Coy) which in my opinion will be some time before they are fit for work – mostly rope galls & kicks due to no heel ropes being issued. 2 of these HD are really small LD horses issued to us when on point of embarkation. ADVS, 18 Div. however only evacuated one of the seven, owing to his reluctance to evacuate & the rapidity with which the RFA have crocked up their horses, I cannot get sufficient remounts demanded to enable the Train Tpt to be efficient – HQ Coy is rapidly getting a collection of temporarily unfit horses.	H.
MONTIGNY	17/8/15		Demanded 7 HD Horses for 150 Coy. (6 evacuated by 51st Div Train 1 by ADVS 18th Div)	
		12 noon	Various moves being discussed nothing settled by D.H.Q.	
			Inspected 1st Line Tpt 53 Bde except Norfolk R, all in excellent condition.	
			151 Coy marched in to camp at BUSSY from VADENCOURT.	H.
MONTIGNY	18/8/15		Demanded 4 HD horses for 150 Coy – 2 evacuated to MVS 5th Div & 2 to replace 2 horses previously evacuated to MVS 18th Div & not demanded	H

1875 Wt. W593/826 1,000,000 4/15 J.B.C. & A. A.D.S.S./Forms/C. 2118.

Instructions regarding War Diaries and Intelligence Summaries are contained in F. S. Regs., Part II. and the Staff Manual respectively. Title Pages will be prepared in manuscript.

WAR DIARY
or
INTELLIGENCE SUMMARY
(Erase heading not required.)

Army Form C. 2118

8

Place	Date	Hour	Summary of Events and Information	Remarks and references to Appendices
MONTIGNY	19/8/15		Div HQ moved to HEILLY.	
			9 HD remounts & 1 R received 17/8/15 disposed of as follows — 150 Coy 7 HD; 153 " 2 "; 152 " 1 R.	
			No definite orders out re moves of troops to occupy line & area allotted to 18th Div. Have asked for Train to be concentrated if possible.	H
HEILLY	20/8/15		HQ Train to HEILLY. 150 (HQ Coy) at FRECHENCOURT; 151 " BUSSY; 152 " MORLANCOURT; 153 " VILLE sur ANCRE.	
			Refilling points at LAHOUSSOYE for Div Troops & 53 Inf Bde Group; MERICOURT " 55th Inf Bde Group; MORLANCOURT " 54th Inf Bde "	
			Orders received to day for move of troops into 18th Div area.	
			Scheme: 1 Inf Bde (53rd) at BRAY (2 Bns in trenches); 55th Inf Bde at MEAULTE (3 Bns in trenches); 54th " at RIBEMONT - DERNANCOURT - MERICOURT.	
			Divisional troops distributed.	
			Train to concentrate at VILLE SUR ANCRE as troops move up into their areas. One Refilling Pt for the Division at VILLE.	H

1875 Wt. W593/826 1,000,000 4/15 J.B.C. & A. A.D.S.S./Forms/C. 2118.

Instructions regarding War Diaries and Intelligence Summaries are contained in F. S. Regs., Part II. and the Staff Manual respectively. Title Pages will be prepared in manuscript.

WAR DIARY
or
INTELLIGENCE SUMMARY
(Erase heading not required.)

Army Form C. 2118

9

Place	Date	Hour	Summary of Events and Information	Remarks and references to Appendices
HEILLY	21/8/15		One Bn 55th Inf Bde in trenches to be fed from BRAY owing to inconvenient situation of communication trench on MEAULTÉ side.	
			D.S.C lorry to run to BRAY with supplies daily from Refilling Pt in stead of 151 Coy horses, too far for latter.	
			DHQ decided that RFA at BRAY should retain Baggage & Supply wagons but not ASC drivers, horses or harness.	
			Promised DHQ to try & get 40 GS wagons for tarring AMIENS - ALBERT road when all these moves of troops are finished.	
			Demanded 1 HD for 152 Coy to replace 1HD evacuated to 18 Div MVS.	
			" 6 HD " 150 Coy " 6 HD " " 51st Div MVS (all RFA Train Tpt)	
			Decided at DHQ this morning that HQ Train should remain at HEILLY with DHQ until troop moves are finished & afterwards join Train at VILLE.	
			No telephone available at present between HEILLY & VILLE	H
HEILLY	22/8/15		Orders re Train moves cancelled. HQ Coy now moves to BONNAY tomorrow	
			151 Coy " " " DAOURS "	
			152 Coy " " " RIBEMONT	
			153 Coy " " " HEILLY.	

1875 Wt. W593/826 1,000,000 4/15 J.B.C. & A. A.D.S.S./Forms/C. 2118.

Army Form C. 2118

10

Instructions regarding War Diaries and Intelligence Summaries are contained in F. S. Regs., Part II. and the Staff Manual respectively. Title Pages will be prepared in manuscript.

WAR DIARY
or
INTELLIGENCE SUMMARY
(Erase heading not required.)

Imp. Hav., 26/7 — 40.000

Place	Date	Hour	Summary of Events and Information	Remarks and references to Appendices
HEILLY	22 8/15		Refilling Points changed as follows. 53rd Bde group at BOIS des TAILLES 2 miles W of BRAY. For remainder of Division at MERICOURT. BRAY was under shell fire today - not advisable to work motor lorries there.	H
HEILLY	23 8/15		Train Coy moves completed as stated yesterday. AQMG. 18 Div does not consider OC Train is responsible for Train Tpt which is with RA Units, & considers it should not be withdrawn. Orders published that Train Tpt may only be withdrawn from Infantry Units. To MERICOURT to see DD S&T re this point, missed him, have asked for an appointment at Army HQ. Also asked AQMG to refer the matter to Superior authority. If this view is to be permitted and also the view of GOC 53rd Inf Bde that OC Train is not responsible for 1st line Tpt the whole of Div ASC organization falls to the ground. There are points which should be made quite clear ~~to all~~ by A.H.Q or GHQ if necessary to all subordinate staffs. A misapprehension concerning the organization & method of running ASC services is likely to lead to a grave risk of a break down in times of stress.	Superior authority. H

Instructions regarding War Diaries and Intelligence Summaries are contained in F. S. Regs., Part II. and the Staff Manual respectively. Title Pages will be prepared in manuscript.

WAR DIARY
or
INTELLIGENCE SUMMARY
(Erase heading not required.)

Army Form C. 2118

11

Imp. Hav., 26/7 — 10,000

Place	Date	Hour	Summary of Events and Information	Remarks and references to Appendices
HEILLY	~~24~~ 24th	Aug.	Division in its new area tonight. Trying to collect baggage wagons from units for carrying sand in connection with laying roads. Hope to get 43 wagons, after leaving 1 baggage wagon ~~with~~ for each Inf Bn to carry forage & vegetables &c.	H
HEILLY	25 8/15		Owing to difficulties re fatigue parties, the D&C lorries are sufficient at present for carrying sand. Train wagons not required. Interview with (Col A Long) DDS&T 3rd Army yesterday re responsibility of OC Train for 1st Line Tpt & withdrawal of R & A Tpt. He entirely supports view taken by me as outlined on 23 8/15 of this Diary, & is taking action to make matters clear through Q.O.C. X Corps.	H.
HEILLY	26 8/15		Nothing of importance.	H.
HEILLY	27 8/15		Requested permission to employ some baggage wagons, now idle, in carrying the harvest at DAOURS - HEILLY - BONNAY - RIBEMONT. Notified 18 HD horses arriving today at MERICOURT { HQ Coy 17 HD. / 152 " 1 " } Owing to shortage of Vet offrs - Lt Rowbotham AVC can only devote portion of his time to the Train. He is i/c several other units at various places.	

Instructions regarding War Diaries and Intelligence Summaries are contained in F. S. Regs., Part II. and the Staff Manual respectively. Title Pages will be prepared in manuscript.

WAR DIARY
or
INTELLIGENCE SUMMARY
(Erase heading not required.)

Army Form C. 2118

12

Imp. Hav., 26/7 — 40,000

Place	Date	Hour	Summary of Events and Information	Remarks and references to Appendices
HEILLY	27 8/15		Lt Col CHATTERTON. O/ Train ordered home by W O for duty at DEPTFORD. 14th Division notifies that Major BERGER will arrive tomorrow to relieve him. Supply wagons of Sussex Pioneers who are now at MEAULTE temporarily posted to No III Coy at RIBEMONT	
HEILLY	28 8/15		All supply wagons of R A Units fed ~~for~~ by 18th Div should be moved up from BONNAY to No III Coy at RIBEMONT, so as to lessen distance. Any supply wagons still with Batteries fed by 18 Div should be withdrawn. Major Berger to see foregoing. Major Berger arrived.	
HEILLY	29 8/15		Lt Col Chatterton left for LONDON.	
Heilly	30 8/15		Visited Hd Qr Company & inspected lines. Went through Office Papers & interviewed S.S.O on supplies.	
HEILLY	31 8/15		Inspected 153 Company Lines & went into questions of general management. Inspected 152 Company Lines & went into question of general management. Arranged for Billeting 151 Company at Vrebemont preparatory to their move from Daours. Baggage Wagons of 151 Company moved out to BRAY by order H Q 18 Div.	
~~Heilly~~	~~1 9/15~~		~~151 Company moved to BILLETS at VIBREMONT from DAOURS~~ ~~Grand Parties~~	

A Berger Major MC
O C 18 Div Train

Instructions regarding War Diaries and Intelligence Summaries are contained in F. S. Regs., Part II. and the Staff Manual respectively. Title pages will be prepared in manuscript.

WAR DIARY
or
INTELLIGENCE SUMMARY.
(Erase heading not required.)

Army Form C. 2118.

Place	Date	Hour	Summary of Events and Information	Remarks and references to Appendices
FLESSELLES	1/8/15		Completing supply & transport arrangements for move of foll. troops:– 53rd Inf. Bde. 79th Coy R. E. Bearer Divn 56th Fd Ambce 1 Coy. R. Cornwall Pioneers } These march on 2nd & 3rd Aug. to join the 51st Div. 84th Bde R.F.A. 1 Battery 85th How. Bde R.F.A. } train on 2nd Aug. to join 5th Division If Pioneer Bns are to be employed by Coys. it will necessitate a reorganization of their Train Transport. Present system does not permit of Coys. being separated.	
FLESSELLES	2/8/15		Railhead fixed at MERICOURT from 3rd Aug. inclusive. 18th Div. Supply Column to fill at 10 a.m.	
FLESSELLES	3/8/15		Excellent accommodation for filling S. Col. lorries at MERICOURT Station In order to issue fresher bread & meat to troops. Reg. train on 5th inst. will bring no bread & meat – this will arrive on 6th & be issued to Supply Secn on 6th for consumption on 7th inst.	

2353 Wt. W2544/1454 700,000 5/15 D. D. & L. A.D.S.S./Forms/C. 2118.

Instructions regarding War Diaries and Intelligence Summaries are contained in F. S. Regs., Part II. and the Staff Manual respectively. Title pages will be prepared in manuscript.

WAR DIARY
or
INTELLIGENCE SUMMARY.
(Erase heading not required.)

Army Form C. 2118.

Place	Date	Hour	Summary of Events and Information	Remarks and references to Appendices
FLESSELLES	4 8/15		Demanded horses to replace casualties as under.	
			150 Coy. (H. Q. Coy.) — Dead: 1; H.D. Left at Havre: 1; H.D. unfit: 5; R. unfit: 1 — Reqd. 10 horses	
			153 Coy. — Dead: 2 — Reqd. to evacuate 6 horses.	
			Total — Dead: 3; H.D. Left at Havre: 1; H.D. unfit: 5; R. unfit: 1	
			of the 5 unfit 2 were issued immediately prior to embarkation & are too small for A.S.C. work.	
			All these casualties in my opinion are due to:-	
			(1) Vet. Authorities at S'hampton taking away our fit horses & replacing by others less fit.	
			(2) Leaving Train Tpt. with Units. Nearly all the casualties are among Baggage Section of R.A. units. Have asked for permission to withdraw all Baggage Secn. transport.	
FLESSELLES	5 8/15		Orders received for 54th & 55th Inf. Bdes. & remaining Div. Troops to march to new Area about St. GRATIEN-BONNAY	
			Baggage section to march with Units	
			Supply Secn. to march by groups, & not split up.	

2353 Wt. W2544/1454 700,000 5/15 D. D. & L. A.D.S.S./Forms/C. 2118.

Instructions regarding War Diaries and Intelligence Summaries are contained in F. S. Regs., Part II. and the Staff Manual respectively. Title pages will be prepared in manuscript.

WAR DIARY
or
INTELLIGENCE SUMMARY.
(Erase heading not required.)

Army Form C. 2118.

Place	Date	Hour	Summary of Events and Information	Remarks and references to Appendices
FLESSELLES	6/8/15		55th Inf. Bde / Bearer Div. 55th Amb.ce / 153 Coy. Train } To Area LA NEUVILLE-BONNAY—LA HOUSSAYE to-day 5-30 p.m.	Refilling Programme see Appendix I (since cancelled)
			Marched with Supply Section loaded for consumption on 7th inst. & will refill at FRANVILLERS at 5 p.m. for consumption on 8th.	
			H.Q. & H.Q. Coy. Train move to MONTIGNY & BEHENCOURT tomorrow respectively,	
			DIV. Troops also move to new Area to-morrow followed by 54th Inf. Bde on 8th inst.	
			Refilling programme Aug. 6th–9th attached	
FLESSELLES	7/8/15		Previous March table & Refilling programme cancelled	
			82nd Bde R.F.A. marched to day to BUSSY les DAOURS. Remainder of Division follows tomorrow –	Refilling Programme App.x I
			Fresh Refilling programme attached. Appendix I.	
MONTIGNY	8/8/15		Left FLESSELLES to-day. H.Q. Train established at Mn. DU. BOIS. MONTIGNY	
			Complaint received from Supply Section 51st Div. Train that 18th Div. Train horses attached to them are unfit for work 13 H.D. complained of, chiefly too small and suffering from debility & defects. Propose to inspect these horses with V.O. to-morrow. We had 38 seasoned L.D. horses taken away at CODFORD & got many others lighter still in exchange. In addition we had to embark with about 100 Remounts which had done no work. It is quite conceivable that some of these horses have broken down	

Army Form C. 2118.

Instructions regarding War Diaries and Intelligence Summaries are contained in F. S. Regs., Part II. and the Staff Manual respectively. Title pages will be prepared in manuscript.

WAR DIARY
or
INTELLIGENCE SUMMARY.
(Erase heading not required.)

Place	Date	Hour	Summary of Events and Information	Remarks and references to Appendices
MONTIGNY	9/8/15		To VADENCOURT & saw 9 out of 13 horses complained of by O.C. 51st Div. Train, remainder were out at work. The horses seen are poor & have been badly used, they were certainly not in their present condition when issued to R.F.A. on 23rd July. They have the appearance of being over-worked & under-fed & watered. Have reported to 18 Div. H.Q. These horses have been away from the Train since we left England. R.F.A are responsible for their present condition. H.Q. Coy. Train to-day to FRECHENCOURT	
MONTIGNY	10/8/15.		G.O.C. informed G.O.C. R.A. that R.A. horses must be used to horse Train Vehicles with R.A. Units, until the 13 horses referred to above, are declared fit for work by V.O.	
			Location of Train to-day. H.Q at MONTIGNY H.Q. Coy. FRECHENCOURT 151 Coy. VADENCOURT 152 Coy. PONT NOYELLES 153 Coy. VILLE sur ANCRE	
			Again ask D.A.D.O.S. to hasten wither pads. Several cases of wither galls caused by lack of wither pads & breechings. Whenever a wagon is backed, the weight is brought on to the neck of the horse. Flies are awful & help to cause the trouble.	
			Communication is bad, it would help if Train Coy. Hd. Qrs. could be linked up with Bde. H.Q.	

2353 Wt. W2544/1454 700,000 5/15 D. D. & L. A.D.S.S./Forms/C. 2118.

Instructions regarding War Diaries and Intelligence Summaries are contained in F. S. Regs., Part II. and the Staff Manual respectively. Title pages will be prepared in manuscript.

WAR DIARY
or
INTELLIGENCE SUMMARY.
(*Erase heading not required.*)

Army Form C. 2118.

Place	Date	Hour	Summary of Events and Information	Remarks and references to Appendices
MONTIGNY	11/8/15		Present system of drawing Bread & Meat from Railhead and issuing same day to troops for following days consumption is unsatisfactory. Troops find difficulty, in cutting up & cooking the meat owing to its hard condition. More over so far as 18th Div. is concerned it means that refilling takes place late (about 4 p.m.). The troops have insufficient time to cut-up & pack rations for carrying to trenches (in sacks). Trench rations are usually sent out about 8 p.m. Also, the late refilling is hard on the Train horses & for that reason alone should, I think be avoided if possible. Under the old system whereby the Supply Column loaded at Railhead for the day after to-morrow's consumption, the Refilling was done early, the horses did not suffer, & the troops got their rations in good time. No complaints were made regarding staleness of bread & meat.	
MONTIGNY	12/8/15		50 zinc wither plates received by 150 Coy., should help to reduce wither galls. Ordered 151 Coy to come in from VADENCOURT to BUSSY LES DAOURS on 17th inst. 53rd Inf. Bde commences moving in to-morrow to area VECQUEMONT - DAOURS. They will be attached to 54th Bde Group for rations until S.O. 53rd Bde comes in on 17th. 51st Div. will continue to ration the 18th Div. troops left in their area	

2353 Wt. W2544/1454 700,000 5/15 D. D. & L. A.D.S.S./Forms/C. 2118.

Instructions regarding War Diaries and Intelligence Summaries are contained in F. S. Regs., Part II. and the Staff Manual respectively. Title pages will be prepared in manuscript.

WAR DIARY
or
INTELLIGENCE SUMMARY.
(*Erase heading not required.*)

Army Form C. 2118.

Place	Date	Hour	Summary of Events and Information	Remarks and references to Appendices
MONTIGNY	13/8/15		Lieut. BROOKE with supply & baggage wagons of R. Fus.rs & Northants Regt moved to SOZANNES. H.Q. of 152 Coy. Train will follow on 17th & billet at MORLANCOURT. 54th Inf. Bde Units in 5th Div. Area are being rationed by S.O. 55th Inf. Bde until 17th inst. when S.O. & R.O. 54th Bde will resume charge.	
MONTIGNY	14/8/15		Saw O.C. 5th Div. Train & he concurs with above arrangements. Communications are very bad. "Signals" are too slow & Push bicycle orderlies inadequate. 2 Motor cycles are badly wanted for H.Q. Train. To SOZANNE – Saw 54th Bde Tpt. Off. re. method of replacement of animals.	
MONTIGNY	15/8/15		Nil.	
MONTIGNY	16/8/15		O.C. 5th Div. Train reports 6 horses with 84th & 85th Bdes R.F.A. require replacing. Wired him I would send him 4 H.D. which form part of 7 now on rail from DIEPPE the remaining 3 are wanted for 83rd R.F.A. Bde with 51st Div. O.C. 51st Div. Train has evacuated 6 H.D. to date, 3 of 83rd Bde & 3 of A/82nd Bde, but the latter move to-day to BUSSY & must carry on with Battery horses. Recd "warning" from D.H.Q. 55th Inf. Bde will move into billets CORBIE–BONNAY–NEUVILLE on night of 18/19 – M. sec. & Bedfords to 5th Div. same night.	

Instructions regarding War Diaries and Intelligence Summaries are contained in F. S. Regs., Part II. and the Staff Manual respectively. Title pages will be prepared in manuscript.

WAR DIARY
or
INTELLIGENCE SUMMARY.
(Erase heading not required.)

Army Form C. 2118.

Place	Date	Hour	Summary of Events and Information	Remarks and references to Appendices
MONTIGNY	16/8/15		Inspected 7 H.D. horses of 150 Coy. (H.Q. Coy.) which in my opinion will be some time before they are fit for work – mostly rope galls & kicks, due to no heel ropes being issued. 2 of these H.D. are really small L.D. horses, issued to us when on point of embarkation. A.D.V.S. 18th Div., however only evacuated one of the seven, owing to his reluctance to evacuate & the rapidity with which the R.F.A. have cracked up their horses. I cannot get sufficient remounts demanded, to enable the Train Tpt. to be efficient. H.Q. Coy is rapidly getting a collection of temporarily unfit horses.	
MONTIGNY	17/8/15		Demanded 7 H.D. Horses for 150 Coy. (6 evacuated by 51st Div. Train 1 by A.D.V.S. 18th Div.)	
		12 noon	Various moves being discussed, nothing settled by D.H.Q.	
			Inspected 1st Line Tpt. 53rd Bde, except Norfolk R., all in excellent condition	
			151 Coy. marched in to camp at BUSSY from VADENCOURT	
MONTIGNY	18/8/15		Demanded 4 H.D. horses for 150 Coy. – 2 evacuated to M.V.S. 5th Div. & 2 to replace 2 horses previously evacuated to M.V.S. 18th Div. & not demanded.	

Army Form C. 2118

Instructions regarding War Diaries and Intelligence Summaries are contained in F. S. Regs., Part II. and the Staff Manual respectively. Title pages will be prepared in manuscript.

WAR DIARY
or
INTELLIGENCE SUMMARY.
(Erase heading not required.)

Place	Date	Hour	Summary of Events and Information	Remarks and references to Appendices
MONTIGNY	19/8/15		Div. H.Q. moved to HEILLY	
			9 H.D. Remounts & 1 R. received 17/8/15 disposed of as follows – 150 Coy. 7 H.D.; 153 " 2 "; 152 " 1 R.	
			No definite orders out re moves of troops to occupy line & area allotted to 18th Div. Have asked for Train to be concentrated if possible	
HEILLY	20/8/15		H.Q. Train to HEILLY 150 (H.Q. Coy.) at FRECHENCOURT; 151 " BUSSY; 152 " MORLANCOURT; 153 " VILLE sur ANCRE	
			Refilling points at LAHOUSSOYE for Div Troops & 53rd Inf. Bde group. MERICOURT " 55th Inf. Bde Group; MORLANCOURT " 54 Inf. Bde Group.	
			Orders received to day for move of troops into 18th Div Area.	
			<u>Scheme</u> 1 Inf. Bde (53rd) at BRAY (2 Bns in trenches)	
			55th Inf. Bde at MEAULTE (3 Bns in trenches)	
			54th " " at RIBEMONT-DERNANCOURT – MERICOURT.	
			Divisional troops distributed	
			Train to concentrate at VILLE sur ANCRE, as troops move up into their Areas. One Refilling PT for the Division at VILLE.	

2353 Wt. W2544/1454 700,000 5/15 D. D. & L. A.D.S.S./Forms/C. 2118.

Army Form C. 2118.

Instructions regarding War Diaries and Intelligence Summaries are contained in F. S. Regs., Part II. and the Staff Manual respectively. Title pages will be prepared in manuscript.

WAR DIARY
or
INTELLIGENCE SUMMARY.
(Erase heading not required.)

Place	Date	Hour	Summary of Events and Information	Remarks and references to Appendices
HEILLY	21/8/15		One Bn 55th Inf. Bde in trenches to be fed from BRAY owing to inconvenient situation of communication trench on MEAULTE side	
			D.S.C. lorry to run to BRAY with supplies daily from Refilling Pt instead of 151 Coy. horses, too far for latter.	
			D.H.Q. decided that R.F.A. at BRAY should retain Baggage & Supply wagons, but not A.S.C. drivers, horses or harness.	
			Promised D.H.Q. to try & get 40 G.S. wagons for tarring AMIENS-ALBERT road. When all these moves of troops are finished	
			Demanded 1 H.D. for 152 Coy. to replace 1 H.D. evacuated to 18 DIV M.V.S.	
			" 6 H.D. " 150 Coy. " 6 H.D. " " 51st Div. M.V.S. (all R.F.A. Train T'pt.)	
			Decided at D.H.Q. this morning that H.Q. Train should remain at HEILLY with D.H.Q. until troop moves are finished & afterwards join Train at VILLE	
			No telephone available at present between HEILLY - VILLE	
HEILLY	22/8/15.		Orders re Train moves cancelled. H.Q. Coy. now moves to BONNAY tomorrow.	
			151 Coy. " " " DAOURS "	
			152 Coy. " " " RIBEMONT.	
			153 Coy. " " " HEILLY	

Instructions regarding War Diaries and Intelligence Summaries are contained in F. S. Regs., Part II. and the Staff Manual respectively. Title pages will be prepared in manuscript.

WAR DIARY
or
INTELLIGENCE SUMMARY.
(Erase heading not required.)

Army Form C. 2118.

Place	Date	Hour	Summary of Events and Information	Remarks and references to Appendices
HEILLY	22/8/15		Refilling Points changed as follows 53rd Bde group at BOIS des TAILLIES 2 miles W. of BRAY For remainder of Division at MERICOURT. BRAY was under shell fire to-day – not advisable to work motor lorries there	
HEILLY	23/8/15		Train Coy. moves completed as stated yesterday A.Q.M.G. 18 DIV. does not consider O.C. Train is responsible for Train Tpt. which is with R.A. Units & considers it should not be with-drawn. Orders published that Train Tpt. may only be withdrawn from Infantry Units. To MERICOURT to see D.D.S&T. re. this point, missed him, have asked for an appointment at Army H.Q. Also asked A.Q.M.G. to refer the matter to superior authority If this view is to be permitted, and also the view of G.O.C. 53rd Inf. Bde that O.C. Train is not responsible for 1st Line Tpt. the whole of our A.S.C. A.S.C. organisation falls to the ground. There are points which should be made quite clear by A.H.Q. or G.H.Q. if necessary to all subordinate staffs. A misapprehension concerning the organization & method of running A.S.C. services, is likely to lead to a grave risk of a breakdown in times of stress.	

2353 Wt. W2544/1454 700,000 5/15 D. D. & L. A.D.S.S./Forms/C. 2118.

Army Form C. 2118.

Instructions regarding War Diaries and Intelligence Summaries are contained in F. S. Regs., Part II. and the Staff Manual respectively. Title pages will be prepared in manuscript.

WAR DIARY
or
INTELLIGENCE SUMMARY.
(Erase heading not required.)

Place	Date	Hour	Summary of Events and Information	Remarks and references to Appendices
HEILLY	24th Aug.		Division in its new area to-night. Trying to collect baggage wagons from Units for carrying Amn., in connection with Tearing [illegible]. Hope to get 43 wagons, after leaving 1 baggage wagon for each Inf. Bn to carry forage + vegetables etc.	
HEILLY	25/8/15		Owing to difficulties re fatigue parties, the D.S.C. Lorries are sufficient at present for carrying Amnl. Train wagons not required. Interview with (Col. A. Long) D.D.S.&T. 3rd Army yesterday re responsibility of O.C. Train for 1st Line Tpt. & withdrawal of R.F.A. Tpt. - He entirely supports view taken by me, as outlined on 23/8/15 of this Diary, & is taking action to make matter clear through G.O.C. X Corps	
HEILLY	26/8/15		Nothing of importance	
HEILLY	27/8/15		Requested permission to employ some baggage wagons, now idle, in carrying the harvest at DAOURS - HEILLY - BONNAY - RIBEMONT Notified 18 H.D. horses arriving to-day at MERICOURT { H.Q. COY 17 H.D. / 152 " 1 " } Owing to Shortage of Vet. Offrs. - Lt. Rowbotham A.V.C can only devote portion of his time to the Train. He is i/c several other units at various places	

Army Form C. 2118.

Instructions regarding War Diaries and Intelligence Summaries are contained in F. S. Regs., Part II. and the Staff Manual respectively. Title pages will be prepared in manuscript.

WAR DIARY
or
INTELLIGENCE SUMMARY.
(Erase heading not required.)

Place	Date	Hour	Summary of Events and Information	Remarks and references to Appendices
HEILLY	27/8/15		Lt. Col. CHATTERTON. O.C. Train ordered home by W.O. for duty at DEPTFORD. 14th Division notifies that Major BERGER will arrive tomorrow to relieve him. Supply wagons of SUSSEX PIONEERS who are now at MEAULTE temporarily posted to No. III Coy. at RIBEMONT	
HEILLY	28/8/15		All supply wagons of R.A. Units fed by 18th Div. should be moved up from BONNAY to No. III Coy. at RIBEMONT, so as to lessen distance. Any supply wagons still with Batteries fed by 18 DIV. should be withdrawn. Major Berger to see foregoing. Major Berger arrived.	
HEILLY	29/8/15		Lt. Col. Chatterton left for LONDON	
HEILLY	30/8/15.		Visited Hd. 2nd Company & inspected lines. Went through Office Papers & interviewed S.S.O. on Supplies.	
HEILLY	31/8/15.		Inspected 153 Company Lines & went into question of general management. Inspected 152 Company Lines & went into question of general management. Arranged for Billeting 151 Company at RIBEMONT preparatory to their move from DAOURS. Baggage Wagons of 151 Company moved out to BRAY by H.Q. 18 Div.	

2353 Wt. W2544/1454 700,000 5/15 D. D. & L. A.D.S.S./Forms/C. 2118.

18th Division

121/699V

18th Divl: Train

Vol III

Sept. 15.

Om/5

—6

Instructions regarding War Diaries and Intelligence Summaries are contained in F. S. Regs., Part II. and the Staff Manual respectively. Title pages will be prepared in manuscript.

WAR DIARY
or
INTELLIGENCE SUMMARY.
(Erase heading not required.)

Army Form C. 2118.

Cleby

Place	Date	Hour	Summary of Events and Information	Remarks and references to Appendices
HEILLY	1.9.15		151 Coy moved in from DAOURS to RIBEMONT. Visited DIV. H Q^rs General duties in HEILLY	
"	2.9.15		Inspected new Billets of 151 Coy and interviewed OC 152 Coy.	
"	3.9.15		Office Work	
"	4.9.15		Office Work. Arranged traffic at Refilling Point at Mericourt	
"	5.9.15		Interviewed A.D.S & T. 3rd Army	
"	6 9.15		Inspected 150 Company in morning. Office Work in afternoon	
"	7.9.15		" 153 " " " " " "	
"	8.9.15		" 152 " " " " " "	
"	9.9.15		" 151 " " " " " "	
"	10.9.15		Office Work " " " " " "	
"	11.9.15		" " " " " " " "	
"	12.9.15		Interviewed all O.C. Coys, S.O^s & R.O^s and lectured to them. Office Work	
"	13.9.15		Interviewed D.D.S & T. 3rd Army at Head Quarters. Inspected 153 Coy horses etc DERNANCOURT	
"	14.9.15		Orders received for Major Whitaker to report to D.D.T. ABBEVILLE; arranged for Captn. Collins to take over etc, etc,	
"	15.9.15		Major Whitaker proceeded to ABBEVILLE, Captain Collins took over S.S.O's duties.	
"	16.9.15		2nd Lt: Curtis reported for duty with Train. Chose new Refilling Point for 17th for 53rd Brigade	

2353 Wt. W2544/1454 700,000 5/15 D. D. & L. A.D.S.S./Forms/C. 2118.

Instructions regarding War Diaries and Intelligence Summaries are contained in F. S. Regs., Part II. and the Staff Manual respectively. Title pages will be prepared in manuscript.

WAR DIARY
or
INTELLIGENCE SUMMARY.
(Erase heading not required.)

Army Form C. 2118.

Place	Date	Hour	Summary of Events and Information	Remarks and references to Appendices
HEILLY	1.9.15		151 Coy moved in from DAOURS to RIBREMONT. Visited Div HQ. General duties in HEILLY	
HEILLY	2.9.15		Inspected new Billets of 151 Coy & interviewed O.C. 152 Coy	
HEILLY	3.9.15		Office Work	
HEILLY	4.9.15		Office Work. Arranged Traffic at R.P. at Méricourt.	
HEILLY	5.9.15		Interviewed A.D.S.T. 3rd Army	
HEILLY	6.9.15		Inspected 150 Company in morning: Office work in afternoon	
"	7.9.15		" 153 " " " " "	
"	8.9.15		" 152 " " " " " " "	
"	9.9.15		" 151 " " " " " "	
"	10.9.15		Office work " " "	
"	11.9.15		Office Work	
"	12.9.15		Interviewed all OC Coys S.O.s & R.O.s & lectured to them: Office Work	
"	13.9.15		Interviewed D.D.S. & T. 3rd Army at Adv 2nd. Inspected 153 Coy Horses at Dernancourt.	
"	14.9.15		Orders received for Major Whitaker to report to D.D.T. Abbeville: arranged for Capt Collins to take over etc etc.	
"	15.9.15		Major Whitaker proceeded to Abbeville. Capt Collins took over S.S.O. duties	
"	16.9.15		2nd Lt Curtis reported for duty with Train. Chose new Refilling Point for 17th for 53rd Bde	

2353 Wt. W2544/1454 700,000 5/15 D. D. & L. A.D.S.S./Forms/C. 2118.

Instructions regarding War Diaries and Intelligence Summaries are contained in F. S. Regs., Part II. and the Staff Manual respectively. Title pages will be prepared in manuscript.

WAR DIARY
or
INTELLIGENCE SUMMARY.
(Erase heading not required.)

Army Form C. 2118.

Place	Date	Hour	Summary of Events and Information	Remarks and references to Appendices
HEILLY	17.9.15		Took Capt Collins to DDS & T to see DADS. Office Work	
"	18.9.15		Office Work: Went round Lines & Billets of Hd Qr Company	
"	19.9.15		Office Work	
"	20.9.15		Office Work visited Refilling Points, inspected new horses, arranged about new Billeting	
"	21.9.15		Office Work visited Refilling Points.	
"	22.9.15		Went to CORBIE to arrange purchase of Lanterns, Visited Hd Qr Company. Office Work.	
"	23.9.15		Went to 54th & 55th Bde Hd Qrs also visited detachment of 152 Coy at DERNANCOURT. Office Work.	
"	24.9.15		Office Work; Visited DDST 3rd Army.	
"	25.9.15		" " Purchased Lanterns at Corbie	
"	26.9.15		Visited Refilling Points. Loaded as experiment supplies of Hd Qr RFA Bde less Hay onto Cooks Cart: satisfactory.	
"	27.9.15		Office Work	
"	28.9.15		Visited Refilling Points & Railhead: Office Work.	
"	29.9.15		Office Work: Inspected Lines & Billets 152 Company	
"	30.9.15		Office Work. Visited Amiens to arrange Wood Supply for The Division	

A Berger
Major ASC
OC Train

2353 Wt. W2544/1454 700,000 5/15 D. D. & L. A.D.S.S./Forms/C. 2118.

18th Division

121/743V

18th Divl. Train

Vol 4

Oct 15

Orig

—6

Army Form C. 2118.

Instructions regarding War Diaries and Intelligence Summaries are contained in F. S. Regs., Part II. and the Staff Manual respectively. Title pages will be prepared in manuscript.

WAR DIARY
or
INTELLIGENCE SUMMARY.

(*Erase heading not required.*)

Place	Date	Hour	Summary of Events and Information	Remarks and references to Appendices
HEILLY	1.10.15		Took Lt Langstaff to D.D.S+T concerning Reg Commission : Visited H.Q. 2nd Coy : Office Work	
"	2.10.15		Office Work : Inspected Lines & Billets of 153 Company	
"	3.10.15		Office Work. Visited OC 5 Clearing Station Corbie to arrange exchange of Chauffeurs.	
"	4.10.15		Visited refilling Points : Office Work. : Inspected Billets of 153 Coy	
"	5.10.15		Office Work.	
"	6.10.15		Inspected Billets & Lines of 151 Coy : Office Work	
"	7.10.15		Office Work : Attended Conference of General Maxse. Inspected Horse Shelters 153 Coy	
"	8.10.15		Office Work : Arranged for Horse shelters for 151 Coy	
"	9.10.15		Met OC 150 Coy & 152 Coy re Horse Shelters for Winter : Visited 150 Coy Lines : Office Work	
"	10.10.15		Office Work. Arranged for departure of Capt Jessiman on 11th & supervised his handing over to Lt Langstaff.	
"	11.10.15		Capt Jessiman left for England to report to W.O. for duty : Visited H.Q. 2nd Coy & attended Foot Parade : Office Work.	
"	12.10.15		Office Work.	
"	13.10.15		Visited Refilling Points : Visited 1st Line of E. ~~Surreys~~ & Queens, Office Work	
"	14.10.15		Office Work : Had conference with OC Coys ~~on~~ on general matters to improve efficiency	
"	15.10.15		Office Work : Visited OC 4th Div Train to obtain information on some points.	
"	16.10.15		Visited Refilling Points & carried on duties of S.S.O. Capt Collins being incapacitated. Office Work	H G Peachey Major for Lt Col ASC 18 Div Train

2353 Wt. W2544/1454 700,000 5/15 D. D. & L. A.D.S.S./Forms/C. 2118.

Army Form C. 21[illegible]

Instructions regarding War Diaries and Intelligence Summaries are contained in F. S. Regs., Part II. and the Staff Manual respectively. Title pages will be prepared in manuscript.

WAR DIARY
or
INTELLIGENCE SUMMARY.

(Erase heading not required.)

Place	Date	Hour	Summary of Events and Information	Remarks and references to Appendices
HEILLY	17.10.15		Office Work. Carried on duties of S S O. Inspected 1st Line of 55th + 56th Fd Amb	
"	18.10.15		Office Work. Put forward Dr Mulham for F.G.C.M. drunk on Duty. Inspected 1st Line of 6th Berks Rgt at BUIRE	
"	19.10.15		Office Work. Inspected 1st Line Transport of 7th Bedfordshire Regt.	
"	20.10.15		Office Work. Inspected 1st Line Transport of East Kent & West Kent Rgts.	
"	21.10.15		Office Work: Instructed Major Peachey in Train office work: Reported on 1st Line taking Supplies to Trenches	
"	22.10.15		Office Work: Arranged with RE to find more Transport. Leave postponed to 29th. Went to Amiens	
"	23.10.15		Office Work: Inspected Horse standings 153 Coy	
"	24.10.15		Office Work: Inspected Horse standings 150 Coy	
"	25.10.15		Off duty owing to slight indisposition	
"	26.10.15		Returned to duty. Office Work.	
"	27.10.15		Office Work inspected Horse Lines 153 Coy	
"	28.10.15		Visited Refilling Points. Office Work. Dined with General	
"	29.10.15		Office Work. Handed over to Major Peachey preparatory to going on 8 day leave on 30th.	
"	30.10.15		Took over from Col Boger. Office work.	
"	31.10.15		Office work. Inspected horse standings 150 Coy.	

H G Peachey Major
for Lt Col ASC
18 Divl Train

2353 Wt. W2544/1454 700,000 5/15 D. D. & L. A.D.S.S./Forms/C. 2118.

121
7621

18th Dist: Train
Vol 5

Nov 15

Instructions regarding War Diaries and Intelligence Summaries are contained in F. S. Regs., Part II. and the Staff Manual respectively. Title pages will be prepared in manuscript.

WAR DIARY
or
INTELLIGENCE SUMMARY.
(Erase heading not required.)

Army Form C. 2118.

Place	Date	Hour	Summary of Events and Information	Remarks and references to Appendices
HEILLY	1/11/15		Office work. inspected horse standings 153 Coy	
"	2/11/15		Office work Capt G T Blackwell left for England to report to WO for duty	
"	3/11/15		Office work. visited refilling point	
"	4/11/15		Office work inspected 152 Cy horse standings 2Lt H D a Dart reported for duty from Base Horse Transport Havre. 2/Lt A E Haynes reported for duty from School of instruction Boulogne.	
"	5/11/15		Office work	
"	6/11/15		Office work Lt C.W. Hughes left to report at the MT School of instruction CALAIS	
	7/11/15		Resumed duty after leave : Office Work	
"	8/11/15		Visited Refilling Points Inspected Horse Lines 151 Coy Office Work Inspected Horse Lines 150 Coy.	
"	9/11/15		Inspected Lines of 153 Company : Office Work.	
"	10/11/15		Office Work	
"	11/11/15		2nd Lt A H Craig reported for duty from School of Instruction BOULOGNE : Inspected Farriers Shops at ALBERT. VILLE. MORLANCOURT : Office Work.	
"	12/11/15		2nd Lieut G.E. Bradfield reported for duty from Base Horse Transport Depot Havre : Office Work	
"	13/11/15		Visited refilling Points : Office Work : Capt Flynn S O 52nd Bde left this Div to report to G.H.Q.	
"	14/11/15		Office Work : Arranged extra Horse Lines in HEILLY for 153 Coy.	

2353 Wt. W2544/1454 700,000 5/15 D. D. & L. A.D.S.S./Forms/C. 2118.

Instructions regarding War Diaries and Intelligence Summaries are contained in F. S. Regs., Part II. and the Staff Manual respectively. Title pages will be prepared in manuscript.

WAR DIARY
or
INTELLIGENCE SUMMARY.
(Erase heading not required.)

Army Form C. 2118.

Place	Date	Hour	Summary of Events and Information	Remarks and references to Appendices
HEILLY	15.11.15		Office Work. Visited 150 Coy BONNAY	
"	16.11.15		Visited Refilling Points. Visited 153 Coy. Office Work. SSO went on leave Lt Hughes answering	
"	17.11.15		Office Work. Visited refilling Points: Assisted acting S.S.O.	
"	18.11.15		Went to see D.D.S & T 3rd Army re 2Lt Craig: assisted acting S.S.O.	
"	19.11.15		Visited 150 Coy Horse Lines: Office Work: assisted acting SSO	
"	20.11.15		Office Work. Assisted acting SSO	
"	21.11.15		Visited 151 Coy & 152 Coy also Div Coal Yard. Office Work Assisted acting SSO	
"	22.11.15		Office Work: Assisted acting SSO.	
"	23.11.15		Office Work: Assisted acting SSO	
"	24.11.15		Office Work: SSO resumed duties. Visited 151 & 152 Horse Lines	
"	25.11.15		Office Work.	
"	26.11.15		Office Work. Lt Langstaff proceeded on leave. Capt Lewis acting as Adjt in his place. Proceeded to St Omer A.B. and returned [redacted]	
"	27.11.15		Office Work: Applied to Div H.Q that 2Lt Craig be given further course of Instruction	
"	28.11.15		Office Work.	
"	29.11.15		Office Work	
"	30.11.15		Visited Refilling Points & Horse Lines of 151 Coy 152 Coy; Sent 2Lt Prince Manchester Regt to G.H.Q.: Office Work.	

30.11.15. A Berger Lt Col ASC
OC Train

2353 Wt. W2544/1454 700,000 5/15 D. D. & L. A.D.S.S./Forms/C. 2118.

18th Divl: Train

Vol: 6

121
7809

Dec 15

Instructions regarding War Diaries and Intelligence Summaries are contained in F. S. Regs., Part II. and the Staff Manual respectively. Title pages will be prepared in manuscript.

A.S.C.
18th Divisional Train

WAR DIARY
or
INTELLIGENCE SUMMARY.
(Erase heading not required.)

Army Form C. 2118.

Vol:- 6.

Place	Date	Hour	Summary of Events and Information	Remarks and references to Appendices
HEILLY	1.12.15		Visited refilling Points : Office Work	
— " —	2.12.15		Office Work : Visited 150 Coy Lines.	
— " —	3.12.15		2nd Lieut Board reported for duty : Office Work	
— " —	4.12.15		2nd Lieut Craig proceeded to Abbeville for duty : Office Work : Visited Hd Qrs 32nd Div FLESSELLE	
— " —	5.12.15		Lieut Langstaff Adjt returned off leave : Orders received for Capt Collins to proceed to G.H.Q Amm Park, Office Work.	
— " —	6.12.15		Office Work : G.O.C. inspected 150 Coy Lines, very satisfactory.	
— " —	7.12.15		Office Work : Inspected 150 Coy Horses & men attached to 153 Coy. satisfactory.	
— " —	8.12.15		Office Work : Inspected 150 Coy Horses & men attached to 152 Coy & 151 Coy. satisfactory	
— " —	9.12.15		Inspected 150 Coy Horses at Dernancourt : Office Work : Capt Collins proceeded to 2 Sub Park G.H.Q, Lieut Smith reported.	
— " —	10.12.15		Office Work. Lt HF Hughes assumed the duties of S.S.O in place of Capt Collins. Lt HF Hughes given local rank of Captain.	
— " —	11.12.15		Visited all refilling points with S.S.O : Office Work.	
— " —	12.12.15		Took S.S.O to see A D S 3rd Army. Office Work	
— " —	13.12.15		Visited La Neuville with S.S.O : Office Work	
— " —	14.12.15		Office Work	
— " —	15.12.15		Office Work	
— " —	16.12.15		Office Work, Went round 153 Coy Lines with GOC Div, very satisfactory	

2353 Wt. W2544/1454 700,000 5/15 D. D. & L. A.D.S.S./Forms/C. 2118.

Army Form C. 2118.

Instructions regarding War Diaries and Intelligence Summaries are contained in F. S. Regs., Part II. and the Staff Manual respectively. Title pages will be prepared in manuscript.

WAR DIARY
or
INTELLIGENCE SUMMARY.
(Erase heading not required.)

Place	Date	Hour	Summary of Events and Information	Remarks and references to Appendices
HEILLY	17.12.15		Visited Refilling Points & Office Work.	
— " —	18.12.15		Office Work.	
— " —	19.12.15		Visited Detachment at DERNANCOURT & arranged for extra Billets: Office Work	
— " —	20.12.15		Interviewed OC Train 32nd Div & arranged to change refilling Point of 96 Bde of 32 Div	
— " —	21.12.15		DCM on Sad Cpl Fletcher: Office Work.	
— " —	22.12.15		Visited Bde H.Qrs 53 Bde	
"	23.12.15		Office Work. Visited 150 Coy Lines.	
"	24.12.15		Office Work.	
"	25.12.15		Office Work. Went round Xmas Dinners at all Coys	
"	26.12.15		Visited Refilling Points & Railhead. Office Work, Chose new RF Point for Div Troops.	
"	27.12.15		Office Work. Lt Banham reported sick. Section 14 Reserve Park reported at Bonnay for duty under Lt Warne	
"	28.12.15		Office Work. Capt Langstaff. Adjt reported sick. Arranged movements of Reserve Park with Lt Warne	
"	29.12.15		Office Work. Capt Beddeley understudying Capt Hughes SSO. Visited Lt Banham in Hospital	
"	30.12.15		Office Work. Lt Col Allen reported from England for Tuition in Local Conditions	
"	31.12.15		Office Work. Capt Hughes proceeded on leave. Visited Refilling Points with Lt Col Allen	

A Berger
Lt. Col. A.S.C.
O.C. 18th Divisional Train

2353 Wt. W2544/1454 700,000 5/15 D. D. & L. A.D.S.S./Forms/C. 2118.

18th Divl: Train
Vol: 7

Jan '16

18th Divisional Train A.S.C.

Instructions regarding War Diaries and Intelligence Summaries are contained in F. S. Regs., Part II. and the Staff Manual respectively. Title pages will be prepared in manuscript.

WAR DIARY
or
INTELLIGENCE SUMMARY.
(Erase heading not required.)

Army Form C. 2118.

Vol:-7

Place	Date	Hour	Summary of Events and Information	Remarks and references to Appendices
HEILLY	1.1.16		Visited refilling points & instructed Lt Col Allen T.F. : Office Work.	
"	2.1.16		Visited Coy Lines of 151, 152, 150 & instructed Lt Col Allen T F. Office Work etc.	
"	3.1.16		Lt Col Allen T F left : Visited Refilling Point 55th Bde : Office Work.	
"	4.1.16		Office Work.	
"	5.1.16		Six men joined from 5th Div to experiment in making Duff Balls for fuel. Office Work.	
"	6.1.16		Office Work	
"	7.1.16		Office Work visited Ribemont & BUIRE	
"	8.1.16		Office Work : Visited Refilling Points.	
"	9.1.16		Went to St Gratien to see OC 14 Reserve Park re Wagons etc : Office Work	
"	10.1.16		Inspected Billets & Horses at 153 Coy Lines : Office Work	
"	11.1.16		Went to interview D D S & T 3rd Army : Office Work	
"	12.1.16		Went to Abbeville re motor repairs : Office Work. Spare parts for motor bus unobtainable !!!	
"	13.1.16		Inspected Horses of 153 Coy. Office Work:	
"	14.1.16		Took over from Lt Col Berger who proceeded on 8 days leave to England. Visited Railhead with SSO	
"	15.1.16		Visited 150, 151, 152 Coy refilling point with SSO.	
"	16.1.16		Office Work 2 men reported from Base Horse Transport Depot for duty with Train	

Instructions regarding War Diaries and Intelligence Summaries are contained in F. S. Regs., Part II. and the Staff Manual respectively. Title pages will be prepared in manuscript.

WAR DIARY
or
INTELLIGENCE SUMMARY.
(Erase heading not required.)

Army Form C. 2118.

Place	Date	Hour	Summary of Events and Information	Remarks and references to Appendices
HEILLY	17.1.16		Visited refilling point accompanied SSO with AMIENS to obtain Clinker	
"	18.1.16		Office work	
"	19.1.16		Visited refilling points with SSO and Lt Col Frewin AA & QMG 18th division	
"	20.1.16		Office Work	
"	21.1.16		Office work	
"	22.1.16		Office Work	
"	23.1.16		Recommenced work. Office Work	
"	24.1.16		Visited refilling Points. Office Work.	
"	25.1.16		Visited DERNANCOURT, MEAULTE. Hdqrs 55th Bde + 54th Bde also Pioneer Battn. Office Work.	
"	26.1.16		Visited RIBEMONT + MERRICOURT Coy lines of 151 + 152 Coys. Office Work.	
"	27.1.16		Visited 150 Coy ASC at BONNAY : Office Work.	
"	28.1.16		Office Work : Div Troops refilling point commenced at BONNAY from LA NEUVILLE	
"	29.1.16		Visited Div Troops Refilling Point. Office Work	
"	30.1.16		Office Work.	
"	31.1.16		Office Work. Reported to X Corps Hdqrs as member of Reconnaissance Committee. Arranged for billets at Pont Noyelles for 150 Coy	

2353 Wt. W2544/1454 700,000 5/15 D. D. & L. A.D.S.S./Forms/C. 2118.

18th Divl: Train

Vol 8

Instructions regarding War Diaries and Intelligence Summaries are contained in F. S. Regs., Part II. and the Staff Manual respectively. Title pages will be prepared in manuscript.

WAR DIARY
or
INTELLIGENCE SUMMARY.
(*Erase heading not required.*)

Army Form C. 2118.

Vol:-8.

18th Divisional Train. A.S.C.

Place	Date	Hour	Summary of Events and Information	Remarks and references to Appendices
HEILLY	1.2.16		Arranged new Billets at RIBEMONT : Office Work	
"	2.2.16		Visited Pont NOYELLES re Billeting : Office Work	
"	3.2.16		Had meeting of S.S.O.s of Division in Xth Corps re reconnaissance Office Work.	
"	4.2.16		Made further arrangements at RIBEMONT re Billets : Office Work	
RIBEMONT	5.2.16		Moved to RIBEMONT. Visited new refilling points & 153 Coy BUIRE : Office Work	
"	6.2.16		Arranged new accomodation at RIBEMONT Office Work	
"	7.2.16		Office Work	
"	8.2.16		Visited new lines of 153 Coy at BUIRE : Visited Xth Corps H.Q. re Committee. Office Work	
"	9.2.16		Office Work	
"	10.2.16		Visited Railhead & made arrangements re doing work of Div S.C. : Office Work	
"	11.2.16		Visited D.D.S.&T. 3rd Army re Vegetables also Amiens on same subject : Office Work.	
"	12.2.16		Office Work	
"	13.2.16		Office Work. Visited Refilling Point	
"	14.2.16		Visited Lines of 153 Coy at BUIRE Office Work	
"	15.2.16		Attended Refilling Points & altered Transport arrangements : Office Work	
"	16.2.16		Visited Railhead. Office Work	

Instructions regarding War Diaries and Intelligence Summaries are contained in F. S. Regs., Part II. and the Staff Manual respectively. Title pages will be prepared in manuscript.

WAR DIARY
or
INTELLIGENCE SUMMARY.
(Erase heading not required.)

Army Form C. 2118.

Place	Date	Hour	Summary of Events and Information	Remarks and references to Appendices
RIBEMONT	17.2.16		Inspected Lines of 150 Coy at RIBEMONT : Office Work	
"	18.2.16		Commenced X^th Corps Area Reconnaissance work as Pres of Committee : Office Work	
"	19.2.16		Checked returns of Reconnaissance : Visited Lines of 152 Coy at PONT NOYELLES : Office Work	
"	20.2.16		Continued Committee work. Office Work.	
"	21.2.16		Received orders to take over X^th Corps Amm Park & hand Train over to Major GROSE, ASC : Office Work	
"	22.2.16		Got ready for handing over	
"	23.2.16		Major Groze arrived 6 a.m. Handed over Train. Reported to X^th Corps	
	24.2.16		Office Work & looking over back orders & correspondence. Roads very slippery owing to frost & snow.	
	25.2.16		At Refilling Stns. Still freezing. DSC dumped loads for to-morrow as they had difficulty in moving having no chains for back wheels, & they might not be able to move to-morrow.	
	26.2.16		Office work. Thaw set in in afternoon. Lorries dumped in afternoon.	
	27.2.16		All lorries had to be off roads by 5 a.m. Pack train in at 4. 20 lorries cleared supplies to RPts. Orders re lorries cancelled about 12.	
	28.2.16		Frost scheme of transport in force. No lorries running. Pack train	

Army Form C. 2118.

WAR DIARY
or
INTELLIGENCE SUMMARY.
(Erase heading not required.)

Instructions regarding War Diaries and Intelligence Summaries are contained in F. S. Regs., Part II. and the Staff Manual respectively. Title pages will be prepared in manuscript.

Place	Date	Hour	Summary of Events and Information	Remarks and references to Appendices
RIBEMONT	28/7/16		cleared by Train transport & all outlets done by lorries done by H.T. Train cleared supplies from Station in 2½ hrs, commencing at 4-10, each Brig going direct to R Pt & issuing beginning at 6.30 am for 53 Brig & others in succession. All coal, fuel etc cleared by H.T during day	
	29/7/16		Re Loading at Railhead at 6-15 am by H.T. finished 8-15. Refilling finished at 10-30. Remounts, post, in F.O. all done by H.T. 10th Essex Regt moved from ALBERT to FRANVILLIERS; 7 Buffs DERNANCOURT to ST GRATIEN, 12 Middlesex FRANVILLERS to CORBIE.	

D. C. E. Grose Lt Col.
O.C. 18th Div Train.

18 [illegible]
Iran
Vol 9
1

Instructions regarding War Diaries and Intelligence Summaries are contained in F. S. Regs., Part II. and the Staff Manual respectively. Title pages will be prepared in manuscript.

WAR DIARY
or
INTELLIGENCE SUMMARY.
(Erase heading not required.)

Army Form C. 2118.

(Vol:-9)

18th Divisional Train A.S.C.

Place	Date	Hour	Summary of Events and Information	Remarks and references to Appendices
RIBEMONT	1.3.16		Same procedure re Railhead & R. Pts as on 29 ulto. Office work. Roads very muddy & getting badly cut up by so much H.T. moving over them	
	2.3.16		D.A.C. pulled from Railhead to R. Pt for 54 Bde, as horses of this Coy had to have a rest. Had great difficulty fixing up how troops were to be fed during move, owing to distance from Rl Head and not being allowed to use M.T.	
	3.3.16		M.T. resumed work. 150 Coy moved from RIBEMONT to DAOURS. 152 Coy PONT NOYELLE to CORBIE 153 Coy BUIRE to PONT NOYELLE	
	4.3.16		R Pts. CORBIE 152 Coy LA NEUVILLE 150 Coy LAHOUSSOYE 153 Coy ALBERT RD 151. Very cold & windy with snow. Visited R. Pts & found all satisfactory & roadways all clear for traffic	
	5.3.16		Fine bright day. Sorting correspondence & checking up office.	
	6.3.16		Hd Qrs of Div moved to MONTIGNY. Move completed about 1-30pm	
	7.3.16		Working on H.T. scheme & Honours Lists. To CORBIE Rly Station & to DAOURS in afternoon re H.T. scheme.	
	8.3.16		Went round 151 & 153 Coys lines & billets. To ETINEHEM with SSO to see 30th Train re supplies offloading from barges & to learn their system.	

Instructions regarding War Diaries and Intelligence Summaries are contained in F. S. Regs., Part II. and the Staff Manual respectively. Title pages will be prepared in manuscript.

WAR DIARY
or
INTELLIGENCE SUMMARY.
(Erase heading not required.)

Army Form C. 2118.

(Vol:-9)

Place	Date	Hour	Summary of Events and Information	Remarks and references to Appendices
			18th Divisional Train A.S.C.	
MONTIGNY	9.3.16		Reported to D.D.S.T. 4th Army at QUERRIEU.	
	10.3.16		Office & general routine work	
	11.3.16		H.T. pulled from Railhead to Dumps in accordance with Div letter 79/Q. Commenced at 9-30 finished 11-15. F.G.C.M. on Sgt Mills 151 Coy.	
	12.3.16		Fine bright day: Roads drying up now. Loading at Rl Hd, took 1½ hours.	
	13.3.16		Inspected 54 F.A transport. Working out scheme for move, & system of supplies at barge head.	
	14.3.16		151 Coy & 53 Bty moved up to new area. Inspected 55 F.A. transport.	
	~~15.3.16~~		L/Cpl Wookey 151 Coy drowned at ETINEHEM whilst watering horses.	
	15.3.16		Office work re moves & barge scheme	
	16.3.16		"	
	17.3.16		53 Bty & 153 Coy moved up to new area.	
	18.3.16		30 Div took over Railhead at CORBIE. 18 Div took over loading from Barges at MERICOURT LOCK.	
	19.3.16		Started Refilling from BARGEHEAD, with 4 groups of dumps. Went over from MONTIGNY, all went off satisfactorily.	

Instructions regarding War Diaries and Intelligence Summaries are contained in F. S. Regs., Part II. and the Staff Manual respectively. Title pages will be prepared in manuscript.

WAR DIARY
or
INTELLIGENCE SUMMARY.
(Erase heading not required.)

Army Form C. 2118.

(Vol:-9)

18th Divisional Train. A.S.C

Place	Date	Hour	Summary of Events and Information	Remarks and references to Appendices
ETINEHEM	20.3.16		Hd Qrs Div & Train moved to ETINEHEM 132 Coy moved there from SAILLY LAIRRETTE & 150 Coy moved to SAILLY LAIRETTE from DAOURS	
	21.3.16		Office work. Scheme for carting straw from SUZANNE. Coys all cleaning up billets which have been left in most filthy condition by 30th Train	
	22.3.16		Normal work	
	23.3.16		Normal work.	
	24.3.16		Snow fell at night & made roads in a very slushy condition.	
	25.3.16		Received 2 chargers for C.O. Train. Complaints re non-issue of vegetables, taken up matter again with D.D.S.T. IV Army.	
	26.3.16		Office work & general routine	
	27.3.16		To Refilling Pt all morning. Inspected 56 F Ambulance in afternoon & also [illegible] at SAILLY LAIRETTE	
	28.3.16		Normal work & inspection of	
	29.3.16		Coys. at ETINEHEM	
	30.3.16		Office & normal work	
	31.3.16			

[illegible] Lt Col
C.O. 18 Div Train

2353 Wt. W2544/1454 700,000 5/15 D. D. & L. A.D.S.S./Forms/C. 2118.

Instructions regarding War Diaries and Intelligence Summaries are contained in F. S. Regs., Part II. and the Staff Manual respectively. Title pages will be prepared in manuscript.

WAR DIARY
or
INTELLIGENCE SUMMARY.
(Erase heading not required.)

Army Form C. 2118.

Vol:- 10

18th Divisional Train. ASC.

Place	Date	Hour	Summary of Events and Information	Remarks and references to Appendices
ETINEHEM	1/4/16		Arranging details of straw convoy from SUZANNE; 20 Wagons sent to collect at night, collected about 7 tons & brought to barn at ETINEHEM finished 2 am.	
	2/4/16		Straw convoy finished at 1 am.	
	3/4/16		Inspected ASC baking offices etc at Bargehead at the ECLUSE	
"	4/4/16		Normal. Inspected billets of 153 Coy	
	5+6/4/16		Normal: Collection of 32 tons of straw from SUZANNE from British Army finished at 1 am 6/4/16. All stored in yard at Train Office	
	7.4.16		Normal.	
	8.4.16		DDST inspected 151, 152 & 153 Coys in the afternoon informally.	
	9.4.16		Inspected 1st Line Transport 8th Suffolk Regt. Very serviceable & smart turn out.	
	10.4.16		Inspected " " 6th Berks Regt - serviceable & in good order.	
	11.4.16		Normal work. Straw convoy (20 wagons) started fetching from SUZANNE to MERICOURT for the French.	
	12.4.16		Inspected 1st line Transport 10th Essex. Machine Gun Coy & 53 Bry Hd Qrs all serviceable & in good order.	

2353 Wt. W2544/1454 700,000 5/15 D. D. & L. A.D.S.S./Forms/C. 2118.

Instructions regarding War Diaries and Intelligence Summaries are contained in F. S. Regs., Part II. and the Staff Manual respectively. Title pages will be prepared in manuscript.

WAR DIARY
or
INTELLIGENCE SUMMARY.
(Erase heading not required.)

Army Form C. 2118.

Vol:- 10.

Place	Date	Hour	Summary of Events and Information	Remarks and references to Appendices
ETINEHEM	13/4/16		Inspected all 1st Line Transport of 53 Bry at SUZANNE. Quite serviceable & in good condition & order.	
	14/4/16		Inspected all 1st L. Transport of 54 Bry at BRAY (also that of [illegible]). Very satisfactory & in excellent condition	
	15 & 16/4/16		Normal work.	
	17/4/16		" "	
	18/4/16		Straw convoys from SUZANNE to MERICOURT for French finished	
	19/4/16		Det. from 4 Div H.T. Coy returned to their H.Qrs.	
	20/4/16		Normal work	
	21/4/16		" "	
	22/4/16		To PICQUIGNY & other places in Reserve area re R Pts.	
	23/4/16		Office work re move	
	24/4/16		" " " " & normal work	
	25 & 26/4/16		Office work & working on scheme & details for move.	
	27/4/16		To CAVILLON. AILLY & BREILLY re billets & R Pts.	
	28/4/16		Normal	
	29 & 30/4/16		Three Battns of 53 Bry commenced to move into Reserve Area	[illegible] 18 Div Tn

2353 Wt. W2544/1454 700,000 5/15 D. D. & L. A.D.S.S./Forms/C. 2118.

Instructions regarding War Diaries and Intelligence Summaries are contained in F. S. Regs., Part II. and the Staff Manual respectively. Title pages will be prepared in manuscript.

WAR DIARY
or
INTELLIGENCE SUMMARY.
(Erase heading not required.)

Army Form C. 2118.

18th Divisional Train ASC Vol 11

Place	Date	Hour	Summary of Events and Information	Remarks and references to Appendices
ETINEHEM	1/5/16		151 Coy marched out.	
	2/5/16		ECLUSE Depot handed over to S.S.O. 30th Div.	
	3/5/16		153 Coy marched out. Railhead at LONGPRE opened for us.	
	4/5/16		Hd Qrs & 152 Coy marched out. D.D.S.T. IV Army inspected Hd Qr Coy at SAILLY LAIRETTE	
CAVILLON	5/5/16		Hd Qrs Div marched in.	
	6/5/16		Normal work. Hd Qrs Train CAVILLON. Hd Qr Coy SAILLY LAIRETTE 151. 152 153 Coys SAILLY. R.Pts Div Troops. R.105. 53 Brig Cross roads S.W. of VAUX. 54th Brig St SAVEUR 55 Brig X Roads NE of FOURDRINOY	
-	7/5/16		Took over from Lt Col Groves who had proceeded on leave to England	
-	8th		Visited refilling points of 151 152, 153 Companies	
-	9th		Visited Head quarters Coy at SAILLY LAURETTE and dealt with local claims	
-	10th		Visited horse lines of 152 Coy. W.C. Yeomanry left the division	
-	11.		Visited 152 Coy and SAILLY LAURETTE. 18th Cyclist Company left for GROVETOWN	
	12		Office work	
	13		Visited 151 152 153 Companies	

2353 Wt. W2544/1454 700,000 5/15 D. D. & L. A.D.S.S./Forms/C. 2118.

Instructions regarding War Diaries and Intelligence Summaries are contained in F. S. Regs., Part II. and the Staff Manual respectively. Title pages will be prepared in manuscript.

WAR DIARY
or
INTELLIGENCE SUMMARY.
(Erase heading not required.)

Army Form C. 2118.

Place	Date	Hour	Summary of Events and Information	Remarks and references to Appendices
CAVILLON	14		Office work	
	15		Office work visited Brigade Companies at AILLY	
	16		President of FGCM at SAISSEVAL	
	17		Lt Col Grose returned from leave. Major Beasley returned to SAILLY LAURETTE	
	18		Office work & routine.	
	19		Visited R.P. at VAUX X Roads & inspected all wagons etc of 151 by there including all baggage wagons	
	20		R.P. at FOURDRINOY & inspected 153 by there	
	21		R.P. at ST SAUVEUR & inspected 152 by there on their way	
	22		R.P. at R 103 & inspected 150 by. A Batt 53 Brig moved up into the forward area.	
	23.		Div Cav & Cyclists struck off strength of Div. B.A.Cs absorbed into D.A.C. surplus Train wagons (4) withdrawn & sent with R.A. details to ABBEVILLE (24/5/16) To S. LAILETTE at 6 pm to settle question of R.E. wagons.	
	24.		Inspected 1st line Transport of 55 Brig. Very good condition & serviceable.	
	25. 26 27		Normal work	
	28.		Normal work. Sports of 53rd Inf Brig.	
	29		Inspected transport of 55th F Ambulance. Very satisfactory.	
	30.		Inspected transport of 54th F.A.	
	31.		Inspected transport of 56th F.A. Satisfactory.	

H. G. Grose LT. COL.
COMDG 18TH DIVISIONAL TRAIN.

2353 Wt. W2544/1454 700,000 5/15 D. D. & L. A.D.S.S./Forms/C. 2118.

18 Div Train

Army Form C. 2118.

Vol:- 12

WAR DIARY
or
INTELLIGENCE SUMMARY.
(Erase heading not required.)

Instructions regarding War Diaries and Intelligence Summaries are contained in F. S. Regs., Part II. and the Staff Manual respectively. Title pages will be prepared in manuscript.

18th Divisional Train. A.S.C.

Place	Date	Hour	Summary of Events and Information	Remarks and references to Appendices
CALLLON	1/6/16		Normal work.	
	2/6/16		Buying sheep in morning for use of Sel^mt 2 I C Div.	
	3/6/16		Normal work, In evening 45000 Iron rations from BRAY to CARNOY.	
	4/6/16		Continuation of transport of 45000 rations. Completed during night.	
	5/6/16		To SAILLY LAIRETTE re Indians in forward area. Left Park subdivision with Iron Rations with dumps as ordered.	
	6/6/16		Normal.	
	7/6/16		To SAILLY LAIRETTE to arrange transport for Ammunition Reserve. Left Park sent to CARNOY to-night re distribution of jam & soup rations.	
	8/6/16		Arranging move of 151 & 153 Coys to forward area on 10th; also move of 55 Bde on 9th/10th.	
	9/6/16		To ETINEHEM with D A Q M G re supply arrangements for move.	
	10/6/16		132 Coy moved to ST PIERRE a GOUY. 54 Bde to PICQUIGNY district.	
	11 & 12/6/16		Normal.	
	13/6/16		To ~~SAIL~~ CHIPILLY re ammunition wagon etc as limits of 150 151 & 153 Coys.	
	14/6/16		C.R.A.s deficiencies & breakages to Bagg & Supply wagons. All clocks put on 1 hour at 11 pm for daylight saving effects to come into line with civil time.	

2353 Wt. W2544/1454 700,000 5/15 D. D. & L. A.D.S.S./Forms/C. 2118.

Instructions regarding War Diaries and Intelligence Summaries are contained in F. S. Regs., Part II. and the Staff Manual respectively. Title pages will be prepared in manuscript.

WAR DIARY
or
INTELLIGENCE SUMMARY.
(Erase heading not required.)

Army Form C. 2118.

Place	Date	Hour	Summary of Events and Information	Remarks and references to Appendices
CAVILLON	15/6/16		Normal.	
	16/6/16		To CHIPILLY to inspect new lines etc of 150. 151 & 153 Coys	
	17/6/16		" " " re accommodation of Train Hd Qrs. 21st Inf Bde left 18 Div area.	
	18/6/16		Moves postponed supply arrangements had to be altered accordingly.	
	19/6/16		To CHIPILLY in morning & to HEILLY Railhead. Trouble with R.A. re supply wagons doing ammunition carrying at night	
	20/6/16		Normal.	
	21/6/16		Normal.	
	22/6/16		3 day of operations. 152 Coy marched out of ST PIERRE à GOUY for CHIPILLY, with all 54th Bde Transport.	
CHIPILLY	23/6/16		"U" day. Hd Qrs Div moved to Battle dugouts. A&Q to ETINEHEM Div Tn to CHIPILLY.	
	24/6/16		"U" day. Round lines of Coys. Ammunition carrying ceased.	
	25/6/16		"V" day.	
	26/6/16		"W" day.	
	27/6/16		"X" day Very wet & heavy showers. Ground very heavy.	
	28/6/16		"Y" day Bgg wagons of Bde went to them at 6 am for loading, when loaded, returned to Train Coys.	

2353 Wt. W2544/1454 700,000 5/15 D. D. & L. A.D.S.S./Forms/C. 2118.

Instructions regarding War Diaries and Intelligence Summaries are contained in F. S. Regs., Part II. and the Staff Manual respectively. Title pages will be prepared in manuscript.

WAR DIARY
or
INTELLIGENCE SUMMARY.
(Erase heading not required.)

Army Form C. 2118.

Place	Date	Hour	Summary of Events and Information	Remarks and references to Appendices
CHIPILLY	29/6/16		"Z" day. Weather brighter: roads drying up well; ~~[illegible]~~	
	30/6/16		Baggage horses & drs lent to R.A. units.	

[illegible signature] LT. COL.
COMDG 18TH DIVISIONAL TRAIN.

2353 Wt. W2544/1454 700,000 5/15 D. D. & L. A.D.S.S./Forms/C. 2118.

18 Vol 13
Train.

18TH DIVISIONAL TRAIN.

Subject:- War Diary.

18TH DIVISIONAL TRAIN.	
No. 1/188.	3/8/16.

Head Quarters.
18th Division.

With reference to Divisional Routine Orders d/ 15.7.16, No 522. I attach herewith original War Diary for the month of July 1916.

Please acknowledge receipt.

[signature]

LT. COL.
COMDG 18TH DIVISIONAL TRAIN.

Instructions regarding War Diaries and Intelligence Summaries are contained in F. S. Regs., Part II. and the Staff Manual respectively. Title pages will be prepared in manuscript.

WAR DIARY
or
INTELLIGENCE SUMMARY.
(Erase heading not required.)

Army Form C. 2118.

VOL:-13

18th Divisional Train. A.S.C.

Place	Date	Hour	Summary of Events and Information	Remarks and references to Appendices
CHIPILLY	1/7/16		To MEAULTE re watering & billeting of train.	
	2/7/16		To MEAULTE re [illegible] with Col Lyon: Train moved to SAILLY LE SEC.	
SAILLY-LE-SEC.	3/7/16		D.H.Q. re wagons for R.A. supplies; horses doing too much; change horses in future at BOIS DES TAILLES	
	4/7/16		To Battle Hd Qrs re transport & to CARNOY to see Divisional Dump.	
	5/7/16		Normal work.	
	6/7/16		" " " Div started coming out of front line	
	7/7/16		Normal work.	
	8/7/16		Div (except R.A.) all out of front line	
	9/7/16		Up to D.H.Q. re baggage wagons & key wagons of R.A.	
	10/7/16		Normal Work	
	11/7/16		"	
	12/7/16		Big movements relieving 30th Div.	
	13/7/16		" " " & normal work.	
	14/7/16		" " "	
	15/7/16		" " " "	

2353 Wt. W2544/1454 700,000 5/15 D. D. & L. A.D.S.S./Forms/C. 2118.

Instructions regarding War Diaries and Intelligence Summaries are contained in F. S. Regs., Part II. and the Staff Manual respectively. Title pages will be prepared in manuscript.

WAR DIARY
or
INTELLIGENCE SUMMARY.
(Erase heading not required.)

Army Form C. 2118.

Vol:- 13

Place	Date	Hour	Summary of Events and Information	Remarks and references to Appendices
SAILLY-LE-SEC	16/7/16		T/3/026312 Sgt. Canty killed by a shell at BRONFAY, also his horse.	
	17/7/16		D.H.Q. to see about R.Pts & R.A Baggage wagons, also move of Train	
	18/7/16		Brigade movements to & from line. D.A.C moved ~~to~~ up from BOIS DE TAILLES	
"	19/7/16		Normal.	
	20/7/16		All transport began march to Back area, except that of R.A. D.A.C & 53 Bny who are remaining behind.	
HALLEN-COURT	21/7/16		Div Hd Qrs moved to HALLENCOURT. 54th & 55 Bny by road to their area.	
	22/7/16		Supply & Bagg horses & vehicles had a most trying march owing to heat & distance & horses were very done. S wagons got to area about 6 am.	
	23/7/16		Div began to entrain for II Army area, 152 & 153 Coy moved this day	
RENESCURE	24/7/16		Hd Qrs moved arrived about 1 pm. Rounds fixing R.Pts & Coy areas. 157 Coy moved. 150 Coy arrived at HALLENCOURT from BRAY area. D.T.S.O has to act S.S.O for D.T till they move.	
	25/7/16		Reported to DDST II Army. R.Pts 53 Bny BLARINGHEM. 54 Bny SERCUS. 55 CAMPAGNE. D Troops. RENESCURE	
	26/7/16		Div Art. begin to leave southern area, also 150 Coy.	

2353 Wt. W2544/1454 700,000 5/15 D. D. & L. A.D.S.S./Forms/C. 2118.

Instructions regarding War Diaries and Intelligence Summaries are contained in F. S. Regs., Part II. and the Staff Manual respectively. Title pages will be prepared in manuscript.

WAR DIARY
or
INTELLIGENCE SUMMARY.
(Erase heading not required.)

Army Form C. 2118.

Vol:-13

Place	Date	Hour	Summary of Events and Information	Remarks and references to Appendices
RENESCURE	27/7/16		Fixing R.Pts in forward area W of BAILLEUL. Div art arrived in forward area.	
	28/7/16		53rd 54th & 55th Bdes with their bgs moved into forward area.	
	29/7/16		53 BODWAERSVERFELDE. 54 METEREN. 55 FLETRE. R.A EECKE.	
	30/7/16		Went round bgs in forward area & found horses better than I expected. All correct near R.Pts. R.A. H.Qrs moved to CROIX DU BEC	
	31/7/16		To forward area to look for R.Pts & bivouacs for bgs.	

[illegible] Lt Col
[illegible]

2353 Wt. W2544/1454 700,000 5/15 D. D. & L. A.D.S.S./Forms/C. 2118.

"A" Form.
Army Form C. 2121.

MESSAGES AND SIGNALS.

No. of Message ....

Prefix .... Code .... m.	Words	Charge	This message is on a/c of:	Recd. at ....m.
Office of Origin and Service Instructions.			.... Service.	Date ....
	Sent			From ....
	At ....m.			
	To			
	By		(Signature of "Franking Officer.")	By ....

TO 18th Divl Train

Sender's Number.	Day of Month.	In reply to Number.	AAA
* A932	4/8/16	T/188	

War diary for July 1916 received

From 18th Div A

Place

Time 10am

The above may be forwarded as now corrected.

.... Censor.

(Z)

[illegible]

Signature of Addressor or person authorised to telegraph in his name.

* This line should be erased if not required.

225,000. W 14042—M 44. H. W & V., Ld. 12/15.

Vol 14

18th Divisional Train

A.S.C

18th Divisional Train A.S.C.

WAR DIARY
or
INTELLIGENCE SUMMARY.
(Erase heading not required.)

Instructions regarding War Diaries and Intelligence Summaries are contained in F. S. Regs., Part II. and the Staff Manual respectively. Title pages will be prepared in manuscript.

18TH DIVISIONAL TRAIN. No. 1/188. 3.9.16.

Army Form C. 2118.

(VOL: 14)

Place	Date	Hour	Summary of Events and Information	Remarks and references to Appendices
RENESCURE	1/8/16		Transport of Div HQ Coys & Train to forward area.	
CROIX DU BAC	2/8/16		HdQrs of Div moved to CROIX DU BAC.	
	3/8/16		53 Bde to ERQUINGHEM & R.A. to CROIX DU BAC areas with Train Coys at CROIX DU BAC	
	4/8/16		Normal.	
	5/8/16		54 Bde moved to ERQUINGHEM + 53rd to ESTAIRES. 151 & 152 Coys to CROIX DU BAC.	
	6/8/16		Commenced drawing supplies from Railhead at BAC ST MAUR by H.T. instead of by D.S.C.	
	7/8/16		Normal	
	8/8/16		53 Bde moved to Reserve Area at ERQUINGHEM. Capt. Stretton W.O. Inspector of Catering arrived to go through Divisional + Regimental Supply System.	
	9/8/16		Inspected casually various vehicles & animals of several units at the foot ground; condition very satisfactory & serviceable.	
	10/8/16		Normal.	
	11/8/16		1 Batt 53 Bde to Training Ground near BAILLEUL. 1 Batt 54 Bde to LA MOTTE	

2353 Wt. W2544/1454 700,000 5/15 D. D. & L. A.D.S.S./Forms/C. 2118.

Army Form C. 2118.

Instructions regarding War Diaries and Intelligence Summaries are contained in F. S. Regs., Part II. and the Staff Manual respectively. Title pages will be prepared in manuscript.

WAR DIARY
or
INTELLIGENCE SUMMARY.
(*Erase heading not required.*)

Place	Date	Hour	Summary of Events and Information	Remarks and references to Appendices
CROIX DU BAC	12/8/16		53 Bry moved to Training ground at BAILLEUL	
	13/8/16 & 14/8/16.		Normal.	
	15/8/16.		Northants (54th Bry) relieved at LA MOTTE by E Surreys. (55 Bry)	
	16/8/16		2Lt. Brand to England for duty with R.F.C.	
	17/8/16.		Normal	
	18/8/16.		Inspected all 1st Line Transport of 53rd & 54th Brig; Animals in good condition. Harness serviceable. Vehicles serviceable (a few wheels want changing this is already in hand) I consider transport most satisfactory considering work they have had to do in the last few months.	
	19/8/16.		Inspected 1st line transport of 55th Bde. Animals good, harness serviceable, Vehicles, serviceable. (wheels as with 53 & 54 Bde.	
	20/8/16.		151 Coy joined 53 Bry at BAILLEUL.	
	21/8/16.		Railhead changed to STEENWERCK & V. Australian S.C. feed from there to dumps.	
	22/8/16.		55 Bry moved to ESTAIRES. 158 Coy also.	

Instructions regarding War Diaries and Intelligence Summaries are contained in F. S. Regs., Part II. and the Staff Manual respectively. Title pages will be prepared in manuscript.

WAR DIARY
or
INTELLIGENCE SUMMARY.
(Erase heading not required.)

Army Form C. 2118.

Place	Date	Hour	Summary of Events and Information	Remarks and references to Appendices
CROIX DU BAC	23/8/16		32 L.D animals (9 Horses + 23 mules) arrived from Remounts, + distributed to Coys: 23 H.D sent away. 17 to Remount Farm 1 back to M.V.S, 5 sick to M.V.S	
BAILLEUL	24/8/16		Div Hd Qrs to BAILLEUL. 11 D.S.C. pulling from Railhead	
ROELLECOURT	25/8/16		Whole Div less R.A. & 150 Coy A.S.C. moved to training area. Third Army. Hd Qrs to ROELLECOURT. Railhead TINQUES. R.P. 53rd Bde CHELERS area 54th Bde MARQUAY 55th MONCHY BRETON area.	
	26/8/16		Watering of horses of 150 & 152 Coys very bad. have to go 2 & 2½ miles for it.	
	27/8/16		3 D.S.C. now pulling from TINQUES Rd Head.	
	28/8/16		Normal.	
	29/8/16		D.D.S.T. inspected 151 & 153 Coys. All satisfactory. R.A. & 150 Coy moved to K area Reserve Army from CROIX DU BAC.	
	30/8/16		8 Sussex Pioneers moved to new area.	
	31/8/16		4 Transport Drs wounded. 2 horses killed. 2 wounded with 150 Coy.	

[illegible signature] LT. COL.
COMDG 18TH DIVISIONAL TRAIN.

2353 Wt. W2544/1454 700,000 5/15 D. D. & L. A.D.S.S./Forms/C. 2118.

Instructions regarding War Diaries and Intelligence Summaries are contained in F. S. Regs., Part II. and the Staff Manual respectively. Title pages will be prepared in manuscript.

WAR DIARY
or
INTELLIGENCE SUMMARY.
(Erase heading not required.)

HEAD QUARTERS No. .... 9 OCT. 1916 * 18TH DIVISION *

Army Form C. 2118.

Vol:-15

Place	Date	Hour	Summary of Events and Information	Remarks and references to Appendices
			18th Divisional Train A.S.C.	
ROELLECOURT	1/9/16		Normal	
	2/9/16		Normal	
	3/9/16		Selected R. Pts for supplies on evening of 6th in LUCHEUX area	
	4/9/16		Refilled twice at old R. Pts for 5th & 6th	
	5/9/16		Man [illegible] off for 4 days	
	6/9/16		Normal	
	7/9/16		Normal. Selected new R Pts for 54th & 55th Brig in B area	
	8/9/16		Normal. Selected R. Pts in 'C' area	
DOULLENS	9/9/16		Hd Qrs to DOULLENS. 53rd 54th & 55th Bdes to A area.	
	10/9/16		Bdes to 'B' area	
ACHEUX	11/9/16		Hd Qrs to ACHEUX. Bdes to 'C' area.	
	12/9/16		Round R. Pts & all bdes. All billets & villages left in a filthy condition	
	13/9/16		To see D.D.S.T. Reserve Army at RAINCHEVAL.	
	14/9/16		All supplies being pulled from ACHEUX Rl Head by H.T. not M.T.	
	15/9/16		Ditto. & normal	
	16/9/16		Normal	
	17/9/16		Bde Hd Qrs [illegible] & 2 Battns 53 Bde to BOUZINCOURT	

2353 Wt. W2544/1454 700,000 5/15 D. D. & L. A.D.S.S./Forms/C. 2118.

Instructions regarding War Diaries and Intelligence Summaries are contained in F. S. Regs., Part II. and the Staff Manual respectively. Title pages will be prepared in manuscript.

WAR DIARY
or
INTELLIGENCE SUMMARY.
(Erase heading not required.)

Army Form C. 2118.

Place	Date	Hour	Summary of Events and Information	Remarks and references to Appendices
ACHEUX	18/9/16		2/Lt Colburn placed in close arrest under sect 16	
	19/9/16		Weather most inclement. Horse lines & mens bivouacs flooded & under water in places.	
	20/9/16		Weather rather bad. Took 2 Lt Haynes to be interviewed by D.D.S.T. R Army	
	21/9/16		Normal. Roads in a terrible state, making work much harder for H.T.	
"	22/9/16		Normal.	
	23/9/16		54 Bde moved to HEDAUVILLE area 48th Div [illegible] falling [illegible] fresh at Railhead. 152 Coy to FORCEVILLE area	
	24/9/16		151 Coy moved up to FORCEVILLE area & 53 Bde up to forward area	
			53 Bde & 54 Bde into line: 49th Div Art & 146th Brig feeding off our pack.	
	25/9/16		53+54 Bde moved into line, in relief of 2 Brig 49th Div. D.H.Q. to HEDAUVILLE	
HEDAUVILLE	26/9/16		Div attacked on THIEPVAL, great success.	
	27/9/16		Normal.	
	28/9/16		Div attacked & took SCHWABEN TRENCH	
	29/9/16		Normal. 146 Brig rejoined their Div & stopped feeding from our supply	
	30/9/16		Normal. Took over 18 water carts 36 L D horses from 49 Div Train	

[illegible] Lt Col.
O.C. 18 Div Train

2353 Wt. W2544/1454 700,000 5/15 D. D. & L. A.D.S.S./Forms/C. 2118.

Instructions regarding War Diaries and Intelligence Summaries are contained in F. S. Regs., Part II. and the Staff Manual respectively. Title pages will be prepared in manuscript.

WAR DIARY
or
INTELLIGENCE SUMMARY.
(Erase heading not required.)

Army Form C. 2118.

VO 16

(VOL:- 16)

18th DIVISIONAL TRAIN. ASC

Place	Date	Hour	Summary of Events and Information	Remarks and references to Appendices
HEDAUVILLE	1/10/16		~~49~~ 48th Div R.A. etc rejoined their own Div for feeding.	
	2/10/16		Normal	
	3/10/16		49th Div R.A. etc rejoined their own Div for feeding. 53rd & 54th Bdes together with 151 Coy & 152 Coy moved back to 'A' area.	
	4/10/16		Railhead CANAPLES. 18 Div R.A. drawing from 2nd Cavalry Park at ACHEUX.	
	5/10/16		Three Regts to A area.	
BERNAVILLE	6/10/16		Hd Qrs of Div moved to BERNAVILLE. 53 Bde to A area.	
	7/10/16		Round all 3 Coys. 151 at OCCOCHES. R.P. at church. 152 153 at MONPLAISIR & MACFER. R.P. at MACFER. 152 at BARLETTE [on Hedauville road] R.P. at Point S of X roads S of RIBEAUCOURT. All horses got over march very well & there were no casualties.	
	8/10/16		M.T. delivering there R.Ps in back area, & H.T. from there to units. 2nd Column tried by G.O.C.	
	9/10/16		Pack train came in very late, causing very late delivery ~~of~~ to units	
	10/10/16		D.S.C. drew from Reserve Dump with them; delivered to R.Ps & then to Railhead & loaded for drawing next day; - back to normal procedure.	

2353 Wt. W2544/1454 700,000 5/15 D. D. & L. A.D.S.S./Forms/C. 2118.

Instructions regarding War Diaries and Intelligence Summaries are contained in F. S. Regs., Part II. and the Staff Manual respectively. Title pages will be prepared in manuscript.

WAR DIARY
or
INTELLIGENCE SUMMARY.
(Erase heading not required.)

Army Form C. 2118.

Place	Date	Hour	Summary of Events and Information	Remarks and references to Appendices
BERNAVILLE	11/10/16		D.S.C. dumped at R.Pt. at 8 a.m. Refilling at 9-30.	
	12/10/16.		All 1st line transport of 53 Bde. 10th Essex & 8 Sussex Pioneers moved to forward area.	
	13/10/16		53 Bde H Q 8th Suffolks. 56 F.A. & 151 Coy A.S.C. T.M.B. & A.D.H.Q. to ALBERT.	
			Inspected 1st line Transport of 53 Bde. Very satisfactory. Animals in excellent condition & with few exceptions harness & vehicles serviceable	
	14/10/16		Berks Regt. ½ Bn of the 150 F.A. to ALBERT by bus.	
	15/10/16		54th & 55 Bde in toto moved to K area.	
ALBERT.	16/10/16		The whole of D.A.Q. moved to forward area.	
	17/10/16		54th Bde reached forward area (BOUZINCOURT) & 53 Bde to ALBERT.	
	18/10/16		D.S.C. drawing altogether from ACHEUX Railhead	
	19/10/16		54th Bde moved to ALBERT	
	20/10/16		Normal. Round horse lines all in bad, muddy condition & bad for both horses & men.	
	21/10/16		Railhead changed to AVELUY	
	22/10/16		Normal.	

2353 Wt. W2544/1454 700,000 5/15 D. D. & L. A.D.S.S./Forms/C. 2118.

Instructions regarding War Diaries and Intelligence Summaries are contained in F. S. Regs., Part II. and the Staff Manual respectively. Title pages will be prepared in manuscript.

WAR DIARY
or
INTELLIGENCE SUMMARY.
(Erase heading not required.)

Army Form C. 2118.

Place	Date	Hour	Summary of Events and Information	Remarks and references to Appendices
ALBERT	23/10/16		D.H.Q. (advanced) to TARA HILL. 55 Bde to Trenches. Promulgation of sentence on 2Lt Callum: Cashiered & 1 year Impt - without H.L. Pulling by HT from AVELUY Railhead vice M.T.	
	24/10/16		Ordinary procedure.	
	25/10/16		Normal. Weather very wet.	
	26/10/16		" " Still very wet	
	27/10/16		" " Rain still on. Roads getting very bad.	
	28/10/16		Pack train 3 hours late.	
	29/10/16		Pulled at 8 am from Railhead from now on. More satisfactory weather last again	
	30/10/16		Normal. Very wet.	
	31/10/16		Pack train 7 hours late. & great shortage of oats (14000 lbs) had to send coal lorries to BELLE EGLISE for them, making delivery very late. 4 Battns moved to WARLOY.	

[signature]
LT. COL.
COMDG 18TH DIVISIONAL TRAIN.

2353 Wt. W2544/1454 700,000 5/15 D. D. & L. A.D.S.S./Forms/C. 2118.

Instructions regarding War Diaries and Intelligence Summaries are contained in F. S. Regs., Part II. and the Staff Manual respectively. Title pages will be prepared in manuscript.

WAR DIARY
or
INTELLIGENCE SUMMARY.
(Erase heading not required.)

Army Form C. 2118.

Vol X

Place	Date	Hour	Summary of Events and Information	Remarks and references to Appendices
BEAUVAL	1/10/16		Column + No 1 W/shop at BEAUVAL No 2 W/shop at HÉDAUVILLE to look after cars of 18th Division (+ Ambulances) ~~Rec^d for repair~~ Rec^d for repair in No 1 W/shop Leyland Lorries 6215, 3568, 6963 of No 3 D.S.C. – Pierce Arrow Lorry 13902 of 29th CCS Daimler Lorry 28308 of 3rd CCS – Daimler Car M105 of 18th Ord^ce W/shop. Sent out of No 1 W/shop Leyland Lorries 6963, 4343, 6774 + Commer Lorry 5121 of No 3 D.S.C. – Pierce Arrow Lorry 13902 of 29th CCS, Napier Box Car M18511 of 16th Adv^d Depot Med Stores, Daimler Car M105 of 18th Ord^ce W/shop Rec^d for repair in No 2 W/shop Vauxhall Cars M17847, M18626 of 18th Div Train, Daimler Car M758 of 18th Div H.Q. Daimler Lorry 28307 of 18th Div Signals, Sunbeam Car M15255 of 18th Div Signals (Last 2 sent out same day) Supplies ~~Dumped~~ for 51st Division and re-loaded for them at BELLE EGLISE Supply arrangements for 18th Division as yesterday. [illegible] Capt O.C. No 3 D.S.C.	

T2134. Wt. W708–776. 500000. 4/15. Sir J. C. & S.

Instructions regarding War Diaries and Intelligence Summaries are contained in F. S. Regs., Part II. and the Staff Manual respectively. Title pages will be prepared in manuscript.

WAR DIARY
or
INTELLIGENCE SUMMARY.
(Erase heading not required.)

Army Form C. 2118.

Place	Date	Hour	Summary of Events and Information	Remarks and references to Appendices
BEAUVAL	2/10/16		Rec^d^ Foregoing in No 1 W/Shop	
			Leyland Lorries 6761, 7163, 6762 of No 3 D.S.C.	
			Austin Car M 14016 of 51st Div HQ + Sunbeam Car M 14074 of 51st D.H.Q.	
			Sent out of No 1 W/Shop Leyland Lorries 3568, 7163, 6762 of No 3 D.S.C.	
			Austin Car M 14016 + Sunbeam Car M 14014 of 51st Div HQ.	
			Rec^d^ for repair in No 2 W/Shop	
			Austin Amb^ce^ A 9801 of 56th F.A, Ford Amb^ce^ A 14596 of 54th F.A,	
			Daimler Car M 14866 of 18th D.H.Q. - Triumph m/c 263891 of 18th Div Signals.	
			Sent out of No 2 W/Shop Austin Amb^ce^ A 9801 of 56th F.A.	
			Ford Amb^ce^ A 14596 of 54th F.A, Daimler Car M 758 of 18th Div HQ,	
			Triumph m/c 263891 of 18th Div Signals.	
			Supply arrangements. Dumped Supplies from Lorries for 51st Div	
			~~+ re-loaded at BELLE EGLISE.~~ (No further loading for this Division)	
			Supplies for 18th Division loaded on Div Train Wagons at	
			ACHEUX as yesterday	
			M2/050619 Pte Burgess S.Q. to 18th Div. HQ	
			M2/076525 Pte Campbell H, M2/074352 Pte Brassler A.W., M2/117547 Pte West L.	
			to 1st Base M.T. Depot, ROUEN.	

Wm. [illegible] Major
O.C. No 3 D.S.C.

T2134. Wt. W708—776. 500000. 4/15. Sir J. C. & S.

Instructions regarding War Diaries and Intelligence Summaries are contained in F. S. Regs., Part II. and the Staff Manual respectively. Title pages will be prepared in manuscript.

WAR DIARY
or
INTELLIGENCE SUMMARY.
(Erase heading not required.)

Army Form C. 2118.

Place	Date	Hour	Summary of Events and Information	Remarks and references to Appendices
BEAUVAL	3/10/16		Rec^d for repair in No 1 W/shop.	
			Commer Lorry 5121 of No 3 D.S.C, Pierce Arrow Lorry 13902 of 29th CCS.	
			Sent out of No 1 W/shop.	
			Leyland Lorry 6761 of No 3 D.S.C, Daimler Lorry 28308 of No 3 CCS	
			Rec^d for repair in No 2 W/shop Austin Ambces A9883, A9888 of 55th FA.	
			Triumph m/c 270385 of 56th FA	
			Sent out of No 2 W/shop. Austin Ambces A9883 A9884 of 55th & 54th	
			Field Ambces respectively - Daimler Car M14866 of 18th Div HQ.	
			Triumph m/c 270385 of 56th FA	
			Supply Railhead for 18th Division changed to CANAPLES -	
			[illegible] Loaded supplies by lorry (less Div Troops)	
			Detail issue from lorries to units of 53rd & 54th Bde &	
			refilled in ordinary way for 55th Bde (supplies issued	
			same day as loaded)	

[illegible]
Comdg No 3 D.S.C

T2134. Wt. W708—776. 500000. 4/15. Sir J. C. & S.

Instructions regarding War Diaries and Intelligence Summaries are contained in F. S. Regs., Part II. and the Staff Manual respectively. Title pages will be prepared in manuscript.

WAR DIARY
or
INTELLIGENCE SUMMARY.
(Erase heading not required.)

Army Form C. 2118.

Place	Date	Hour	Summary of Events and Information	Remarks and references to Appendices
BEAUVAL	4/10/16		Recd for repair in No 1 W/Shop Vauxhall Car M17847 of 18th Div Train, Commer Lorry 6752 & Leyland Lorries 6963, 6760, 6765, 5505 of No 3 D.S.C.	
			Sent out after repair from No 1 W/Shop. Vauxhall Car M17847 of 18th Div Train, Pierce Arrow Lorry 13902 of 29th C.C.S. Leyland Lorries 6765, 5505, 6760 of No 3 Div Supply Col.	
			Recd for repair in No 2 W/Shop Austin Amb^ce A9802 of 55th F.A., Commer Lorry 6750 of No 3 D.S.C., Austin Amb^ce A9749 & Talbot Amb^ce A15629 of 54th F.A. – Sent out of No 2 W/Shop Austin Amb^ce A9882 & A9888 of 55th F.A. & A9749 of 54th F.A. – Commer Lorry 6750 of No 3 D.S.C.	
			Supply arrangements as yesterday	
			Feeding strength of 18th Div (less R.A.) 11423 men, 1115 Horses, Supply Col 466 men (Including details rationed in BEAUVAL)	
			20 Tons coal carted by Lorry	
			7 Lorries detailed to move No 4 C.C.S.	
			[signature] Capt. Comdg No 3 D.S.C.	

Instructions regarding War Diaries and Intelligence Summaries are contained in F. S. Regs., Part II. and the Staff Manual respectively. Title pages will be prepared in manuscript.

WAR DIARY
or
INTELLIGENCE SUMMARY.
(Erase heading not required.)

Army Form C. 2118.

Place	Date	Hour	Summary of Events and Information	Remarks and references to Appendices
BEAUVAL	5/10/16		Rec'd for repair in No 1 W/Shop & sent out same day Leyland Lorries 6878, 20980, 3584, 7164 of No 3 D.S.C. Commer Lorry 7715 of No 3 D.S.C, Daimler Lorry 26239 of 44th C.C.S. Daimler Lorry 27603 of 29 CCS, Daimler Car M 758 of 18th D.H.Q. Singer Car M 19404 of 17th Mob Lab Y.- In addition rec'd in No 1 W/Shop Leyland Lorry 6761 of No 3 DSC In addition sent out of No 1 W/Shop Commer " 6752 " " " Rec'd in No 2 W/Shop & sent out same day Daimler Car M 18409 of No 3 D.S.C, Douglas m/c 28335 of 54th F.A Supply arrangements as yesterday Feeding strength of 18th Div 12257 men, 1791 Horses, Supply Col including attached 466 men 7 Lorries provided for the move of No 4 C.C.S	

[illegible]
Comdg No 3 D.S.C.

T2134. Wt. W708—776. 500000. 4/15. Sir J. C. & S.

Instructions regarding War Diaries and Intelligence Summaries are contained in F. S. Regs., Part II. and the Staff Manual respectively. Title pages will be prepared in manuscript.

WAR DIARY
or
INTELLIGENCE SUMMARY.
(Erase heading not required.)

Army Form C. 2118.

Place	Date	Hour	Summary of Events and Information	Remarks and references to Appendices
BEAUVAL	6/10/16		Rec'd for repair in No 1 W/shop & sent out same day Leyland Lorries 6214, 6223 & Commer Lorry 13131 of No 3 D.S.C. Daimler Lorry 27523 of 29th CCS, Ford Box Car 24304 of 18th ADMS	
			In addition sent out of No 1 W/shop Commer Lorry 5121 of No 3 DSC	
			No 2 W/shop moves from HEDAUVILLE to BEAUVAL to rejoin the Column (18th Division moving to rest in back area)	
			Supply arrangements as yesterday but no detail issuing done by lorries.	
			Feeding strength of 18th Division 11950 men, 1804 Horses, Supply Col 397 men. (including attached)	
			Extras carried – Coal 10 Tons	
			7 lorries provided for No 4 CCS, 2 for miscellaneous duties.	
			M2/120370 Pte Cartwright F from No 20 D.S.C.	

[signature] Capt.
Comdg No. 3 D.S.C.

Instructions regarding War Diaries and Intelligence Summaries are contained in F. S. Regs., Part II. and the Staff Manual respectively. Title pages will be prepared in manuscript.

WAR DIARY
or
INTELLIGENCE SUMMARY.
(Erase heading not required.)

Army Form C. 2118.

Place	Date	Hour	Summary of Events and Information	Remarks and references to Appendices
BEAUVAL	7/10/16		No 2 W/shop moves to BERNAVILLE (new Hd Qrs of 18th Div.)	
			Received for repair in No 1 W/shop	
			Packard Lorry 26045 of 35th CCS	Sent out same day.
			Singer Car M 19190 of 13th Mob Lab'y	
			Leyland Lorries 3585, 6769, 6765 of No 3 D.S.C.	
			Daimler Lorry 26339 of 49th CCS, Leyland Lorry 6882 of No 3 DSC	
			Commer Lorries 7715, 5121 of No 3 D.S.C	
			Supply arrangements as yesterday	
			Feeding Strength of 18th Division 12978 men, 1749 Horses.	
			S.C. 512 men (including attached)	
			Extras carried Coal 25 Tons	
			M2/136901 Pte Watterson E to No 20 D.S.C	

[illegible]
[illegible]
Comdg No 3 D.S.C.

Instructions regarding War Diaries and Intelligence Summaries are contained in F. S. Regs., Part II. and the Staff Manual respectively. Title pages will be prepared in manuscript.

WAR DIARY
or
INTELLIGENCE SUMMARY.
(Erase heading not required.)

Army Form C. 2118.

Place	Date	Hour	Summary of Events and Information	Remarks and references to Appendices
BEAUVAL	8/10/16		Rec^d for repair in No 1 W/Shop Leyland Lorries 7164, 4696 of No 3 D.S.C. Sent out after repair from No 1 W/Shop Leyland Lorries 4696, 6761, 6963, 6882 of No 3 D.S.C. – Crossley Lorry 7715 of No 3 D.S.C. Rec^d for repair in No 2 W/Shop. Austin Amb^ce A 9749 of 54th F.A. Talbot Amb^ce A 9887 of 55th F.A, Austin Amb^ce A 9886 of 56th F.A. Rec^d for repair in No 2 W/Shop & sent out same day Triumph m/c 71225 of 55th F.A, 270385 of 56th F.A. Douglas m/c 23008 of 56th F.A. Supply arrangements as yesterday. Feeding strength of Division 12901 men, 1959 Horses, Supply Col (including attached) 479 men Extras obtained from No 3 Field Supply Depot	

[illegible] Capt.
Comdg No 3 D.S.C.

Instructions regarding War Diaries and Intelligence Summaries are contained in F. S. Regs., Part II. and the Staff Manual respectively. Title pages will be prepared in manuscript.

WAR DIARY
or
INTELLIGENCE SUMMARY.
(Erase heading not required.)

Army Form C. 2118.

Place	Date	Hour	Summary of Events and Information	Remarks and references to Appendices
BEAUVAL	9/10/16		Received for repair in No 1 W/Shop	
			Leyland Lorries 7133, 4761, 6211 of No 3 D.S.C.	Sent out same day
			Sunbeam Car M 14027 of 3 D.S.C, Sunbeam Car M 14657 of 15 Ord W/Shops	
			Pierce Arrow Lorry 13902 of 29th C.C.S.	
			Dennis Lorry 26240 of 49th CCS, Commer Lorry 26260 of 2/1 S Midland CCS	
			Leyland Lorries 6779, 6769 of No 3 D.S.C.	
			Rec^d from Adv^d M.T. Depot Triumph m/c 272692, Douglas S/c 3553	
			Rec^d for repair in No 2 W/Shop Austin Amb^ce A 9000 of 54th F.A, Talbot Amb^ce A 9747 of 55th F.A, Daimler Car M 1906 of 18th D.H.Q.	
			Triumph m/c 265402, 264505, 712 m/s	
			Sent out of No 2 W/Shop Austin Amb^ce A 9000, of 54th F.A, Talbot Amb^ce A 9887 of 55th F.A – Triumph m/cs 265402, 264505, 712 m/s.	
			Supply arrangements as before.	
			Feeding strength of Division 12429 men, 1872 Horses, Supply Col (including attached) 479 men – Extras carted Coal 30 Tons c/640 Pte Ayres Pk to 47th CCS	
			5 Lorries employed on carting stores –	
				[illegible] Major Comdg No 3 D.S.C.

T2134. Wt. W708–776. 500000. 4/15. Sir J. C. & S.

Instructions regarding War Diaries and Intelligence Summaries are contained in F. S. Regs., Part II. and the Staff Manual respectively. Title pages will be prepared in manuscript.

WAR DIARY
or
INTELLIGENCE SUMMARY.
(Erase heading not required.)

Army Form C. 2118.

Place	Date	Hour	Summary of Events and Information	Remarks and references to Appendices
BEAUVAL	10/10/16		Rec'd for repair in No 1 W/Shop. Leyland Lorries 5647, 5505, 4161 of No 3 DSC	
			Commer Lorries 10070, 26261 of No 3 DSC + 2/1 S Midland CCS respectively	
			Packard Lorry 26045, Vauxhall Car M17644 of 35th CCS + 18th Div Train "	
			Sunbeam Cars M15255 + M14112 of 18th Div Signals + 33rd Ord W/Shops "	
			Sent out of No 1 W/Shop Leyland Lorries 21121, 6215, 6772 of No 3 DSC	
			Commer Lorries 10070, 26260 of No 3 DSC + 2/1 S Midland CCS respectively	
			Packard Lorry 26045 of 35th CCS, Vauxhall Car M17644 of 18th Div Train	
			Sunbeam Car M15255 of 18th Div Signals.	
			Rec'd for repair in No 2 W/Shops Ford Amb'ces A14596, A9750 of 54th & 55th	F.A
			Sent out of No 2 W/Shop Daimler Car M1906 of 18th D.H.Q	
			Talbot Amb'ce A9774 of 55th F.A.	
			M/Cs. has received + sent out after repair - Triumph M/C 262365	
			+ Douglas M/C 28335 both of 54th F.A.	
			Supply arrangements ~~[illegible]~~ become normal except	
			for Div Troops (R.A) Group. i.e. Reserve Supplies picked up	
			+ delivered to refilling Points - Feeding Strength 12532 men, 1924 Horses	
			Supply Col 519 men (including attached)	
			20 Tons Coal carted by Column	
			R. Ba[illegible] Major Comdg No 3 D.S.C	

T2134. Wt. W708—776. 500000. 4/15. Sir J. C. & S.

Instructions regarding War Diaries and Intelligence Summaries are contained in F. S. Regs., Part II. and the Staff Manual respectively. Title pages will be prepared in manuscript.

WAR DIARY
or
INTELLIGENCE SUMMARY.
(Erase heading not required.)

Army Form C. 2118.

Place	Date	Hour	Summary of Events and Information	Remarks and references to Appendices
BEAUVAL	11/10/16		Recd for repair in No 1 W/shop. Commer Lorry 13131 of No 3 D.S.C.	
			Pierce Arrow Lorry 13902 of 29th CCS, Leyland Lorries 13207, 20980 of No 3 D.S.C	
			Commer Lorry 3994 of No 3 D.S.C, Commer Lorry 26259 of 2/1 S.M. CCS	Sent out same day
			Leyland Lorries 3560, 7167, 6765	
			In addition sent out after repair - Sunbeam Car M14112 of 35th Div'l Supply Col	W/shops
			Recd for repair in No 2 W/shop Daimler Lorry 11211 of 35th San Sec.	
			Talbot Amb 9889 + Ford Amb A9744 of 56th F.A.	
			Talbot Amb A19246 of 55th F.A.	
			Sent out of No 2 W/shop after repair Daimler Lorry 11211 of 35 San Sec.	
			Ford Amb A14596 of 54th F.A.	
			Supply arrangements as yesterday.	
			Feeding strength of Division 12970 men, 1882 Horses	
			Supply Col 578 (including attached).	
			Extras carted Coal 20 Tons.	
			2 Lorries employed on miscellaneous duties	
			[signature] Major Comdg No 3 D.S.C	

T2134. Wt. W708—776. 500000. 4/15. Sir J. C. & S.

Army Form C. 2118.

Instructions regarding War Diaries and Intelligence Summaries are contained in F. S. Regs., Part II. and the Staff Manual respectively. Title pages will be prepared in manuscript.

WAR DIARY
or
INTELLIGENCE SUMMARY.
(*Erase heading not required.*)

Place	Date	Hour	Summary of Events and Information	Remarks and references to Appendices
BEAUVAL	12/10/16		Recd for repairs in No 1 W/shop	
			Leyland Lorry 3568 of No 3 D.S.C	
			Leyland Lorries 21119, 5647 + Commer Lorry 3990 of No 3 DSC	Sent out
			Sunbeam Car M14034 of No 3 DSC, Wolseley Car M974 of Graves Registration Committee	Same day
			Recd for repairs in No 2 W/shop + sent out same day	
			Vauxhall Car M17847 of 18th Div Train, Daimler Car M1274 of 18 D H.Q.	
			Sunbeam Car M15255 ~~of 18~~, + Daimler Lorry 28307 of 18th Div Signals	
			Austin Ambce A9886 of 56th F.A	
			In addition recd for repair Talbot Amb A 15629 of 54th F.A	
			In addition sent out after repair Talbot Amb A19246 of 55th F.A.	
			Feeding strength of 18th Division 14491 men, 1802 Horses,	
			Supply Col (including attached) 516 men.	
			Supply arrangements as before.	
			1 Lorry to POZIERES with 1 Battalion's rations	
			[illegible] Major	
			Comdg No 3 D.S.C	

Instructions regarding War Diaries and Intelligence Summaries are contained in F. S. Regs., Part II. and the Staff Manual respectively. Title pages will be prepared in manuscript.

WAR DIARY
or
INTELLIGENCE SUMMARY.
(Erase heading not required.)

Army Form C. 2118.

Place	Date	Hour	Summary of Events and Information	Remarks and references to Appendices
BEAUVAL	13/10/16		Recd for repair in No 1 W/shop Leyland Lorries 4670, 6963 of	No 3 D.S.C
			Austin Amb A9882 + Talbot Amb A19246 of 55th F.A.	
			Austin Amb A9747 of 54th F.A.	
			Sent out of No 1 W/shop Leyland Lorries 6963, 6769, 5505, +	Commer
			Lorry 13131 of No 3 D.S.C. – Austin Amb A9747 of 54th F.A	
			Austin Amb A9882 + Talbot Amb A19246 of 55th F.A	
			Recd for repair in No 2 W/shop + Sent out same day	
			Austin Ambs A9748, A9888, A9890 of 54th, 55th + 56th F.A's respectively	
			In addition sent out Ford Amb A9750 of 55th F.A, Talbot Amb A15629 of 54th F.A.	
			Supply arrangements as before	
			Feeding strength of Division 9964 men, 12451 Horses (less R.A + 53rd Bde)	
			S.C. 574 men.	
			1 lorry to POZIERES with rations of 1 Bn –	
			Lorries delivered from refilling point of 53rd Bde	
			rations direct to units of this Bde at	
			ALBERT (going into the line)	
			M2/153492 Pte Rogers CA to 29th C.C.S	
			[signature] Major Comdg No 3 D.S.C.	

Instructions regarding War Diaries and Intelligence Summaries are contained in F. S. Regs., Part II. and the Staff Manual respectively. Title pages will be prepared in manuscript.

WAR DIARY
or
INTELLIGENCE SUMMARY.
(Erase heading not required.)

Army Form C. 2118.

Place	Date	Hour	Summary of Events and Information	Remarks and references to Appendices
BEAUVAL	15/10/16		Rec^d for repair in No 1 W/Shop. – Leyland Lorries 5505, 6766, 6870 of No 3 DSC. Commer Lorries 7714, 5210 of No 3 DSC.	
			Sent out of No 1 W/Shop. Leyland Lorries 7167, 6766 of No 3 DSC. Commer Lorry 7714 of No: 3 D.S.C.	
			Rec^d for repair in No 2 W/Shop	
			Talbot Amb^ce A 9809 of 56th F A	
			Triumph m/c 265402 of 18th Div Train (Sent out same day)	
			5 Lorries employed on carting stores, 3 on miscellaneous duties	
			Wm. Ley Pruss (?) Major Comdg No 3 DSC.	

Instructions regarding War Diaries and Intelligence Summaries are contained in F. S. Regs., Part II. and the Staff Manual respectively. Title pages will be prepared in manuscript.

WAR DIARY
or
INTELLIGENCE SUMMARY.
(Erase heading not required.)

Army Form C. 2118.

Place	Date	Hour	Summary of Events and Information	Remarks and references to Appendices
BEAUVAL	16/10/16		Rec^d for repair in No 1 W/shop. Commer Lorry 3990 of No 3 D S C	
			Daimler Lorry 26241 of 44th CCS, Ford Box Car M 24304 of 18th O D S	
			Sent out of No 1 W/shop. Commer Lorries 3990, 5210 of No 3 D S C	
			Leyland Lorries 6878, 3568, 20980 of No 3 D.S.C.	
			Daimler Lorry 26241 of 44th CCS, Dennis Lorry 36340 of 49th CCS.	
			Singer Car M 19190 of 13th MOB Lab, Triumph m/c 270811 of 18th Div Signals	
			Rec^d for repair in No 2 W/shop - Nil	
			Sent out of No 2 W/shop A 9744 of 56th F A.	
			18th Div HQ moves to ALBERT, the Division going into the line.	
			Railhead ACHEUX (refilling point for 53rd Bde in ALBERT area)	
			5 lorries employed on carting stores.	
			Feeding strength of Division (18th) 17999 men, 4841 Horses, S.C. 574 men	
			3 Infy Bdes loaded by M.T, Div^l Troops by Train wagons.	
			[signature] Capt Commdg No 3 D.S.C.	

Instructions regarding War Diaries and Intelligence Summaries are contained in F. S. Regs., Part II. and the Staff Manual respectively. Title pages will be prepared in manuscript.

WAR DIARY
or
INTELLIGENCE SUMMARY.
(Erase heading not required.)

Army Form C. 2118.

Place	Date	Hour	Summary of Events and Information	Remarks and references to Appendices
BEAUVAL	17/10/16		Recd for repair in No 1 W/Shop Leyland Lorries 3561, 6760 of No 3 DSC	
			Daimler Car M412 of Branch Requ Office, Dennis Lorry 26338 of 49th CCS	
			Napier Box Car 18571 of 16th A.D.M.S	
			Sent out of No 1 W/Shop Leyland Lorries 4343, 6760 of No 3 D.S.C	
			Daimler Car M412 of Branch Requ Office, Ford Box Car M24304 of 18th A.D.M.S.	
			Napier Box Car M18511 of 16th A.D.M.S	
			Railhead ACHEUX (refilling points all in ALBERT area)	
			No 2 W/Shop rejoins Column from BERNAVILLE.	
			5 Lorries employed on carting stores.	
			M2/053989 Pte Windle A to No 3 CCS.	
			Feeding strength of 18th Division 18100 men, 4773 Horses	
			S.C. 518 men (including attached)	
			Loaded by M.T.	

[illegible signature]
Comdg No 3 D.S.C.

T2134. Wt. W708—776. 500000. 4/15. Sir J. C. & S.

Instructions regarding War Diaries and Intelligence Summaries are contained in F. S. Regs., Part II. and the Staff Manual respectively. Title pages will be prepared in manuscript.

WAR DIARY
or
INTELLIGENCE SUMMARY.
(Erase heading not required.)

Army Form C. 2118.

Place	Date	Hour	Summary of Events and Information	Remarks and references to Appendices
BEAUVAL	18/10/16		Recd for repair in No 1 W/Shop & sent out same day –	
			Leyland Lorry 6223, Commer Lorries 5121, 7715, 6750 of No 3 DSC	
			Singer Car M 19190 of 13th Rof Lab?	
			In addition recd for repair (not sent out)	
			Vauxhall Car M 17644 of 18th Div Train, Sunbeam Car M 14112 of 33rd Ord W/Shops	
			In addition sent out (recd for repair yesterday) Dennis Lorry 26338 of 49th CCS	
			Railhead ACHEUX.	
			No 2 W/Shop moves to ALBERT	
			M2/022225 Pte Jackson H. C. from 55th F A, M/38130 Pte Eyre S to	47 CCS
			Feeding strength of Division 18253 men, 4768 Horses,	
			S C. 539 men.	

[illegible] [illegible]
Major
Comdg No 3 DSC

Instructions regarding War Diaries and Intelligence Summaries are contained in F. S. Regs., Part II. and the Staff Manual respectively. Title pages will be prepared in manuscript.

WAR DIARY
or
INTELLIGENCE SUMMARY.
(Erase heading not required.)

Army Form C. 2118.

Place	Date	Hour	Summary of Events and Information	Remarks and references to Appendices
BEAUVAL	19/10/16		Rec^d for repair in No 1 W/shop. Commer Lorry 6752 of No 3 D.S.C.	
			Sent out of No 1 W/shop. Leyland Lorries 6779, 3561 of No 3 DSC	
			Vauxhall Car M 17644 of 18th Div Train.	
			Rec^d for repair in No 2 W/shop Daimler Car M 116 of 18th Div HQ	
			Talbot Amb A 15629 of 54th F.A	
			Sent out of No 2 W/shop. Talbot Amb A 9809 of 56th F.A	
			Supply arrangements as yesterday.	
			Feeding strength of Division (18th) 19583 men, 5200 Horses. S.C 419 men.	
			R/Head - ~~AVELUY~~ ACHEUX [illegible]	

[illegible]
Major
Comdg No: 3 D.S.C.

Instructions regarding War Diaries and Intelligence Summaries are contained in F. S. Regs., Part II. and the Staff Manual respectively. Title pages will be prepared in manuscript.

WAR DIARY
or
INTELLIGENCE SUMMARY.
(Erase heading not required.)

Army Form C. 2118.

Place	Date	Hour	Summary of Events and Information	Remarks and references to Appendices
BEAUVAL	20/5/16		Recd for repair in No 1 W/Shop - Leyland Lorry 6761 of No: 3 D.S.C	
			Sunbeam Cars M14027, M14034 of No 3 D.S.C	
			Commer Lorry 26259 of 2/1 S. Midland CCS, Daimler Car M758 of 18th D HQ.	
			Sent out of No 1 W/Shop Commer Lorry 6752 of No 3 D.S.C	
			Daimler Car M758 of 18th D.HQ., Sunbeam Car M14034 of No 3 D.S.C	
			MS/12 P.O Pte Burchatt C to 1st Base M.T Depot	
			Recd for repair in No 2 W/Shop Talbot Amb.ce A15628 of 56th F.A	
			Sent out of No 2 W/Shop. M116 Daimler Car of 18th D.H.Q	
			Supply arrangements as yesterday	
			Feeding Strength of Division 19094 men, 5037 Horses, S.C. 629 men	
			R/Head ~~AVELUY~~ ACHEUX	
			[illegible] Major Comdg No 3 D S C	

T2134. Wt. W708—776. 500000. 4/15. Sir J. C. & S.

Instructions regarding War Diaries and Intelligence Summaries are contained in F. S. Regs., Part II. and the Staff Manual respectively. Title pages will be prepared in manuscript.

WAR DIARY
or
INTELLIGENCE SUMMARY.
(Erase heading not required.)

Army Form C. 2118.

Place	Date	Hour	Summary of Events and Information	Remarks and references to Appendices
BEAUVAL	21/10/16		Recd for repair in No 1 W/shop. & sent out same day Leyland Lorries 7163, 20980, 13207, 6773 & Commer Lorry 7714 of No 3 D.S.C.	
			In addition sent out of No 1 W/shop. Leyland Lorry 6761 of No 3 D.S.C. Commer Lorry ~~7714~~ 26259 of 2/1 S. Midland CCS, Triumph m/c 26346 of No 3 DSC	
			Recd for repair in No 2 W/shop. Daimler Car M1274 of 18th Div HQ. Vauxhall Car M17847 of 18th Div Train	
			Sent out of No 2 W/shop. Talbot Amb^ce A 15629 of 54th FA.	
			Supply arrangements as yesterday.	
			Feeding Strength of 18th Division 18002 men, 5012 Horses	
			S.C. 522 men	
			Railhead AVELUY.	
			M. [illegible] Major	
			Comdg No 3 D.S.C.	

Instructions regarding War Diaries and Intelligence Summaries are contained in F. S. Regs., Part II. and the Staff Manual respectively. Title pages will be prepared in manuscript.

WAR DIARY
or
INTELLIGENCE SUMMARY.
(Erase heading not required.)

Army Form C. 2118.

Place	Date	Hour	Summary of Events and Information	Remarks and references to Appendices
BEAUVAL	22/10/16		Recd for repair in No 1 w/shop (+ all sent out same day except last 2 mentioned Commers)	
			Commer Lorries 7715, 5121, 13131, 21015, 6750, 3989 of No 3 D.S.C.	
			Leyland Lorries 4585, 7163, 3568 of No 3 D.S.C.	
			Recd for repair in No 2 w/shop + sent out same day	
			Austin Amb. A 9748 of 54th F.A, Daimler Car M 14855 of 11th Div R.A.	
			Douglas m/c 28335 of 54th F.A	
			In addition sent out of No 2 w/shop.	
			Daimler Car M 1274 of 18th Div HQ, Vauxhall Car M 17847 of 18th Div Train	
			Feeding strength of 18th Division 20,000 men*, 5006 Horses	
			S.C 517 men	
			* Pack Train of 20,000 men's rations drawn by M.T + stored on Supply Col. (Dumped)	
			R/Head AVELUY.	
			Extras Carted – Coal 40 Tons, Coke 24000 lbs, Charcoal 6000 lbs.	
			[illegible] Major Comdg No 3 D.S.C.	

T2134. Wt. W708–776. 500000. 4/15. Sir J. C. & S.

Instructions regarding War Diaries and Intelligence Summaries are contained in F. S. Regs., Part II. and the Staff Manual respectively. Title pages will be prepared in manuscript.

WAR DIARY
or
INTELLIGENCE SUMMARY.
(Erase heading not required.)

Army Form C. 2118.

Place	Date	Hour	Summary of Events and Information	Remarks and references to Appendices
BEAUVAL	23/10/16		Rec^d^ for repair in No 1 w/shop. Commer Lorries 4409, 3255, 7714 of No 3 DSC. Daimler Lorry 11211 of 35 San Sec, Ford Amb^ce^ A 9744 of 56th F A. Leyland Lorries 4343 + 21119 of No 3 D.S.C. Commer Lorry 10070 + Leyland Lorries 3584, 13207, 3561 of No 3 DSC (These 4 sent out same day)	
			Rec^d^ for repair in No 2 w/shop. Austin Amb^ces^ A 9747, A 9749 of 54th F.A, Douglas m/c 2300-8 of 55th FA	
			Sent out of No 2 w/shop. – Nil.	
			M2/101195 Pte Cuffs R to 55th Field Amb^ce^.	
			23 (3 Ton) lorries on Stones to AVELUY for C.E. II Corps.	
			Supplies for 18th Div loaded by Horse Transport.	
			Supply Det^t^ of No 3 DSC. proceeds to ALBERT (attached 18th Div Train)	
			[signature] Major Comdg No 3 D.S.C.	

T2134. Wt. W708—776. 500000. 4/15. Sir J. C. & S.

Army Form C. 2118.

WAR DIARY
or
INTELLIGENCE SUMMARY.
(Erase heading not required.)

Instructions regarding War Diaries and Intelligence Summaries are contained in F. S. Regs., Part II. and the Staff Manual respectively. Title pages will be prepared in manuscript.

Place	Date	Hour	Summary of Events and Information	Remarks and references to Appendices
BEAUVAL	24/10/16		Recd for repair in No 1 W/Shop.	
			Commer Lorry 21075 + Leyland Lorries 6963, 6769, 3568, 3914 of No 3 D.S.C.	
			Commer Lorry 5121 + Leyland Lorries 7167, 6762, 4254, 21121 of No 3 D.S.C. (Sent out same day).	
			Recd from A.M.T. Depot for issue	
			Triumph m/cycles 264420, 954 M.S, 703 M.S.	
			Recd for repair in No 2 W/Shop. Ford Amb^ce A 9750 of 55th F.A.	
			Triumph m/c 264505 of 18th Div Signals, Leyland Lorry 7165 of No 3 DSC (Sent out same day)	
			M2/045572 Pte Bowner S to No: 2 Special Coy. R.E.	
			Supply arrangements as yesterday	
			[signature] Major Comdg No 3. D.S.C.	

T2134. Wt. W708—776. 500000. 4/15. Sir J. C. & S.

Instructions regarding War Diaries and Intelligence Summaries are contained in F. S. Regs., Part II. and the Staff Manual respectively. Title pages will be prepared in manuscript.

WAR DIARY
or
INTELLIGENCE SUMMARY.
(Erase heading not required.)

Army Form C. 2118.

Place	Date	Hour	Summary of Events and Information	Remarks and references to Appendices
BEAUVAL	25/10/16		Recd for repair in No. 1 w/shop. Dennis Lorry 26339 of 49th CCS	
			Commer Lorries 3255, 5121, 7715 + Leyland Lorry 6765 of No 3 D.S.C	
			(all except Commer 7715 sent out same day).	
			M/cycles sent to 2nd A.S.C. Repair Shop	
			Douglas m/cycles 24822, 2992 + Triumph m/c 263925	
			Recd for repair in No 2 w/shop Ford Ambce A14596 of 54th F.A,	
			Vauxhall Car M 18626 of 18th Div Train, Douglas m/c 23008 of 55th FA	
			Sent out of No 2 w/shop. Austin Ambce A 9747 + Ford Ambce A14596	
			of 54th FA, Douglas m/c 23008 of 55th FA	
			Supply arrangements as before	
			5 lorries employed at AVELUY for stores - C.E II Corps	
			15 " " " ACHEUX " supplies of 2nd Corps T.S.C.	
			[signature] Major	
			Comdg No 3 D.S.C	

Instructions regarding War Diaries and Intelligence Summaries are contained in F. S. Regs., Part II. and the Staff Manual respectively. Title pages will be prepared in manuscript.

WAR DIARY
or
INTELLIGENCE SUMMARY.
(Erase heading not required.)

Army Form C. 2118.

Place	Date	Hour	Summary of Events and Information	Remarks and references to Appendices
BEAUVAL	26/10/16		Rec^d for repair in No 1 w/shop. Napier Car M18511 of 16th D.M.S Commer Lorry 6752, Leyland Lorries 6211, 6765 of No 3 D.S.C Sent out of No 1 w/shop Napier Box Car M18571 of 16th D.M.S. Commer Lorry 6752, Leyland Lorries 6765, 5647, 4343 of No 3 D.S.C Rec^d for repair in No 2 w/shop. Daimler Car M18623 of 18th D.HQ Triumph m/c 719 MS of 55th F A. Sent out of No 2 w/shop Talbot Amb^ce A15628 of 56th F.A, Vauxhall Car M10626 of 18th Div Train. Supply arrangements as before 21 lorries employed on stores for C E II Corps – M2/103421 Pte Gradwell H to No 2 Special Coy R.E. [illegible] Capt Comdg No 3 D.S.C.	

T2134. Wt. W708–776. 500000. 4/15. Sir J. C. & S.

Instructions regarding War Diaries and Intelligence Summaries are contained in F. S. Regs., Part II. and the Staff Manual respectively. Title pages will be prepared in manuscript.

WAR DIARY
or
INTELLIGENCE SUMMARY.
(Erase heading not required.)

Army Form C. 2118.

Place	Date	Hour	Summary of Events and Information	Remarks and references to Appendices
BEAUVAL	27/10/16		Recd for repair in No 1 W/shop Commer Lorry 3990, 13131 & Sunbeam Car M 14034 of No 3 D.S.C Sent out of No 1 W/shop Commer Lorries 21075, 13131, 3255, 77148 Leyland Lorries 3584, 21119, 6769 & Sunbeam Car M14034 of No 3 D.S.C Recd for repair in No: 2 W/shop Austin Amb.ce A 9740 of 54th F.A, Talbot Amb.ce A 19246 of 55th F.A Sent out of No 2 W/shop – Nil. Supply arrangements as before 12 Lorries employed at BELLE EGLISE for 2nd Corps T.S.C. – (Supplies) – 5 Lorries working from CONTAY on Stores & 6 from AVELUY on Stores for 2nd Corps –	

[illegible]
Major
Cmdg No 3 D.S.C.

Army Form C. 2118.

WAR DIARY
or
INTELLIGENCE SUMMARY.
(Erase heading not required.)

Instructions regarding War Diaries and Intelligence Summaries are contained in F. S. Regs., Part II. and the Staff Manual respectively. Title pages will be prepared in manuscript.

Place	Date	Hour	Summary of Events and Information	Remarks and references to Appendices
BEAUVAL	28/10/16		Recd for repair in No 1 w/shop. Leyland Lorry 4585 of No 3 D.S.C	
			Sent out of No 1 w/shop Sunbeam Car M14112 of 33rd Ord w/shops.	
			Commer Lorries 3989, 6750 + Leyland Lorries 4670, 7163, 6963, 3568, 3914	
			4 Austin Ambulances received from 51st D.S.C } for 18th Division	of No 3 D.S.C
			2 Ford Ambulances " " No 5 D.S.C }	
			Received for repair in No 2 w/shop Talbot Amb A9794 of 55th F.A, Daimler Car M18409 of 18th D HQ, Daimler Car M14855 of 11th Div RA HQ, Triumph m/c 719 M.S of 55th F.A	
			Sent out of No 2 w/shop Talbot Ambce A9794 + Triumph m/c 719 M.S of 55th F.A – Ford Ambce A9750 of 55th F.A. Daimler Cars M18409, M18623 of 18th Div HQ	
			T4/124446 Pte John B [illegible] to 47th CCS.	
			Supply arrangements as before.	
			12 Lorries on stores at AVELUY, 11 on supplies at BELLE EGLISE, 4 on blankets for 25th Division.	

[illegible]
Comdg No 3 D.S.C

T2134. Wt. W708–776. 500000. 4/15. Sir J. C. & S.

Army Form C. 2118.

Instructions regarding War Diaries and Intelligence Summaries are contained in F. S. Regs., Part II. and the Staff Manual respectively. Title pages will be prepared in manuscript.

WAR DIARY
or
INTELLIGENCE SUMMARY.
(Erase heading not required.)

Place	Date	Hour	Summary of Events and Information	Remarks and references to Appendices
BEAUVAL	29/10/16		Recd for repair in No 1 W/shop & sent out same day - Leyland Lorries 6223, 6215, 3584, 3561 + Commer Lorry 6750 of No 3 D.S.C. Motor Box Car M 18719 of No 2 Special Coy R.E. In addition sent out of No 1 W/shop Leyland Lorry 5505 of No 3 DSC	
			Vehicles transferred 7 Talbot ambulances of 18th Division to 19th Division (No 5 D.S.C.)	
			Recd for repair in No 2 W/shop Austin Ambces A371, A372 of 55th F.A.	
			Sent out of No 2 W/shop Daimler Car M14855 of 11th Div R.A.	
			M2/139148 Pte Brown C H from No 2 Spec Coy R.E.	
			Supply arrangements as before	
			11 Lorries employed on Stones at AVELUY,	
			3 " " " blankets for 25th Division	
			[signature] Major Comdg No 3 D.S.C.	

Instructions regarding War Diaries and Intelligence Summaries are contained in F. S. Regs., Part II. and the Staff Manual respectively. Title pages will be prepared in manuscript.

WAR DIARY
or
INTELLIGENCE SUMMARY.
(Erase heading not required.)

Army Form C. 2118.

Place	Date	Hour	Summary of Events and Information	Remarks and references to Appendices
BEAUVAL	30/10/16		Recd for repair in No 1 w/shop Commer Lorry ~~12217~~ 3255 of No 3 D.S.C	
			Leyland Lorries 12217, 6214, 11076, 6223 of No 3 D.S.C.	
			Sent out of No 1 w/shop Commer Lorry 3255 of No 3 D.S.C	
			Leyland Lorries 6223, 7164 of No 3 D.S.C.	
			Recd for repair in No: 2 w/shop & sent out same day	
			Sunbeam Car M 15255 of 18th Div Signals, Leyland Lorry 6206 of 3 D.S.C	
			Ford Ambce A 14596 of 54th F A	
			In addition sent out after repair Austin Ambce A 9740 of 54th FA	
			Supply arrangements as yesterday.	
			12 Lorries employed on Supplies at BELLE EGLISE for 2nd Corps	T.S.C.
			5 on Stones at AVELUY, 5 on fuel wood at CANDAS for 4th Canadian Divn	
			[signature] Capt Comdg No 3 D.S.C.	

T2134. Wt. W708—776. 500000. 4/15. Sir J. C. & S.

Instructions regarding War Diaries and Intelligence Summaries are contained in F. S. Regs., Part II. and the Staff Manual respectively. Title pages will be prepared in manuscript.

WAR DIARY
or
INTELLIGENCE SUMMARY.
(Erase heading not required.)

Army Form C. 2118.

Place	Date	Hour	Summary of Events and Information	Remarks and references to Appendices
BEAUVAL	31/10/16		Rec^d for repair in No 1 w/shop Commer Lorries 7714, 6750 of No 3 D.S.C	
			Leyland Lorries 6774, 21120, 5505 of No 3 D.S.C.	
			Sent out of No 1 w/shop. Commer Lorry 6750 of No 3 D.S.C.	
			Leyland Lorries 6774, 5505, 11076, 12217 of No 3 D.S.C.	
			Vehicles transferred 1 Ford Amb^ce received from No 5 DSC	
			(feeding 19th Division) to complete transfer commenced on 28th inst.	
			Supply arrangements as before –	
			M2/117249 Pte Manwaring C to 47th CCS –	
			12 Lorries employed on Supplies at BELLE EGLISE for 2nd Corps T.S.C	
			9 " " " Stores " AVELUX.	
			2 " " " RE material at VARENNES.	
			Rec^d for repair in No 2 w/shop Leyland Lorry 6882 of No 3 D.S.C,	
			Ford Amb^ce A15697 of 54th F.A, Daimler Lorry 28301 of 18th Div Sigs	
			Triumph m/cycles 265402 of 18th Div Train	
			Sent out of No 2 w/shop Triumph m/c 265402 of 18th Div Train, Leyland Lorry	
			6882 of No 3 DSC, Daimler Lorry 28301 of 18th Div Signals, Austin Amb^ces	
			A371, A372 of 55th FA	

[illegible] Major
Comdg No 3 D.S.C

Instructions regarding War Diaries and Intelligence Summaries are contained in F. S. Regs., Part II. and the Staff Manual respectively. Title pages will be prepared in manuscript.

WAR DIARY
or
INTELLIGENCE SUMMARY.
(*Erase heading not required.*)

18TH DIVISIONAL TRAIN.
No. 7/577 7/12/16

Army Form C. 2118.

Vol 17

18th Divisional Train ASC

VOL:-17

Place	Date	Hour	Summary of Events and Information	Remarks and references to Appendices
ALBERT	1/11/16		Refilling from railhead by H.T. from AVELUY. Trains running very late	
			2Lt Clift joined from 14 R Park	
	2/11/16		Lt Collins wounded on stone carting. Very wet & rainy	
	3/11/16		Train 12 hours late owing to a derailment, refilling consequently very late.	
	4/11/16		Capt Brooke transferred to 9 Reserve Park. 4 Regts to & 4 from WARLOY	
	5/11/16		Capt McCall & 2Lt Jennings joined Train.	
	6/11/16		Lt Antrim taking over duties of Adjt vice Capt Lewis who is to report to M.T. School as soon as possible. Very windy with occasional very heavy rain.	
	7/11/16		Weather still very bad. Capt Hewson transferred to Rouen.	
	8/11/16		Lorries all off the roads, owing to weather & condition of roads. Food etc all fetched by H.T. To see Capts in each Coy but could get no satisfaction	
	9/11/16		All wagons very busy all day on supplies & coal. 2Lt Palmer joined from B.H.T.D. Capt Lewis went to M.T. School St Omer.	
	10/11/16		abroad. Bosch planes very busy overhead in ALBERT with machine gun	

2353 Wt. W2544/1454 700,000 5/15 D. D. & L. A.D.S.S./Forms/C. 2118.

Instructions regarding War Diaries and Intelligence Summaries are contained in F. S. Regs., Part II. and the Staff Manual respectively. Title pages will be prepared in manuscript.

WAR DIARY
or
INTELLIGENCE SUMMARY.
(Erase heading not required.)

Army Form C. 2118.

Place	Date	Hour	Summary of Events and Information	Remarks and references to Appendices
ALBERT	11/11/16		Road Precautions withdrawn.	
	12/11/16		Normal Work	
	13/11/16		" " Work. All Brigades on the move to & from Trenches	
	14/11/16		Normal Work. Shelling in vicinity of Train HdQrs.	
	15/11/16		Work as usual.	
	16/11/16		To see D.D.S.T. in morning. Frost at night.	
	17/11/16		R.A. of 39th Div pulled off on Rlh. ALBERT badly shelled & bombed in the night. Keen frost at night.	
	18/11/16		Keen frost at night but changed to rain at 8-30 am	
	19/11/16		Normal. 53 Brig began to march to back area.	
	20/11/16		151 Bg moved out. Train 10 hours late at Railhead.	
	21/11/16		152 Bg moved out. R.A. group drawing off 61st Train Park. We issued our reserve day pack & DSR pulled supplies from BELLE EGLISE. 54 Brig began march to back area. Park Train not in till 9 pm	
CONTAY.	22/11/16		Div HdQrs. of 18th back area. R & Train to CONTAY. 55 Brig moved out to back area. Supplies dumped at 8 am. Cleared at 9 am	

2353 Wt. W2544/1454 700,000 5/15 D. D. & L. A.D.S.S./Forms/C. 2118.

Instructions regarding War Diaries and Intelligence Summaries are contained in F. S. Regs., Part II. and the Staff Manual respectively. Title pages will be prepared in manuscript.

Army Form C. 2118.

WAR DIARY
or
INTELLIGENCE SUMMARY.
(Erase heading not required.)

Place	Date	Hour	Summary of Events and Information	Remarks and references to Appendices
DOULLENS	23/11/16		Div HQ Crs & Co DOULLENS. 53 Bry + 54 to DOULLENS area. 53 to BEAUVAL	
BERNAVILLE	24/11/16		" " " " BERNAVILLE. 53 Bry to LE MEILLARD area. 54th to BERNAVILLE area 55 Bde. same as 28/11/16. D.S.C. moved from PIERREGOT	
YVRENCH	25/11/16		Div HQ Crs. Co to YVRENCH. 53 Bry to CRAMONT area. 54th to RIBEAUCOURT. 55th Bde to PROUVILLE area. Railhead. STRIQIER. Very wet.	
	26/11/16		Div HQ Crs & Co BOIGNY. 53 Bry to BRAILLY 54 to ST RIQUIER 55th to MAISON PONTHIEU	
	27/11/16		53 Bry to LE TITRE area. 54th to DRUCAT. 55th to CANCHY.	
Buigny St Maclou	28/11/16		D.S.C. continuing to ~~pulling~~ from Railhead.	
–	29/11/16		Took over from Lt Col D.C.E. Grose who proceeded to England on leave. Office work	
–	30/11/16		Capt M Williams proceeded to DDS&T Reserve Army to relieve Lt Curtis as forward purchasing Officer	

H S Peachey Major
OC 18 Div. Train.

2353 Wt. W2544/1454 700,000 5/15 D. D. & L. A.D.S.S./Forms/C. 2118.

18th Divisional Train.

Vol

Army Form C. 2118.

WAR DIARY
or
INTELLIGENCE SUMMARY.
(Erase heading not required.)

(Vol:- 18.) 18

Instructions regarding War Diaries and Intelligence Summaries are contained in F. S. Regs., Part II. and the Staff Manual respectively. Title pages will be prepared in manuscript.

Place	Date	Hour	Summary of Events and Information	Remarks and references to Appendices
Bugny St Maclow	1/12/16		Accompanied the ~~DAD~~ AMG to see the new billeting area allotted to Head Quarter Coy	
–	2/12/16		Office work	
–	3 –		Office work.	
–	4		Office work. Present at 1st Round of Divisional Football competition in which ASC Train team beat the Buffs	
–	5th		Met advanced party of 150 Coy + showed them their new Billets at Pte LAVIERS.	
–	6		Lt Curtis reported for doing duty with DDST 5th Army. Head Quarter Coy marched in to Pte LAVIERS	
–	7		Visited Refilling point + 150 Company. 21 Reinforcements arrived from Base	
–	8		Office work	
–	9		Visited Head Quarter Company Billet.	
–	10		Office work	
–	11		Office work	
–	12		Road Precautionary Period came into force 2 pm. Visited DSC to fix DIVISIONAL Refilling Point	
–	13		Refilling from Divisional Dump quite satisfactory. 2/Lt. Jennings proceeded to join the 12th E. Yorks	
	14		Office work all day till 4-30, to see 151 Coy in evening	
	15		Inspected D. R. Pt + transport working there. 2Lt Bishop joined from 4 C D R Park	
	16		D Troops pulled from old D. T. ~~D~~ R. Pt.	

2353 Wt. W2544/1454 700,000 5/15 D. D. & L. A.D.S.S./Forms/C. 2118.

Army Form C. 2118.

WAR DIARY
or
INTELLIGENCE SUMMARY.
(Erase heading not required.)

Instructions regarding War Diaries and Intelligence Summaries are contained in F. S. Regs., Part II. and the Staff Manual, respectively. Title pages will be prepared in manuscript.

Place	Date	Hour	Summary of Events and Information	Remarks and references to Appendices
BUIGNY	17/12/16		Train sports to select teams etc for Divisional Sports.	
ST MACLOU	18/12/16		53 Bde Sports. The turn out of the various transport competitions was most extraordinarily good & reflected great credit on all.	
	19/12/16		Inspected 150 Coys lines, billets etc.	
	20/12/16		" " " 151 Coys lines, billets etc. & part of 1st line transport of 53 Bde.	
	21/12/16		Inspection by Corps Commander.	
	22/12/16		Round 152 Coys lines, billets etc.	
	23/12/16		Road Precautions scheme in force. Awful rain & hailstorms	
	24/12/16		Very fine football match D.S.C. v ? Coys, latter won by 2–1. Two dumpings at R.P. & one refill in morning & one in afternoon	
	25/12/16		Round all Coys. during day. Men quite happy & enjoying themselves.	
	26/12/16		Divisional Sports all day.	
	27/12/16		Inspected 1st line transport of 54th Brig	
	28/12/16		Normal.	
	29/12/16		53rd Bde moved to DRUCAT area & 55th to LE TITRE area.	
	30/12/16		To ST RIQUIER re-loading by H.T. at Railhead. Rugby match 18th v 63rd Div, good game 18th won 13 [illegible]	
	31/12/16		Normal.	

[signature]
LT. COL.
COMDG 18TH DIVISIONAL TRAIN.

2353 Wt. W2544/1454 700,000 5/15 D. D. & L. A.D.S.S./Forms/C. 2118.

Army Form C. 2118.

Vol 19

(Vol:- 19)

Instructions regarding War Diaries and Intelligence Summaries are contained in F. S. Regs., Part II. and the Staff Manual respectively. Title pages will be prepared in manuscript.

WAR DIARY
or
INTELLIGENCE SUMMARY.
(Erase heading not required.)

18th Divisional Train

Place	Date	Hour	Summary of Events and Information	Remarks and references to Appendices
BUIENY	1/7		Normal	
ST MACLOU	2/7		R.A. & H.Q. Cn Coy moved out of this area for the front area. Inspected 54th F.A. Transport. Very satisfactory	
	3/7		Normal	
	4/7		Normal. Rugby match v 2nd Div. 18th won by 48 points to nil	
	5/7		Rounds 151 Coy billets at DRUCAT. R.A. & H.Q. Cos Coy moved in front area.	
	6/7		A.Q.M. of II Corps inspected R. Pts.	
	7/7		Normal	
	8/7		Transport of 53rd & 54th Bdes inspected by Corps Commander. Very good turn out. Weather vile, snow & rain. O.C. 157 Coy complimented.	
	9/7		Transport of 55 Bde inspected by Corps Commander. Very good turn out. O.C. 153 Coy complimented on his turn out. Rugby match v 63rd Div. 18th won by 13 points to nil	
	10/7		Normal	
YRENCH	11/7		Whole Division moved one days march into new area. 53rd Bde PROUVILLE. 54th DOMQUEUR 55th CRAMONT. H.Q. Cos ([illegible]) at YRENCH. Weather very cold & windy	

2353 Wt. W2544/1454 700,000 5/15 D. D. & L. A.D.S.S./Forms/C. 2118.

Instructions regarding War Diaries and Intelligence Summaries are contained in F. S. Regs., Part II. and the Staff Manual respectively. Title pages will be prepared in manuscript.

WAR DIARY
or
INTELLIGENCE SUMMARY.
(*Erase heading not required.*)

Army Form C. 2118.

Place	Date	Hour	Summary of Events and Information	Remarks and references to Appendices
BERNA-VILLE	12/1/17		53rd Bde to BEZAINCOURT 54th to FIENVILLIERS 55th to MONPLAISIR area. Hd Qrs at BERNAVILLE. Weather cold.	
	13/1/17		Did not move.	
MARIEUX	14/1/17		53 Bde to PUCHEVILLIERS 54 to RUBEMPRE 55 to BEAUQUESNE. Hd Qrs to MARIEUX	
	15/1/17		53 Bde to MARTINSART 54 to ~~[illegible]~~ TRENCHES.	
BOUZIN-COURT	16/1/17		55 Bde to HEDAUVILLE. H.Q. Qrs to HUTS at BOUZINCOURT. Hq lines very bad & unpassable & left in filthy condition by 61st Train.	
	17/1/17		Snowed all night. Roads very bad for horses. R.Pts MARTINSART for 53rd & 54th. D.T. & 55th on HEDAUVILLE main road.	
	18/1/17		All supplies drawn by H.T. at Railhead.	
	19/1/17		Work at Railhead delayed greatly by intermittent shelling. All clear at 1-45 pm.	
	20/1/17		Normal work. Very cold & still freezing	
	21/1/17		" " " Still freezing	

Instructions regarding War Diaries and Intelligence Summaries are contained in F. S. Regs., Part II. and the Staff Manual respectively. Title pages will be prepared in manuscript.

WAR DIARY
or
INTELLIGENCE SUMMARY.
(Erase heading not required.)

Army Form C. 2118.

Place	Date	Hour	Summary of Events and Information	Remarks and references to Appendices
BOUZINCOURT	22/1/17		Normal. Freezing very hard.	
	23/1/17		To see D.D.S.T. re supply Personnel. Very cold & frosty. Roads very slippery.	
	24/1/17		Normal.	
	25/1/17		Railhead (AVELUY) heavily shelled. Supplies (Hay) for 2 days. Thaw Dump began to be drawn. Lt Hamford left to join forming Company in England.	
	26/1/17		Normal. Very cold & freezing hard. Two days rations for thaw scheme began to be issued to units.	
	27/1/17		Railhead shelled. Units continuing to draw for thaw scheme.	
	28/1/17		Frost still very keen.	
	29/1/17		D.D.S.T. inspected lines of 151.152.153 Coys. Frost still on.	
	30/1/17		Still freezing. Normal work.	
	31/1/17		Frost still on & roads very slippery. Normal work.	

[signature]
LT. COL.
COMDG 18TH DIVISIONAL TRAIN.

2353 Wt. W2544/1454 700,000 5/15 D. D. & L. A.D.S.S. Forms/C. 2118.

Instructions regarding War Diaries and Intelligence Summaries are contained in F. S. Regs., Part II. and the Staff Manual respectively. Title pages will be prepared in manuscript.

WAR DIARY
or
INTELLIGENCE SUMMARY.
(Erase heading not required.)

Army Form C. 2118.

(Vol:- 20)

Vol 20

18th Divisional Train A.S.C.

Place	Date	Hour	Summary of Events and Information	Remarks and references to Appendices
BOUZINCOURT	1/2/17		Very cold & still freezing. Normal work	
	2/2/17		Still freezing. Normal	
	3/2/17		Very heavy shelling at AVELUY. Cold & freezing but no wind. 2 Lt Smallwood joined from B.H.T.D. after a journey of 11 days owing to congestion of traffic.	
	4/2/17		Normal work. Still very cold & freezing hard	
	5/2/17			
	6/2/17			
	7/2/17		Normal work. Very cold & freezing wind & frost still holding	
	8/2/17		Wind still holding & very cold	
	9/2/17		Normal. Frost still holding.	
	10/2/17		31st Div RA & HQ Sn by 31st Train arrived & are attached to us. Wind has dropped	
	11/2/17		Warmer. 1 Batt R.F.A 11th Div & 1 Batt 51st Div joined to complete A.R.F.A Bny	
	12/2/17		31st Div R.A. feeding from us & on front at Railhead	
	13/2/17		Much milder. Normal work	
	14/2/17		Normal. All H.T. employed owing to Bde movements } Weather milder but still freezing at night	
	15/2/17			

2353 Wt. W2544/1454 700,000 5/15 D. D. & L. A.D.S.S. Forms/C 2118.

Instructions regarding War Diaries and Intelligence Summaries are contained in F. S. Regs., Part II. and the Staff Manual respectively. Title pages will be prepared in manuscript.

WAR DIARY
or
INTELLIGENCE SUMMARY.
(Erase heading not required.)

Army Form C. 2118.

Place	Date	Hour	Summary of Events and Information	Remarks and references to Appendices
BOUZIN-COURT	16/2/17		Thaw commencing. Normal work.	
	17/2/17		Thaw going on & roads, lines etc getting in an awful state.	
	18/2/17		Thaw Precautions scheme came into force at 12 noon. [illegible] rather mixed up at Railhead, but soon got straightened out & all went off successfully. 8 E Surreys had their Reserve rations. Horses very hard worked.	
	19/2/17		HQ Coy moved to BOUZINCOURT. E. Surreys found their rations with Buffs. Roads very slushy & covered with water. Every wagon on duty. Horses won't stand this heavy work very long	
	20/2/17		All wagons out again to-day & roads getting heavier, will lead to a lot of wastage amongst the animals.	
	21/2/17		All wagons out & some of 31st Div Tr. The work for II C.T. S.C. is getting heavier & heavier.	
	22/2/17		All wagons out. Roads awfully heavy & are getting badly cut up.	
	23/2/17		~~[illegible]~~ Normal & same as last 5 days.	
	24/2/17		All wagons out & work very heavy on horses. Working for II Corps S.C. Royal	
	25/2/17		Engineers & food from ACHEUX	
	26/2/17		Lorries for Corps Troops S.C. running, but all wagons & horses out on R.E. & food	

2353 Wt. W2544/1454 700,000 5/15 D. D. & L. A.D.S.S. Forms/C 2118.

Instructions regarding War Diaries and Intelligence Summaries are contained in F. S. Regs., Part II. and the Staff Manual respectively. Title pages will be prepared in manuscript.

WAR DIARY
or
INTELLIGENCE SUMMARY.
(Erase heading not required.)

Army Form C. 2118.

Place	Date	Hour	Summary of Events and Information	Remarks and references to Appendices
BOUZIN-COURT	26/2/17		Horses are beginning to show signs of this awfully heavy work & I am afraid wastage will soon begin to increase.	
	27/2/17		H.T. very heavy, also particularly in R.E. work	
	28/2/17		R.F.A. moved up to forward area. Roads awfully bad & lorries not allowed to run generally. Transport work piling up.	

A. E. Grose
LT. COL.
COMDG 18TH DIVISIONAL TRAIN.

2353 Wt. W2544/1454 700,000 5/15 D. D. & L. A.D.S.S./Forms/C. 2118.

Instructions regarding War Diaries and Intelligence Summaries are contained in F. S. Regs., Part II. and the Staff Manual respectively. Title pages will be prepared in manuscript.

WAR DIARY
or
INTELLIGENCE SUMMARY.
(Erase heading not required.)

Army Form C. 2118.

VOL ~~21~~ Vol 21

18th DIVISIONAL TRAIN ASC

Place	Date	Hour	Summary of Events and Information	Remarks and references to Appendices
BOUZINCOURT	1/3/17		Lines of 63rd Bde R.A. found to be full of mange. None of the 4 Coys in 2nd [illegible].	
	2/3/17		53rd Bde moved to NAB ROAD area: 54th to THIEPVAL + 55th to AUTHUILE WOOD. Congestion on AVELUY-AUTHUILE road very bad, but will be better in future as baggage of Brigades will not be moving. R.Ps for all four groups at L.5.d.9.0.	
	3/3/17		Horses falling away badly, & work getting heavier; question of horse flesh is going to be very serious.	
	4/3/17		Hd Qrs Div (except Train Hd Qrs) moved to NEW WARWICK HUTS	
	5/3/17		Snowed hard all night. 4 Train Coys moved to W.12.c.	
	6/3/17		Capt [illegible] took over command of Hd Qr Coy from Major [illegible] who went away to 3rd Can R. Park	
	7/3/17		To Hd Qrs re horses & this heavy work & put in letter D.T. 438 pointing out seriousness of the horses getting debilitated. Very windy & cold.	
	8/3/17		Lorries still off road. Very cold.	
	9/3/17		Warm snow. Received 14 H.D. 2 L.D. 1 R from Remounts.	
	10/3/17		All horses out & work very heavy.	

Instructions regarding War Diaries and Intelligence Summaries are contained in F. S. Regs., Part II. and the Staff Manual respectively. Title pages will be prepared in manuscript.

WAR DIARY
or
INTELLIGENCE SUMMARY.
(Erase heading not required.)

Army Form C. 2118.

Place	Date	Hour	Summary of Events and Information	Remarks and references to Appendices
BOUZIN-COURT	11/3/17		A.D.V.S. inspected all horses of Train & has agreed that they are being overworked.	
	12/3/17		Lorries still off the road & work very hard on horses.	
	13/3/17		Weather very mild, & lorries still off the road.	
	14/3/17		Lorries still off the ~~road~~ road.	
	15/3/17		" " " " " " 54 Bde 1st line transports all at CHALK PALACE Rations loaded in supply wagons at AVELUY this evening	
	16/3/17		132 Coy moved up to CHALK PALACE. Supplies dumped & carried to units on spot. Rations for 18th loaded on trucks at AVELUY railed to BEAUCOURT, then to supply wagons, which conveyed them to IRLES, ~~thence by pack to line~~. Worked all right.	
	17/3/17		Supply wagons pulled to IRLES & from there to line by pack animals.	
	18/3/17		Loaded supplies for R.A. R.E. & Pioneers at AVELUY at 2 a.m. & they went on. H.Q. Coy moved to GRANDCOURT	
	19/3/17		Line of supply getting very long, from railhead to line. Train wagons & horses doing very heavy work. 45 Wagons of 63rd D.A.C. left this Division	

2353 Wt. W2544/1454 700,000 5/15 D. D. & L. A.D.S.S. Forms/C. 2118.

Instructions regarding War Diaries and Intelligence Summaries are contained in F. S. Regs., Part II. and the Staff Manual respectively. Title pages will be prepared in manuscript.

WAR DIARY
or
INTELLIGENCE SUMMARY.
(Erase heading not required.)

Army Form C. 2118.

Place	Date	Hour	Summary of Events and Information	Remarks and references to Appendices
BOUZINCOURT	20/3/17		53rd Bde moved to WARLOY area. 54th to MIRAUMONT & 53rd to HUTS at W12 d central.	
	21/3/17		54 Bde to W12 d central: 53 Bde to CONTAY area.	
	22/3/17		53 Bde to MOLLIENS area. 54 to CONTAY. 55th to VILLERS BOCAGE	
	23/3/17		53 Bde to SALEUX. 54 to VILLERS BOCAGE 55 to SALEUX. D.H.Q. to DURY	
	24/3/17		Div began to entrain at SALEUX & BACOUEL for 1st Army area. Moved to new area & camp at STEENBECQUE. Bdes returned to 2 for 26th.	
STEENBECQUE	~~25/3/17~~ 25/3/17		Trains very late & irregular, & only two arrived during the day. D.L.I. detraining from LILLERS for 27th [illegible]	
	26/3/17		Trains coming in very irregularly, & supply arrangements becoming somewhat involved. Trains 20-25 being retained in S area for 27 & 28th. Trains 16.18.19 to be arranged for here. 151 & 153 Bdes arrived.	
	27/3/17		Trains still coming irregularly. Units are however getting their food. 151 Bde at LE CORNET BRALSART. 153 LE MARTIN.	
	28/3/17		152 Bde arrived at 7 am & went to GUARBECQUE. All Div detrained.	

• Instructions regarding War Diaries and Intelligence Summaries are contained in F. S. Regs., Part II. and the Staff Manual respectively. Title pages will be prepared in manuscript.

WAR DIARY
or
INTELLIGENCE SUMMARY.
(Erase heading not required.)

Army Form C. 2118.

Place	Date	Hour	Summary of Events and Information	Remarks and references to Appendices
STEENBECQUE	29 3/17		Took over temporary duties of O/C Train, visited Railhead and Refilling Point. Captn Williams reported for duty, work normal. Attended to my own duties as SSO	
"	30 3/17		Got into communication with O/C H.Qrs Coy previous to arriving this area to inform O/C HQ Coy the lines etc allotted also supply arrangements this end. Major Ruckle ADS 1st Army visited Train Office also Field Purchasing Officer re extra forage for horses of this Division. Office duties normal. Attended to my own duties as SSO	
"	31 3/17		Interviewed Company Officers, no complaints, new horse lines and watering arrangements found satisfactory. Attended funeral of Lt Col Pierre-Louis Constant at Steenbecque by request DHQ, 18th Div General & Staff present. Rained most of day. Office duties normal. Attended to my own duties as SSO.	

H. F. Hughes Major –
T. O/C 18th Div Train

18th Divisional Train. A.S.C.

WAR DIARY
or
INTELLIGENCE SUMMARY.
(Erase heading not required.)

Army Form C. 2118.

Instructions regarding War Diaries and Intelligence Summaries are contained in F. S. Regs., Part II. and the Staff Manual respectively. Title pages will be prepared in manuscript.

Vol 22 (Vol:- 22)

Place	Date	Hour	Summary of Events and Information	Remarks and references to Appendices
STEEN-BECQUE	1/4/17		Div R.A. arrived in area & billeted in MORBECQUE area. Report asked for as to how many horses died on march up to 1st Army area. Only one of the Train horses died (152 Coy) & was buried. Full ration of oats ~~only~~ allowed for R.A. horses only from 1st inst. 150 Coy at MORBECQUE	
	2/4/17		Meeting at H.Q. Div re sports. Orders received that H.T. are to draw from Railhead from 3rd inst. at STEENBECQUE, except 151 Coy who are too far away & lorries will continue for this group. Supplies drawn from R.Pts by 1st line transport from 3rd. Extra forage drawn to supplement rations [illegible]	
	3/4/17		Supplies from Railhead by H.T. & from R.Pts by 1st line. Heavy snow fell at 2 am. Only 9 lbs of hay per horse arrived on pack train, extra forage demanded.	
	4/4/17		Major Blackburn reported for duty. Weather fine. D.A.D.S called re change of railhead to AIRE.	
	5/4/17		Normal work, fine weather. 152 Coy moved from GUARBECQUES to STEENBECQUE	
	6/4/17		Normal work, weather fine. Football D. Train v Berks Regt. Train won 2-1.	
	7/4/17		Normal	
	8/4/17		Railhead changed to AIRE. Supplies drawn by H.T. for 53. 54. 55 Bdes. by M.T. for D. Troops. Cross country relay race of 10 miles, won by Buffs.	
	9/4/17		Turn-out competitions at AIRE for all units of Div. & all vehicles. Train won 1st & 2nd in G.S. wagons, 150 Coy 1st, 151 Coy 2nd. Splendid turn outs, in fact the whole exhibition of vehicles, harness & horses could not be beaten. Corps Commander very pleased. Snowed heavily in afternoon & night.	

2353. Wt. W2544/1454 700,000 5/15 D. D. & L. A.D.S.S./Forms/C. 2118.

Instructions regarding War Diaries and Intelligence Summaries are contained in F. S. Regs., Part II. and the Staff Manual respectively. Title pages will be prepared in manuscript.

WAR DIARY
or
INTELLIGENCE SUMMARY.
(Erase heading not required.)

Army Form C. 2118.

Place	Date	Hour	Summary of Events and Information	Remarks and references to Appendices
STEEN-BECQUE	10/4/17		Five mile cross country race won by Queens. Major Blackburn took over HdQrs by [illegible]	
			Went round lines & billets of 150 & 153 Bty & also the R. Bts. Football	
	11/4/17		Team v D.A.C. We won after extra time had been played 2-1. Weather very bad Snow & sleet. Major Blackburn to Hospital with German measles	
	12/4/17		Inspected all Bty at Railhead & also R. Bts of 53rd & 54th Bdes: Football v R. Sussex Pioneers. We won 13-2.	
	13/4/17		F.G.C.M. proceedings on Sgt. Beadle promulgated Reduction to Cpl. Inspected 152 Bty lines & billets	
	14/4/17		Football final. Team v E Surreys. latter won after a good game 3-2. Capt Williams took over duties of Adjt.	
	15/4/17		Work normal. Weather most inclement.	
	16/4/17		" " " Weather still wet	
	17/4/17		Inspection of all 1st line of 55 Bde. Fairly satisfactory on the whole, some units very good, others fair. Snow & sleet & rain on & off all day	
	18/4/17		Inspection of all 1st line 53 Bde. Fairly satisfactory, Essex particularly good. Wet & cold	
	19/4/17		Inspected 1st line of 54 Bde. Satisfactory & quite serviceable. 53 Bde moved to BETHUNE area for night. Supplies drawn by D.T. & taken forward	
	20/4/17		53 Bde still at BETHUNE. 55 Bde moved to BERGETTE. both groups drawing supplies by D.T.	
	21/4/17		53 Bde moved to NOEUX-LES-MINES area. 157 Bty at ANNEZIN 54 Bde to LA MIQUELLERIE area. 152 Bty at CANTRAINE 55 Bde to BETHUNE area. 153 Bty at LE REVEILLON. Drs Tordoff & Mair & Moore rejoined from 14th R. Park.	

2353 Wt. W2544/1454 700,000 5/15 D. D. & L. A.D.S.S./Forms/C. 2118.

Instructions regarding War Diaries and Intelligence Summaries are contained in F. S. Regs., Part II. and the Staff Manual respectively. Title pages will be prepared in manuscript.

WAR DIARY
or
INTELLIGENCE SUMMARY.
(Erase heading not required.)

Army Form C. 2118.

Place	Date	Hour	Summary of Events and Information	Remarks and references to Appendices
STEEN-BECQUE.	22/4/17		D. Troops drawing by D.S.C. } from Railhead LILLERS to R. Pts 53 Bde " " D.S.C. } 54 Bde drawing by H.T. } from Railhead LILLERS to R. Pts 55 Bde " " H.T. } 1st line feeding from R. Pts to units, except 53 Bde who are supplying wagons from [illegible] to units. 8th Norfolks detached to 6th Div. & 7th R. [illegible] to 6th Div. I went round Coys & R. Pts. 151 at ANNEZIN with R.P. chosen to billet: 152 Coy at CANTRAINE R.P. near LILLERS. 153 Coy at LEREVEILLON R.P. at CHOCQUES.	
	23/4/17		Capt Randall R.A.M.C. to No 7 Gen Hospital with German measles.	
	24/4/17		R.A. moved to MT BERNENCHON area. Hd Qr Coy to BAS RIEUX. R.P. at a farm on LILLERS – BAS RIEUX road. Part of [illegible] in fire at 150 billet in MORBECQUE. Dr. Holmes inspected 151 Coy from 14 R. [illegible]	
	25/4/17		Remounts arrived 24 for Hd Qr Coy, 1 for 151, 14 for 152, 9 for 153 Coy. Major Blackburn back from Hospital. Round transport of 55 F. Ambulance satisfactory.	
PERNES	26/4/17		D.H.Q. & 54 Bde moved to PERNES area. R.A. to BURBURE area. all by road.	
	27/4/17		54 Bde (men by tactical trains) transport by road to NEUVELLE VITESSE area. 53 Bde by road to VALHUON & 55 Bde to PERNES. R.A. to ~~[illegible]~~ ANVIN area	
	28/4/17		53 Bde (men by tactical trains) transport by road to NEUVELLE VITESSE. R.A. to ETREE WAMIN. ~~Railhead~~ Railhead ST POL	

Instructions regarding War Diaries and Intelligence Summaries are contained in F. S. Regs., Part II. and the Staff Manual respectively. Title pages will be prepared in manuscript.

WAR DIARY

or

INTELLIGENCE SUMMARY.

(Erase heading not required.)

Army Form C. 2118.

Place	Date	Hour	Summary of Events and Information	Remarks and references to Appendices
ACHICOURT	29/4/17		Hd Qrs. Advanced to NEUVELLE VITESSE but Bde. Hd Qrs ACHICOURT. 53 Bde to NEUVELLE VITESSE. R A to AGNY area. Railhead ARRAS. 54 & 55 Bdes supplying by H.T.	
	30/4/17		151 Coy mobilised at 9 am. All Coys have done their long marches very well, & only two rubbed shoulders have occurred. R.A. & abt 130 Coy move up to BOYELLES area. H.T. is being very heavily taxed in the Division at present owing to D.S.C. being taken off supply work & put on blankets, water, bomb wagon work, & H.T. are clearing railhead & also marching loaded. The question of communication between Hd Qrs Train & Coys is most unsatisfactory, a push bike or horse are useless when Coys are scattered in a circle of 8 or 9 miles from Hd Qrs. I think Train Hd Qrs should have at least 1 motor cycle attached to them.	
			Reinforcements received this month 2 H.T. Sgts. 10 Supply men. 1 H.T. Dr. 1 Dr Wheeler. 44 H.D. 1 R. Casualties during month 1 Cpl H.T. 1 L Cpl S. 2 Drs. 1 Sgt H.T. to England re commission 1 S.S.M. (attd to A (H.Q.) Coy) sent to Base.	

LT. COL.
COMDG 18TH DIVISIONAL TRAIN.

2353 Wt. W2544/1454 700,000 5/15 D. D. & L. A.D.S.S./Forms/C. 2118.

Instructions regarding War Diaries and Intelligence Summaries are contained in F. S. Regs., Part II. and the Staff Manual respectively. Title pages will be prepared in manuscript.

WAR DIARY
or
INTELLIGENCE SUMMARY.
(Erase heading not required.)

18th Divisional Train. A.S.C.

18TH DIVISIONAL TRAIN.
No. 37/169 4/6/17.

Army Form C. 2118.

Vol 23

VOL:- 23

Place	Date	Hour	Summary of Events and Information	Remarks and references to Appendices
ACHICOURT	1/5/17		All Sups drawn from Railhead, ARRAS, by H.T. & also delivering to Q.M. stores	
	2/5/17		Attended conference at VII Corps HdQrs re S.S. & H.T. arrangements from Railhead. 58 Bde moved to WANCOURT. 151 Coy & R.A. to M.15 b.7.8.	
	3/5/17		Division engaged on general action. Bombardment most intense. about 4 am. Result of action not too satisfactory	
	4/5/17		Normal, in that supply section pulls from Railhead & Baggage from R.Pts.	
	5/5/17		Railhead 7-45 am	
	6/5/17		Railhead shelled at 9-30 no casualties. Major Lockhill D.A.Q.M.G. appointed A.A.& Q.M.G.	
	7/5/17		Railhead shelled at 9-10. One H.D killed 4 H.D. wounded. 1 L.D. mule & 2 loaders hit by stones & splinters not serious. 1 Bombr. R.A. (loader) wounded & taken to hospital.	
	8/5/17		Complete change of weather, raining hard.	
	9/5/17		Beautiful weather. Pack train not in till 2-30, great inconvenience caused.	
	10/5/17		Pack train not in till 12-30.	
	11/5/17		HdQrs Coy badly shelled in their camp, 1 H.D. killed, Capt Pike & 4 men wounded very lucky not to have had more casualties. Pike returned to duty also Sgt Davies & Sc Cliff: slight wounds. Drs Marfleet & Petchy severely wounded & detained in hospital.	

2353 Wt. W2544/1454 700,000 5/15 D. D. & L. A.D.S.S./Forms/C. 2118.

Instructions regarding War Diaries and Intelligence Summaries are contained in F. S. Regs., Part II. and the Staff Manual respectively. Title pages will be prepared in manuscript.

WAR DIARY
or
INTELLIGENCE SUMMARY.
(Erase heading not required.)

Army Form C. 2118.

Place	Date	Hour	Summary of Events and Information	Remarks and references to Appendices
ARRAS	12 5/17		Hd Qrs Bdg moved to S 20 b. as R. A Bdes have moved to BOIRY ST MARTIN. Very hot & dusty.	
	13 5/17		54th Bde moved to S17 area	
	14 5/17		55 Bde moved to S17 area. 152 Bdg moved to M 15 b. R. Pk at Camp. Capt Rhodes [illegible] detailed to take over duties of Staff Capt CHERBOURG Base. Lt Antoine took over command of 153 Bg	
	15 5/17		153 Bdg moved to M 15 d. R Pk at Camp. Lt Antoine in command of 153 Bdg Hd Qrs Div moved to S 17 a 6.8	
BOISLEUX ST MARC	16 5/17		Hd Qrs Train moved to S 17 a 6.8.	
	17 5/17		Normal work.	
	18 5/17			
	19 5/17		Round all Bdgs. & R.Pks All satisfactory.	
	20 5/17		Horses all improving in condition, owing to getting grazing. Animals all out everyday & mileage done is considerable. Train running	
	21 5/17		to worked pretty punctually so animals are not kept	
	22 5/17		standing about too long	
	23 5/17		To BEAUMETZ re transfer of supplies. It [illegible] not possible as it [illegible] without	
	24 5/17		To ARRAS re same, & dept. with 17 Hd Qrs, not possible under present conditions	

2353 Wt. W2544/1454 700,000 5/15 D. D. & L. A.D.S.S./Forms/C. 2118.

Instructions regarding War Diaries and Intelligence Summaries are contained in F. S. Regs., Part II. and the Staff Manual respectively. Title pages will be prepared in manuscript.

WAR DIARY
or
INTELLIGENCE SUMMARY.
(Erase heading not required.)

Army Form C. 2118.

Place	Date	Hour	Summary of Events and Information	Remarks and references to Appendices
BOIS LEUX ST MARC	25/5/17		Awfully hot.	
	26/5/17		Very hot. Had to move our lines to valley below ... [illegible] ... [illegible] from BOIS VERT, moved to S 16 a 8.0	
	27/5/17		Shelling very heavy all night, some unpleasantly close to our lines.	
			14 H.D. & 4 L.D. horses arrived. 150 Coy 10 H.D. 151 — 2 L.D 152 3 Coy — 153 1 2 L.D	
	28/5/17		Major A. H. Maxwell 5th D. Train reported & took over command of HQ Co Coy from Major Blackburne who proceeded to 5th Div Train.	
	29/5/17		Lt Col Grose. Major Hughes. Capt West. Lts Ford & Arthur S. Sergts Fairhead & Whittlesey & Cpl Dawes mentioned in despatches of May 21st	
	30/5/17		Very heavy rain for three hours in afternoon, turned all lines into swamps. A.A.& Q.M.G. looked round 156 Coy horses & was satisfied.	
	31/5/17		157 Coy moved to S 8 a 9.5 — A.A.& Q.M.G. looked round 151 152 " " " " S 8 b central Coy horses & was very pleased. 153 " " " " S 9 a central	
			Arrivals during month. T/Major Maxwell 3 Supply O.Rs 2 H.T. Drs. 2 Corps. 1 Wheeler. 2 Farriers	
			Departures " T/Major Blackburne. T/Capt Chichester. 4 Supply det. 3 H.T. Drivers	
			Horses received. 4 Chargers. 1 Rider. 4 L.D. 14 H.D. Horses evacuated 4 " "	

2353 Wt. W2544/1454 700,000 5/15 D. D. & L. A.D.S.S./Forms/C. 2118.

D H Grose
LT. COL.
COMDG 18TH DIVISIONAL TRAIN

Instructions regarding War Diaries and Intelligence Summaries are contained in F. S. Regs., Part II. and the Staff Manual respectively. Title pages will be prepared in manuscript.

June 1917

WAR DIARY or INTELLIGENCE SUMMARY.

18th Divisional Train A.S.C.

(Erase heading not required.)

Army Form C. 2118.

Vol (Vol:- 2A) 24

Place	Date	Hour	Summary of Events and Information	Remarks and references to Appendices
BOISLEUX ST MARC	1/6/17		Railhead at BOISLEUX AU MONT. 11 am. Much better for the horses	
	2/6/17		R.Pts. D.T. at S.4 b.4.8 53 Bde. at S 8 a 9.1. 54 Bde at S 8 b 2.5 55 Bde at S 8 b 3.8. Inspected 55 F A transport, condition of animals good, grooming only fair.	
	3/6/17		Loading at Railhead done very quickly, only 50 minutes, very smart & each done like clockwork	
	4/6/17		58 men of the Labour Corps arrived to take over duties of loaders in supply wagons, not too bad looking, a lot on the whole. Regimental loaders sent back to their Regts.	
	5/6/17		Lt Col Grove & Major Hughes awarded D.S.O. in London Gazette of June 4th.	
	6/6/17		S.S.M. Harper awarded M. Cross in London Gazette of 4th inst. Labour Corps loaders not doing too badly, but am afraid they would be much worse at marching.	
	7/6/17		Lts Ford & Antoine promoted Capt. Gazette 5/6/17	
	8/6/17		Sgt Davies & Dr Rawsthorne 150 Coy awarded Military Medal for bravery under shell fire at BOYRY BECQUERELLE. Inspected Queens 1st Line	
	9/6/17		A.A.& Q.M.G. round Coy horses in afternoon. Railhead shelled in morning 35 casualties, fortunately for us it was too early for our loading	

Instructions regarding War Diaries and Intelligence Summaries are contained in F. S. Regs., Part II. and the Staff Manual respectively. Title pages will be prepared in manuscript.

WAR DIARY
or
INTELLIGENCE SUMMARY.
(Erase heading not required.)

Army Form C. 2118.

Place	Date	Hour	Summary of Events and Information	Remarks and references to Appendices
BOISLEUX ST MARC	10/6/17		Very violent thunderstorm at night, camps all turned into mud but it soon dries.	
	11/6/17		Normal.	
	12/6/17		Inspected all 1st line transport of 53rd Bde, very satisfactory & showed much improvement	
	13/6/17		To look over A.H. billets etc in new area, R Pts & Regt lines	
	14/6/17		Normal, weather very hot.	
	15/6/17		153 Regt & 53rd Bde moved to BAYENCOURT area. R.Pt at Regt's lines.	
	16/6/17		To new area & saw 153 Regt	
	17/6/17		151 Regt & 53 Bde moved to SOUASTRE area. R.Pt at Regt's lines	
COUIN	18/6/17		D. Hd Qrs & Train Hd Qrs moved to COUIN area, also 54 Bde to BAUDIEMPRE area. R.Pt at Regt's lines. Very hot march & billets in [illegible] huts very warm. All Regts' vets uncomfortable.	
	19/6/17		H.T. from Railhead for 151 & 152 Regts. M.T. delivering to 153 Regt. Two violent thunderstorms during night.	
	20/6/17		Sent 7 farriers to shoe 123 animals of water carts concentrated at AUTHIE	
	20/6/17		Presentation of medal ribbons to W.O. [illegible] by Corps Commander	

Instructions regarding War Diaries and Intelligence Summaries are contained in F. S. Regs., Part II. and the Staff Manual respectively. Title pages will be prepared in manuscript.

WAR DIARY
or
INTELLIGENCE SUMMARY.
(Erase heading not required.)

Army Form C. 2118.

Place	Date	Hour	Summary of Events and Information	Remarks and references to Appendices
COOIN	21/6/17		Round all Coys & all R.Eq.: Sussex Pioneers. [illegible] R.E. & 3 Field Coys all left Division to go to Fifth Army up north	
	22/6/17		Inspected 55 Bde 1st line Transport. Great improvement all round except Bde Hd Qrs.	
	23/6/17		All mules & horses of Ammunition Park at AUTHIE passed as satisfactorily shod	
	24/6/17		Normal	
	25/6/17		Over Coy Hd Qrs Coy. Horses greatly improved.	
	26/6/17		Inspected 1st Line Transport of 54th Bde, very satisfactory & serviceable on the whole. D.A.C. & D. Train in football competition D.A.C. won 3-1	
	27/6/17		Normal	
	28/6/17		Normal. Exceedingly heavy thunderstorm & torrential rain in evening. 22 Remounts arrived for the Coys.	
	29/6/17		Organising Hd Qrs Sports for Divisional Sport. Train Officers beat R.A.M.C. at wrestling on horseback.	
	30/6/17		Busy arranging details of supply & transport arrangements. Divisional Sports. Train officers in final [illegible]	
During month			Arrivals 10 H.T. Drs. 1 Dr Wheeler. 1 Pte Supply 1 Pte M.T. 24 H.D. horses 1 L.D.	
			Departures 1 S.S.M. 1 Saddler S. 1 Pte (Supply) 1 Pte (M.T.) 8 H.T. Drs. 7 H.D. horses	

[illegible] Lt Col
O.C. [illegible] Div Train

2353 Wt. W2544/1454 700,000 5/15 D. D. & L. A.D.S.S./Forms/C. 2118.

17

Instructions regarding War Diaries and Intelligence Summaries are contained in F. S. Regs., Part II. and the Staff Manual respectively. Title pages will be prepared in manuscript.

WAR DIARY or INTELLIGENCE SUMMARY.

18th Divisional Train. A.S.C.

(Erase heading not required.)

Army Form C. 2118.

8 VI 25

(Volume 25)

Place	Date	Hour	Summary of Events and Information	Remarks and references to Appendices
COUIN	1/7/17		Arranging further details of T & S. for the move of Division & R.A to new area. Most complicated.	
	2/7/17		55 Bde moved to GRENAS area so as to shorten march to entraining stations on 3rd.	
	3/7/17		Division commenced entraining for new area. 53rd Bde from MONDICOURT 54 Bde. DOULLENS N. & 55 Bde DOULLENS S; detraining respectively at CASSEL. GODESWAERFELDE & HOPOUTRE. S.S.O. & myself by car to new Hd Qrs at STEENVOORDE	
STEEN-VOORDE	4/7/17		Division (less R.A & 150 Coy) completed move to new area. Hd Qrs at STEENVOORDE, 53rd Bde ditto 54th BEAUVOORDE 55th at WIPPENHOOK area. R. Pts. 53rd STEENVOORDE. 54th GODERSVELDE 55th HOPOUTRE	
	5/7/17		Up to see Hd Qrs 31st Train at RENINGHELST re taking over Coy lines R. Pts etc. 55 Bde into the line	
	6/7/17		Round Coys & work normal. 54 Bde into support.	
BUSSEBOOM G22 d 1.7	7/7/17		Hd Qrs Div moved to RHENINGHELST. Hd Qrs Train to G22 d central 152 & 153 Coys also there; very crowded camp. 30 Pairs & 30 wagons out all night on R.E. work, as I only have 22 Baggage wagons here, I foresee great difficulty in carrying out these duties nightly.	
	8/7/17		Distribution of supplies difficult owing to trains being very late & also on account of horses having been out all night.	

2353 Wt. W2544/1454 700,000 5/15 D. D. & L. A.D.S.S./Forms/C. 2118.

Instructions regarding War Diaries and Intelligence Summaries are contained in F. S. Regs., Part II. and the Staff Manual respectively. Title pages will be prepared in manuscript.

WAR DIARY
or
INTELLIGENCE SUMMARY.
(Erase heading not required.)

Army Form C. 2118.

Place	Date	Hour	Summary of Events and Information	Remarks and references to Appendices
f.22.d.1.7.	9/7/17		2 H.D horses killed on night work with R.E. & the driver wounded. This night work is most trying on horses & men & they will soon begin to lose condition	
	10/7/17		Railhead changed to RENINGHELST ROAD	
	11/7/17		R.A. HQ. Or by formed Division & R.A moved to H20. HQ Or by to f.22.b.9.2. Tried 2nd Coy's loading scheme at Railhead the whole traffic in roads, but could not do it properly as so much had to be drawn off R.S.O. dumps all over the ground owing to new sets, hay, biscuits or forage being on the train.	
	12/7/17		Train awfully late at Railhead, not in till 2-3 a.m. so had to work out Loading Stunt for to-day.	
	13/7/17		Train very late at Railhead so could not do refilling "stunt" properly, as congestion of traffic arose. Roads forward heavily shelled. 2 horses bolted & were lost, 1 wagon smashed badly [interlined, unclear: Roads seriously congested at night]	
	14/7/17		Train not in till 3 a.m. 2 wagons smashed, 10 wagons left on road. Sgt Hooper badly wounded & Dr Goddard & Cpl Tomkins slightly wounded. Very heavy shelling all night.	
	15/7/17		Train again late. 2 Wagons destroyed & left on road.	
	16/7/17		S.S.O. & myself up at 4-30 to ZILLIEBEKE to look for a site for Pack Mule Trains & for coke & rum dump. Found suitable place	

2353 Wt. W2544/1454 700,000 5/15 D. D. & L. A.D.S.S./Forms/C. 2118.

Army Form C. 2118.

Instructions regarding War Diaries and Intelligence Summaries are contained in F. S. Regs., Part II. and the Staff Manual respectively. Title pages will be prepared in manuscript.

WAR DIARY
or
INTELLIGENCE SUMMARY.
(Erase heading not required.)

Place	Date	Hour	Summary of Events and Information	Remarks and references to Appendices
I 22 C 1.7	16/7/17		at I 22 c central. Fairly quiet except bad shelling at certain points on the road	
	17/7/17		Ten wagons had to be left out loaded last night owing to gas [LB Riders] shells & bad shelling. 10 pairs of H.D of 157 & 8 pairs of H.D of 150 gassed & can't be used for at least 48 hours. Some men also gassed. 1 wagon destroyed by shell fire	
	18/7/17		No casualties to convoys at night	
	19/7/17		No casualties to convoys at night	
	20/7/17		Lt Smallwood lost his horse. no further casualties, the horse found at night. No casualties to convoy	
	21/7/17		Conference at Q re Administrative arrangements. No casualties	
	22/7/17		Capt May to Q office as understudy. No casualties	
	23/7/17		No casualties. Bosch planes have been flying very low over lines the last two nights & firing machine guns.	
	24/7/17		No casualties. 30 Train moved into our camp & occupied [illegible] south of us.	
	25/7/17		No casualties. 151 Coy moved to this camp. Moves of 53rd & 54 Bdes put off temporarily	
	26/7/17		No casualties	

Instructions regarding War Diaries and Intelligence Summaries are contained in F. S. Regs., Part II. and the Staff Manual respectively. Title pages will be prepared in manuscript.

WAR DIARY
or
INTELLIGENCE SUMMARY.
(Erase heading not required.)

Army Form C. 2118.

Place	Date	Hour	Summary of Events and Information	Remarks and references to Appendices
f 22 d 1.7	27/7		No casualties at night.	
	28/7		No casualties. 53 & 54 Bdes still in back area, but 53 Bde moved up at night (W day).	
	29/7		No casualties (X day). Sgt Sanders, Cpl [illegible], & Dr Shepherd awarded Military Medal. 54 Bde moved up.	
	30/7		(Y day) Supply Park Train formed at H 33 a 5.7. All Bdes moved up.	
RENINGHELST	31/7		Battle began early dawn. Park Train moved up to CHATEAU SEGARD. All [illegible] moved to NEW DICKEBUSCH CAMP.	
			Casualties for month.	
			Joined 2 Officers. 1 Saddler Sgt. 1 H.T. Corp. 1 H.T. Sgt. 7 Drivers 11 H.D	
			Evacuated 1 Dr Wheeler. 1 L. Corp. 2 Sgts (1 wounded). 3 Drs. (2 wounded) 1 Pte (wounded). 10 H.D 4 Riders (2 killed. 1 gassed. 3 H.D & 3 Riders bolted & are still missing)	

[illegible] Lt Col
C.O. 18 Div Tn

2353 Wt. W2544/1454 700,000 5/15 D. D. & L. A.D.S.S./Forms/C. 2118.

Instructions regarding War Diaries and Intelligence Summaries are contained in F. S. Regs., Part II. and the Staff Manual respectively. Title pages will be prepared in manuscript.

WAR DIARY
or
INTELLIGENCE SUMMARY.
(Erase heading not required.)

August 1917

Army Form C. 2118.

(Vol:-26)

Vol 26

Place	Date	Hour	Summary of Events and Information	Remarks and references to Appendices
			18th Divisional Train: A.S.C.	
RENINGHELST.	1/8/17		Poured with rain all night & all day. Ground a regular quagmire. Pack Train & Bdes moved back from extreme front. Railhead at DICKEBUSH & loading in detail there. Pack Train disbanded.	
	2/8/17		Divisional Pack Train is not to be reformed, (thank Heavens, far too unwieldy & large for practical purposes), Bdes will run their own Pack animals on similar lines. Still raining & the whole place a quagmire.	
	3/8/17		Still pouring with rain. Railhead detail loading improving.	
CANAL RESERVE AREA	4/8/17		D.H.Q. including HdQrs Train moved up to H27 b central. Rain has at last stopped, but only for a short time. Railhead at OUDERDOM (altered in middle of night) as train cannot get up to DICKEBUSH owing to rain	
	5/8/17		Still at OUDERDOM Railhead. Rain stopped & warm sunshine ground drying up well.	
	6/8/17		1st Aust. A.T. [illegible] 113 A.F.A. Bde. 65 A.F.A. Bde. No 3 Special Coy R.E. [illegible] + Canadian Tunnellers all added to us for rations, but nothing in Pack for them; great inconvenience caused at Railhead as all supplies for [illegible] had to be fetched by lorries, [illegible]	

2363 Wt. W2544/1454 700,000 5/15 D. D. & L. A.D.S.S. Forms/C. 2118.

Instructions regarding War Diaries and Intelligence Summaries are contained in F. S. Regs., Part II. and the Staff Manual respectively. Title pages will be prepared in manuscript.

WAR DIARY
or
INTELLIGENCE SUMMARY.
(Erase heading not required.)

Army Form C. 2118.

Place	Date	Hour	Summary of Events and Information	Remarks and references to Appendices
CANAL RESERVE AREA	7/8/17		All correct at Railhead, & supplies all on time with exception of a little forage. 30 Div R.A. & 11 A.F.A. Bde & 23rd Div R.A. all on our hands to-day total 31000 men & 15000 horses	
	8/8/17		Much work at Railhead, all finished by 12 o'clock	
	9/8/17		Very much at Railhead & finished by 11. Very glad as Bosch planes were about & I expected shelling. 30 Div Troops left us & 23 Div Tr. 21st [illegible] R.A. filled for last time	
	10/8/17		Work normal. Aeroplanes (Bosch) very busy at night, dropped bombs quite close to [illegible] lines.	
	11/8/17		Railhead DICKEBUSH. 53 Bde moved to WIPPENHOEK area. Supply columns filled from Railhead. All transport marched Brigaded under O.C. 155 Coy.	
	12/8/17		54 Bde moved to STEENVOORDE EAST area. All transport brigaded & marching under O.C. 152 Coy.	
RENINGHELST	13/8/17		Divisional H.Q. moved to RHENINGHELST.	
	14/8/17		Round all Coys & fixing up details of [illegible], handing over etc.	
LEDERZEELE	15/8/17		Div H.Q. to LEDERZEELE. 53 Bde to ERINGHEM 54 Bde to BOYSSCHEURE area. Railhead RHENICHELST. Lorries brought supplies through.	

Instructions regarding War Diaries and Intelligence Summaries are contained in F. S. Regs., Part II. and, the Staff Manual respectively. Title pages will be prepared in manuscript.

WAR DIARY
or
INTELLIGENCE SUMMARY.
(Erase heading not required.)

Army Form C. 2118.

Place	Date	Hour	Summary of Events and Information	Remarks and references to Appendices
LEEDERZEELE	16/8/17		To forward area in afternoon. Saw 150 & 151 Coys.	
	17/8/17		To forward area & arranged about move of 53 Bde to new area, also feeding of R.A. & HdQrs by whom will be attached to 47th Divn. 2 Battns 53 Bde moved to new area.	
Answered for O/c Train from 5.30pm	17/8/17		O/c left for leave to England. Essex & Suffolk Regts arrived by lorries at Rubrouck area 7.30. pm – with rations in lorries, went to ABEELE for O/c Train re rations. Railhead ARNEKE for 3 Bdges. Artilly attached 47th Div drawing at Reninghelst	H. J. Hughes for O/c Train
	18/8/17		attended Railhead. 151 Coy S/o & details arrived 3 pm. Office duties normal.	
	19/8/17		Attended Railhead & Refilling Points. Work normal. 53rd Bdge arrived night of 18th into their rest area. Suggestion made by DAQMG that supplies will be drawn by H.T. on 21st from Arneke Railhead all lorries required for shooting range to convey troops (151 Coy ASC arrived 2 pm)	
	20/8/17		Brigade Refilling Points, called on O/c 151 Coy attended Railhead & 3 Brigade Refilling Points, called on O/c 151 Coy work normal weather fine Capt. Williams (Adgt) dislocated his shoulder continued bed	
	21/8/17		151 Coy & 152 Coy ASC drew supplies from Arneke Railhd by H.T lorries for 153 Coy. H.T cleared in 3/4 hour both Brigades. work normal. 18 Div HQ V. 8 Corps cricket result HQ 18 Div 85 runs 8 Corps 35. weather very hot. 153 Coy ordered to pull by H.T. Railhead on 22/8/17, supplies.	
	22/8/17		attended Railhead & Refilling Point. Handed over duties of O/c Train to Major Newell 10 A.M.	H. J. Hughes Major for O/c Train
			Took over duties of O/c Train from Major Hughes. DSO at 10 AM. – Capt WILLIAMS sent to Hospital at ST OMER. — Visited 151 & 153 Coys – Arranged for Lieut BISHOP to come to Train HQ to-morrow morning to take over duties of Adjutant.	
		11-45 pm	Received instructions from Q to arrange to draw mails from Supply Train until further notice, issued necessary instructions to Coys.	L. M. Newell Major for O.C.

A7092 Wt. W125 9/M1293 750,000. 1/17. D. D & L. Ltd. Forms/C2118/14.

Instructions regarding War Diaries and Intelligence Summaries are contained in F. S. Regs., Part II. and the Staff Manual respectively. Title pages will be prepared in manuscript.

WAR DIARY
or
INTELLIGENCE SUMMARY.
(Erase heading not required.)

Army Form C. 2118.

Place	Date	Hour	Summary of Events and Information	Remarks and references to Appendices
LEDERZEELE	23.8.17		2nd Lieut. BISHOP reported to take over duties of Adjutant at 8.30 a.m. — Visited Railhead & saw Supplies drawn.	
"	24.8.17		Visited Railhead and saw Supplies drawn. — Visited No 1 (150) Company at DICKEBUSCH also R.A. Hqrs. was informed that the intended move of the Artillery out of the Line on 25th was cancelled.	
"	25.8.17		Visited Railhead and 152 Company — everything going smoothly. (12-0 midnight) Instructions received from D.H.Q. to detail 11 G.S. Wagons to collect Stores from [illegible] OOZENEGHEM on evening of 27th wagons to return on morning of 28th.	
"	26.8.17		Detail for 11 G.S. Wagons altered to 24. Orders issued to 151-152-153 Coys to supply necessary Wagons. Instructions received to send party to CALAIS to collect horses. — Party detailed.	
"	27.8.17		Capt. FORD left for England on leave. Horse collecting party proceeded from here to WATTEN Railhead at 9.30 a.m. Capt. PIKE returned from leave, reports having great difficulty in finding where his unit was stationed, very wet day. 2nd Lieut. Smallwood returned from leave midnight 27/28th. Called at R.A. H.Qrs. — no	
"	28.8.17		Visited Railhead — also visited 150 Coy. — all leave postponed for one day — Weather very stormy & wet. information as to Artillery coming out of line. —	
"	29.8.17		Received 7 HD horses from Remount Depot CALAIS — distributed 2 to 151 Coy & 5 to 150 Coy — took over two riding horses for 150 Coy. Instruction received for all General Duty men, Spare men & issuers to be medically examined, issued instruction to 151-152-153 Coy. for these men to be examined. Information received that Div. Artillery move tomorrow to OUDERZEELE — Weather wet and windy.	S. M[illegible] Major for O.C.
"	30.8.17		Visited Railhead to see supplies drawn. Saw Capt. Spooner re lorries for supplies for Artillery. 2 Corps providing lorries for supplies on 30th. H.d. Qr. Coy. moved back to OUDERZEELE	
	31.8.17		To inspect H.d. Qr. Coy. [illegible] moved to HOUTKERK to join XVIII Corps. [illegible]	
			Casualties [illegible] 7 H.D. horses. 2 L.D. 1 [illegible] 2 [illegible]	
			Joined 1 [illegible] 1 Sgt. 5 Drs. 1 Pte. [illegible] 1 Cpl. 4 Drs. 1 Pte. 11 H.D. 3 L.D.	
			Departures [illegible]	[illegible] Lt. Col. [illegible] Div. Train

A7092 Wt. W128/9/M1293 750,000. 1/17. D. D & L. Ltd. Forms/C2118/14.

11

Instructions regarding War Diaries and Intelligence Summaries are contained in F. S. Regs., Part II. and the Staff Manual respectively. Title pages will be prepared in manuscript.

WAR DIARY or INTELLIGENCE SUMMARY.

(Erase heading not required.)

18th Divisional Train A.S.C.

Army Form C. 2118.

(Vol:- 27)

Vol 27

Place	Date	Hour	Summary of Events and Information	Remarks and references to Appendices
LEDERZEELE	1/7/17		Railhead & R Pts. Inspected 153 Coy, full strength & marching order in afternoon. Satisfactory.	
	2/7/17		Normal. Inspected 150 Coy in afternoon, full strength & marching order. Most exceedingly good turn out, would not have recognised it as the same Coy as it was 6 months ago.	
ESQUELBECQ	3/7/17		Divisional HdQrs to ESQUELBECQ area. 54 Bde to WORMHOUDT (C) area.	
	4/7/17		Weather fine & warm. Divisional Gymkhana. Train won mounted tug of war easily.	
	5/7/17		Round all 3 Bde Coys & R. Pts & Railhead. All billets etc quite satisfactory. Divisional Boxing Matches.	
	6/7/17		Inspected 152 Coy all ranks marching order, not at all satisfactory.	
	7/7/17		HdQrs Coy drawing from ARNEKE railhead for R A	
	8/7/17		Q staff of HdQrs & Bdes. Col Train & S.S.O. & all Regtl Qr Mrs to CALAIS & were shown over Bakery, Supply Depot, M.T. Depot, Petrol Refilling Depot, Salvage Depot – most interesting day.	
	9/7/17		Lt B[illegible] A.S.C. & 2 Lt Toogood A.S.C. joined Train for duty. 2Lt Toogood posted to 152 Coy.	
	10/7/17		Capt Martin joined as Adjt. Inspected 151 Coy marching order.	
	11/7/17		Normal.	

A7092 Wt. W128-9/M1293 750,000. 1/17. D. D & L. Ltd. Forms/C2118/14.

Instructions regarding War Diaries and Intelligence Summaries are contained in F. S. Regs., Part II. and the Staff Manual respectively. Title pages will be prepared in manuscript.

WAR DIARY
or
INTELLIGENCE SUMMARY.
(Erase heading not required.)

Army Form C. 2118.

Place	Date	Hour	Summary of Events and Information	Remarks and references to Appendices
ESQUELBECQ	12/9/17		Normal. Open air Divisional smoking concert 6 – 8.30 pm.	
	13/9/17		Normal. Looked at 1st line at R. Pts & on road.	
	14/9/17		Normal. Looked at 1st line of R. Pts & on their lines at various places.	
	15/9/17		Normal. D.D.S.T came to see me re green forage. Officers smoking concert in evening at ZEGGERS CAPPEL.	
	16/9/17		Normal.	
	17/9/17		Normal.	
	18/9/17		53rd Bde Assault at Arms. Went off very successfully, although it was raining nearly all the time.	
	19/9/17		I2H book formed, posted to 157 Coy.	
	20/9/17		R A Hd Qrs & 2 Bdes, D.A.C & 150 Coy Train moved to SERGUES area. Round all Coys, (own 150 on the march) & R Pts.	
	21/9/17		Visited HdQr Coy & R Pts in SERGUES area, not very comfortable.	
	22/9/17		54 Bde & 152 Coy moved to forward area 54 Bde to Tunnelling Camp	
	23/9/17		53 Bde moved to ST JAN DER BIEZEN area. 53 Bde to School Camp. 151 Coy to F28 b 7.1. 152 Coy to F28 c 2 6. 153 Coy to F29 c 1.2. all near POPERINGHE	
POPERINGHE	24/9/17		DHQ & Train HdQrs moved to POPERINGHE. R A HdQrs & Bdes to BERLINGHEM area. Railhead PROVEN.	

A7092 Wt. W128 9/M1293 750,000. 1/17. D. D & L. Ltd. Forms/C2118/14.

Instructions regarding War Diaries and Intelligence Summaries are contained in F. S. Regs., Part II. and the Staff Manual respectively. Title pages will be prepared in manuscript.

WAR DIARY
or
INTELLIGENCE SUMMARY.
(Erase heading not required.)

Army Form C. 2118.

Place	Date	Hour	Summary of Events and Information	Remarks and references to Appendices
POPERINGHE	25 9/17		All supplies except R.A. group drawn by H.T. from PROVEN at 7-30. R.A. from WATTEN, being on moving to 26-day to PESELHOEK	
	26 9/17		Railheads at PROVEN & PESELHOEK for R.A. R.A. & H.Q. Coy in PESELHOEK area.	
	27 9/17		All supplies by H.T. from Railheads. 2Lt Moore joined the Train from HAVRE	
	28 9/17		Lt Clift left to join Infantry Class in England.	
	29 9/17		155 & 282 A.F.A. Bdes falling off our Rich at PROVEN	
	30 9/17		Bosche planes very busy all night. dropped bombs in POPERINGHE & close to our lines. Major Hughes wounded by a bomb & admitted to 46 C.C.S.; flesh wound in left shoulder. Capt Dwight took over duties of S.S.O.	
			Arrivals	
			Capt Marton & Lts Toogood, Cook, Moore. Lt Bassett (A.V.C.)	
			1 Sgt. 1 Corpl. 8 Drivers. 11 Infantrymen (Batmen) 2 Ptes.	
			6 H.D. 1 L.D. 1 Charger horses.	
			Departures	
			Lt Clift. 11 Category A. Drs. 2 Ptes (Clerks) 9 Drivers. 1 S.Q.M.S.	
			5 H.D horses.	

[signature] LT. COL.
COMDG 18TH DIVISIONAL TRAIN.

A7092 Wt. W128 9/M1293 750,000. 1/17. D. D & L. Ltd. Forms/C2118/14.

16

Instructions regarding War Diaries and Intelligence Summaries are contained in F. S. Regs., Part II. and the Staff Manual respectively. Title pages will be prepared in manuscript.

WAR DIARY of 18th Divisional Train A.S.C. INTELLIGENCE SUMMARY.

(Erase heading not required.)

Army Form C. 2118.

(Vol:-28.)

Vol 28

Place	Date	Hour	Summary of Events and Information	Remarks and references to Appendices
POPERINGHE	1/10/17		Normal work. Bombing not so bad at night.	
	2/10/17		2 A Forage[?] evacuated to 56 F.A.	
	3/10/17		Normal. Rain at night.	
	4/10/17		Normal. A good deal of rain.	
	5/10/17		Normal. Still raining & ground getting very bad.	
	6/10/17		Normal. Very wet & muddy. 2 A.F.A. Bdes ceased to draw off our Pack.	
	7/10/17		Normal. Weather very wet.	
	8/10/17		Normal. Very wet. To army ie Railheads etc.	
PISELHOEK	8/10/17		Nos 2, 3, 4 Coys & Hd Qrs moved to A21.a.6.5. Took over from 4th Train. Railhead PISELHOEK most congested & bad traffic management. Train very late (7 hrs) & a great shortage. Round to see REGERSBURG SIDING & new R.Ph. for 53 & 55 Bdes.	
	10/10/17		Railhead REGERSBURG. Very congested owing to R.A drawing ammunition there too; ground very uneven and limited in size. Strength 23,400 men 9754 horses. Round looking for horse lines with A A Q M G in afternoon.	
	11/10/17		Railhead very bad & congested. Grand is too small for big fresh lorries[?] like they are at present, only takes 30 lorries for working easily, this morning 55 & 20 of these could not be got off without shunting	

A7092 Wt. W128 9/M1293 750,000. 1/17. D. D & I. Ltd. Forms/C2118/14.

Instructions regarding War Diaries and Intelligence Summaries are contained in F. S. Regs., Part II. and the Staff Manual respectively. Title pages will be prepared in manuscript.

WAR DIARY
or
INTELLIGENCE SUMMARY.
(*Erase heading not required.*)

Army Form C. 2118.

Place	Date	Hour	Summary of Events and Information	Remarks and references to Appendices
PISELHOEK	12/10/17		Train very late at Railhead, did not get in till 12.	
	13/10/17		Railhead PISELHOEK. Much better arrangement. Very wet & muddy	
	14/10/17		Normal	
	15/10/17		53 & 54 Bdes changed over & former came back to TUNNELING CAMP	
	16/10/17		11th Div R.A. left for 1st Army. 282 A.F.A. Bde on our pack.	
	17/10/17		Major Walker joined as S.S.O.	
	18/10/17		Normal.	
	19/10/17		51st Div R.A. drew off our pack for last time.	
	20/10/17		32nd Div R.A. drew off our pack for first time. 2 Lts Seedman, Everett & Brown joined Train from B.H.T. Depot. Lt Haynes left to join Infantry [illegible]	
	21/10/17		2 Lt [illegible] joined Train. Very frequent bombing at night.	
	22/10/17		Normal. Whole of 53 Bde to TUNNELING CAMP.	
	23/10/17		To see C.R.58 D.T. re taking over & handing over.	
	24/10/17		Train very late & great difficulty getting supplies up to batteries. Train not in till 3.	
PROVEN ROAD.	25/10/17		Divisional HQ has moved to POPERINGHE. Train HQrs to PROVEN ROAD. Train Coys (2, 3, 4) to F 28. 53 Bde at TUNNELING CAMP. 54 at DIRTY BUCKET CAMP. 55 Bde at POPERINGHE. Railhead PROVEN. Div A.F.A. Bdes handed over to 58 Train. Lt [illegible] joined Train.	

A7092 Wt. W125 9/M1293 750,000. 1/17. D. D & I. Ltd. Forms/C2118/14.

Army Form C. 2118.

WAR DIARY
or
INTELLIGENCE SUMMARY.
(Erase heading not required.)

Instructions regarding War Diaries and Intelligence Summaries are contained in F. S. Regs., Part II. and the Staff Manual respectively. Title pages will be prepared in manuscript.

Place	Date	Hour	Summary of Events and Information	Remarks and references to Appendices
POPERINGHE	26/10/17		General Bozzie D.T. inspected 151. 152. 153 Bys & horsed limbers. Pleased with the horses, given the wet & mud he simply went round horse lines. Lt Isaac to ST POL to Purchase Board vice Williams	
	27/10/17		Normal.	
	28/10/17		Round new area, very bad accommodation for men & horses & the whole place a sea of mud.	
	29/10/17		~~53 Bde moved to P4 area. 151 Bty to PELERIN CAMP R.A. at CAMP~~ 152 Bty to POPLAR CAMP R.A. at F10d2.8	
			54 Bde moved to P2 area. 153 Bty to PORTOBELLO. R.A. at X roads near camp	
			55 Bde to P3 area. 163 Bty to PORTOBELLO	
			Div Hd Qrs to PROVEN. Train Hd Qrs E12 d 6.8	
	30/10/17		Div Hd Qrs to PROVEN... 151 Bty to PELERIN CAMP. R.A. at camp. 53 Bde to P4 area	
	31/10/17		Normal. Capt Randall late M.O. of Train killed whilst with a R.A. Battery.	
			Taken on strength. Major Walker. Lt Isaac. 2 Lts Witt, Deacon, Leadman, from Motor. 2 Suppl. Offrs 1 H.T. Sergt 1 Cpl 9 Drs 13 Infantry from B. 8 H.D. horses.	
			Struck off. Major Hughes. Capt Pike. Capt Williams. Lt Clift. Lt [illegible] 2 Lts 6 Drs. 1 [illegible]. Horses. 13 H.T. Drs Category A. 1 [illegible] 2 Sgts. 2 Cpls. 4 H.D. 1 L.D. 12 R. [illegible] (12 Bicycles issued in lieu)	[illegible] Lt Col. [illegible] 16 Div Tn.

A7092 Wt. W128 9/M1293 750,000. 1/17. D. D & L. Ltd. Forms/C2118/14.

Confidential. 17

Instructions regarding War Diaries and Intelligence Summaries are contained in F. S. Regs., Part II. and the Staff Manual respectively. Title pages will be prepared in manuscript.

WAR DIARY
of :~ *18th Divisional Train A.S.C.*
INTELLIGENCE SUMMARY.
(*Erase heading not required.*)

Army Form C. 2118.

Volume :~ 29.

Vol 29

Place	Date	Hour	Summary of Events and Information	Remarks and references to Appendices
PROVEN	1/11/17		To see Bde 35 Train & arrange with him re taking over [illegible]	
	2/11/17		Normal.	
	3/11/17		53 Bde moved to Support area. 153 Coy to B.6.b.5.8. R.R. in Coy lines	
	4/11/17		Railhead ELVERDINGHE 53 Bde to Line. 157 Coy to B.6.b.3.2 R.R. in lines	
J.CAMP	5/11/17		Hd Qrs Div & Train to J Camp. 54 Bde to BENSONSFARM. 153 Coy to B.8.b.5.8 R.R. in camp.	
	6/11/17		Normal work.	
	7/11/17		2Lt Morton left Division for Special Purchase Board. PARIS.	
	8/11/17		2Lt Robertson joined & was ~~[illegible]~~ posted to 153 Coy.	
	9/11/17		Normal. Weather awfully wet.	
	10/11/17		Normal. Horse lines & camps getting in a most awful state owing to rain & mud.	
	11/11/17		Hd Qrs moved to ELVERDINGHE. CHATEAU.	
	12/11/17		Weather much brighter & drier.	
	13/11/17		Weather better. Work normal	
	14/11/17		Normal. F.G.C.M. on Dr. Waring.	
	15/11/17		Normal. 157 Coy's lines are too close to the shells that have been coming over the last 2 days, must be moved if possible	
	16/11/17		as although at present shells are going just over & just short	

A7092 Wt. W123.9/M1293 750,000. 1/17. D. D & L. Ltd. Forms/C2118/14.

Instructions regarding War Diaries and Intelligence Summaries are contained in F. S. Regs., Part II. and the Staff Manual respectively. Title pages will be prepared in manuscript.

WAR DIARY
or
INTELLIGENCE SUMMARY.
(*Erase heading not required.*)

Army Form C. 2118.

Place	Date	Hour	Summary of Events and Information	Remarks and references to Appendices
J CAMP	16/11/17		+ at any moment one may come into the camp	
	17/11/17		151 Bty moved to B.1.c.9.2.	
	18/11/17		Normal. Weather fine & ground drying up well.	
	19/11/17		Normal.	
	20/11/17		} Normal.	
	21/11/17		}	
ELVERDINGHE	22/11/17		242 & 315 A.F.A Bdes attached for feeding. Train HdQrs moved to ELVERDINGHE CHATEAU. Met A.Q.M.G. XIX Corps at Railhead to discuss scheme of loading on Decauville at Railhead & delivering direct by it to Bde Transport lines so as to relieve congestion of traffic on roads	
	23/11/17		Normal.	
	24/11/17			
	25/11/17		Capt. Mg left to join infantry. 2/19 London Regt. returned to 58 Div.	
	26/11/17		Normal.	
	27/11/17		Normal.	
	28/11/17		Normal.	
	29/11/17		Heavy shelling of back areas in evening & at night. 153 Coy's Officers mess kitchen blown to bits, but no casualties.	

Instructions regarding War Diaries and Intelligence Summaries are contained in F. S. Regs., Part II. and the Staff Manual respectively. Title pages will be prepared in manuscript.

WAR DIARY
or
INTELLIGENCE SUMMARY.
(Erase heading not required.)

Army Form C. 2118.

Place	Date	Hour	Summary of Events and Information	Remarks and references to Appendices
ELVERDINGHE	30.11.17.		Normal. Arrivals 2Lt Robertson, 2 Sgts, 2 Sgts, 1 Cpl. 5 Ptes, 12 drivers 5 H.D horses 1 L D horse Departures 2Lt Morton, Cpl Maj, 1 C.S.M. 1 Sergt 1 Cpl 8 drivers. 2 Ptes. 21 H D horses 1 Rider.	

[illegible] Lt Col
OC [illegible] Div Tr.

A7092 Wt. W128 9/M1293 750,000. 1/17. D. D & L. Ltd. Forms/C2118/14.

Instructions regarding War Diaries and Intelligence Summaries are contained in F. S. Regs., Part II. and the Staff Manual respectively. Title pages will be prepared in manuscript.

WAR DIARY of 18th Divisional Train. A.S.C. **INTELLIGENCE SUMMARY.**

(*Erase heading not required.*)

Army Form C. 2118.

VIII (VOL:- 30)

30

Place	Date	Hour	Summary of Events and Information	Remarks and references to Appendices
ELVERDINGHE	1/12/17		Normal	
	2/12/17		To see D.D.S.T. II Army at CASSEL	
	3/12/17		A.A. & Q.M.G. round lines & we went thoroughly into the question of how to drain them. Very cold & frosty	
	4/12/17		Went into question of permanent huts & lines with C.O. R.E. Difficulty is want of labour, owing to sick men & other causes. 2/Lt Hanse joined Train	
	5/12/17		G.O.C. Division inspected lines etc of 151, 152, & 153 Coys. Capt. Mason [illegible] Quite satisfactory. Bosch planes active at night. [illegible]	
	6/12/17		Normal. Freezing all day " " " "	
	7/12/17		C.R.E. round Coys re siding of [illegible]. 2/Lt Tucker joined Train from HAVRE. 2/Lt Fowler to 3rd Dival A.S.C.	
	8/12/17		Pack train never arrived having been run into en route. Supplies had to be drawn from GRUBBEN & [illegible] inconvenience & delay was caused by Corps not being able to give us enough lorries, only 6 being forthcoming, & also 2 S.S. lorries. Oats & groceries drawn from GRUBBEN by 4 p.m. 2 lorries had managed to get through with Bread, Meat, Bacon & [illegible]. These were emptied & supplies were completed at R.P. by 7 p.m.	

A7092 Wt. W128_9/M1293 750,000. 1/17. D. D & I. Ltd. Forms/C2118/14.

Army Form C. 2118.

Instructions regarding War Diaries and Intelligence Summaries are contained in F. S. Regs., Part II. and the Staff Manual respectively. Title pages will be prepared in manuscript.

WAR DIARY
or
INTELLIGENCE SUMMARY.
(Erase heading not required.)

Place	Date	Hour	Summary of Events and Information	Remarks and references to Appendices
ELVERDINGHE	9 12/17		33rd Divnl R.A. left us, & 87 Divnl R.A. came in to us on 10th for feeding.	
	10 12/17		Proceeded to ROUSBRUGGE & saw O.C. 57 D Train & found out [illegible] location & R.Ps of his Coys; also proceeded to HERZEELE & saw [illegible] of [illegible]	
	11 12/17		Normal.	
	12 12/17		Divisional R.A. & H.Q. Coy moved to CROMBEKE area.	
	13.12/17.		Took over duties as O.C. Train.	Entries from 13-12-17 by Major L.M. Howell? O.C. 151 Coy.
	14.12/17.		Went through particulars of move with O.C. Companies. (move of 55 Brigade altered) Capt West went over to see camp in new area.	
	15.12/17		Adjutant went over to RUSBRUGGE to arrange for the taking over of quarters in new area. S.S.O. 57. Div. called.	
	16 12/17.		152 Company left ELVERTINGE for HARINGE 153 Coy moved from ELVERTINGE proceeding to NORDAUSQUES area staying at ZEEGERS CAPPEL for one night, one half the Brigade transport remains behind and proceeds on 18th	
	17 12/17		151 Coy moved to HERZEELE - new railhead at RUSBRUGGE 151 Coy draw by lorries	
	18 12/17		Train Headquarters moved to RUSBRUGGE remainder of 153 Coy proceeded to NORDAUSQUES area. Visited 150 Coys lines	
	19 12/17		Visited Railhead and also refilling points & Company lines of 151 & 152 Coys.	
	20 12/17.		Visited 153 Coy. found Company comfortably accommodated. S.S.O. arranged with 550? 8th Train for 55 Bde drawing rations off 8th Train Pelke? at WATTEN.	
	21 12/17		Railhead for 55 Bde changed from ARNEKE to WATTEN. Instructions received for BISHOP - PALMER & SMALLWOOD to proceed to England for Infantry. O.C's Motor Car into 2nd D.C.S. for overhaul.	
	22 12/17		2nd Lieut PALMER left for ENGLAND. Attended at Railhead.	
	23 12/17.		Nothing to be noted.	

A7092 Wt. W128 9/M1293 750,000. 1/17. D. D & L., Ltd. Forms/C2118/14.

Instructions regarding War Diaries and Intelligence Summaries are contained in F. S. Regs., Part II. and the Staff Manual respectively. Title pages will be prepared in manuscript.

WAR DIARY

or

INTELLIGENCE SUMMARY.

(Erase heading not required.)

Army Form C. 2118.

Place	Date	Hour	Summary of Events and Information	Remarks and references to Appendices
ROUSSBRUGGE 24-12-17.			Preparations are being made for the adoption of these precautions and also for 1st Line Transport to draw Supplies at Railhead	
25-12-17			Christmas Day. ~~[illegible]~~ first fall of snow.	
26-12-17			Went to Railhead & saw supplies drawn. Issued instructions with regard to move of Division.	
27-12-17.			Transport of 55th Brigade move from NORDAUSQUES AREA to LEDERZEELE	
28-12-17			55 Brigade moved from NORDAUSQUES AREA to PROOSDY AREA also 153 Coy moved from LEDERZEELE to PROOSDY rations drawn from WATTEN by MT for this Brigade. 53 Bde moves to CANADA FARM AREA. Supplies drawn by MT	
29-12-17			53rd Bde moves to BOESINGHE AREA supplies drawn by MT at ELVERTINGHE. Thaw Precaution Warning received.	
30-12-17.			54 M.G.C. Transport moves to NORDAUSQUES AREA taking rations for consumption 1st.	
31-12-17.			55 Bde moved from Proosdy area to ELVERTINGHE, rations drawn for this Brigade at ELVERTINGHE by 151 Coy	
			Arrivals: Two 2nd Lieutenants; ONE S.S.M. (IC); Two CSMs; one Wheeler Corporal; Two H.T. Corporals; One Dr H.T.; one Staff Sgt.	
			Departures: One Captain; Four 2nd Lieutenants; one SSM (IC); one Wheeler Cpl; Two H.T. Cpls; one S/Cpl (supply); Four H.T. Drivers; one Private Infantry	
			arrivals: H.D 6, L.D –, R 1 — Departures: H.D. 4, L.D. 1, R. –	
1-1-18.			~~Cold frosty weather. 8A and 153 Coy moved from ROUSSBRUGGE to DROMORE CORNER (ELVERTINGHE). Supplies drawn at ELVERTINGHE Railhead by M.T. Visited 151 – 153 – and 150 Coy at ELVERTINGHE. [illegible] for [illegible] Brigade [illegible] Infantry.~~	
2-1-18				

L. M. Newell
Major,
O.C. 18th Divisional Train.

A7092 Wt. W128 9/M1293 750,000. 1/17. D. D & L. Ltd. Forms/C2118/14.

7

Instructions regarding War Diaries and Intelligence Summaries are contained in F. S. Regs., Part II. and the Staff Manual respectively. Title pages will be prepared in manuscript.

WAR DIARY
of 18th DIVISIONAL TRAIN A.S.C
INTELLIGENCE SUMMARY.
(Erase heading not required.)

Army Form C. 2118.

(Vol:-31)
Vol 31

Place	Date	Hour	Summary of Events and Information	Remarks and references to Appendices
ROUSSBRUGGE 1-1-18			Cold frosty weather. R.F.A. and 150th Coy moved from ROUSSBRUGGE AREA to BOSINGHE AREA. Supplies drawn at ELVERTINGHE Railhead by M.T. Visited 151. 153-150 Coys Camps at ELVERTINGHE. Lieut Smallwood left for ENGLAND to join infantry.	
2-1-18.			Weather Cold & frosty.	
3-1-18 ELVERTINGHE			DIVISION H.Q. & Train office move from ROUSSBRUGGE to ELVERTINGHE. Cold frosty weather & roads frozen. Supplies for Units on the move drawn at Railhead & delivered by Coy already in the area.	
4-1-18.			54 Brigade & 152 Coy ASC moved from Herzeele Area to BOSINGHE AREA. Supplies drawn for this Brigade by 157 Coy. weather still cold & frosty.	
5-1-18.			1st Line Transport drawing supplies at Railhead for Infantry Brigade. Considerably less time was taken than was estimated for. 25 G.S. wagons were detailed for General duties. 1st Line continues to draw at Railhead until further orders.	
6-1-18			Supplies drawn in much less time by 1st Line. Went with Major Campbell to look at suggested new Coal dump at [illegible]. [illegible] of 53rd Brigade by ASC called here. 40 GS wagons detailed for general duties. 1 days extra forage drawn at Railhead for thaw precautions.	
7-1-18.			27th Inf Bde come under 18th Divisional administration, 1st Line transport draw supplies from 18th Div Pack at ELVERTINGHE Railhead. 65 wagons detailed for general duties. 1 days extra forage drawn at Railhead	
8-1-18.			3rd days extra forage drawn at Railhead for thaw precautions, snow fell during the morning 65 GS wagons for general duties	
9-1-18.			Weather Cold & frosty some snow. 89 wagons employed on general duties	
10-1-18			Rained during the night, most of the snow & ice on the ground has gone. 84 wagons employed on general duties.	
11-1-18			Thawing – 85 wagons employed on General duties	
12-1-18			Thaw precautions come into force at 11-0 AM to-day – extra wagons required for [illegible], [illegible] & fuel wood 101 wagons employed on General duty work	
13-1-18			No forage drawn from Railhead to-day, forage drawn from thaw ration dump, this procedure for 3 days. Car sent to ~~[illegible]~~ to pick up Col [illegible] [illegible]. ELVERDINGHE [illegible] [illegible] [illegible] 6 G.S. wagons	
14.1.18			Thaw precautions off. [illegible] all night. 71 G.S. wagons on duty	
15.1.18			Raining all day, ground in a very bad state 71 G.S. wagons on duty	
16.1.18			Awful rains & wind in the night, & rivers flooded. big [illegible] in a most awful state – 143 G.S. wagons at duty including those on supplies which have not been shown before	
			151 Coy [illegible] [illegible] [illegible] [illegible]	

A7092 Wt. W.128 9/M1293 750,000. 1/17. D. D & L. Ltd. Forms/C2118/14.

Instructions regarding War Diaries and Intelligence Summaries are contained in F. S. Regs., Part II. and the Staff Manual respectively. Title pages will be prepared in manuscript.

WAR DIARY
or
INTELLIGENCE SUMMARY.
(Erase heading not required.)

Army Form C. 2118.

Place	Date	Hour	Summary of Events and Information	Remarks and references to Appendices
ELVERDINGHE	17/1/18		Cold & damp. 149 G.S. wagons on duty. [illegible] all [illegible] [illegible] all day	
	18/1/18		Muggy & warm. Major Hardcastle A/A.D.S.T. XIX Corps came round Bdes & lines. 130 wagons out on duty	
	19/1/18		Quite warm. 121 G.S. wagons on duty. Thaw precautions off	
	20/1/18		Round all R. Pts, & Bdes lines. Also inspected [illegible] 53rd Bde. [illegible] very satisfactory. 129 G.S. wagons on duty.	
	21/1/18		At [illegible] & inspected all 1st line vehicles & [illegible] of Division [illegible] there. [illegible] in good condition also harness, but vehicles very dirty; this can hardly be avoided owing to nature of ground in camps & horse lines. 115 G.S. wagons on duty	
	22/1/18		117 G.S. wagons on duty. Ch. 32 Train [illegible] me about [illegible]	
	23/1/18		91 G.S. wagons on duty. To HARINGHE [illegible] camp for 157 Coy. [illegible] PROBBEM [illegible] change of [illegible] on 26th for them	
	24/1/18		Fixing up all details of 53 Bde move. 99 G.S. wagons on duty.	
	25/1/18		53 Bde moved to HARINGHE area. 157 Coy [illegible] good camp. 90 G.S. wagons on duty. R.P. for 157 Coy in their camp	
	26/1/18		85 G.S. wagons on duty. [illegible] to HARINGHE [illegible] 157 Coy & [illegible] [illegible] [illegible] satisfactory & men & horses comfortable	

A7092 Wt. W128.9/M1293 750,000. 1/17. D. D & L. Ltd. Forms/C2118/14.

Army Form C. 2118.

Instructions regarding War Diaries and Intelligence Summaries are contained in F. S. Regs., Part II. and the Staff Manual respectively. Title pages will be prepared in manuscript.

WAR DIARY
or
INTELLIGENCE SUMMARY.

(Erase heading not required.)

Place	Date	Hour	Summary of Events and Information	Remarks and references to Appendices
ELVERDINGHE	27/1/18		83 G.S. Wagons on duty. Capt. 32 Train to see [illegible] re change of [illegible] & camps.	
	28/1/18		86 G.S. wagons on duty.	
	29/1/18		98 G.S. wagons on duty. [illegible] 153 Bde to HERZEELE [illegible] billets lines. [illegible] good & [illegible] from Railhead.	
ROUSBRUGGE	30/1/18		D.H.Q. moved to ROUSBRUGGE. 54 Bde to CROMBEKE area. 152 Bde at lines close to WAAYENBERG STATION. R.Pt at Station. Train H.Q. in ROUSBRUGGE [illegible] [illegible] on the march [illegible] looked [illegible] well.	
	31/1/18		To [illegible] [illegible] Train [illegible] transfer of 8th Berks Regt [illegible] Division. Also [illegible] 153 Bde at DROMORE CORNER. 53 Bde to HERZEELE area; 153 Bde to HERZEELE. R.Pt in village. Very cold & damp weather.	
			Arrivals: 1 [illegible] H.T. [illegible]. 4 H.D. horses. 1 L.D. horse.	
			Departures: [illegible] [illegible] Pte [illegible] (H.T.) 1 [illegible] Pte. 1 [illegible] (H.T.) 6 Drivers. 7 H.D. horses. 1 Charger. 1 Rider.	
			[illegible] Lt Col. C.O. [illegible] Div Tn.	

11

18th Divisional Train.

Instructions regarding War Diaries and Intelligence Summaries are contained in F. S. Regs., Part II. and the Staff Manual respectively. Title pages will be prepared in manuscript.

WAR DIARY
or
INTELLIGENCE SUMMARY.
(Erase heading not required.)

Army Form C. 2118.

Vol 32

VOL:- 32.

Place	Date	Hour	Summary of Events and Information	Remarks and references to Appendices
ROUSBRUGGE	1/2/18		To HERZEELE to see 153 Coy in their new lines & billets. Billets very satisfactory. Very muddy, cold & damp.	
	2/2/18		Normal. 2nd ~~[illegible]~~ Artillery Supply Officer joined Train from HAVRE	
	3/2/18		To see 150 Coy at DROMORE CORNER re move of Pioneers & R.A. 8 Berks Regt joined Division from 1st Div.	
	4/2/18		Normal work. 5 H.D., R & 1 Kruger (for L.G.) received, very poor condition.	
	5/2/18		Dry pack drawn from GRUBHEM RAILHEAD ~~drawn~~ at 2 p.m. for 53 Bde group taken to R.P. & issued to units, these rations are for consumption 8th & to be taken on train. Rode over to 153 Coy & settled details of S & T arrangements for move.	
	6/2/18		Dry pack drawn & issued to 55 Bde for consumption 9th. Over to 150 Coy & saw C.O. & S.O. re final arrangements for move of R.A. 6 Berks, 1st Lincs & Train transport transferred to 1st Division. Large detachments of 8 Norfolks, 8 Suffolks, 6th Berks transferred to other Divisions on reduction of infantry brigades.	
	7/2/18		Division commenced to entrain at PROVEN at 10 a.m. for Fifth Army detraining station NOYON. 53 Bde first units to go. Dry Pack ~~issued~~ drawn & issued to 54 Bde for consumption 10th	
	8/2/18		55 Bde entraining. Dry Pack for R.A. drawn from GRUBHEM & stacked at PROVEN STATION for issue to R.A. before entrainment.	
	9/2/18		54 Bde entraining. Train H.Q. Crs with 152 Coy left PROVEN 1 p.m.	
NOYON.	10/2/18		arrived NOYON 5-45 a.m. D.H.Q. at SALENCY. also T.H.Q. R.A. & H.Q. Coy for entrainment. Round lines & R.Pts of Coys in new area	

A7092 Wt. W12859/M1293 750,000. 1/17. D. D. & L. Ltd. Forms/C2118/14.

Instructions regarding War Diaries and Intelligence Summaries are contained in F. S. Regs., Part II. and the Staff Manual respectively. Title pages will be prepared in manuscript.

WAR DIARY
or
INTELLIGENCE SUMMARY.
(Erase heading not required.)

Army Form C. 2118.

Place	Date	Hour	Summary of Events and Information	Remarks and references to Appendices
NOYON	10/2/18		Hd Qrs by will be at BRETIGNY area. 150 by at BABOEUF R.R. at same place. 151 by at R.R. at SALENCY 153 by & R.R. at VARESNES	
	11/2/18		55 Bde moved forward with Hd Qrs Bde at ROUEZ. 153 by at MAREST – DAMPCOURT R.R. on NOYON – CHAUNY road. Bomb on SALENCY in evening; 10 killed. Q. Transport Office windows broken.	
	12/2/18		Railhead changed to APPILLY. 2 bys H.T. D.To & 55 Bde M.T. to 150 & 153 bys they are very comfortable.	
	13/2/18		54 Bde moved to BETANCOURT area en route to JUSSY area. Railhead & bys H.T. D.To & 54 Bde M.T. latter will be M.T. till further orders.	
	14/2/18		All bys except 152 fuelling by H.T. from Railhead. Pioneers to CHAUNY SUD area. Inspected 56 F.A. Camfort not very satisfactory. 54 Bde to JUSSY area	
	15/2/18		All spare pairs ploughing & doing agricultural work for people around. To see 152 by at FLAVY ST MARTEL & found them very comfortably settled in, all under cover. R.R. at M 26 d 8.3. Supplies by M.T. from APPILLY. RA & HdQrs by moved to GUISCARD area. by & R.R. at GUISCARD	
	16/2/18		Cold & frosty. 53 Bde moved to CAILLOUEL area: 151 by to NEUFLIEUX R.R. at K6.c central (Sheet 70E). Saw them in evening & found them very comfortable	

2353 Wt. W2544/1454 700,000 5/15 D. D. & L. A.D.S.S. Forms/C. 2118.

Instructions regarding War Diaries and Intelligence Summaries are contained in F. S. Regs., Part II. and the Staff Manual respectively. Title pages will be prepared in manuscript.

WAR DIARY
or
INTELLIGENCE SUMMARY.
(Erase heading not required.)

Army Form C. 2118.

Place	Date	Hour	Summary of Events and Information	Remarks and references to Appendices
NOYON.	16/8/18		Carrying on with agricultural work. HdQrs Bde, 152 Bde & Remount [illegible] camp are [illegible] by M.T. from Railhead. Planes over in evening.	
BABOEUF	17/8/18		HdQrs moved to BABOEUF, Inspected 151 Bde at GUISCARD, found them most comfortably settled & all supply arrangements satisfactory. Planes over in evening.	
	18/8/18		1st Line Transport of 8th Norfolks, 8th Suffolks & 12th Middlesex was under Train for administration & discipline. Round 151, 152 & 153 Bdes in afternoon.	
	19/8/18		Inspected 54 F.A., very good turnout on the whole, but some horses were badly groomed, & the harness not cleaned [illegible] even on the inside of buckles, whips.	
	20/8/18		Normal; first [illegible] ploughing but [illegible] on mowing the ground instead. About 56 H.D. horses have been working for the last four days dead [illegible].	
	21/8/18		Inspected 8th Berks Transport. Quite satisfactory. [illegible] precautions in force from 6 pm.	

Instructions regarding War Diaries and Intelligence Summaries are contained in F. S. Regs., Part II. and the Staff Manual respectively. Title pages will be prepared in manuscript.

WAR DIARY
or
INTELLIGENCE SUMMARY.
(Erase heading not required.)

Army Form C. 2118.

Place	Date	Hour	Summary of Events and Information	Remarks and references to Appendices
BABOEUF	22/2/18		Thaw precautions on: All Coys drawing by M.T. from Railhead: 152 Coy are doing 32 miles, & Hd Qrs Coy 22.	
	23/2/18		Thaw precautions still on, although roads are in good condition & lots of lorries are on the road but no supply lorries. It is a long pull for horses of 152 Coy & another day will effect efficiency of Coy. 53 M.T. Coy moved to FRIERES CAMP.	
	24/2/18		53 M.T. Coy moved to forward area. Thaw precautions still on. To all Cos. 5th Train re change of Rds etc. & also are billets etc.	
	25/2/18		53 Bde moves to LIEZ section. 153 Coy & R.P. at VILLEQUIER-AUMONT. Thaw precautions off 6 pm on 24th.	
	26/2/18		53 Bde moved to LY FONTAINE area. 151 Coy & R.P. at FLAVY-LE-MARTEL. 54 Bde moved to CAILLOUEL area. 152 Coy to NEUFLEUX R.P. K.6.c (70 [illegible])	
	27/2/18		Hd Qrs 18 Div moved to VILLEQUIER-AUMONT. Corps detail of wagons for R.E. work trying as very hard, every horse & wagon employed on supplies & R.E.	
	28/2/18		Hd Qrs Coy moved to COMMENCHON. R.P. in village.	

2353 Wt. W2544/1454 700,000 5/15 D. D. & L. A.D.S.S./Forms/C. 2118.

Instructions regarding War Diaries and Intelligence Summaries are contained in F. S. Regs., Part II. and the Staff Manual respectively. Title pages will be prepared in manuscript.

WAR DIARY
or
INTELLIGENCE SUMMARY.
(Erase heading not required.)

Army Form C. 2118.

Place	Date	Hour	Summary of Events and Information	Remarks and references to Appendices
During Month:			Arrivals 2 Corporals 2 Drivers 1 Private 1 Charger 2 Riders & H D	
			Evacuations 6 Drivers 1 Private 6 H D 1 R horses.	

[illegible signature]

LT. COL
COMDG 18TH DIVISIONAL TRAIN.

2353 Wt. W2544/1454 700,000 5/15 D. D. & L. A.D.S.S. Forms/C. 2118.

47

Instructions regarding War Diaries and Intelligence Summaries are contained in F. S. Regs., Part II. and the Staff Manual respectively. Title pages will be prepared in manuscript.

18th Divisional Train

WAR DIARY
or
INTELLIGENCE SUMMARY.
(Erase heading not required.)

Army Form C. 2118.

(VOL:- 33.) Vol 33

Place	Date	Hour	Summary of Events and Information	Remarks and references to Appendices
VILLEQUIER-AUMONT	1/3/18		53 Bde group feeding by H T from III Corps Troops Park at FLAVY-LE-MARTEL	
	2/3/18		Snowed hard all day. Roads in a most awful state.	
	3/3/18		Thawed during night & much slush very bad. Roads very heavy on H.T.	
	4/3/18		More snow & frost at night. Thaw all day & roads in a very bad state	
	5/3/18		Transport work getting very heavy & practically every wagon is out every day & some of them half the night too	
	6/3/18		All of the wagons out on duty. Italian Labour Coys arrived. 2 Coys are supplied with transport of the Suffolk 1st Line	
	7/3/18		Normal work as for the last few days.	
	8/3/18		Inspected 1st Line transport of 54 Bde. Very good & in serviceable condition	
	9/3/18		Various moves notified at very short ~~with~~ notice, have made supply & transport arrangements very intricate & worrying, but we pulled through alright. Higher commands do not seem to realise that ~~two~~ ~~days~~ supplies are drawn from Railhead two days before they are required to be consumed.	

Instructions regarding War Diaries and Intelligence Summaries are contained in F. S. Regs., Part II. and the Staff Manual respectively. Title pages will be prepared in manuscript.

WAR DIARY
or
INTELLIGENCE SUMMARY.
(Erase heading not required.)

Army Form C. 2118.

Place	Date	Hour	Summary of Events and Information	Remarks and references to Appendices
VILLEQUIER-AUMONT	10/3/18		To 151 Bty. Weather very warm. Summer time came into force at 11 pm last night.	
	11/3/18		Normal. Weather very fine & warm	
	12/3/18		Normal. Very hot all day.	
	13/3/18		Normal		
	14/3/18		Groceries short on both [illegible] at FLAVY & APPILLY & great inconvenience & delay caused	
			Groceries short on 14th which not arrived at HAM till 11 am. 15th,	
	15/3/18		Every wagon on the road, some of the work is very heavy on the horses & it is wonderful how well in condition they keep, a few are falling off but not badly	
	16/3/18		Railhead changes to FLAVY-LE-MARTEL for all Divn except 54 Bde group which stays at APPILLY. Drawing at 8-45 am found very congested & full of lorries & wagons.	
	17/3/18		Railhead put back to 9-30 am. much better & no congestion in yard at all. R.A.A. Mounted Sports at CAUMONT	
	18/3/18		Normal: 6th detachments moved back at very short notice to 54th Bde, a bit awkward over supplies but it was managed alright	

2353 Wt. W2544/1454 700,000 5/15 D. D. & L. A.D.S.S./Forms/C 2118.

Instructions regarding War Diaries and Intelligence Summaries are contained in F. S. Regs., Part II. and the Staff Manual respectively. Title pages will be prepared in manuscript.

WAR DIARY
or
INTELLIGENCE SUMMARY.
(Erase heading not required.)

Army Form C. 2118.

Place	Date	Hour	Summary of Events and Information	Remarks and references to Appendices
VILLEQUIER-AUMONT	19/3/18		Complete change in weather. Rained all day.	
	20/3/18		Still raining. "Prepare for attack" wire received at 3 pm.	
	21/3/18		Bosch started bombardment at 3-30 a.m. Very heavy & consistent. Gas alert given at 5 a.m. Front line pushed back & Battle line manned. All civilians moved from villages close up, at 10 p.m. whole division ordered to fall back on Green Line. Train marched to BABOEUF.	
BABOEUF	22/3/18		All billeted in village. Railhead ROYE, & we also had to clear FLAVY supply Reserve. M.T. used. Some of the distances were very great for horses. Bosch still pushing on.	
	23/3/18		Fierce fighting still going on. French Divisions coming up to hold front line taking over from English Divisions on ours & right hand sector, 18th still left in & fighting magnificently, under French Divisional Command.	
DIVE-LE-FRANC	24/3/18		Train & Baggage moved back to PASSEL & DIVE-LE-FRANC. Bosch coming on fast.	
PIMPREZ	25/3/18		Train & Baggage to PIMPREZ. D.S.S. delivering supplies. Train to draw stores at Baggage taking it on. Standing to all night, horses hooked in.	

2353 Wt. W2544/1454 700,000 5/15 D. D. & L. A.D.S.S. Forms/C. 2118.

Instructions regarding War Diaries and Intelligence Summaries are contained in F. S. Regs., Part II. and the Staff Manual respectively. Title pages will be prepared in manuscript.

WAR DIARY
or
INTELLIGENCE SUMMARY.

(Erase heading not required.)

Army Form C. 2118.

Place	Date	Hour	Summary of Events and Information	Remarks and references to Appendices
CARLEPONT	26/3/18		Moved at 6 am to CARLEPONT. Owing to suddenness of move we had to load off lorries on to wagons directed by commandant des a dump a group at other end.	
ADINCLI-COURT	27/3/18		Moved at 5 am to ADINCLICOURT, but on arrival I had to go select another site & it was most difficult owing to scarcity of water, finally got them to a place near ATTICHY. We have had great difficulty all day with locating units attached to Division being no one's children, no one can notify us of their whereabouts. T.H.Q. is at ADINCLICOURT.	
"	28/3/18		Moved Tvans by Q HAUTBRAYE. R.P. there too.	
CHOISY	29/3/18		Moved ½ of all 1st line Transport to CHOISY. Arrived very late. All in the open.	
ARSY	30/3/18		R.P. in CHOISY & marched loaded to ARSY. All under cover.	
LA NEUVILLE	31/3/18		R.P. outside village. Marched loaded. Traffic very congested owing to M.T. movement. All out in the open at night in the woods.	

[signature] Lt Col
[signature]

Instructions regarding War Diaries and Intelligence Summaries are contained in F. S. Regs., Part II. and the Staff Manual respectively. Title pages will be prepared in manuscript.

WAR DIARY
or
INTELLIGENCE SUMMARY.
(Erase heading not required.)

Army Form C. 2118.

9/51 34 VOL:- 34.

Place	Date	Hour	Summary of Events and Information	Remarks and references to Appendices
			18th Divisional Train A.S.C	
AUCHY LA-MONTAGNE	1/4/18		Moved with loaded wagons to AUCHY-LA-MONTAGNE, & managed to get all men under cover. No checks on the road.	
LOEUILLY	2/4/18		Very badly congested roads & progress very slow, to LOEUILLY. Had trouble to get men billeted as it is all French Zone. The whole of this trek has been constant trouble with the French over billets etc; we seem to be given villages full of French troops.	
SALEUX	3/4/18		More than half 1st line back to their units at BOVES area remainder still with me to SALEUX. All bivouacked out. D.H.Q. at BOVES. The whole march has been most annoying as the orders re railheads, supplies & billeting places has been most vague.	
	4/4/18		Orders from Q that 2nd days rations are to be kept with the Train & not in the 1st Line, this appears to me to be going to lead to confusion in moving as we cannot carry 2 days supplies in wagons, if lorries have to come & load it will mean congestion of traffic. If the normal procedure was adopted it would mean much less worry & anxiety.	

2353 Wt. W2544/1454 700,000 5/15 D. D. & L. A.D.S.S. Forms/C. 2118.

Instructions regarding War Diaries and Intelligence Summaries are contained in F. S. Regs., Part II. and the Staff Manual respectively. Title pages will be prepared in manuscript.

WAR DIARY
or
INTELLIGENCE SUMMARY.

(Erase heading not required.)

Army Form C. 2118.

Place	Date	Hour	Summary of Events and Information	Remarks and references to Appendices
SALEOUX	5/4/18		Suffolk transport joined up with Division again. Weather awfully wet & men are living in great discomfort. Location of Train. HdQrs & 3 Bde Coy at SALEOUX, forward detachment under Capt Ford at BOVES; HdQrs Coy at FRESNOY-AU-VAL	
	6/4/18		Making up deficiencies of 1st line transport from 7th Norfolk & 8th Suffolk transport.	
	7/4/18		Round 1st line to see if refitting was going on satisfactorily	
	8/4/18		Round A echelon transport at BOVES & GENTILLES to see what further requirements for refitting were required	
	9/4/18		To see HdQrs Coy at CHARGNY (30 miles away). All rations have now been cleared off Reserve Dump & are on wagons of R.P.	
	10/4/18		Normal work. HdQrs Coy & R.A. group moving very erratically impossible	
	11/4/18		to keep track as there no means of communication for long distances	
	12/4/18		HdQrs Train Coys moved to camp on SALEOUX-DURY road.	
			153 Coy & 53 Bde moved out at 6-30pm to CAVILLON area	
	13/4/18		HdQrs to ST FUCIEN. 53 Bde to ST FUCIEN. 54 Bde to SAULEUX area	

2353 Wt. W2544/1454 700,000 5/15 D. D. & L. A.D.S.S./Forms/C. 2118.

Instructions regarding War Diaries and Intelligence Summaries are contained in F. S. Regs., Part II. and the Staff Manual respectively. Title pages will be prepared in manuscript.

WAR DIARY
or
INTELLIGENCE SUMMARY.
(Erase heading not required.)

Army Form C. 2118.

Place	Date	Hour	Summary of Events and Information	Remarks and references to Appendices
SALEUX area.	14/4/18		T. H. Qr move into SALEUX.. Reinforcements for 55 Bde about 600 came up. Very young looking lot of men.	
	15/4/18		Reinforcements for 54 Bde, similar to those for 55 Bde.	
	16/4/18		Railhead AILLY-SUR-SOMME.	
	17/4/18		Normal.	
	18/4/18		Hd Qr Coy & R A drawing off own truck at AILLY	
	19/4/18 – 22/4/18		Normal, except 1st line drawing from R Pts	
	23/4/18		53. 54. 55 Bdes drawn by H T from AILLY-SUR-SOMME.	
			O. C Train evacuated to 47 C.C.S. Major NEWELL (O.C. 150 Coy) assumes command of Train.	
	24/4/18		Supply train 16 hours late. Lorries authorised to draw supplies from Railhead for Bdes on 25th inst.	
	~~25/4/18~~ 25/4/18		55th Bde move from CAVILLON to St FUSCIEN. 153 Coy CAVILLON to SALEUX.	
			Lorries draw all supplies for Division until further notice	

2353 Wt. W2544/1454 700,000 5/15 D. D. & L. A.D.S.S./Forms/C. 2118.

Instructions regarding War Diaries and Intelligence Summaries are contained in F. S. Regs., Part II. and the Staff Manual respectively. Title pages will be prepared in manuscript.

WAR DIARY
or
INTELLIGENCE SUMMARY.
(Erase heading not required.)

Army Form C. 2118.

Place	Date	Hour	Summary of Events and Information	Remarks and references to Appendices
SALEUX	26/4/18		Division commence moving back to CAVILLON – OISSY Area (D.H.Q, PIONEERS & M.G. BAT:)	
– do –	27/4/18		Movement back continued. 54th Brigade to BELLOY-ST. LEONARD.	
RIENCOURT	28/4/18		Division moves to CAVILLON; Train Head Quarters to RIENCOURT.	
– do –	29/4/18		Waggons overhauled and grazing.	
– do –	30/4/18		Supplies drawn from HANGEST Railhead by M.T. with exception of R.A and 55th Bde.	

Personnel

Arrivals	Departures
1 Captn	2nd Lieut.
1 Lieut:	12 Drs
Whlr Cpl	2 H.T. Cpls.
Sh: Smith	
Dr Farr	
4 H.T. Drs	

Horses

Arrivals.	Departures.
5. H.D	11. H.D 2 R's

L. M. Newell
Major
O.C. 18th Divisional Train

D. D. & L., London, E.C.
(A8004) Wt. W1771/M2-31 750,000 5/17 Sch. 52 Forms/C2118/14

Army Form C. 2118.

Instructions regarding War Diaries and Intelligence Summaries are contained in F. S. Regs., Part II. and the Staff Manual respectively. Title pages will be prepared in manuscript.

WAR DIARY
or
INTELLIGENCE SUMMARY.
(Erase heading not required.)

18th Divisional Train **VOL:- 35.**

Vol 35

Place	Date	Hour	Summary of Events and Information	Remarks and references to Appendices
~~SAIGUY~~	~~26 4/18~~		~~Division commence moving back to CAVILLON - OISSY area (D.H.Q. Pioneers + M.G. Battalion)~~	Shewn on Diary for month of April 1918.
	~~27 4/18~~		~~Movement back continued 54th Bde to BELLOY - St LEONARD~~	
~~RIENCOURT~~	~~28 4/18~~		~~Div moves to CAVILLON. Train H^d Qrs to RIENCOURT.~~	
~~"~~	~~29 4/18~~		~~Waggons washed + greasing.~~	
~~"~~	~~30 4/18~~		~~Supplies drawn from HANGEST Railhead by M.T. with exception of R.A. + 55th Bde.~~	
	1 5/18		Unsuccessfully try to purchase locally wood for repairing waggons at MOLLIENS VIDAME + AIRAINES. Am told there is a good supply at PICQUIGNY.	
	2 5/18		No Change. Refitting proceeding.	
	3 5/18		Divisional Cold shoeing board assembled at 152 Coy SOUES. A high standard of efficiency throughout. Out of thirty candidates only 3 failed to pass.	
	4 5/18		Division less 55th Bde, 2 Coys M.G. Battn + Arty transferred from III Corps to Australian Corps. Divisional Transport moved by march route to BERTICOURT.	
BAVELINCOURT.	5.5.18.		Personnel of Division moved by bus to MONTIGNY area, from CAVILLON. Transport from BERTICOURT to MONTIGNY by march route. Div Artillery from BETHENCOURT area to MONTIGNY area.	
	6.5.18.		Heavy rain during night	
	7.5.18. 8.5.18		151 + 152 Coys. moved camp to West side river. L'HULLE on instructions from Q.	

2353 Wt. W2544/1454 700,000 5/15 D. D. & L. A.D.S.S./Forms/C. 2118.

Instructions regarding War Diaries and Intelligence Summaries are contained in F. S. Regs., Part II. and the Staff Manual respectively. Title pages will be prepared in manuscript.

WAR DIARY
or
INTELLIGENCE SUMMARY.
(Erase heading not required.)

Army Form C. 2118.

Place	Date	Hour	Summary of Events and Information	Remarks and references to Appendices
BAVELINCOURT	9.5.18.		150th + 153 Coys moved to new camp areas, to be out of 47th Divisional area.	
	10.5.18			
	11-5-18		Notification from 18th Div Q that Lt Col D.C.E Grose. has been transferred to ENGLAND and struck off the strength from 27-4-18. 2 Corporals 1 Shoeing Smith + 7 drivers arrived from Base, instructions received to arrange for grazing for horses of the Division.	
	12-5-18		Inspected AA. machine gun posts of Coys. 1-30 + 2-0 pm.	
	13-5-18		Four pairs of H.D. horses despatched to ETAPLES to bring back water tanks. Some shells fell in this locality between	
	14-5-18		Railhead from 15th to be at POULANVILLE. SSO located new refilling points nearer to Railhead to lessen mileage of supply lorries. Location of RPs. D.T.s B25 b 7·1 53rd Bde B21 C. 54th Bde B21 a 7·6 55 Bde B21·a 9·5.	
	15-5-18		Lorries drawing supplies at POULANVILLE. time of drawing at Railhead 4-30 AM. Proceeded with SSO to allotment gardens AMIENS to arrange collection of vegetables for Division. Lt KIRKWOOD in charge of gardens.	
	16-5-18		1 NCO + 5 men proceeded to PICQUIGNY. to collect 11 HD horses for the Train	
	17-5-18		11 HD Horses arrived for Train distributed 4 to 150 Coy 1 to 151 Coy 2 to 152 Coy 4 to 153 Coy. Weather fine all day.	
	18-5-18			
	19-5-18		Visited Refilling points between 9 + 10 o'clock. lorries for 53 Bde stopped by traffic control, application made for permit for lorries to proceed to R.P. Shoeing Board assembled to test Shoeing Smiths. Board Capt West, Capt Mortlock, Capt Russell	
	20-5-18		Shoeing Board reassembled to test further batch of men as Shoeing Smiths.	
	21-5-18		Locating new sites for Camps for Train Coys nearer to Railhead, watering for horses can only be got in the villages sites located at Rainneville, where pumping station in course of completion.	
	22-5-18		Orders received for relief of Division on nights 23/24th + 24/25th relieved by 47th Division. Went to see OC 47th Div. Train re moving.	
	23-5-18		Train Coys will not move from their present camps during period Division is out of the line. Inspected turn out of Supply wagons of 150 Coy. The turnout was good.	
	24-5-18			
MOLIENS au BOIS.	25-5-18		Division HQ including Train HQ moved to MOLIENS au Bois to-day, situation 1049 Sutherland St. One Saddler Corporal + 7 drivers as reinforcements reported from the base. Capt Parritt admitted to Field Ambulance. Notified that Lt Cox struck off strength	
	26-5-18		Two drivers as reinforcements arrived from base, posted to 150 + 153 Coys.	
	27-5-18		Visited refilling points + Company lines.	
	28-5-18		Capt Bell returned from 7th Suffolks attached to the Train for duty.	
	29-5-18		2nd Lieut. Moore reported for temporary duty from Guards Divl Train posted to 152 Coy. MO detailed to go round Coys to inoculate men	
	30-5-18		normal.	
	31-5-18		16 H.D. Remounts arrived for Division.	

L M Newell Major
COMDG 18TH DIVISIONAL TRAIN

D. D. & L., London, E.C.
(A8004) Wt. W1771/M2 31 750,000 5/17 Sch. 52 Forms/C2118/14

*Instructions regarding War Diaries and Intelligence Summaries are contained in F. S. Regs., Part II. and the Staff Manual respectively. Title pages will be prepared in manuscript.

WAR DIARY
or
INTELLIGENCE SUMMARY.
(Erase heading not required.)

18TH DIVISIONAL TRAIN No. .... Date. .... A. S. C.

VR 36 Army Form C. 2118.

(VOL:-36)

Place	Date	Hour	Summary of Events and Information	Remarks and references to Appendices
MOLLIENS-AU-BOIS	1.6.18		18th Division taking over left sector of Corps front fr 58th Division. Advanced DHQ moves to CONTY. Instructions received from DDS+T 4th Army to send surplus Infantry Baggage + supply wagons to ABBEVILLE	
	2-6-18		8 GS wagons of Train proceeded to ABBEVILLE.	
	3-6-18		Q office moved from MOLLIENS au Bois to CONTY. located & marked camp sites for Train Coys, in wood EAST of MOLLIENS au BOIS.	
	4-6-18		150 + 153 Coys moved from BAVLINCOURT AREA to wood EAST of MOLLIENS au BOIS. 4 LD & 8 HD horses arrived as remounts for Division. 2nd Lieut E.W. HENSON reported from Base for temp. duty with Train	
	5-6-18		Remounts distributed 2 LD 55 Bde Hq 2 HD 150 Coy 2 HD 153 Coy 1 HD MGB 1 HD 8th E Surrey 1 HD 10th Essex 1 HD 54 Bde 2 LD 54 Bde HQ 151 + 152 Coy moved camp into wood EAST of MOLLIENS au BOIS.	
	6-6-18		Instructions received to draw supplies from POULAINVILLE by H.T. Time of drawing 9-30 pm. Lieut Col. R R B JACKSON takes over command of the Train	L.M. Newell Major
	7.6.18		Bomb protection work on horse lines accelerated.	
	8.6.18		53rd Inf Bde relieve 55th Inf Bde in the line.	
	9.6.18		G.O.C. inspected Train Coys. Everything very satisfactory.	
	10.6.18		Advised by Division that 714th Labour Coy will be rationed by us for consumption 12th inst	
	11.6.18		1 Rider (remount) drawn ~~from~~ PICQUIGNY for O.C. 153 Coy.	
	12.6.18		Advised by Division that 34th M.G Battalion will be rationed by 47th Div for consumption 15th inst + that 55th Inf Bde relieve 54th Inf Bde in the line on night 13th/14th inst.	

G. R. M. Morton Capt-
for Lt. Col.
COMDG 18TH DIVISIONAL TRAIN.

D. D. & L., London, E.C. (A8004) Wt. W1771/M2031 750,000 5/17 Sch. 52 Forms/C2118/14

Instructions regarding War Diaries and Intelligence Summaries are contained in F. S. Regs., Part II. and the Staff Manual respectively. Title pages will be prepared in manuscript.

WAR DIARY
or
INTELLIGENCE SUMMARY.
(Erase heading not required.)

18TH DIVISIONAL TRAIN
No. ....
Date ....
A. S. C.

Army Form C. 2118.

Place	Date	Hour	Summary of Events and Information	Remarks and references to Appendices
MOLLIENS-au-BOIS	13.6.18		R E material collected for Dump shelters + anti bomb walls on horse lines.	
"	14.6.18			
"	15.6.18		Refilling Points inspected by O C Train. Brick dome solder kiln not a success, impossible to moderate the combustion. Directions given for erecting shelters in which to hang the meat.	
"	16.6.18		O C Train visits 54th + 55th Bde HQ to discuss supply situation. No complaints, everything satisfactory.	
"	17.6.18		Many drivers laid up with P. U. O. 35 in 152 Coy. Necessary measures taken to isolate P.U.O cases in Coys only slightly affected.	
	18.6.18		Number of P. U. O cases increasing in 152 Coy. No fresh cases in other Coys. Camps inspected by ADMS. Solder kiln inspected by DADMS.	
	19.6.18		P.U.O increasing 19 men of 151 Coy laid up. Arrangements made with Division to lend 9 infantrymen from Brigade training camps for 3 days to tide over the epidemic.	
	20.6.18		P. U. O still increasing, + has spread to the other Coys.	
	21.6.18			
	22.6.18		O C Train goes on leave for the period 23rd 6.18 – 7.7.18. Major L.M. NEWELL assumes command of Train ~~[illegible]~~ temporarily.	
	23.6.18		Division commences to draw from VIGNACOURT by ~~#~~ M.T. Train	

E. R. M. Horton Capt.
for
COMDG 18TH DIVISIONAL TRAIN.

D. D. & L., London, E.C.
(A8004) Wt. W1771/M2 31 750,000 5/17 Sch. 53 Forms/C2118/14

Instructions regarding War Diaries and Intelligence Summaries are contained in F. S. Regs., Part II. and the Staff Manual respectively. Title pages will be prepared in manuscript.

WAR DIARY
or
INTELLIGENCE SUMMARY.
(Erase heading not required.)

18TH DIVISIONAL TRAIN No. .... Date .... A.S.C.

Army Form C. 2118.

Place	Date	Hour	Summary of Events and Information	Remarks and references to Appendices
Field	23.6.18		Vehicles deliver supplies from Refilling points to units	
MOLLIENS-au-BOIS	24.6.18		7 waggons found for R.E. work in forward area. P.U.O. on the wane. 34th M.G. Battn + Australian reinforcement camp taken on feeding strength consumption 26th	
	25.6.18		Informed by Division that 53rd Inf Bde will relieve 55th Inf Bde on night 26th/27th	
	26.6.18		4 Bombs dropped near Train HQ by E.A at about 11.20. Splinters through tents & mess. Everyone dug down, no casualties sustained by our detachment.	
	27.6.18		A Battn M.G. Corps ~~xxx~~. 2 Guards M.G. Battn taken on feeding strength for consumption 28th inst	
	28.6.18		34th M.G. Battalion cease to be administered by Division	
	29.6.18		'A' Battn M.G. Corps drew rations from us for consumption 30th, & cease to be administered from 18th Division from this date	
	30.6.18		T/Lt E.W. HENSON (attached) sent to report to 8th Div Train for duty. Authy A.Q.M.G.(P) A.S.C. G.H.Q. No A.S.C./20779	
	~~1.7.18~~		~~Railhead changes to POULAINVILLE. Continue to draw by M.T. Notified that 55th Inf Bde relieve 54th Bde in line on night 2nd/3rd inst.~~	

E. R. M. Morton Capt
Lt. COL.
COMDG 18TH DIVISIONAL TRAIN.

2353 Wt. W2544/1454 700,000 5/15 D. D. & L. A.D.S.S./Forms/C. 2118.

Instructions regarding War Diaries and Intelligence Summaries are contained in F. S. Regs., Part II. and the Staff Manual respectively. Title pages will be prepared in manuscript.

WAR DIARY
or
INTELLIGENCE SUMMARY.
(Erase heading not required.)

Army Form C. 2118.

18th DIVISIONAL TRAIN. A.S.C.

(VOL:- 37.)

Vol 37

Place	Date	Hour	Summary of Events and Information	Remarks and references to Appendices
MOLLIENS-au-BOIS.	1.7.18		Supply Railhead changes to POULAINVILLE from 1st inst inclusive. M.T. continues to draw.	
	2.7.18		55th Bde relief of 54th Bde in line postponed 24 hours.	
	3.7.18		55th Bde relieves 54th Bde in the line.	
	4.7.18		Train draws from Railhead (H.T.) 1st Line transport draws from Refilling Point.	
	5.7.18			
	6.7.18			
	7.7.18		Supplies drawn from POULAINVILLE Railhead (Broad Gauge) to CONTAY (South) by light Railway. Supplies for Brigade groups loaded on to 5 Trucks. Supplies for R.A group on to 10 Trucks. To avoid congestion at light Railway ~~Railhea~~ Siding (CONTAY South) 53 Bde + 54th Bde units hold 2 days rations. 55th Bde + R.A units continue to hold one days supplies only. Lt Col R.R.B. JACKSON D.S.O. returned from leave to England + re-assumes command of the Train.	
	8.7.18		46 wagons found by Train for Road work + R.E. work in forward area. To ensure that supply dumps at light Railhead are clear on arrival of train (time of which varies) all units will hold 2 days rations.	
	9.7.18		Notified that Division will shortly move back into rest area. O.C. Train + S.S.O. go to reconnoitre new Refilling Points etc.	
	10.7.18		Arrangement for move completed. Move commences 12th inst. Division less R.A to be clear of this area by 14th inst. R.A by 16th inst. Relieved	

Army Form C. 2118.

Instructions regarding War Diaries and Intelligence Summaries are contained in F. S. Regs., Part II. and the Staff Manual respectively. Title pages will be prepared in manuscript.

WAR DIARY
or
INTELLIGENCE SUMMARY.
(Erase heading not required.)

Place	Date	Hour	Summary of Events and Information	Remarks and references to Appendices
MOLLIENS-au-BOIS	10.7.18		by 47th Division. Division to move back to CAVILLON area, where it will be in G.H.Q. Reserve.	
"	11.7.18		notified that 54th Bde move back into G.H.Q Reserve on 12th inst instead of 14th inst, as had been expected. Supply arrangements adjusted accordingly.	
"	12.7.18		54th Bde move back to BOVELLES area + 53rd Bde move back to PICQUIGNY area 152 Coy at BOVELLES, 151 Coy at BREILLY. Bde 1st Line Transports march under command of ~~OC~~ respective O.C. Coys. Field Ambulances march independently in rear.	
"	13.7.18		Div Hd Qrs + Train H.Q. move back to CAVILLON, + 55th Bde to BRIQUEMESNIL. Bde 1st Line Transport marches under orders of O.C. 152 Coy ASC. ~~55~~ 55th Field Ambulance marches independently in rear. From 10 AM Division in G.H.Q Reserve at 9 hours notice.	
CAVILLON	14.7.18		150 Coy move back to St SAUVEUR. Supplies for Division drawn from AILLY by M.T.	
"	15.7.18		Supplies for whole Division drawn from AILLY by H.T.	
	16.7.18		O.C. Train inspected 53rd Bde 1st Line Transport.	
	17.7.18			
	18.7.18		O.C. Train inspected 1st Line Transport of 55th Bde + Sussex Pioneers.	
	19.7.18		O.C. Train inspected 1st Line Transport of 54th Bde.	
	20.7.18			
	21.7.18			
	22.7.18			
	23.7.18			

A7092 Wt. W128 9/M1293 750,000. 1/17. D. D & L. Ltd. Forms/C2118/14.

Instructions regarding War Diaries and Intelligence Summaries are contained in F. S. Regs., Part II. and the Staff Manual respectively. Title pages will be prepared in manuscript.

WAR DIARY
or
INTELLIGENCE SUMMARY.
(Erase heading not required.)

Army Form C. 2118.

Place	Date	Hour	Summary of Events and Information	Remarks and references to Appendices
CAVILLON	24.7.18		O.C. Train inspected Transport of 18th R.S. Battalion & of 54th Field Ambl.	
	25.7.18		Divisional Steeplechase meeting, attended by Sir Douglas Haigh & others – a great success. Men's Totalisator run by the Train, & a substantial balance obtained to be devoted to Charity.	
	26.7.18		Train Sports. Large attendance, & went off well.	
	27.7.18		O.C. Train inspected 55th & 56th Field Ambulances.	
	28.7.18		R A Horse Show. 150 Coy & 152 Coy got 1st & 3rd prizes respectively in the "Best turned out G.S waggon H.D" competition. 150 Coy got 2nd prize in the best turned out G.S Limber (C.–T.). 152 Coy won first prize for best pair of H.D horses.	
	29.7.18		18th Div commences to relieve 5th Australian Division in the line from the SOMME to 62D/K.1.d.6.3. Relief (less RA) to be completed by Dawn August 1st. 18th Div Arty & 50th Div Arty relieve 4th & 5th Australian Div Artys under orders of G.O.C. R.A. 3rd Corps. Relief to be complete by 10 AM. Aug 3rd. 54th Bde move by bus to forward area. Debussing point 62D/I.7 central. Transport moves Brigaded under orders of O.C. 152 Coy to the following destinations. 1st Line Transport. C.20, 2.1. 152 Coy ASC. H.11.C.	
	30.7.18		55th Bde moves forward, Personnel by bus. Transport by road under orders of O.C. 153 Coy. Destination of 1st Line Transport C.25.c. 153 Coy ASC. 62D/H.11.C.	

A7092 Wt. W128 9/M1293 750,000. 1/17. D. D & I. Ltd. Forms/C2118/14.

Instructions regarding War Diaries and Intelligence Summaries are contained in F. S. Regs., Part II. and the Staff Manual respectively. Title pages will be prepared in manuscript.

WAR DIARY
or
INTELLIGENCE SUMMARY.
(Erase heading not required.)

Army Form C. 2118.

Place	Date	Hour	Summary of Events and Information	Remarks and references to Appendices
QAVILLON	31.7.18		53rd Bde moves forward. Personnel by buss. Transport by road under orders of O.C. 151 Coy ASC. Destination of 1st Line Transport. 151 Coy ASC.	
			Supplies for whole division less ~~S~~ DAC (moving forward on 2nd inst) drawn from POULAINVILLE Railhead by Decauville & delivered to Refilling Points at QUERRIEU.	
			150 Coy move forward from St SAUVEUR to bivouacs near QUERRIEU.	
			E. R. M. Morton Capt ASC. 18th Div Train	

A7092 Wt. W125 9/M1293 750,000. 1/17. D. D & L. Ltd. Forms/C2118/14.

Instructions regarding War Diaries and Intelligence Summaries are contained in F. S. Regs., Part II. and the Staff Manual respectively. Title pages will be prepared in manuscript.

WAR DIARY
or
INTELLIGENCE SUMMARY.
(*Erase heading not required.*)

Army Form C. 2118.

18th Divisional Train A.S.C.

Vol 38

Vol:- 38.

Place	Date	Hour	Summary of Events and Information	Remarks and references to Appendices
QUERRIEU	1.8.18		Div HQ moved to St GRATIEN. Train HQ to QUERRIEU. RA less DAC moved from rest area ARGOEUVES – St-SAUVEUR to HEILLY area	
"	2.8.18		RA HQ St-GRATIEN. DAC move forward from ARGOEUVES area to 62D/B.29.b.2.4.	
	3.8.18		20 waggons for R.E work, found by Train. T1/3720 Sgt SANDERS. 153 Coy drowned.	
	4.8.18		– Normal	
	5.8.18		– Normal	
	6.8.18		Busy filling petrol tins with drinking water	
St-GRATIEN	7.8.18		Train HQ move to St GRATIEN	
"	8.8.18		Battle commences. Up to date 2365 petrol tins filled with water & delivered to supply tanks & dumps in forward area. Stoppers for 800 of these tins made by Train whalers.	
	9.8.18		Further 500 Petrol tins (filled) delivered to BOMB STORE forward.	
	10.8.18		54th Bde move to CONTAY area	
	11.8.18		53rd + 55th Bdes move to CONTAY area. 151, 152 + 153 Coys move to ROSSIGNOL wood.	
	12.8.18		Division HQ move to CONTAY.	
	13.8.18		Normal.	

A7092 Wt. W125 9/M1293 750,000. 1/17. D. D & L. Ltd. Forms/C2118/14.

Instructions regarding War Diaries and Intelligence Summaries are contained in F. S. Regs., Part II. and the Staff Manual respectively. Title pages will be prepared in manuscript.

WAR DIARY
or
INTELLIGENCE SUMMARY.
(Erase heading not required.)

Army Form C. 2118.

Place	Date	Hour	Summary of Events and Information	Remarks and references to Appendices
~~14.8.18~~ CONTAY	14.8.18		Supply section of 150 Coy moved from QUERRIEU to new Camp at 57D/T.29.b.2.3. 151 Coy. 152 Coy + 153 Coy move to adjacent camps.	
"	15.8.18		Remainder of 150 Coy joined supply section in new Camp.	
"	16.8.18		Supplies less RA, are drawn from CONTAY SOUTH DECAUVILLE SIDING by 1st Line Transport. RA supplies delivered by Train waggons as usual.	
	17.8.18		Many waggons detailed for R.E + road work. Average detail 30 waggons	
	18.8.18		T3/022488 Dr PHILLIPS R.J. 151 Coy awarded 'Meritorious Service Medal' by 3rd Corps Commander for saving a comrade from drowning on 18.7.18. Auth 3rd Corps R.O. No 506 d. 13.8.18.	
	19.8.18		Many waggons still employed on RE + road work, with consequent deterioration + disintegration ~~of waggons~~. ~~The~~ Several supply waggons having been filled with tarred stones are temporarily hors de combat for carrying supplies. Effective protest lodged by O.C. Train.	

A7092 Wt. W128.9/M1293 750,000. 1/17. D. D & I. Ltd. Forms/C2118/14.

Army Form C. 2118.

Instructions regarding War Diaries and Intelligence Summaries are contained in F. S. Regs., Part II. and the Staff Manual respectively. Title pages will be prepared in manuscript.

WAR DIARY
or
INTELLIGENCE SUMMARY.
(Erase heading not required.)

Place	Date	Hour	Summary of Events and Information	Remarks and references to Appendices
CONTAY.	20.8.18		12 waggon loads of Salvage cleared from forward area	
"	21.8.18		Supply arrangements for Div attack tomorrow, completed.	
"	22.8.18		Extra issue of Rum to 54th Bde. Batmen from Train assist M.M.P in collection of prisoners in forward area. Com	
"	23.8.18		Extra Rum issue to 54th Bde. 3rd issue in 4 days to this Bde. 150 Coy move to ~~[illegible]~~ MERICOURT.	
"	24.8.18		151, 152 + 153 Coys move forward to new camps near HEILLY	
RIBEMONT	25.8.18		Train HQ moves to RIBEMONT.	
"	26.8.18		Supply Railhead changes to MERICOURT L'ABBE. Coys move to new camps at 62D/D.30.central.	
	27.8.18		Normal	
	28.8.18		Railhead moves forward to ~~DERNANCOURT~~ EDGE HILL. Refilling points moved from RIBEMONT SUCRERIE to EDGE HILL (near DERNANCOURT).	
	29.8.18		Normal	
	30.8.18		Normal	
	31.8.18		Train + all 4 Refilling points move to X.29.d.5.4. near (MAMETZ) Supplies from 31st inclusive drawn from EDGE HILL Railhead by M.T.	

E.R.M. Morton Captain & ADJT.
for O.C., 18TH DIVISIONAL TRAIN.

A7092 Wt. W125 9/M1293 750,000. 1/17. D. D & I. Ltd. Forms/C2118/14.

Sub. [illegible]:- War Diary.

Confidential.

Head Quarters, "A".
18th Division.

I beg to forward, herewith, War Diary, Vol:39 for month ending 30th Septr last, for the Unit under my Command. Kindly acknowledge receipt.

L. M. Newell
Major,
for O.C.; 18th Divisional Train.

7/10/1918.

Instructions regarding War Diaries and Intelligence Summaries are contained in F. S. Regs., Part II. and the Staff Manual respectively. Title pages will be prepared in manuscript.

WAR DIARY
or
INTELLIGENCE SUMMARY.
(Erase heading not required.)

Army Form C. 2118.

VOL:- 39

Vol. 40

Place	Date	Hour	Summary of Events and Information	Remarks and references to Appendices
ALBERT combined 62 sheet X.29.d. central	1.9.18			
	2.9.18		Train moved to new camp at S.23 Albert combined sheet.	
	3.9.18			
	4.9.18			
	5.9.18			
	6.9.18			
	7.9.18			
	8.9.18		-Railhead changed from ALBERT to TRONES WOOD -150 Co. ASC move to new camp at S 6 d. 7 8 ALBERT combined sheet.	
	9.9.18			
	10.9.18			
	11.9.18			
	12.9.18			
	13.9.18			
	14.9.18			
	15.9.18		150 Co A.S.C. move to new camp at C 24 a Sh 62 c	
MOBLAINS	16.9.18		H.Q. Train and 151 152 & 153 Co. move to C 24 a Sh 62 c at 3 a.m. storm of cyclonic violence. All tents and shelters blown down. Many office records destroyed by rain or blown away by gale.	

Instructions regarding War Diaries and Intelligence Summaries are contained in F. S. Regs., Part II. and the Staff Manual respectively. Title pages will be prepared in manuscript.

WAR DIARY
or
INTELLIGENCE SUMMARY.
(Erase heading not required.)

Army Form C. 2118.

Place	Date	Hour	Summary of Events and Information	Remarks and references to Appendices
MOSLAINS	17.9.18			
	18.9.18			
	19.9.18			
	20.9.18			
	21.9.18			
	22.9.18			
	23.9.18			
	24.9.18			
	25.9.18		Train HQ. DHQ 53rd & 55th Bdes move to Combles. RA & 54th Bde remain in forward area. Supply Railhead changed to LE PLATEAU.	
	26.9.18			
	27.9.18			
	28.9.18		Train HQ moved to LIERAMONT. 151 & 153 Coy to 62c/D.14.d. Supply Railhead changes to QUINCONCE. All 4 Refilling Points moved forward to 62c/D.9.d.	
	29.9.18			
	30.9.18			

L.M. Newell LT. COL.
COMDG 18TH DIVISIONAL TRAIN.

A7092 Wt. W128.9/M1293 750,000. 1/17. D. D & L. Ltd. Forms/C2118/14.

Instructions regarding War Diaries and Intelligence Summaries are contained in F. S. Regs., Part II. and the Staff Manual respectively. Title pages will be prepared in manuscript.

WAR DIARY
or
INTELLIGENCE SUMMARY.
(*Erase heading not required.*)

Army Form C. 2118.

Vol:- 40

Place	Date	Hour	Summary of Events and Information	Remarks and references to Appendices
MONTIGNY.	1.10.18		Division move out of line + go back to following areas. Div HQ BEAUCOURT 53rd Bde. ALLONVILLE. 54th Bde. MOLLIENS-au-BOIS. 55th Bde. CONTAY. Infantry travel back by bus in one day. Transport travel by road taking 2 days over the move.	
	2.10.18			
	3.10.18		Railhead changes to POULAINVILLE. Supplies for 54th + 55th Bde drawn from R'head by MT 53rd Bde by H.T.	
	4.10.18			
	5.10.18			
	6.10.18.			
	7.10.18		150 Coy moved forwards to VILLERS FAUCON.	
	8.10.18		Sussex Pioneers move forward to relieve American Pioneers. Men by bus. Transport by road. Transferred to Corps Troops. S. Column for feeding consumption 11th inst + onwards.	
	9.10.18		150 Coy moved forward to LE CATELET.	
	10.10.18		150 Coy move forward to ~~ST~~ ELINCOURT.	
	11.10.18			
	12.10.18		54th Bde supplies drawn from Railhead by H.T. 1st Line Transport of that group draw from Refilling Point.	
	13.10.18.			

A7092 Wt. W128 9/M1293 750,000. 1/17. D. D & L. Ltd. Forms/C2118/14.

Instructions regarding War Diaries and Intelligence Summaries are contained in F. S. Regs., Part II. and the Staff Manual respectively. Title pages will be prepared in manuscript.

WAR DIARY
or
INTELLIGENCE SUMMARY.
(Erase heading not required.)

18TH DIVISIONAL TRAIN No.......... Date.......... A. S. C.

Army Form C. 2118.

Place	Date	Hour	Summary of Events and Information	Remarks and references to Appendices
MONTIGNY	14.10.18			
"	15.10.18			
"	16.10.18		orders received for Division (less RA) to move up to NURLU area on 17th inst. M.G. Battalion move up by buss today. Div Transport moves by train (tactical) night 16th/17th at MARETZ. Move taking place at 4 hours notice entailed long + tiring marches for HQT. today + stages	
RONSSOY WOOD	17.10.18		Div + T HQ move to RONSSOY WOOD.	
"	18.10.18		151 + 152 Coys move up to GOUY. 153 Coy to RONSSOY wood. Supply R'head changes to EPEHY.	
SERAIN	19.10.18		Div HQ + THQ move to SERAIN. 3 Bde Coys to 57B/U.10.a.3.5.	
MARETZ	20.10.18		Div HQ + T.HQ move to MARETZ. RA rejoin Div for Railhead drawing 20th inst.	
	21.10.18			
	22.10.18		Broad guage R'head changes to BELLICOURT. Thence supplies taken to BOHAIN by Light Railway + delivered to Supply dumps at ELINCOURT + U.10.a. by M.T.	
LE CATEAU.	23.10.18		Division + Train (Coys included) move to LE CATEAU. All 4 dumps on CAMBRAI LE CATEAU Rd at 57B/K.32.b.9.8	
	24.10.18		Coys move to another part of the Town & Supply dumps are moved to K.34.c. central. Train is instructed by Division to take over enemy fuel (Coal, coke charcoal + wood.) Immense quantities	

A7092 Wt. W12819/M1293 750,000. 1/17. D. D & L. Ltd. Forms/C2118/14.

Instructions regarding War Diaries and Intelligence Summaries are contained in F. S. Regs., Part II. and the Staff Manual respectively. Title pages will be prepared in manuscript.

WAR DIARY
or
INTELLIGENCE SUMMARY.
(Erase heading not required.)

18TH DIVISIONAL TRAIN
No.............
Date.............
A. S. C.

Army Form C. 2118.

Place	Date	Hour	Summary of Events and Information	Remarks and references to Appendices
LE CATEAU	24.10.18		left behind by enemy. also a quantity of maize flour.	
"	25.10.18		Large enemy straw dump found in Town & taken over by Train arrangements made to deliver direct to units + to underdraw from R'head.	
	26.10.18		Large quantity of flour found in a mill in the town. Machinery practically intact. Guard found by 10th R.G. Coy	
	27.10.18		Shelling of LE CATEAU resumed.	
	28.10.18		Continued shelling of LE CATEAU.	
	29.10.18		Supply Railhead changes to BOHAIN. supplies continue to be drawn from R'head by M.T.	
	30.10.18		Personnel R'head changes to BUSIGNY	
	31.10.18		Train 8 hours late. Supply Convoy kept waiting whole day at Railhead.	

E. R. R. Roskin [signature] Captain & Adjt.
for LT. COL.
COMDG 18TH DIVISIONAL TRAIN.

D. D. & L., London, E.C.
(A800.) Wt. W1771/M2031 750,000 5/17 Sch. 52 Forms C2118/14

Instructions regarding War Diaries and Intelligence Summaries are contained in F. S. Regs., Part II. and the Staff Manual respectively. Title pages will be prepared in manuscript.

WAR DIARY
or
INTELLIGENCE SUMMARY.
(Erase heading not required.)

Army Form C. 2118.

VOL:- 41

41

Place	Date	Hour	Summary of Events and Information	Remarks and references to Appendices
LE CATEAU	1.11.18.		Supply Train again late Train Transport waited at Railhead from 9AM till arrival of train at 10PM.	
	~~1.11.18~~			
	2.11.18		no supply Train arrived.	
	3.11.18		Supply Train with rations for consumption 4th arrived at BUSIGNY R'head at 5PM. M.T to deliver to Refilling Points. 1st Line Transport drawing from R.P to save time.	
	4.11.18		Train again late Bridge blown up between BUSIGNY & BOHAIN. One days complete reserve rations delivered to R.P by Corps	
	5.11.18			
	6.11.18			
	7.11.18			
	8.11.18		2 days supplies delivered to dumps.	
	9.11.18		normal	
	10.11.18			
	11.11.18		Hostilities cease; otherwise normal.	
	12.11.18			
SERAIN	13.11.18		Train & Division move back to SERAIN area.	
	14.11.18			

D. D. & L., London, E.C. (A8001) Wt. W1771/M2031 750,000 5/17 Sch. 52 Forms C2118/14

Instructions regarding War Diaries and Intelligence Summaries are contained in F. S. Regs., Part II. and the Staff Manual respectively. Title pages will be prepared in manuscript.

WAR DIARY
or
INTELLIGENCE SUMMARY.
(Erase heading not required.)

Army Form C. 2118.

Place	Date	Hour	Summary of Events and Information	Remarks and references to Appendices
SERAIN	15.11.18		Salvage work	
	16.11.18		..	
	17.11.18		..	
	18.11.18		..	
	19.11.18		..	
	20.11.18		..	
	21.11.18		..	
	22.11.18			
	23.11.18		..	
	24.11.18			
	25.11.18		..	
	26.11.18		..	
	27.11.18		..	
	28.11.18		..	
	29.11.18		..	
	30.11.18		..	

E.R.M. Morton Captain & Adjt.
for LT. COL.
COMDG 18TH DIVISIONAL TRAIN.

D. D. & L., London, E.C.
(A8001) Wt. W1771/M2031 750,000 5/17 Sch. 52 Forms C2118/14

Confidential.

Subject:- War Diary

18TH DIVISIONAL TRAIN
No. DT/0101
Date.............
A. S. C.

Head Quarters "A"
18th Division

I beg to forward herewith original Diary (Vol:-42) for month of December 1918, for Unit under my Command.

E R K Rowbin
Captain & Adjt.
for OC.; 18th DIV: TRAIN

10-1-1919

Instructions regarding War Diaries and Intelligence Summaries are contained in F. S. Regs., Part II. and the Staff Manual respectively. Title pages will be prepared in manuscript.

WAR DIARY
or
INTELLIGENCE SUMMARY.
(Erase heading not required.)

18 D Train

Army Form C. 2118.

VOL: NO:- 42

V8 42

Place	Date	Hour	Summary of Events and Information	Remarks and references to Appendices
SERAIN	1.12.18		Normal.	
"	2.12.18		Divisional Review by G.O.C Div. went off very well.	
"	3.12.18			
"	4.12.18		SERAIN visited by H.M. the King during his tour of 3rd Army area.	
"	5.12.18			
	6.12.18			
"	7.12.18		Supply R'head changes to CAUDRY	
"	8.12.18		~~Do~~ RA & 55th Inf Bde groups draw from R'head by H.T. Supplies ~~delivd~~ delivered from R.P. by baggage waggons in the case of R.A, & by 1st Line Transport in the case of 55th Bde.	
	9.12.18			
	10.12.18		150 Coy move to CAUDRY. R.P. at CAUDRY	
	11.12.18			
	12.12.18		152 Coy move to CAULLERY. R.P also there	
	13.12.18			
	14.12.18			
	15.12.18			
	16.12.18			
LIGNY	17.12.18		Div HQ + Train HQ move to LIGNY-en-CAMBRESIS.	
"	18.12.18			
"	19.12.18			
"	20.12.18			
"	21.12.18		~~152 Coy RASC move from PREMONT to SERAIN.~~	

A7092 Wt. W123 9/M1293 750,000. 1/17. D. D & I. Ltd. Forms/C2118/14.

Instructions regarding War Diaries and Intelligence Summaries are contained in F. S. Regs., Part II. and the Staff Manual respectively. Title pages will be prepared in manuscript.

WAR DIARY
or
INTELLIGENCE SUMMARY.
(Erase heading not required.)

Army Form C. 2118.

Place	Date	Hour	Summary of Events and Information	Remarks and references to Appendices
LIGNY.	22.12.18.		151 Coy RASC move from PREMONT to SERAIN	
"	23.12.18			
"	24.12.18			
"	25.12.18			
"	26.12.18			
"	27.12.18			
"	28.12.18			
"	29.12.18			
"	30.12.18			
"	31.12.18			

E.R.M. Morton Capt.
ADJT.
[illegible]TH DIVISIONAL TRAIN.

A7092 Wt. W128 9/M1293 750,000. 1/17. D. D & L. Ltd. Forms/C2118/14.

Instructions regarding War Diaries and Intelligence Summaries are contained in F. S. Regs., Part II. and the Staff Manual respectively. Title pages will be prepared in manuscript.

WAR DIARY
or
INTELLIGENCE SUMMARY.
(Erase heading not required.)

14/

Vol 43

Army Form C. 2118.

Place	Date	Hour	Summary of Events and Information	Remarks and references to Appendices
Field.	1.1.19			
	18.1.19		153 Coy moved to AUDENCOURT	
	27.1.19		151 Coy moved to CLARY.	

E.R.M. Morton Capt.
for LT. COL
COMDG 18TH DIVISIONAL TRAIN.

Instructions regarding War Diaries and Intelligence Summaries are contained in F. S. Regs., Part II. and the Staff Manual respectively. Title pages will be prepared in manuscript.

WAR DIARY
or
INTELLIGENCE SUMMARY.
(Erase heading not required.)

Army Form C. 2118.

(VOL:- 44)

VOL 44

Place	Date	Hour	Summary of Events and Information	Remarks and references to Appendices
			18th Divisional Train R.A.S.C.	
Ligny en Cambresis	1 2/19			
	2nd			
	3rd			
	4th			
	5th			
	6th			
	7th			
	8th			
	9th			
	10th			
	11th			
	12th			
	13th			
	14th			
	15th			
	16th			
	17th			
	18th		OC. Train (Lt Col. R R B. Jackson. D.S.O.) left to assume Command of 2nd Div: Train	
	19th			
	20th			
	21st			
	22nd			
	23rd			
	24th			
	25th			
	26th			
	27th			
	28th			

E. W. Best.
Captain ~~LT. COL.~~
COMDG 18TH DIVISIONAL TRAIN.

A7092 Wt. W128 9/M1293 750,000. 1/17. D. D & L. Ltd. Forms/C2118/14.

Subject:- War Diaries.

18th DIVISIONAL TRAIN.
No DT29 8/5/19.

Head Quarters. "A".
18th Divis-ion.

I beg to forward herewith War Diary, Vol.46, for the month of April last, for the Unit under my Command, receipt of which kindly acknowledge hereon.

8th May 1919.

C W Walker
Major.
Commanding, 18th Divisional Train.

HEAD QUARTERS
No
8 MAY 1919
18th DIVISION

Instructions regarding War Diaries and Intelligence Summaries are contained in F. S. Regs., Part II. and the Staff Manual respectively. Title pages will be prepared in manuscript.

WAR DIARY
or
INTELLIGENCE SUMMARY.
(Erase heading not required.)

18TH DIVISIONAL TRAIN
No. DT.29.
Date 8.9.19.
A. S. C.

Army Form C. 2118.

VOL:-46.

Vol 46

Place	Date	Hour	Summary of Events and Information	Remarks and references to Appendices
Ligny en Cambresis	1 11/19			
	2 "			
	3 "			
	4 "			
	5 "			
	6 "			
	7 "			
	8 "			
	9 "			
	10 "			
	11 "			
	12 "			
	13 "		— Nil —	
	14 "			
	15 "			
	16 "			
	17 "			
	18 "			
	19 "			
	20 "			
	21 "			
	22 "			
	23 "			
	24 "			
	25 "			
	26 "			
	27 "			
	28 "			
	29 "			
	30 "			

Major.
COMDG 18TH DIVISIONAL TRAIN.

(3)

WO 95/2032

18 Division
Divisional Troops.

Divisional Salvage Company

Jul 1916 - June 1917

18TH DIVISION

SALVAGE COY.

JLY 1916-JUN 1917

WAR DIARY

SALVAGE COY

War Diary

18th Div. Salvage Coy

Jly '16
June '17

Instructions regarding War Diaries and Intelligence Summaries are contained in F. S. Regs., Part II. and the Staff Manual respectively. Title Pages will be prepared in manuscript.

WAR DIARY
or
INTELLIGENCE SUMMARY
(Erase heading not required.)

18
Salvage Coy. Vol 1.

Army Form C. 2118

July

Place	Date	Hour	Summary of Events and Information	Remarks and references to Appendices
Etinehem	1/7/16		Salvage & Convalescent Co. moved to Sapper's Corner, Grovetown, under bivouacs. Sent party to dressing station (main) to collect helmets etc.	
Grovetown & Carnoy	2/7/16		Reported to 55th Bde HQ at Billon Wood & received orders to report to Capt Mitchell, Town Major at Carnoy. At 7.30 PM moved up to battlefield under Revd [illegible] Mather, to bury dead, which were collected at craters, searched, & then buried in craters & large shell holes. Men available not sufficient for job so applied to DHQ for reinforcements. One man shut down with shell shock. Worked until dark. Many unauthorised men were observed searching battlefield (for souvenirs) including French gunners. This also reported to DHQ.	
Carnoy	3/7/16		Started at 4 AM & continued burying. Sent out party to search for machine guns & drums. Reinforcements arrived from HQ platoon, 13 men. Collection of bodies difficult, being hampered by barbed wire, shell holes & trenches. Owing to urgency of getting bodies buried, as decomposition in some cases had set in, applied for more reinforcements, which arrived next day.	
Carnoy	4/7/16		Officer of 11th R.F. reported, to superintend 54th Bde area.	
Carnoy	5/7/16		Cavalry & cyclists took over work of burying, & Salvage Co. started salving. One dump was formed for each Bde. area. Received orders from Corps to collect rifles quickly, owing to change in weather expected.	

1875 Wt. W593/826 1,000,000 4/15 J.B.C. & A. A.D.S.S./Forms/C. 2118.

Instructions regarding War Diaries and Intelligence Summaries are contained in F. S. Regs., Part II. and the Staff Manual respectively. Title Pages will be prepared in manuscript.

WAR DIARY
or
INTELLIGENCE SUMMARY
(Erase heading not required.)

Army Form C. 2118

Place	Date	Hour	Summary of Events and Information	Remarks and references to Appendices
Carnoy	6/7/16		Formed dump at Granetown to receive salvage from trenches, & arranged for lorries to take it to D.A.D.O.S. & railhead.	
Carnoy	7/7/16		Sergeant Burn & Private Catt wounded by shrapnel searching for 60 lb. [illegible] in valley. Sgt Burn evacuated. Four G.S. waggons were attached, & utilised for carting from forward area to dump at Granetown. Very slow work, owing to amount of traffic, & bad state of roads.	
Carnoy	7/7/16 to 11/7/16		Continued with collection & disposal of salvage. Found various buried dumps of stores & ammunition, & dug out as much as possible. All serviceable rations & boxes of ammunition collected in dumps & placed in accessible positions on Montauban Road for transmission forward. Received plan of machine gun emplacements & signal dugouts from 55th Bde. These were well searched, but most of the stores must have been buried & destroyed, as only one machine gun was salved, in a damaged condition, & two West Spring Guns. Collected as much as possible, & were relieved on 10th July by 3rd Div. Salvage Coy. Moved to Granetown on 11th.	
Granetown	13/7/16		24 men of Convalescent Co. sent to Divisional School, in place of Band who joined Salvage Co.	

1875 Wt. W593/826 1,000,000 4/15 J.B.C. & A. A.D.S.S./Forms/C. 2118.

Instructions regarding War Diaries and Intelligence Summaries are contained in F. S. Regs., Part II. and the Staff Manual respectively. Title Pages will be prepared in manuscript.

WAR DIARY
or
INTELLIGENCE SUMMARY
(Erase heading not required.)

Army Form C. 2118

Place	Date	Hour	Summary of Events and Information	Remarks and references to Appendices
Grovetown	13/7/16 to 19/7/16		Men employed on sorting salvage, cleaning rifles & machine gun drums etc & loading on lorries. Large quantities of stores were issued to various units as replacements & exchanges, especially machine gun drums, steel helmets & equipment. About three thousand rifles & bayonets were salved, but many of these had been rendered unserviceable by shell fire. Besides large quantity of stores issued to units, 12 lorry loads were despatched to Railhead & D.A.D.O.S. On 16th party proceeded to Maricourt under Capt. Golding Sanitary Section to bury mules. Four men were wounded & one evacuated. Parties were sent out every day to different areas, & brought in large amount of ammunition etc.	
Grovetown	20/7/16 to 24/7/16		Marched to Meaulte, unloaded shell train, & entrained for Pont St. Remy. Marched to billets at Hallencourt.	
Hallencourt Renescure	24/7/16 to 31/7/16		Marched to Pont St Remy & entrained for Renescure. Sent parties to Bde areas, but very little salvage was found.	

Lieut
O.C. Salvage Convalescent Coy.

1875 Wt. W593/826 1,000,000 4/15 J.B.C. & A. A.D.S.S./Forms/C. 2118.

War Diary of Salvage Co: 18 Division

Instructions regarding War Diaries and Intelligence Summaries are contained in F. S. Regs., Part II. and the Staff Manual respectively. Title Pages will be prepared in manuscript.

WAR DIARY
or
INTELLIGENCE SUMMARY
(Erase heading not required.)

'Army Form C. 2118

Place	Date	Hour	Summary of Events and Information	Remarks and references to Appendices

1875 Wt. W593/826 1,000,000 4/15 J.B.C. & A. A.D.S.S./Forms/C. 2118.

War Diary August

Salvage Coy 18 Division

Instructions regarding War Diaries and Intelligence Summaries are contained in F. S. Regs., Part II. and the Staff Manual respectively. Title Pages will be prepared in manuscript.

WAR DIARY
or
~~INTELLIGENCE SUMMARY~~
(Erase heading not required.)

Salvage Coy 18 Division — Army Form C. 2118

18 Vol 2

Place	Date	Hour	Summary of Events and Information	Remarks and references to Appendices
	7/8/16		Left Rincoure, entrained to Steenwerck Station, & marched to billets at Croix du Bac. Men had good billets in large grain shed.	
	8/8/16		Sent party to Estaires to 53rd Bde billets Found large number of 4.5 shell boxes at Croix du Bac	
	9/8/16		Salved 41 slightly damaged G.S. wheels & despatched to Railhead.	
	10/8/16		Found 15,000 rounds of S.A.A. in billet vacated by Australians	
	11/8/16		Found 44,000 rounds of S.A.A. in billet at Erquinghem, apparently part of a discarded dump.	
	12/8/16		Despatched large amount of stores to Railhead. Sent party to Le Petit Mortier, to billets vacated by Norfolks.	
	17/8/16		Found 12,000 rounds of S.A.A. in Erquinghem & district near	
	19/8/16		Despatched stores to Railhead.	
	24/8/16		Received 45000 rounds S.A.A. from Buffs, & sent them to D.A.C. Despatched stores to Railhead	

1875 Wt. W593/826 1,000,000 4/15 J.B.C. & A. A.D.S.S./Forms/C. 2118.

Instructions regarding War Diaries and Intelligence Summaries are contained in F. S. Regs., Part II. and the Staff Manual respectively. Title Pages will be prepared in manuscript.

WAR DIARY
or
INTELLIGENCE SUMMARY
(Erase heading not required.)

Army Form C. 2118

Place	Date	Hour	Summary of Events and Information	Remarks and references to Appendices
	23/8/16		Despatched Stores Railhead	
	24/8/16		Moved from [illegible] Bois de Buillens [illegible]	
	25/8/16		Entrained for [illegible] Station, arrived at 1.45 A.M., unloaded train, & arrived at Rollencourt at 6.30 A.M.	
	27/8/16		Sent party to St Pol [illegible]	

[illegible] Lieut
O.C. 18th Division Salvage Coy.

1875 Wt. W593/826 1,000,000 4/15 J.B.C. & A. A.D.S.S./Forms/C. 2118.

1916

OCTOBER.

WAR DIARY.

SALVAGE COY.

Instructions regarding War Diaries and Intelligence Summaries are contained in F. S. Regs., Part II. and the Staff Manual respectively. Title Pages will be prepared in manuscript.

WAR DIARY
or
INTELLIGENCE SUMMARY
(Erase heading not required.)

October 1916

Salvage Coy
18th Division

Vol 4

Army Form C. 2118

Place	Date	Hour	Summary of Events and Information	Remarks and references to Appendices
	OCTOBER			
PIONEER ROAD	1.		Main Dump HEDAUVILLE in charge of 1 L/C. & 10 men. Remainder of Coy billeted in PIONEER ROAD.	
	2		Attached to Sussex Pioneers clearing dugouts in THIEPVAL & dumping. Shelled for 3 hours.	
	3.		6th & 7th Cavalry Brigade reported for dumping & salvage. Formed dump at WOOD POST	
	4		Salved from THIEPVAL 2 Snipers Rifles, 3 Minenwerfers 4 M Gs, 1 Trench Mortar. Found Flammenwerfer but could not move it, as dugout had been built round it.	
	5		Taken off dumping. Relieved by Cavalry.	
	6.		Found 1 Bosch M/G & 1 Automatic Rifle in Chatham. Cavalry buried 144 British & 43 German	

Instructions regarding War Diaries and Intelligence Summaries are contained in F. S. Regs., Part II. and the Staff Manual respectively. Title Pages will be prepared in manuscript.

WAR DIARY
or
INTELLIGENCE SUMMARY
(Erase heading not required.)

Army Form C. 2118

Place	Date	Hour	Summary of Events and Information	Remarks and references to Appendices
	7.		Cavalry reported area S of THIEPVAL cleared of dead. Large amount of Salvage brought to TRAMWAY CORNER	
	8.		4 men from 53rd Bde attached to Coy	
	9.		Cavalry reported 725 British & 182 Germans buried to date.	
	10.		84 British & 45 German buried. Large quantity salvage sent in. German bombs sent by lorry to D.H.Q.	
	11.		1 M.G. 250 short rifles & 2 Stokes salved. Cavalry reported heavy shell fire prevented work.	
	12		130 Rifles 50 boxes Mills 64 M.G. drums salved. 4 British 9 German buried	

1875 Wt. W593/826 1,000,000 4/15 J.B.C. & A. A.D.S.S./Forms/C. 2118.

Army Form C. 2118

Instructions regarding War Diaries and Intelligence Summaries are contained in F. S. Regs., Part II. and the Staff Manual respectively. Title Pages will be prepared in manuscript.

WAR DIARY
or
INTELLIGENCE SUMMARY
(Erase heading not required.)

Place	Date	Hour	Summary of Events and Information	Remarks and references to Appendices
	13		6 men of 54 Bde ^ 55th Bde attached.	
	15		Cavalry reported area clear of dead.	
	16		194 boxes of Mills etc. salved.	
	17		2 German Canister throwers salved & sent to D.H.Q. 1100 shell cases 198 boxes Mills salved. Picks & shovels sent to R.E.	
	18		53 gas cylinders salved.	
ALBERT.	22		Moved to ALBERT.	
OVILLERS	25		Moved to OVILLERS	
	28 to 31.		Hut building at OVILLERS	

G B Clare[?] Lieut.
Salvage Coy 18th Divn[?]

1875 Wt. W593/826 1,000,000 4/15 J.B.C. & A. A.D.S.S./Forms/C. 2118.

War Diary

18th Div Salvage Coy

November 1916

Salvage Coy.

Army Form C. 2118

Vol 5

WAR DIARY
or
INTELLIGENCE SUMMARY
(Erase heading not required.)

Instructions regarding War Diaries and Intelligence Summaries are contained in F. S. Regs., Part II. and the Staff Manual respectively. Title Pages will be prepared in manuscript.

Place	Date	Hour	Summary of Events and Information	Remarks and references to Appendices
Albert	1/11/16		Party attached to Camp Commandant Tara Hill for fatigues	
do	2/11		Party detailed to take over Camp from Suffolks at Tara Hill. Men salving at Pozieres warned off by Artillery, as they were in view & drawing fire onto batteries	
do	3/11		Started collecting shell cases in Mash Valley. Collected German bombs for Corps	
do	4/11		Supplied large quantity of bully & biscuits to 55th Brigade for men in trenches	
do	6/11		Bombs dropped on ALBERT. Small damage	
do	8/11		Divisional School left for back area, & attached 10 men to Salvage Coy.	

Instructions regarding War Diaries and Intelligence Summaries are contained in F. S. Regs., Part II. and the Staff Manual respectively. Title Pages will be prepared in manuscript.

WAR DIARY
or
INTELLIGENCE SUMMARY
(Erase heading not required.)

Army Form C. 2118

Place	Date	Hour	Summary of Events and Information	Remarks and references to Appendices
ALBERT. 9/11/16			Party detailed as loading fatigue for R E material at AVELUY railhead etc (This party was shelled out 2 days after)	
			Eight shells dropped very near our marquee at the Quarry Ovillers. Enemy searching for our 8" hows.	
do	10/11		Gas shells dropped in Mash Valley. Gas got as far as Ovillers. Men used smoke helmets. Four R E casualties on Bapaume Road.	
			All available men attached to 92nd R.E. to level ground, fill in trenches, unload waggons etc at Ovillers where camp of 90 huts was started.	
do	11/11		All available men with R Es.	
do	12/11		Detailed 1 N.C.O. 3 men to run coffee stall, Red Cross Corner.	
			All men turned on to salvage	

Instructions regarding War Diaries and Intelligence Summaries are contained in F. S. Regs., Part II. and the Staff Manual respectively. Title Pages will be prepared in manuscript.

WAR DIARY
or
INTELLIGENCE SUMMARY
(Erase heading not required.)

Army Form C. 2118

Place	Date	Hour	Summary of Events and Information	Remarks and references to Appendices
ALBERT	12/11		Men salving in Mash Valley. All good shell cases cleared from large shell dump W of La Boiselle which had been blown up by shell. Mostly 13 pdr. cases. S.A.A. cases all destroyed.	
do	13/11		Aeroplane fired machine gun along Bapaume road in Albert. Afterwards dropped bombs near Railroad, Albert.	
do	14/11		Owing to urgency of completing dump, Ovillers, men attached to R.Es again.	
do	15/11		Red Cross Corner badly shelled with gas shells. Mules & horses gassed.	
do	16/11		Sent party of men back to the School	
do	19/11		Men turned on to salving again. Collected about 6000 shell cases	

Army Form C. 2118

Instructions regarding War Diaries and Intelligence Summaries are contained in F. S. Regs., Part II. and the Staff Manual respectively. Title Pages will be prepared in manuscript.

WAR DIARY
or
INTELLIGENCE SUMMARY
(Erase heading not required.)

Place	Date	Hour	Summary of Events and Information	Remarks and references to Appendices
ALBERT	20/11		Appointed Camp Commandant Ovillers Camp. Whole day duty. Started incinerator, & detailed party to clean up. Drafted out orders for sanitation etc, & had various sign boards made.	
do	21/11		Foggy day. Sent men salving E of Pozieres. At 10.15 AM received orders from A.A.&Q.M.G. to send all available men to report to Staff Captain 65th Brigade for burying. Found 32 after difficulty owing to parties being widely scattered. At 10.30 met Brigade Salvage Officers of 61st Div. Div Salvage Officer turned up 2 hours late. Took them over ground, handed over billets etc, & returned at 4 PM. Burying party returned about same time, having knocked off early owing to fog lifting & being under	

1875 Wt. W593/826 1,000,000 4/15 J.B.C. & A. A.D.S.S./Forms/C. 2118.

Instructions regarding War Diaries and Intelligence Summaries are contained in F. S. Regs., Part II. and the Staff Manual respectively. Title Pages will be prepared in manuscript.

WAR DIARY
or
INTELLIGENCE SUMMARY
(Erase heading not required.)

Army Form C. 2118

Place	Date	Hour	Summary of Events and Information	Remarks and references to Appendices
ALBERT	21/11 contd		Party were sniped the whole time. One man hit in leg.	
			Party attached to me from 35th Sanitary Section for transportation to back area.	
do	22/11		Orders to entrain at Acheux on 23rd. One lorry detailed. Not sufficient, as I had all Band instruments, cooking apparatus & blankets etc for 200 men. Searched Albert for transport, & borrowed lorry from Advanced Workshop. Sent as much baggage as possible to Railhead.	
do	23/11		Party from 35th Sanitary Section disappeared. Eventually found had gone on lorry. No notification caused lot of trouble. Sent one lorry load off with orders to return as soon as possible. Road blocked by Artillery for 5 miles. Lorry took 8 hours for	

1875 Wt. W593/826 1,000,000 4/15 J.B.C. & A. A.D.S.S./Forms/C. 2118.

Instructions regarding War Diaries and Intelligence Summaries are contained in F. S. Regs., Part II. and the Staff Manual respectively. Title Pages will be prepared in manuscript.

Army Form C. 2118

WAR DIARY
or
INTELLIGENCE SUMMARY
(Erase heading not required.)

Place	Date	Hour	Summary of Events and Information	Remarks and references to Appendices
ACHEUX			double journey, & missed train.	
	23/11/16		Lt Winton with men & left C.Sgt. to collect rest of baggage	
			Left Acheux 5.30 PM arrived Abbeville 6 AM. 24/11.	
ABBEVILLE	24/11		Arrived Abbeville, marched to Buigny	
BUIGNY	25/11		Went to station to wait for C.S.M. No sign of him. Phoned Acheux & found party had left.	
do	26/11		Found C.S.M. & baggage & got transport from A.H.T.D. Abbeville.	
			Sent parties to all Town Majors in Div. Area.	
do	28/11		Party from Corps Staff Red Cross Barn relieved & arrived 2 days after.	
do	30/11		Sent parties to 3 farms to assist in threshing.	

W. B. McClean Lieut.
O.C. 18th Div. Salvage & Conservancy

1875 Wt. W593/826 1,000,000 4/15 J.B.C. & A. A.D.S.S./Forms/C. 2118.

Salvage Coy

Instructions regarding War Diaries and Intelligence Summaries are contained in F. S. Regs., Part II. and the Staff Manual respectively. Title Pages will be prepared in manuscript.

18th Divn

WAR DIARY
or
INTELLIGENCE SUMMARY
(Erase heading not required.)

Salvage Coy 18 D

Army Form C. 2118

Vol 7

Place	Date	Hour	Summary of Events and Information	Remarks and references to Appendices
BUIGNY	3/1/17		Went to Havre to see Salvage Depot at GRAVILLE.	
HAVRE	4/1/17		Arrived HAVRE, reported to C.O.O. who sent guide to GRAVILLE. Had very interesting & instructive day, seeing the various processes through which salvage material passes.	
HAVRE	5/1/17		Went to Graville again.	
BUIGNY	7/1/17		Arrived back at BUIGNY	
do	9/1/17		Saw Colonel Wright V.C. D.S.O. & Capt Meartys. Took over Camp Commandant from Capt Neville A.D.C. who was joining 18th Corps with General Maxse. Went to BOUZINCOURT to have a look at Camp.	
MARIEUX	10/1/17		Went to MARIEUX & arranged billets for D.H.Q. Sent men to laundry at ABBEVILLE	

Instructions regarding War Diaries and Intelligence Summaries are contained in F. S. Regs., Part II. and the Staff Manual respectively. Title Pages will be prepared in manuscript.

WAR DIARY
or
INTELLIGENCE SUMMARY
(Erase heading not required.)

Army Form C. 2118

Place	Date	Hour	Summary of Events and Information	Remarks and references to Appendices
MARIEUX	11/1/17		D.H.Q. arrived MARIEUX, & turned in comfortably. Salvage Coy send 9 men to Div. School at ABBAYE, BUIGNY	
BOUZINCOURT	12/1/17		Went BOUZINCOURT arranged billets, & took over from C.C. 61st Div. Accomodation poor, men in tents.	
do	13/1/17		D.H.Q. arrived.	
AVELUY	14/1/17		Took over Salvage dumps at DONNET'S POST, AVELUY & TRAMWAY CORNER. Large amount of salvage left at each.	
do	18/1/17		Arranged dumps at HEDAUVILLE, MARTINSART, VARENNES. & attached men for rations to Town Majors.	
do	19/1/17		1 G.S. limber attached from D.H.Q.	
do	25/1/17		2/Lt. Rendle 11 R.F. & 2/Lt. Hewlett 8th Norfolks attached to Coy	

1875 Wt. W593/826 1,000,000 4/15 J.B.C. & A. A.D.S.S./Forms/C. 2118.

Instructions regarding War Diaries and Intelligence Summaries are contained in F. S. Regs., Part II. and the Staff Manual respectively. Title Pages will be prepared in manuscript.

WAR DIARY
or
INTELLIGENCE SUMMARY
(Erase heading not required.)

Army Form C. 2118

Place	Date	Hour	Summary of Events and Information	Remarks and references to Appendices
AVELUY	27/1/17		Conference with Corps, 63rd & 2nd Division Salvage Officers. Chief trouble discussed was Transport. Salvage Companies not on War Establishment, so that all transport required has to be asked for as a favour. Agreed by all that work accomplished by Companies, warrants permanent transport, lorries for preference.	
do	28/1/17		1 G.S. wagon & 2 limbers ordered to report daily.	
do	29/1/17		Railhead shelled, also sorting place in AVELUY. Horse in our G.S. wagon killed.	
do	30/1/17			
do	31/1/17		Borrowed horse from M.V.S	

G B Clare
Lieut
O.C. Salvage Coy
18th Div

1875 Wt. W593/826 1,000,000 4/15 J.B.C. & A. A.D.S.S./Forms/C. 2118.

Vol 8.

WAR DIARY

SALVAGE COY. 18 DIV

February 1917

FEBRUARY

WAR DIARY
or
INTELLIGENCE SUMMARY
(Erase heading not required.)

Salvage Coy 18th Division

Army Form C. 2118

Instructions regarding War Diaries and Intelligence Summaries are contained in F. S. Regs., Part II. and the Staff Manual respectively. Title Pages will be prepared in manuscript.

Place	Date FEB	Hour 1917	Summary of Events and Information	Remarks and references to Appendices
AVELUY	3		Sorting place in Scotch St shelled. 5 men wounded. Horse attached to our G.S. waggon killed.	
"	4		Made my Headquarters at DONNETS POST. Shared an office with Bomb Store Officer.	
	6		Formed a dump near advanced S.H.Q. on NAB ROAD of 1 Corporal & 6 men, to collect shells & shell cases left on sides of road.	
	7		Sent off 2 truck loads shell cases from DONNETS POST to Railhead	
	10		DONNET'S POST shelled with 13. 8" No damage done.	

1875 Wt. W593/826 1,000,000 4/15 J.B.C. & A. A.D.S.S./Forms/C. 2118.

Instructions regarding War Diaries and Intelligence Summaries are contained in F. S. Regs., Part II. and the Staff Manual respectively. Title Pages will be prepared in manuscript.

WAR DIARY
or
INTELLIGENCE SUMMARY
(Erase heading not required.)

Army Form C. 2118

Place	Date	Hour	Summary of Events and Information	Remarks and references to Appendices
	FEB 1917.			
	11		Large quantity of bombs, loose S.A.A. etc sent to Moulin de Vivier, the Div. Ammunition Railhead	
	13		Applied for more lorries, but none available. Corps Officer visited area.	
	14		Received 2 lorries, which took loads from TRAMWAY CORNER. Enormous explosion near TULLOCHS CORNER which broke windows in AVELUY	
	15		Received 1 lorry	
	16		124 shells dropped in AVELUY & district. Ptes Dunn & Bull wounded.	

1875 Wt. W593/826 1,000,000 4/15 J.B.C. & A. A.D.S.S./Forms/C. 2118.

Instructions regarding War Diaries and Intelligence Summaries are contained in F. S. Regs., Part II. and the Staff Manual respectively. Title Pages will be prepared in manuscript.

WAR DIARY
or
INTELLIGENCE SUMMARY
(Erase heading not required.)

Army Form C. 2118

Place	Date	Hour	Summary of Events and Information	Remarks and references to Appendices
	FEB 1917			
	18.		Handed over serviceable Mills Bombs & 75 boxes SAA to Bomb Store.	
			Applied to D.H.Q. for bombers to undetonate Mills & Stokes at TRAMWAY CORNER. No men available.	
	19.		ALBERT & AVELUY shelled again. One shell just missed our sorting place.	
	21		Half the Salvage Coy detailed for burying. Started on SCHWABEN REDOUBT.	
			Formed a dump at NAB JUNCTION.	
	22		Went to SCHWABEN REDOUBT.	
	23		Party burying between FIELD TRENCH & TRAMWAY	

1875 Wt. W593/826 1,000,000 4/15 J.B.C. & A. A.D.S.S./Forms/C. 2118.

Instructions regarding War Diaries and Intelligence Summaries are contained in F. S. Regs., Part II. and the Staff Manual respectively. Title Pages will be prepared in manuscript.

WAR DIARY
or
INTELLIGENCE SUMMARY
(Erase heading not required.)

Army Form C. 2118

Place	Date	Hour	Summary of Events and Information	Remarks and references to Appendices
	FEB 1917			
	25		Received report that Main Railway Line N. of AVELUY strewn with empty cases. Visited same & found it blocked by Corps Ammunition Dump.	
	26		Party detailed to report to Town Major THIEPVAL for burying.	
	27		Collected large quantity salvage from THIEPVAL.	
			[illegible] Lieut. O.C. Salvage Coy 18th Division	

1875 Wt. W593/826 1,000,000 4/15 J.B.C. & A. A.D.S.S./Forms/C. 2118.

18th Div. SALVAGE COY MARCH 1917

Army Form C. 2118.

Instructions regarding War Diaries and Intelligence Summaries are contained in F. S. Regs., Part II. and the Staff Manual respectively. Title pages will be prepared in manuscript.

WAR DIARY
or
INTELLIGENCE SUMMARY.
(Erase heading not required.)

Vol 9

Place	Date	Hour	Summary of Events and Information	Remarks and references to Appendices
AVELUY	4th		Went round area with General Lee & arranged scheme of evacuation by tramline.	
	5th		Cleared Main Dump at Scotch St. AVELUY.	
	6th		Moved HQ to TULLOCHS CORNER. Handed over Scotch St. Dump to 2nd Division, & formed sorting dump on tramline at Railhead. Utilised 10 G.S. wagons.	
	7th		Removed 7000 shell cases from NAB JUNCTION.	
	8th		Sent party to SCHWABEN REDOUBT, who were billeted & rationed by Town Major THIEPVAL.	
	9th		Cleared NAB JUNCTION.	
	10th		Removed many thousand shell cases from TULLOCHS CORNER by trucks.	

A5834 Wt. W4973/M687 750,000 8/16 D. D. & L. Ltd. Forms/C.2118/13.

Instructions regarding War Diaries and Intelligence Summaries are contained in F. S. Regs., Part II. and the Staff Manual respectively. Title pages will be prepared in manuscript.

WAR DIARY MARCH contd.
or
INTELLIGENCE SUMMARY.
(*Erase heading not required.*)

Army Form C. 2118.

Place	Date	Hour	Summary of Events and Information	Remarks and references to Appendices
AVELUY	11th		Withdrew men from ST. PIERRE DIVION dump as men could be better employed on right of our area.	
	12th		Utilised 14 G.S. wagons. Handed over BOUZINCOURT to 63rd Division. Started dump at RIFLE DUMP.	
	13th		Started subsidiary dump near BOOM RAVINE. Utilised 14 G.S. wagons. 22 men attached from 53rd & 55th Brigades.	
	14th		Closed RIFLE DUMP & opened up at ZOLLERN TRENCH.	
	17th		Sent 10 extra men to sorting dump to help with large accumulation of stores. Had 3 lorries from Corps to assist clearing TRAMWAY CORNER of S.A.A., bombs etc.	

A5834 Wt. W4973/M687 750,000 8/16 D. D. & L. Ltd. Forms/C.2118/13.

Instructions regarding War Diaries and Intelligence Summaries are contained in F. S. Regs., Part II. and the Staff Manual respectively. Title pages will be prepared in manuscript.

WAR DIARY *or* INTELLIGENCE SUMMARY.

MARCH contd

(*Erase heading not required.*)

Army Form C. 2118.

Place	Date	Hour	Summary of Events and Information	Remarks and references to Appendices
AVELUY	19th		Private Short wounded accidentally by Mills Bomb	
	20th		Finished clearing TRAMWAY CORNER with help of 6 trucks & 4 G S wagons. Also cleared RIFLE DUMP & GRAVEL PITS.	
	22nd		Received orders to collect men preparatory to entraining	
	23rd		Cleared up Main Dump. Arranged with R.T.O to move us to SALEUX. Had another bomb accident while moving boxes of Mills. Pte Hayward killed. L/C Cable & Pte Patrick wounded.	
	25th		Left AVELUY for STEENBECQUE.	
	27th		Arrived at STEENBECQUE	

A5834 Wt. W4973/M687 750,000 8/16 D. D. & L. Ltd. Forms/C.2118/13.

Instructions regarding War Diaries and Intelligence Summaries are contained in F. S. Regs., Part II. and the Staff Manual respectively. Title pages will be prepared in manuscript.

WAR DIARY
or
INTELLIGENCE SUMMARY.
(*Erase heading not required.*)

MARCH contd

Army Form C. 2118.

Place	Date	Hour	Summary of Events and Information	Remarks and references to Appendices
STEENBECQUE				
	30th		Sent 6 men to work at Baths at AIRE.	
	31st		Men surplus to establishment of 67 O.R.s returned to their units	

G B Clare
Lieut
O.C. Salvage Coy
18th Division

A5834 Wt. W4973/M687 750,000 8/16 D. D. & L. Ltd. Forms/C.2118/13.

APRIL

WAR DIARY

SALVAGE COY

18th DIVISION

18th DIVISION

SALVAGE COY

APRIL 1917

Army Form C. 2118.

Instructions regarding War Diaries and Intelligence Summaries are contained in F. S. Regs., Part II. and the Staff Manual respectively. Title pages will be prepared in manuscript.

WAR DIARY
or
INTELLIGENCE SUMMARY.

(Erase heading not required.)

Vol 10

Place	Date	Hour	Summary of Events and Information	Remarks and references to Appendices
STEENBECQUE	1st		Rest area at STEENBECQUE	
	2nd		Attached men to Town Majors of villages in Divisional Billeting Area for salvage work. Arrangements made for units to return all clothes to D.A.D.O.S. Supplied party to deal with same.	
	18th		Evacuated to hospital ST. OMER with measles.	
	20th		2 Lt. Rendle took over Company.	
	23rd		2 Lt. Rendle evacuated with measles.	
	25th		2 Lt. Hull took over Company.	
	26th		Sent G.S. wagons to collect Salvage left by troops in villages in our area.	

A5834 Wt. W4973/M687 750,000 8/16 D. D. & L. Ltd. Forms/C.2118/13.

Instructions regarding War Diaries and Intelligence Summaries are contained in F. S. Regs., Part II. and the Staff Manual respectively. Title pages will be prepared in manuscript.

WAR DIARY
or
INTELLIGENCE SUMMARY.
(*Erase heading not required.*)

APRIL 1917
contd.

Army Form C. 2118.

Place	Date	Hour	Summary of Events and Information	Remarks and references to Appendices
PERNES	27th		Moved to forward area Stopped at PERNES en route	
ACHICOURT	28th		Arrived ACHICOURT & took over from 30th Division	
NEUVILLE VITASSE	30th		Moved to NEUVILLE VITASSE & formed dump at head of tramway. Arranged with tramway Officer for trucks to evacuate salvage to BEAUMETZ Sent 10 men to BEAUMETZ & arranged sorting dump	
			G B Clare Lieut O C Salvage Coy 18th Division	

Savage Company

War Dept

MAY 1917

1/

SALVAGE COY

18th Division

Instructions regarding War Diaries and Intelligence Summaries are contained in F. S. Regs., Part II. and the Staff Manual respectively. Title pages will be prepared in manuscript.

MAY 1917

WAR DIARY
or
INTELLIGENCE SUMMARY.
(Erase heading not required.)

Army Form C. 2118.

18 Div Salvage Coy

Vol XI

Place	Date	Hour	Summary of Events and Information	Remarks and references to Appendices
NEUVILLE VITASSE	1st		Moved to NEUVILLE VITASSE & formed Dump at Tramway Head. O/c Tramway gave every facility for evacuating salvage to Corps Dump at BEAUMETZ where 1 N.C.O. & 9 men from Company dealt with same. Most articles brought to dump noticed to be in good condition	
	2nd		Brigade Dumps formed at BEAURAINS & NEUVILLE VITASSE. Area much cleaner than that last occupied on the SOMME	
	4th		17 men attached for work from VII Corps Salvage Coy P.B. men & not much good for the work	
	7th		53rd Brigade doing good Salvage work & bringing in large quantity of articles	
	10th		Obtained Corps Lorries to remove bombs etc to Q. dump ARRAS.	

II

Instructions regarding War Diaries and Intelligence Summaries are contained in F. S. Regs., Part II. and the Staff Manual respectively. Title pages will be prepared in manuscript.

WAR DIARY
or
INTELLIGENCE SUMMARY.

(Erase heading not required.)

Army Form C. 2118.

Place	Date	Hour	Summary of Events and Information	Remarks and references to Appendices
	11th		Visit from A.D.O.S. & advice given re storage etc of explosives. 36 trucks of salvage sent away from 6th to 11th	
MERCATEL	15th		Owing to Division taking over different back area, closed dump at NEUVILLE VITASSE & formed one at MERCATEL close to siding. Also separate explosive dump. Moved HQ to MERCATEL road. Attached 20 men to Brigade in line to work under them	
	18th		Attached 5 men to Bomb Store to undergo course. Issued orders that no man was to detonate unless he had been to course. The cause of many explosions being put down to unskilled men tampering with bombs.	

A5834 Wt. W4973/M687 750,000 8/16 D. D. & L. Ltd. Forms/C.2118/13.

111

Instructions regarding War Diaries and Intelligence Summaries are contained in F. S. Regs., Part II. and the Staff Manual respectively. Title pages will be prepared in manuscript.

WAR DIARY
or
INTELLIGENCE SUMMARY.
(Erase heading not required.)

Army Form C. 2118.

Place	Date	Hour	Summary of Events and Information	Remarks and references to Appendices
BOISLEUX ST MARC	24th		Moved HQ to BOISLEUX ST MARC to be nearer HQ. Sent half the men for Medical Inspection	
	26th		Received orders to start work at BOISLEUX AU MONT and work along valley of COJEUL RIVER.	
	29th		Sent large quantity of shell cases to Corps Dump at BOISLEUX AU MONT railhead	

G B Clear [?] Lieut
O.C. Salvage Coy
18th Division

A5834 Wt. W4973/M687 750,000 8/16 D. D. & L. Ltd. Forms/C.2118/13.

WAR DIARY

JUNE

JUNE 1917

Vol 12

Army Form C. 2118.

WAR DIARY
or
INTELLIGENCE SUMMARY.
(Erase heading not required.)

Instructions regarding War Diaries and Intelligence Summaries are contained in F. S. Regs., Part II. and the Staff Manual respectively. Title pages will be prepared in manuscript.

SALVAGE COY
18th Division

Place	Date	Hour	Summary of Events and Information	Remarks and references to Appendices
BOISLEUX ST MARC	JUNE 1st		Made suggestion to Q Office that units should collect French Agricultural Implements in British zone, in order to help farmers. Taken up by Corps & orders issued re collection & evacuation. Men working at BOIRY BECQUERELLE & adjacent country	
	10th		Asked Q Office if they would publish a list of ~~the~~ the prices of certain Ordnance Stores, as most of the Officers & men of the Army have a very underestimated idea of the value of the more expensive stores:– Lewis Gun £175, Machine Gun handcart £20.18. A.D.O.S. consulted, & permission given to publish.	
	14th to 24th		On leave. Handed over to Lieut Wootton of Employment Company.	
			G B Clare Lieut OC Salvage Coy 18th Division	

A5834 Wt. W4973/M687 750,000 8/16 D. D. & L. Ltd. Forms/C.2118/13.

(4)

WO 95/2032

18 Division
Divisional Troops

Divisional Anti-Gas School

Jul 1916 - Nov 1918

18TH DIVISION

DIVL ANTI-GS SCHOOL

JLY 1916-NOV 1918.

WAR DIARY

JULY 1916

Nov '18

18TH DIV. ANTI-GAS SCHOOL.

18/July
Anti Gas
School
Vol 1

R. T. Thompson. LIEUT.
ANTI-GAS INSTRUCTOR
18TH DIVISION.

A.G.-18/61

18th Division.

Herewith War Diary for July 1916

McPherson Lieut.
Anti Gas Instructor
18th Division.

18th Div. Gas School
13 — viii — 16

Instructions regarding War Diaries and Intelligence Summaries are contained in F. S. Regs., Part II. and the Staff Manual respectively. Title Pages will be prepared in manuscript.

WAR DIARY ~~or~~ ~~INTELLIGENCE SUMMARY~~

(Erase heading not required.)

Army Form C. 2118

Place	Date	Hour	Summary of Events and Information	Remarks and references to Appendices
BRAY	July 1		Sent Sergeants Snowden and Chatterley and Corpl Bailey to inspect gas-proof doors at each Brigade H.Q., also to improve existing arrangements for gas protection at 55th Advanced Dressing Station near BRONFAY FARM. I did not consider that anywhere in that area S. of CARNOY valley would be very much affected by hostile gas. BILLON Wood would also be pretty safe	R/T.T.
BRAY	July 2		Moved to GROVETOWN with N.C.O's, BRAY being evacuated by all British Troops.	
GROVETOWN	July 3 " 4 " 5 " 6 " 7 " 8 " 9 " 10		Paid occasional visits to captured German trenches to see if I could gather any information about result of our gas attack, but did not find anything useful. All dead Germans were wearing their respirators slung. Could not find out anything about their method of gas alarm: everything was smashed up by shell fire. It struck me that their deep dug-outs would be particularly dangerous in gas attack owing to the amount of gas they would swallow. It would be very difficult to clear such dug-out of gas, and I did not notice any arrangements for protecting them*. Some Germans were found dead from gas in a dug-out, apparently killed before they had time to remove respirators from their tins. Gas would flow like water into these dug-outs.	* Some did have a blanket rolled up ready for covering the doorway; others were fitted with wooden doors but I should not say this was a precaution against gas R/T.T.

1875 Wt. W593/826 1,000,000 4/15 J.B.C. & A. A.D.S.S./Forms/C. 2118.

Instructions regarding War Diaries and Intelligence Summaries are contained in F. S. Regs., Part II. and the Staff Manual respectively. Title Pages will be prepared in manuscript.

WAR DIARY
~~or~~
~~INTELLIGENCE SUMMARY~~
(Erase heading not required.)

Army Form C. 2118

Place	Date	Hour	Summary of Events and Information	Remarks and references to Appendices
	July			
GROVETOWN	11		Held Class of Instruction for N.C.O's from all battalions of 53rd Brigade in examination of helmets	[illegible]
	12			
	13			
	14			
	15			
	16			
	17			
	18		Rumours of a gas alarm somewhere on the front. Visited Divisional H.Q. to find out whether they had had any news: thought it peculiar because wind had been in wrong direction for hostile gas attack. Could not ascertain anything. On return to GROVETOWN found that Assistant Chemical Adviser, 4th Army, had been down to investigate German gas shell bombardment. I made my own enquiries - discovered that the transport of the ARGYLLS, 9th Division, had been caught in a gas shelling W. of MONTAUBAN. Men and horses gassed, but effect not felt till two or three hours after in some cases, particularly horses.	
	19		Dispatched Sgt. CHATTERLEY to investigate the gas shells. Saw affected horses at GROVETOWN. Four had already been killed and others were in a bad way. Appearances pointed to use of PHOSGENE shells, particularly from smell at locality of shelling. Apparently they	

1875 Wt. W593/826 1,000,000 4/15 J.B.C. & A. A.D.S.S./Forms/C. 2118.

Instructions regarding War Diaries and Intelligence Summaries are contained in F. S. Regs., Part II. and the Staff Manual respectively. Title Pages will be prepared in manuscript.

WAR DIARY
or
~~INTELLIGENCE SUMMARY~~
(Erase heading not required.)

Army Form C. 2118

Place	Date	Hour	Summary of Events and Information	Remarks and references to Appendices
	July			
GROVETOWN	19		is the German K-STOFF II Shell, which is the asphyxiating gas shell, and not the tear shell. Sgt CHATTERLEY reported shelling very local, intense, and severe in effects, probably 77 m.m. shells, muffled explosion, and appearance of shell pieces as if "ripped up", pointing to minimum explosive power. Lieut OSCROFT, 18th Dn. Sig Coy R.E. told me that he and some of his men were also caught in this shelling. It was pitch dark, but they all got their helmets on, and found them complete protection. One man became ill and Lieut. OSCROFT carried him for about a mile out of the gas. It turned out that the man had a small hole in the outer fabric of his helmet. This is a unique case, and a good example of pressure of gas on least point of resistance in a helmet. 10th Corps wired Division asking for particulars of shells. I sent in report as far as I could gather nature of shells.	R.T.T.
GROVETOWN	20			
GROVETOWN	21		Moved to HALLENCOURT with N.C.O's. by Charabanc	R.T.T.

1875 Wt. W593/826 1,000,000 4/15 J.B.C. & A. A.D.S.S./Forms/C. 2118.

Army Form C. 2118

Instructions regarding War Diaries and Intelligence Summaries are contained in F. S. Regs., Part II. and the Staff Manual respectively. Title Pages will be prepared in manuscript.

WAR DIARY
or
~~INTELLIGENCE SUMMARY~~
(Erase heading not required.)

Place	Date	Hour	Summary of Events and Information	Remarks and references to Appendices
HALLENCOURT	22			
	23			
	24		Moved to RENESCURE.	R.T.T.
RENESCURE	25		Conference with Staff of Division re new part of line Division would take over	
	26		Interview with Chemical Adviser 2nd Army, who made enquiries about	
	27		Existing anti-gas measures in the Division. Told him that nearly all the Company gas N.C.O's in the Division had become casualties in the advance on July 1. Advised setting up School at once for training new ones. The C.A. also advised lectures to Battalions on account of so many new drafts probably arriving soon. N.C.O's. sent out to inspect helmets in 53rd Brigade.	R.T.T.
	28		Obtained a motor-lorry and moved to PICQUIGNY to fetch all stores belonging to the Divisional Gas School left there. This journey	
	29		took two days. Left stores at FLÊTRE	R.T.T.
	30		Sent Sgt. CHATTERLEY to C.R.E. HQ CROIX DU BAC to inspect helmets, and also those of the 79th, 80th and 92nd Field Companies R.E.	R.T.T.
	31		Myself, Sergt. SNOWDON, and Cpl. BAILEY started off on a tour of inspection of the Smoke Helmets of the Division, reporting to-day at the 55th Bde. H.Q. THIESHOUK.	R.T.T.

1875 Wt. W593/826 1,000,000 4/15 J.B.C. & A. A.D.S.S./Forms/C. 2118.

ANTI - GAS SCHOOL

18th Division

Vol 2

SECRET

WAR DIARY

FOR

AUGUST 1916

R. J. T. Thompson Lieut.

DIVISIONAL GAS OFFICER

18TH DIVISION.

Instructions regarding War Diaries and Intelligence Summaries are contained in F. S. Regs., Part II. and the Staff Manual respectively. Title Pages will be prepared in manuscript.

WAR DIARY

~~or~~

~~INTELLIGENCE SUMMARY~~

(Erase heading not required.)

Army Form C. 2118

Place	Date	Hour	Summary of Events and Information	Remarks and references to Appendices
THIESHOUK	Aug. 1 " 2	}	Myself, Sergt. SNOWDON, & CORPL. BAILEY, inspected helmets &c, and lectured to all battalions of the 55th Bde.	R.P.T. Major
METEREN	" 3 " 4	}	Reported to 54th Bde and visited all four battalions	R.P.T.
CROIX DU BAC	"		Sergt CHATTERLEY examined the helmets &c, & lectured to Field Companies, R.E.	R.P.T.
CROIX DU BAC	" 5		Arrived at CROIX DU BAC with Anti-Gas School stores, etc.	R.P.T.
	" 6		Sent my 2 senior NCOs to visit front line trenches of 55th Bde and report on anti-gas appliances. They found everything very satisfactory. Much more care was evidently taken in this part of the line than previously on the SOMME over anti-gas measures. Sent in report to 18th Division	R.P.T.
	" 7 " 8		Preparing School for next class. Fitted up gas proof dug-out. Made an excellent "class-room" with a large tarpaulin lent by Camp Commandant. 23 N.C.O's reported for Course of Instruction.	R.P.T.
	9 10		Course begins.	R.P.T.

1875 Wt. W593/826 1,000,000 4/15 J.B.C. & A. A.D.S.S./Forms/C. 2118.

Army Form C. 2118

Instructions regarding War Diaries and Intelligence Summaries are contained in F. S. Regs., Part II. and the Staff Manual respectively. Title Pages will be prepared in manuscript.

WAR DIARY

~~or~~

~~INTELLIGENCE SUMMARY~~

(Erase heading not required.)

Place	Date	Hour	Summary of Events and Information	Remarks and references to Appendices
CROIX DU BAC	Aug 11		Sent 2 N.C.O's. to visit trenches of 56th Brigade and again all anti-gas appliances were found in a very satisfactory state. I had arranged with the Chemical adviser 2nd Army to give a gas demonstration to the 8th Norfolks, and he did so very successfully. The Chemical Adviser informed me that in the German Gas attack near YPRES ~~#~~ the day before or so that considerable casualties were caused through the unpreparedness of our men. The same night I wrote out 18 Div G 268 "Precautions against Surprise Gas Attacks" & this was circulated at once among our units.	RPT
	13		Course ends. Gas "Alert" on Divisional front.	RPT
	14		24 N.C.O's. report for next course of instruction. I visited 54th Bde trenches & organised a smoke wave for the dummy raid, which went off very successfully	RPT
			Next course commences.	RPT
	15		N.C.O's. return to their units	
	19		Gas Alert on front of 54th Bde, and revised & completed	
	23		"Standing Orders" for Gas Alert, etc. circulated in the Division.	RPT

1875 Wt. W593/826 1,000,000 4/15 J.B.C. & A. A.D.S.S./Forms/C. 2118.

Instructions regarding War Diaries and Intelligence Summaries are contained in F. S. Regs., Part II. and the Staff Manual respectively. Title Pages will be prepared in manuscript.

WAR DIARY

~~or~~

~~INTELLIGENCE SUMMARY~~

(Erase heading not required.)

Army Form C. 2118

Place	Date	Hour	Summary of Events and Information	Remarks and references to Appendices
BAILLEUL	24		Moved to BAILLEUL.	RJTT.
BAILLEUL	25		Moving to ROELLECOURT.	RJTT.
ROELLECOURT	26		Arrived at ROELLECOURT.	RJTT.
"	27		Arranging for re-installation of Div. Gas School.	RJTT
"	28.		Inspected helmets of 7th Royal West Kent Regt. and arranged with the adjutant for more facilities to be given to the Company Gas N.C.O's. of this Battalion.	RJTT
"	29		Interviewed Chemical Adviser IIIrd Army with reference to the work to be done while at ROELLECOURT.	RJTT.
	30		Course begins for 53 Company Gas NCO's.	RJTT.

1875 Wt. W593/826 1,000,000 4/15 J.B.C. & A. A.D.S.S./Forms/C. 2118.

Vol 3

ANTI-GAS SCHOOL,
18TH DIVISION.
No. 114
Date 3-10-16

WAR DIARY
FOR
- SEPTEMBER -
1916

R J Thompson Lt.
DIVISIONAL GAS OFFICER
18 TH DIVISION.

HEAD QUARTERS
No.
3 OCT. 1916
18TH DIVISION

Army Form C. 2118

Instructions regarding War Diaries and Intelligence Summaries are contained in F. S. Regs., Part II. and the Staff Manual respectively. Title Pages will be prepared in manuscript.

WAR DIARY
or
INTELLIGENCE SUMMARY

(*Erase heading not required.*)

18th DIV. ANTI GAS SCHOOL

Place	Date	Hour	Summary of Events and Information	Remarks and references to Appendices
ROELLE-COURT	Sept 1		Flammenwerfer display by Chemical Adviser 3rd Army near MONCHY BRETON. Took NCO's attending Gas School over to see this.	RJTT.
"	Sept 4		Class ends, and NCOs return to units.	RJTT.
"	Sept 5		I visited units of infantry brigades to ascertain whether	
"	6		Coy Gas N.C.O's. were carrying out their duties and were	
"	7		given proper facilities. I found everything going on well. Only one or two N.C.OS complained, and I spoke to the Adjutant of the Battalions concerned in each case, who promised to put matters right	RJTT.
"	" 8		Myself and Staff of N.C.O's visited 3rd Army Anti-Gas School for lecture & demonstration by Chem. Adviser on the new Box Respirator. Major Harvey, General Staff, 18th Divn. & D.A.D.M.S. of Division also attended	RJTT.
DOULLENS	9		Moved from ROELLECOURT to DOULLENS by lorry, with Stores.	
DOULLENS	10		Instructional practices at DOULLENS with small box respirator for Gas School Staff.	RJTT.
ACHEUX	11		Moved to ACHEUX by lorry, with stores.	RJTT.

1875 Wt. W593/826 1,000,000 4/15 J.B.C. & A. A.D.S.S./Forms/C. 2118.

Instructions regarding War Diaries and Intelligence Summaries are contained in F. S. Regs., Part II. and the Staff Manual respectively. Title Pages will be prepared in manuscript.

Army Form C. 2118

WAR DIARY
or
INTELLIGENCE SUMMARY

18th DIV ANTI GAS SCHOOL *(Erase heading not required.)*

Place	Date	Hour	Summary of Events and Information	Remarks and references to Appendices
ACHEUX	Sept 12		Instructional exercises with Small Box Respirator, for School Staff.	R.J.T.
LEALVILLERS	13		Instruction to 53rd Bde in New Small Box Respirator	R.J.T.
ARQUEVES	14		Similar instruction to 54th Bde.	R.J.T.
PUCHEVILLERS	15		" " " 55th Bde.	R.J.T.
ACHEUX	16			R.J.T.
	17		1 Offr. and 31 O.R. report for class of instruction	
	18		Course starts	
	22		Commenced monthly inspection of Div. Reserve Gas helmets. Visited Reserve Army H.Q. to see C.A. Reserve Army.	R.J.T.
	24		N.C.O's. returned to their units	R.J.T.
			Moved to HEDAUVILLE.	
HEDAUVILLE	25			R.J.T.
	26		Sent an N.C.O. to report on gas shelling in MESNIL VALLEY.	
	27		I visited MESNIL VALLEY and found that it was shelled nearly every evening with the 77 mm. gas shell and the 15 cm and 10.5 cm Tear shells	R.J.T.
	29		Concluded inspection of 10% of Gas Helmets in Div. Reserve.	R.J.T.
	30		I visited 53rd Bde battalions at FORCEVILLE and offered assistance if required to adjutants.	R.J.T.

1875 Wt. W593/826 1,000,000 4/15 J.B.C. & A. A.D.S.S./Forms/C. 2118.

Vol. 4

SECRET
To 18th Division

WAR DIARY

ANTI-GAS SCHOOL,
18TH DIVISION.
No. Vol. IV
Date 31-X-16

FOR

OCTOBER, 1916.

R. J. Thompson Lieut.
Divisional Gas Officer
18th Division.

Instructions regarding War Diaries and Intelligence Summaries are contained in F. S. Regs., Part II. and the Staff Manual respectively. Title Pages will be prepared in manuscript.

OCT., 1916.

WAR DIARY
or
~~INTELLIGENCE~~ SUMMARY
(Erase heading not required.)

Volume IV (1)

Army Form C. 2118.

18th Divisional Anti-Gas School.
Capt. Thompson Lieut. O.C.

Place	Date	Hour	Summary of Events and Information	Remarks and references to Appendices
HEDAUVILLE	OCT. 1		Sgt. CHATTERLEY visited Company Gas NCOs in the 54th Brigade. Only 9 out of 16 were found present, the remainder having become casualties at THIEPVAL.	
"	2		I and my NCOs visited the captured German trenches at THIEPVAL to examine any German gas apparatus we could find – we discovered among other things the "box" or "drum" of a German respirator which had only been a month out of the factory, and this was immediately forwarded to the Chemical Adviser, Reserve Army, for examination at the Central Laboratory, G.H.Q., together with other specimens. I opened one drum, and found the chemicals of precisely the same nature as those in the original drums found, so evidently the Germans have made a thorough test of the drum, and found it's contents quite satisfactory and efficient.	
HEDAUVILLE	4		Moving to BERNAVILLE with D.H.Q.	

2449 Wt. W14957/M90 750,000 1/16 J.B.C. & A. Forms/C.2118/12.

Instructions regarding War Diaries and Intelligence Summaries are contained in F. S. Regs., Part II. and the Staff Manual respectively. Title Pages will be prepared in manuscript.

OCT., 1916.

WAR DIARY ~~or~~ INTELLIGENCE SUMMARY

(Erase heading not required.)

Volume IV (2) Army Form C. 2118.

18th Divisional Anti: Gas School.

[illegible] Lieut. OC.

Place	Date	Hour	Summary of Events and Information	Remarks and references to Appendices
BERNAVILLE	7th		Made arrangements with G.O.C. 53rd Brigade for a series of demonstrations to battalions.	
	8th		2 officers and 16 N.C.O.s report for course of instruction	
	9th		I and three N.C.O's. gave a demonstration to 8th Suffolk Regt. at HEUZECOURT. the battalion was massed, and I opened out ~~two~~ cylinders of gas on them to prove the efficiency of the helmets they were wearing: they marched back through a "barrage" of lachrymatory gas	
	10th		Class	
	14th		Class ended. All arrangements for further demonstrations had to be cancelled owing to projected move of D.H.Q.	
ALBERT	16th		Moved to ALBERT with D.H.Q.	
	17th		Interviewed General Staff of Division and asked for class: G.S. consented if it could be arranged, but very doubtful.	
	18th		Visited 11th Royal Fusiliers and lectured on gas shells to new drafts. Visited Brigade Office to arrange for lectures and demonstrations to other battalions, but was informed they were moving next day.	

2449 Wt. W14957/M90 750,000 1/16 J.B.C. & A. Forms/C.2118/12.

Instructions regarding War Diaries and Intelligence Summaries are contained in F. S. Regs., Part II. and the Staff Manual respectively. Title Pages will be prepared in manuscript.

OCT. 1916.

Volume IV (3)

WAR DIARY
or
INTELLIGENCE SUMMARY

(Erase heading not required.)

Army Form C. 2118

18th Divisional Anti. Gas School.

R.f. Thompson Lieut. R.

Place	Date	Hour	Summary of Events and Information	Remarks and references to Appendices
ALBERT	19th		Visited IInd Corps HQ to see flammenwerfer.	
"	20th		Visited HEDAUVILLE to inspect supposed German gas cylinders on Salvage Dump there: found they were English.	
"	22nd		Visited units of 56th Brigade to ascertain whether their equipment in gas helmets was up to scale: found all satisfactory except that drafts had no PHG Helmets with them when they arrived from the Base. I visited D.A.D.O.S., found that deficiencies could be made up next day, and notified the Brigade Office accordingly: also suggesting that further cases, if deficient of a helmet altogether, should be issued with a PH temporarily, which I consider really more satisfactory than the P.H.G. It is certainly more popular with the men.	
"	23rd		Visited IInd Corps Salvage Dump, and found two specimens of gas shells on the Ammunition (German) Dump — one a 7.7, the other a 10.5 cm. Instructed my NCOs to examine some salved box respirators & helmets. Visited units of 55th Brigade.	

Instructions regarding War Diaries and Intelligence Summaries are contained in F. S. Regs., Part II. and the Staff Manual respectively. Title Pages will be prepared in manuscript.

OCT. 1916.

WAR DIARY
or
INTELLIGENCE SUMMARY
(Erase heading not required.)

Army Form C. 2118.

Volume IV (4)
18th Divisional Anti-Gas School.
[signature] Lieut. Ol.

Place	Date	Hour	Summary of Events and Information	Remarks and references to Appendices
ALBERT	24th		Visited "KAY" DUMP, nr. POZIÈRES, at request of Staff Captain of 55th Brigade, to inspect some supposed German gas cylinders there, which were feared on account of likelihood of a shell bursting them. Discovered they were small air cylinders, belonging to STROMBOS Horns!	
	26th		Arranged with D.A.D.O.S. 18th Divn. a scheme for keeping a check on the indents for gas helmets — beneficial to him because he has very little opportunity, and for me because it gives me some idea as to what the consistency in the demand per week from a unit is like. If it is abnormal, I visit the unit and find out why: I shall also be able to tell whether the helmets are inspected regularly enough in each case.	
	29th		Examination of 800 of the 2,000 gas helmets in Divisional Reserve completed. Percentage of defects very small.	
			Sergts. SNOWDON and CHATTERLEY visited 12th Middlesex Regt. to interview Coy. Gas N.C.Os and inspect any doubtful helmets.	

2449 Wt. W14957/M90 750,000 1/16 J.B.C. & A. Forms/C.2118/12.

Instructions regarding War Diaries and Intelligence Summaries are contained in F. S. Regs., Part II. and the Staff Manual respectively. Title Pages will be prepared in manuscript.

OCT. 1916.

WAR DIARY
or
~~INTELLIGENCE SUMMARY~~
(Erase heading not required.)

Army Form C. 2118.

Volume iv (5)
18th Divisional Anti-Gas School.
R. Thompson Lieut. O.C.

Place	Date	Hour	Summary of Events and Information	Remarks and references to Appendices
ALBERT	31st		8th R. Sussex and 11th R. Fusiliers visited: the former unit particularly was found to be very well equipped with gas NCOs and shows great interest in gas precautions. Three companies in the Fusiliers had no gas NCO whatever: they had become casualties recently.	

2449 Wt. W14957/M90 750,000 1/16 J.B.C. & A. Forms/C.2118/12.

18

SECRET.

18th Divisional Gas School.

Vol 5

WAR DIARY.

Vol. V

NOVEMBER, 1916.

R. J. Thompson Lieut.
Divl. Gas Offr.
18th Division.

Army Form C. 2118.

WAR DIARY
or
~~INTELLIGENCE SUMMARY~~

Instructions regarding War Diaries and Intelligence Summaries are contained in F. S. Regs., Part II. and the Staff Manual respectively. Title Pages will be prepared in manuscript.

NOVEMBER (Erase heading not required.) VOL V (1)
18th Div Gas School.

Place	Date	Hour	Summary of Events and Information	Remarks and references to Appendices
ALBERT	1st to 10th		Visits to units, inspection of anti-gas helmets etc, and three short classes of instruction held for N.C.O's of 11th R. Fusiliers, 7th Buffs, and 7th R.W. Kent Regt., also 53rd T. M. Battery	The usual classes were not practicable owing to active operations during the whole of this month.
"	10th		Div'l Gas Officer visited POZIERES CEMETERY and reported to Div'l Staff re the severe gas shelling in that vicinity in the early hours of the morning. The enemy fired about 3,000 gas shells into a large back-area, all di-phosgene, the usual gas shell, mixed with tear shells. Hardly any casualties among 18th Div'l troops, & helmets reported to be very effective protection.	
"	10 - 13th		Div'l Gas Officer and his N.C.O's inspected the	

2449 Wt. W14957/M90 750,000 1/16 J.B.C. & A. Forms/C.2118/12.

Instructions regarding War Diaries and Intelligence Summaries are contained in F. S. Regs., Part II. and the Staff Manual respectively. Title Pages will be prepared in manuscript.

WAR DIARY
or
~~INTELLIGENCE SUMMARY~~

NOVEMBER (*Erase heading not required.*)

Army Form C. 2118.

Vol V (ii) 18th Div. Gas School

Place	Date	Hour	Summary of Events and Information	Remarks and references to Appendices
ALBERT	8th – 12th		box respirators & helmets of various units in the Division relieved from the trenches: also examined anti-gas protection and advised re blanket doors at Brigade, etc. H.Q. at POZIERES, MOUQUET FARM, R. 29 Central, and DRESSING STATION, POZIÈRES.	
"	14th –		Invented and arranged for issue a PH helmet adapted for use by horses & mules	
"	20th		Inspected helmets returned to Ordnance deciding whether they should be condemned or re-dipped only.	
"	21st		Dipping and issuing blankets to 18th Div RA. for protecting against gas the doors of dug-outs.	

2449 Wt. W14957/M90 750,000 1/16 J.B.C. & A. Forms/C.2118/12.

Army Form C. 2118.

Instructions regarding War Diaries and Intelligence Summaries are contained in F. S. Regs., Part II. and the Staff Manual respectively. Title Pages will be prepared in manuscript.

WAR DIARY
or
INTELLIGENCE SUMMARY
(Erase heading not required.)

NOVEMBER

Vol. V (iii)
18th Div. Gas School.

Place	Date	Hour	Summary of Events and Information	Remarks and references to Appendices
BUIGNY ST MACLOU	23rd		Moved to BUIGNY ST. MACLOU from ALBERT.	
"	24th		Divl. Gas Officer left for ten days leave to England. Sgt. W. SNOWDON in charge of School.	
"	24th – 30th		Preparing School for class, digging trench, dug-out, etc.	

R.P. Thompson Lieut.
Divl. Gas Offr.
18th Division

2449 Wt. W14957/M90 750,000 1/16 J.B.C. & A. Forms/C.2118/12.

Vol 6

18 DIV. GAS SCHOOL

WAR · DIARY

DECEMBER, 1916.

Vol. VI

R. J. Thompson Lt

Gas Officer
18th Division

8/1/17.

Army Form C. 2118.

Instructions regarding War Diaries and Intelligence Summaries are contained in F. S. Regs., Part II. and the Staff Manual respectively. Title Pages will be prepared in manuscript.

WAR DIARY
or
~~INTELLIGENCE SUMMARY~~

DECEMBER (Erase heading not required.) 18 DIV. Gas School. Vol. VI.

Place	Date	Hour	Summary of Events and Information	Remarks and references to Appendices
BUIGNY ST MACLOU	1 to 14		Class for Company Gas N.C.O's. Divl. Gas Officer returned from leave and resumed duty.	
"	15 to 19		Daily classes for representatives of all units in the 18th Division in the use of the small box respirator.	
	20 -24		Examining salved anti-gas apparatus. Two further small box respirator classes.	
	25 -27		Superintending the fitting of the small box respirator to various units	
	28		Class of instruction for 1 officer and N.C.O's. of II Corps Troops commenced.	

2449 Wt. W14957/M90 750,000 1/16 J.B.C. & A. Forms/C.2118/12.

Army Form C. 2118.

WAR DIARY
or
~~INTELLIGENCE SUMMARY~~
(Erase heading not required.)

Instructions regarding War Diaries and Intelligence Summaries are contained in F. S. Regs., Part II. and the Staff Manual respectively. Title Pages will be prepared in manuscript.

DECEMBER 18 Div. Gas School Vol. VI

Place	Date	Hour	Summary of Events and Information	Remarks and references to Appendices
BUIGNY ST MACLOU	29 -31		Daily supervising the fitting of the small box respirator to units. It has been difficult to impress on units that the small box respirator is a far different thing from the smoke helmet and requires ten times more care in training. The men themselves are delighted with it on account of its comparative comfort when adjusted, and the cool & easy breathing afforded. In addition the protection afforded against gases used for military purposes appears to be most complete. R. J. Thompson Lt. Divl. Gas Officer 18 Division	

2449 Wt. W14957/M90 750,000 1/16 J.B.C. & A. Forms/C.2118/12.

WAR DIARY Vol 7

18 TH DIV: GAS SCHOOL

JANUARY 1917.

ANTI-GAS SCHOOL,
18TH DIVISION.
No. ....
Date 11/2/17

R. J. T. Thompson, Lieut,
Div. Gas Officer,
18th Div.

Army Form C. 2118.

Instructions regarding War Diaries and Intelligence Summaries are contained in F. S. Regs., Part II. and the Staff Manual respectively. Title Pages will be prepared in manuscript.

WAR DIARY
or
~~INTELLIGENCE SUMMARY~~

(Erase heading not required.)

JANUARY 1917

18 DIV. Gas School.
Vol. VII

Place	Date	Hour	Summary of Events and Information	Remarks and references to Appendices
BUIGNY ST MACLOU	1-9		Superintending fitting of small box respirator to units of the 18th Division	
"	10-16		18th Division left training area and marched to the line. 18 Div. Gas School took over Gas School of 61st Division at HEDAUVILLE.	
HEDAUVILLE	17-19		Taking stock of stores and preparing for demonstrations. Submitted plan to 18 Div. "G" for alterations and additions to Gas School.	
"	19		Put gas cloud over 7th Bn Buffs, wearing their small box respirators, to give them confidence in the efficacy of the means of protection.	
"	21		D.G.O. fitted small box respirators of 55th Bde HQ.	
"	22		Gas cloud demonstration to 7th Queens, 1 Coy 7 R.W.K. Regt, 3 coys 8th E. Surrey Regt.	

2449 Wt. W14957/M90 750,000 1/16 J.B.C. & A. Forms/C.2118/12.

Army Form C. 2118.

Instructions regarding War Diaries and Intelligence Summaries are contained in F. S. Regs., Part II. and the Staff Manual respectively. Title Pages will be prepared in manuscript.

WAR DIARY
or
INTELLIGENCE SUMMARY
(Erase heading not required.)

JANUARY 1917 — 18 DIV GAS SCHOOL — Vol. VII P. 2.

Place	Date	Hour	Summary of Events and Information	Remarks and references to Appendices
HEDAUVILLE	23		Owing to lack of accommodation, the School was removed to "Black Hut" HEDAUVILLE Village	
"	24.		Gas alarms, etc. in camps of support brigades inspected. Artillery N.C.O. visited batteries of 83rd Bde R.F.A.	
"	25		Gas test for 3 Coys of 7th R.W. Kent Regt. About 30 men had to leave cloud because their expiratory valves froze. Reported this to G.S., also to C.A. 5th Army and advised precautionary measures	
"	26		Visited line and inspected anti-gas measures.	
"	27		N.C.O.'s inspected STROMBOS Horns on KAY DUMP.	
"	29		Sgt. CHATTERLEY of Bde CAITHNESS, R.F.A. attached to H.Q of Bde in line.	
"	30-31		Visits to forward area, & arranging for distribution of glycerine to prevent freezing of box respirator valves. Arranging School for class of instruction.	

R.F. Thorp[?] Lt.
Div. Gas Officer, 18th Div.

2449 Wt. W14957/M90 750,000 1/16 J.B.C. & A. Forms/C.2118/12.

ANTI-GAS SCHOOL,
18TH DIVISION.
No. ....
Date 7/3/17

Vol 8

WAR DIARY

FEBRUARY, 1917

R. J. T. Thompson Lt.,
Divl. Gas Officer
18th Division

HEAD QUARTERS
No ....
7 MAR. 1917
18TH DIVISION

Instructions regarding War Diaries and Intelligence Summaries are contained in F. S. Regs., Part II. and the Staff Manual respectively. Title Pages will be prepared in manuscript.

WAR DIARY
~~or~~
~~INTELLIGENCE SUMMARY~~
(Erase heading not required.)

ANTI-GAS SCHOOL,
18TH DIVISION.
No.
Date VOL. VIII.

Army Form C. 2118.

Place	Date	Hour	Summary of Events and Information	Remarks and references to Appendices
HEDAUVILLE	1st to 9th		Class of instruction for Company Gas N.C.Os. Anti-gas measures of batteries of corps heavy artillery inspected by Div. Gas N.C.Os in forward area.	
	10th to 12th		Inspection of salvaged respirators etc. — Gas-proofing blankets. 18th Div. Artillery batteries visited.	
	12th 13th		Gas shell attack S. of GRANDCOURT. Reported on to Headquarters 18th Div. and Chemical Adviser, 5th Army. No casualties. Divl. Gas N.C.Os in forward area superintended the glycerining of expiratory valves of small box respirators.	
	13th -17th		Various units visited in forward area. Sgt. CHATTERLEY & BOMBDR. CAITHNESS working in forward area relieved by Sgt. SNOWDON & Corpl. BAILEY. D.G.O. visited Chemical Adviser at Army H.Q.	
	19th		Anti-Gas School moved to BOUZINCOURT.	
	20-21st		Spraying gas-proof blankets. Visits to Corps H.A. batteries St. PIERRE DIVION by Gas N.C.Os.	

2449 Wt. W14957/M90 750,000 1/16 J.B.C. & A. Forms/C.2118/12.

Instructions regarding War Diaries and Intelligence Summaries are contained in F. S. Regs., Part II. and the Staff Manual respectively. Title Pages will be prepared in manuscript.

WAR DIARY
or
INTELLIGENCE SUMMARY
(Erase heading not required.)

ANTI-GAS SCHOOL, 18TH DIVISION. No. VIII Date. Vol VIII P. 2.

Army Form C. 2118.

Place	Date	Hour	Summary of Events and Information	Remarks and references to Appendices
BOUZINCOURT	22		D.G.O. visited line and reported to H.Q. Division that men were not wearing their respirators in "Alert" position in trench system contrary to 5th Army Orders. "G" issued memo. re this to units.	
	24 – 28		Class of instruction for Coy. Gas N.C.O.s. Demonstration gas cloud over 6th Northants. R. and 11th R. Fusiliers to give men confidence in Small Box Respirator. Divl. Gas N.C.O.s in turned [?] visited the Company Gas N.C.O.s of various units, & gave them technical information on various new points.	

R. J. T. Thompson Lt.
D. Gas Officer
18th Div:

2449 Wt. W14957/M90 750,000 1/16 J.B.C. & A. Forms/C.2118/12.

SECRET

18th Divisional Anti-Gas School.

Vol 9

War Diary
Vol. IX

For March 1917.

R. J. T. Thompson Lt.

Jm

GAS OFFICER,
18th DIVISION.

Instructions regarding War Diaries and Intelligence Summaries are contained in F. S. Regs., Part II. and the Staff Manual respectively. Title Pages will be prepared in manuscript.

WAR DIARY
or
~~INTELLIGENCE SUMMARY~~
(Erase heading not required.)

Army Form C. 2118.

Place	Date	Hour	Summary of Events and Information	Remarks and references to Appendices
BOUZINCOURT	March 1		Gas cloud demonstration with 12th Middlesex and 7th Bedford Regiments	
	2		Class of instruction at Gas School returned to their units.	
	3		Experiments to determine absorption of water by small box respirator.	
	4		D.G.O. and Bombdr. CAITHNESS investigated gas shelling in BOOM RAVINE. Trichloromethylchloroformate and benzyl bromide gas shells used.	
	5		Reported to 18th Div. about casualties from this gas shelling and recommended that in future men slightly gassed must be given as little exertion as possible. This was circulated among units.	
	7 – 10		New class of instruction for Company Gas N.C.O's	
	11 – 12		Classes of instruction in the fitting and use of the small box respirator to officers and N.C.O's. of IInd Corps Heavy Artillery.	
	14		Class of instruction for Company gas NCOs ended.	
	15 – 17		Small box respirator classes for officers & NCOs of corps troops.	

2449 Wt. W14957/M90 750,000 1/16 J.B.C. & A. Forms/C.2118/12.

Instructions regarding War Diaries and Intelligence Summaries are contained in F. S. Regs., Part II. and the Staff Manual respectively. Title Pages will be prepared in manuscript.

WAR DIARY
or
~~INTELLIGENCE SUMMARY~~
(Erase heading not required.)

Army Form C. 2118.

ANTI-GAS SCHOOL, 18TH DIVISION.
Vol. No. IX p. 2
Date

Place	Date	Hour	Summary of Events and Information	Remarks and references to Appendices
BOUZINCOURT	17		D.G.O. and Bombdr. CAITHNESS investigated gas shelling at MIRAUMONT. Normal shells used, scattered indiscriminately. Class of instruction for Company Gas N.C.O.s commenced.	
	21		Class returned to units on Division moving.	
	23		Sergt. SNOWDON and Corpl. BAILEY returned to re-join Gas School staff from their work in forward area.	
	24-26		Moving to STEENBECQUE with D.H.Q.	
STEENBECQUE	27		School established at STEENBECQUE, D.H.Q.	
	28		D.G.O. visited Chemical Adviser, First Army.	
	29-30		Fitting up School and arranging work.	
	31		D.G.O. and N.C.O's. toured 53rd Brigade, supervising fitting of small box respirators. Visited C.A. IInd Corps.	

R. J. T. Thompson Lt.
GAS OFFICER,
18th DIVISION.

2449 Wt. W14957/M90 750,000 1/16 J.B.C. & A. Forms/C.2118/12.

Secret

ANTI-GAS SCHOOL.
18TH DIVISION.
No. ....
Date 9/5/17

Vol 10

WAR DIARY

APRIL, 1917

VOL. X.

HEAD QUARTERS
No. ....
11 MAY. 1917
18TH DIVISION

R. J. T. Thompson. Lieut.

GAS OFFICER,
18th DIVISION.

Instructions regarding War Diaries and Intelligence Summaries are contained in F. S. Regs., Part II. and the Staff Manual respectively. Title Pages will be prepared in manuscript.

WAR DIARY

~~or~~ ~~INTELLIGENCE SUMMARY~~

(Erase heading not required.)

Army Form C. 2118.

VOL. X.

Place	Date	Hour	Summary of Events and Information	Remarks and references to Appendices
STEENBECQUE	1917 APRIL 1–26		During the month while the 18th Division was resting in the First Army area, numerous parades for the fitting of the small box respirator were supervised both for troops in the Division and for Corps Troops.	
			Four successive gas clouds were passed over all units of the 53rd Brigade to give them confidence in the small box respirator.	
			The Divl. Gas Officer lectured to and drilled each battery of the Divisional Artillery in the use of the respirator. They were specially practised in those points of the drill which they required particularly as gunners to defend themselves against hostile gas shelling.	
			Two classes of instruction for Company and Battery Gas N.C.O.s were held, and a third class begun.	
			R. J. Thompson Lt. GAS OFFICER, 18th DIVISION.	

2449 Wt. W14957/M90 750,000 1/16 J.B.C. & A. Forms/C.2118/12.

SECRET

18TH DIVISIONAL ANTI-GAS SCHOOL

Vol XI

WAR DIARY

VOL. XI

MAY 1917

R. J. T. Thompson Lt.

GAS OFFICER.
18th DIVISION.

HEAD QUARTERS
5 JUN 1917
18TH DIVISION

Instructions regarding War Diaries and Intelligence Summaries are contained in F. S. Regs., Part II. and the Staff Manual respectively. Title Pages will be prepared in manuscript.

WAR DIARY
~~INTELLIGENCE SUMMARY~~
(Erase heading not required.)

Army Form C. 2118.

VOL. XI.

Place	Date	Hour	Summary of Events and Information	Remarks and references to Appendices
	MAY.			
AGNY.	1 -10		Cpls. Lettington (55th) Gutteridge (54th) Pettit (52nd) and Caithness (Divl. Artillery) attached to the Headquarters of Infantry Brigades and the Divl. Artillery as Brigade Gas N.C.Os The state of anti-gas defence in the line and artillery reported on – more gongs and STROMBOS Horns required – In co-operation with D.A.D.O.S. secured 13 of the latter and had them placed in the line On 3/5/17 82nd Bde. R.F.A. were subjected to 100 gas shells of new variety – diphosgene and chlorpicrin asphyxiant and strongly lachrymatory. Reported on this, also on a bombardment with same gas shell on night of 2/3rd May in valley E. of NEUVILLE VITASSE. No casualties. Reports to "G" 18th Division and Chemical Advisor, 7th Corps Divl. Artillery Gas NCO brought in a sample of earth from gas shell hole near D/148 Battery R.F.A. on night of 10th May. This was analysed at Central Laboratory	

2449 Wt. W14957/M90 750,000 1/16 J.B.C. & A. Forms/C.2118/12.

Instructions regarding War Diaries and Intelligence Summaries are contained in F. S. Regs., Part II. and the Staff Manual respectively. Title Pages will be prepared in manuscript.

WAR DIARY
or
INTELLIGENCE SUMMARY

(Erase heading not required.)

Army Form C. 2118.

Place	Date	Hour	Summary of Events and Information	Remarks and references to Appendices
AGNY	1-10		and proved to be phosgene mustard oil, a new lachrymator.	
	11		Demonstration to transport officers etc in use of anti-gas horse respirator.	
			Visiting line, batteries, etc as to anti-gas precautions	
	-16		moved to new site where R.E.'s built 3 huts for the School about ½ mile S.W. of AGNY.	
			Two classes of instruction in anti-gas measures	
	18-31		Sgt. Snowden sent to Reinforcement Depot at LE SOUICH to train drafts	
			Smoke barrage in practice attack of 54th Brigade	
			Visits to line and artillery and reinforcement camp.	
			Selection of dug-outs & erection of gongs seen to	
			Various inspections of respirators and fitting respirators to units of Corps Troops	
			All the Corps Heavy artillery in Divisional area visited – their state of anti-gas defence reported on to C.A. VII Corps. On the whole it is good.	
			R.P. Thompson [signature]	

2449 Wt. W14957/M90 750,000 1/16 J.B.C. & A. Forms/C.2118/12.

Vol 12

WAR DIARY

OF

18TH DIVL. ANTI-GAS SCHOOL

VOL. XII.

JUNE 1917

HEAD QUARTERS
No.
8 - JUL. 1917
18TH DIVISION

R. F. Thompson Lt.
GAS OFFICER,
18th DIVISION.

Instructions regarding War Diaries and Intelligence Summaries are contained in F. S. Regs., Part II. and the Staff Manual respectively. Title Pages will be prepared in manuscript.

WAR DIARY
or
~~INTELLIGENCE SUMMARY~~
(Erase heading not required.)

Army Form C. 2118.

VOL. XII.

Place	Date JUNE	Hour	Summary of Events and Information	Remarks and references to Appendices
AGNY.	1st – to 17th		Two classes of instruction for N.C.Os in anti-gas duties were held during this period and work in the line such as arranging for the distribution and testing of Strombos Horns & other gas appliances in the line, inspections & so forth.	
COUIN	17th		Moved to COUIN with 18th Divl. H.Q.	
	17th-30th		One class of instruction. Gas Officer on leave from the 24th. Sgt. Challenley left in charge. All box respirators of units in Rest Area re-fitted in lachrymatory gas under Brigade Gas N.C.Os	

[illegible signature]

GAS OFFICER,
18th DIVISION.

2449 Wt. W14957/M90 750,000 1/16 J.B.C. & A. Forms/C.2118/12.

Secret

Vol / 3

WAR DIARY

FOR

JULY.

VOL. XIII

[signature]

LIEUT.,

GAS OFFICER 18TH DIVISION.

Instructions regarding War Diaries and Intelligence Summaries are contained in F. S. Regs., Part II. and the Staff Manual respectively. Title Pages will be prepared in manuscript.

WAR DIARY

~~or~~

~~INTELLIGENCE SUMMARY~~

(Erase heading not required.)

July, 1917

Vol. XIII

Army Form C. 2118.

Place	Date	Hour	Summary of Events and Information	Remarks and references to Appendices
COUIN	1st-4th		Moved to STEENVOORDE with D.HQ.	
	6th		D.G.O. returned from leave.	
STEENVOORDE	7th		Moved to RENINGHELST. Took over anti-gas appliances in the line from D.G.O., 30th Division.	
RENINGHELST	10th-16th		Class of instruction held for 12 NCOs	
	19th-25th		Class of instruction held for 17 NCOs	
			Handed over anti-gas appliances in line to D.G.O. 30th Division	
	26th-31st		Gas Cloud demonstration to all units of 53rd Inf. Bde.	
			Inspection of all small box respirators in 55th Inf. Brigade.	
			"Extensions" for small box respirators demonstrated to all units and issued to all units. These were quickly fitted.	
			During the month several gas shell bombardments were investigated and reported on. In one instance a cloud the result of a severe gas shell bombardment of ZILLEBEKE and locality, travelled back to D.HQ. and further – probably about 8 miles. The Germans commenced the use of a new type of gas in their gas shells, producing blistering effects all over the body. The box respirator will give perfect protection to the lungs, but the effects on the skin have so far baffled us as regards safeguarding the soldier from them in time to prevent development.	

[signature] Gas Officer 18th Division

2449 Wt. W14957/M90 750,000 1/16 J.B.C. & A. Forms/C.2118/12.

Secret

Vol 14

W A R   D I A R Y

for

A U G U S T , 1 9 1 7.

- - - - - - - - - - - -

[signature]

Lieut., R. E.

D.G.O., 18th. Division.

Instructions regarding War Diaries and Intelligence Summaries are contained in F. S. Regs., Part II. and the Staff Manual respectively. Title Pages will be prepared in manuscript.

WAR DIARY
or
~~INTELLIGENCE SUMMARY~~
(Erase heading not required.)

ANTI-GAS SCHOOL. 18TH DIVISION.
No.........
Date........

Army Form C. 2118.

VOL. XIV

Place	Date	Hour	Summary of Events and Information	Remarks and references to Appendices
RENINGHELST	1-14		Several gas shell attacks in which the enemy made much use of the new di-chlorethyl sulphide gas, took place. Nightly the enemy harrassed our communications and artillery with gas shells. The ~~c~~ gas casualties were very much more ~~numerous~~ than during any previous period in the line, but a large number were accounted for by the blistering effects. A scheme was arranged with D.A.D.O.S. by which all anti-gas Ordnance supplies were taken over by the D.G.O. for administration.	
	15		Handed over to D.G.O. 56th Division and moved to LEDERZEELE with D.H.Q. on Division going out to rest.	
LEDERZEELE	19-30		73 N.C.O.s from all units trained as gas N.C.O.s to replace casualties. Re-fitting of box respirators in all units arranged and supervised	

R. J. Ahayneult(?) Lt.
D.G.O. 18th Division

2449 Wt. W14957/M90 750,000 1/16 J.B.C. & A. Forms/C.2118/12.

SECRET 1

Anti Gas School
Vol 15

WAR DIARY

FOR

SEPTEMBER.

ANTI-GAS SCHOOL,
18TH DIVISION.
No. WAR DIARY
Date.

H G Hughes
2nd LIEUT. R.E
for GAS OFFICER,
18th DIVISION.

Vol 28/10

Instructions regarding War Diaries and Intelligence Summaries are contained in F. S. Regs., Part II. and the Staff Manual respectively. Title Pages will be prepared in manuscript.

WAR DIARY
or
~~INTELLIGENCE SUMMARY~~
(Erase heading not required.)

Army Form C. 2118.

VOL. XV.

Place	Date SEPTEMBER	Hour	Summary of Events and Information	Remarks and references to Appendices
LEDERZEELE.	1-2		Class of instruction for Company Gas NCOs.	
	3.		School moved to ESQUELBECQ.	
ESQUELBECQ.	4-12.		Class of instruction held for 37 N.C.Os. Inspection of the P.H. Helmets of all units of the 53rd Inf. Bde, & all units completely equipped with serviceable P.H. Helmets	
	13-18		Class of instruction held for "Refresher" Course for Company Gas NCO's.	
	19-22		Class of instruction held for "Refresher" Course for Coy. Gas NCOs. Lectures given to Officers & NCOs of 54th & 55th Infantry Brigades.	
	24		School moved to POPERINGHE.	
POPERINGHE.	25-30		Inspection of Small Box Respirators of all Units of the Division carried out & all units equipped with serviceable Anti-Gas Equipment.	

H. G. Hughes.
2nd Lieut. R.E.
for D.G.O. 18th DIVISION.

2449 Wt. W14957/M90 750,000 1/16 J.B.C. & A. Forms/C.2118/12.

16

Anti Gas School
Vol 16

War Diary

for

October. 1917.

Vol. XVI.

Instructions regarding War Diaries and Intelligence Summaries are contained in F. S. Regs., Part II. and the Staff Manual respectively. Title Pages will be prepared in manuscript.

WAR DIARY

~~or~~

~~INTELLIGENCE SUMMARY~~

(Erase heading not required.)

Army Form C. 2118.

VOL. XVI.

Place	Date	Hour	Summary of Events and Information	Remarks and references to Appendices
	OCTOBER.			
POPERINGHE.	1		Class of instruction being held for Officers of the Division.	
	2-5		Second class of instruction for Officers. Lectures given to all Companies of the 18th Divisional Train on Gas Defence.	
	6-10		Class of instruction for 28 NCOs of the Division & 8 NCOs from Corps Troops for training as Company Gas NCOs.	
BORDER CAMP.	11		Moved to BORDER CAMP. Took over Anti-Gas Trench Stores in Divisional Area from D.G.O. 51st (Highland) Division.	
	12-24		Weekly inspections of all Anti-Gas Trench Stores in the Divisional Area, & reports on the same. Investigations & reports on all gas shellings & gas shell bombardments. Visits to various units of the Division, Corps Troops, Dumps Etc. in Divisional Area. Inspection of the Anti-Gas Appliances of the 53rd & 55th Infantry Brigades.	
	25.		Handed over Anti-Gas Trench Stores to D.G.O. 58th Division.	
POPERINGHE.			Moved to POPERINGHE.	
	26-29		Brigade Gas NCOs holding inspections of Anti-Gas Appliances of Units in	

2449 Wt. W14957/M90 750,000 1/16 J.B.C. & A. Forms/C.2118/12.

Army Form C. 2118.

Instructions regarding War Diaries and Intelligence Summaries are contained in F. S. Regs., Part II. and the Staff Manual respectively. Title Pages will be prepared in manuscript.

WAR DIARY
or
INTELLIGENCE SUMMARY

(Erase heading not required.)

Place	Date	Hour	Summary of Events and Information	Remarks and references to Appendices
			Brigades.	
PROVEN.	30.		Moved to PROVEN.	
			[illegible] Lieut. R.E. D.G.O. 18th Division.	

2449 Wt. W14957/M90 750,000 1/16 J.B.C. & A. Forms/C.2118/12.

SECRET

17

18 D Gas Officer
Vol 17

War Diary.

for

November. 1917.

Vol. XVII

GAS
18TH DIVISION.
No. WAR DIARY.
Date. NOVEMBER.

H. A. Stillman.
2nd Lieut.,
for GAS OFFICER,
18th DIVISION.

Army Form C. 2118.

Instructions regarding War Diaries and Intelligence Summaries are contained in F. S. Regs., Part II. and the Staff Manual respectively. Title Pages will be prepared in manuscript.

WAR DIARY

or

~~INTELLIGENCE SUMMARY~~

(Erase heading not required.)

VOL. XVII

Place	Date	Hour	Summary of Events and Information	Remarks and references to Appendices
NOVEMBER.				
PROVEN.	1-4th		Units of the Division visited and inspections of Anti-Gas appliances held.	
"J" Camp.	5th		Moved to "J" Camp, & took over trench stores, reserve stores etc from D.G.O., 35th Division.	
	6-8th		Inspection of trench stores in the Divisional area. Divisional Baths, ELVERDINGHE visited & arrangements made for the erection of an Anti-blister bath, to be run in conjunction with the Divisional Baths.	
	9th		2nd Lieut. Hillman, 7th R. West Kent Regt. attached to School at "J" Camp, to take charge of & run the Courses of Instruction for Company Gas N.C.O's.	
	10th		Class of 21 N.C.O.s reported to "J" Camp for a 7 day course of instruction in Anti-Gas measures.	
ELVERDINGHE CHATEAU.	11th		D.G.O. moved with Divisional H.Q. to ELVERDINGHE CHATEAU, the School & Stores of Anti-Gas appliances remaining at "J" Camp.	
	12-18		10th Batt. Essex Regt., 11th Batt. R. Fusiliers & 6th Batt. Northants Regt. visited with regard to the casualties sustained in gas shell bombardment. Suggestions given and inspections carried out. The line & various pill-boxes in the area were visited with regard to the protection of shelters & dugouts against gas. Arrangements made for the completion of the Anti-blister baths, & the necessary chemicals and clothing obtained to run the baths.	
	19th		Class of 16 N.C.O.s reported to "J" Camp for a 7 day course of instruction.	

2449 Wt. W14957/M90 750,000 1/16 J.B.C. & A. Forms/C.2118/12.

Army Form C. 2118.

Instructions regarding War Diaries and Intelligence Summaries are contained in F. S. Regs., Part II. and the Staff Manual respectively. Title Pages will be prepared in manuscript.

WAR DIARY
or
INTELLIGENCE SUMMARY
(Erase heading not required.)

Place	Date	Hour	Summary of Events and Information	Remarks and references to Appendices
	20-27th		The Battalion Hd Qtrs of units in the line visited. Plans of Anti-Gas Doorframes submitted for the protection of these & other Hd Qtrs, Aid Posts & dugouts. Various units of the R.F.A. and R.G.A. in the Divisional Area were visited, & suggestions & advise given regarding the protection of men & shelters against gas. Gas shell bombardments investigated & reports on them submitted. Anti-blister Baths completed & opened for use.	
	28th		Class of 21 N.C.O's, including 5 from Corps Troops reported to "J" Camp for a 7 day course of instruction in anti-gas measures.	
	30th		D.G.O. proceeded to ENGLAND on leave. 2nd Lieut. Hillman acting as Div. Gas Officer pending the return of the D.G.O.	

A. J. Hillman 2Lt.
for. D.G.O.

2449 Wt. W14957/M90 750,000 1/16 J.B.C. & A. Forms/C.2118/12.

SECRET

18 D Gas School
Vol 18

War Diary

for

December/17.

Vol. XVIII.

GAS
18TH DIVISION.
No. 1/19
Date 9-1-18

Instructions regarding War Diaries and Intelligence Summaries are contained in F. S. Regs., Part II. and the Staff Manual respectively. Title Pages will be prepared in manuscript.

WAR DIARY or ~~INTELLIGENCE SUMMARY~~

(Erase heading not required.)

Army Form C. 2118.

VOL. XVIII.

Place	Date	Hour	Summary of Events and Information	Remarks and references to Appendices
DECEMBER.				
ELVERDINGHE CHATEAU.	1st - 16th.		Visits to the line & Brigades in Reserve & Support. Inspections of anti-gas appliances, protected shelters, battery positions etc., & reports on the condition of same. Gas shell bombardments investigated & reported on.	
			Class of instruction in Anti-Gas Measures held at "J" Camp from the 7th to the 14th.	
	16th		D.G.O. returned from ENGLAND off leave.	
ROUSBRUGGE.	18th		Moved with stores to ROUSBRUGGE. All Anti-Gas Appliances, Trench Stores & Stores at "J" & "H" Camps handed over to the D.G.O. 57th Division.	
	19th - 21st.		Arrangements made for the refitting of Small Box Respirators throughout the Division.	
	22nd		D.G.O. lecturing to the Officers & N.C.Os of 54th Brigade.	
	23rd - 31st		All units refitting Small Box Respirators. Visits to units & refitting parades. General supervision of fitting & Anti-Gas Training of units.	

[signature]

2449 Wt. W14957/M90 750,000 1/16 J.B.C. & A. Forms/C.2118/12.

SECRET

18 D Gas School
Vol 19

War Diary

for

January 1918.

Vol. XIX.

HEAD QUARTERS
No. ______
6 FEB. 1918
18TH DIVISION

GAS
18TH DIVISION.
No. 111
Date 6-2-18.

Army Form C. 2118.

Instructions regarding War Diaries and Intelligence Summaries are contained in F. S. Regs., Part II. and the Staff Manual respectively. Title Pages will be prepared in manuscript.

WAR DIARY
or
~~INTELLIGENCE~~ SUMMARY
(Erase heading not required.)

18th Div
Anti-Gas School
VOL. XIX

Place	Date	Hour	Summary of Events and Information	Remarks and references to Appendices
JANUARY 1918				
ROUSBRUGGE	1st +	2nd.	Refitting of Box respirators of 55th Inf. Bde. + RA. supervised by D.G.O.	
	3rd		Division moves to ELVERDINGHE CHATEAU. D.G.O. took over from D.G.O. 57th Division.	
ELVERDINGHE CHATEAU	8th.		Arrangements made for gas proof entrances to be built at 12 of the important concrete shelters in the Divisional sector.	
	11th + 12th		Line + artillery visited by D.G.O. to inspect protection of shelters against gas.	
	13th		Labour Coys respirators inspected by D.G.O.	
	14th		From 9 pm to 10.45 pm salvoes of Yellow Cross (dichlorethylsulphide) 77 m.m. shell were fired against our batteries in the BROEMBEEK. A few also against batteries in WIJDENDRIFT ROAD + the STEENBEEK. On account of the high wind – 20 miles per hr – gas was ineffective. Rounds fired about 300. Casualties NIL.	
	15th		Arrangements made for rattle shell alarms to be carried in each of line by reliefs, so that alarm can be spread when enemy shells our duck-board tracks, with gas shell.	
	17th.		D.G.O. went on special leave to renew kit burnt by fire at ELVERDINGHE chateau on Jan. 13th 1918. LT. J.C.S. BRANSON 8th Norfolks took over duty.	

2449 Wt. W14957/M90 750,000 1/16 J.B.C. & A. Forms/C.2118/12.

Army Form C. 2118.

Instructions regarding War Diaries and Intelligence Summaries are contained in F. S. Regs., Part II. and the Staff Manual respectively. Title Pages will be prepared in manuscript.

WAR DIARY
or
~~INTELLIGENCE SUMMARY~~

(Erase heading not required.)

Place	Date	Hour	Summary of Events and Information	Remarks and references to Appendices
JANUARY	1918			
ELVERDINGHE CHATEAU	17th		Arrangements made for issue of glycerine to units to treat expiratory valves of respirators to prevent moisture freezing in them & blocking them.	
	18th.		Refitting of respirators to 55th Inf. Brigade starts.	
	19th.		Gas proof entrances to dugouts finished. (See Jan 8th 1918, above)	
	22nd.		1 officer + 3 O.R. ranks reported gassed by enemy gas shell, & showing peculiar symptoms. Later, found to be due to carbon-monoxide formed by explosion of enemy H.E. shell in doorway of concrete "pill-box".	
	23rd.		Refitting of 55th Inf. Brigade finished. 8th Sussex (pioneers) respirators inspected & fitted.	
	25th.		D.G.O. returned from special leave.	
	26th.		Concrete shelters recently protected against gas reported on as efficient after inspection by D.G.O.	
	28th.		Lt. A.R. GREGORY 1/4th BORDER RGT. reported, to take over duty of D.G.O., who was appointed Chemical Adviser XVIII Corps.	
	29th		Lt R.J. THOMPSON proceeded to XVIII Corps.	
	30th		Division moved to Army reserve, being relieved by 32nd Divn.	
ROUSBRUGGE	31st.		D.G.O's office opened at ROUSBRUGGE	A.R. Gregory Lt. 1/4th Border Rgt. D.G.O. 18th Divn.

2449 Wt. W14957/M90 750,000 1/16 J.B.C. & A. Forms/C.2118/12.

Instructions regarding War Diaries and Intelligence Summaries are contained in F. S. Regs., Part II. and the Staff Manual respectively. Title pages will be prepared in manuscript.

WAR DIARY
or
INTELLIGENCE SUMMARY.
(Erase heading not required.)

Army Form C. 2118.

ROUSBRUGGE	Date	Hour	Summary of Events and Information	Remarks and references to Appendices
	Feb. 1-4		Inspections & lectures for all arms arranged in so far as movement of troops would allow.	
	5		Meeting of Brigade Gas officers at Divisional Gas officers office. Considered the principal steps which would have to be taken in the event of 18th Divn taking over part of line from the FRENCH. Decided that STROMBOS horns could be taken in by reliefs & posted as a temporary emergency measure at all headquarters. Decided that lectures on the German GAS-PROJECTORS which had recently been used for the first time should be given in all units – also lectures on the persistency of gas shell fillings, seeing that the country which Divn was probably going into would offer numerous suitable targets for enemy gas shell with a filling of high persistence. Decided that considerably more attention be paid to demonstration & instruction in HORSE-RESPIRATOR since a document recently captured from the enemy stated that the loss of guns & failure of ammunition supply at the battle of ARRAS was attributed largely to the effect of our gas on enemy horses.	

(A7092). Wt. W12839/M1293. 750,000. 1/17. D. D. & L., Ltd. Forms/C.2118/14.

Instructions regarding War Diaries and Intelligence Summaries are contained in F. S. Regs., Part II. and the Staff Manual respectively. Title pages will be prepared in manuscript.

WAR DIARY
or
INTELLIGENCE SUMMARY.
(Erase heading not required.)

Army Form C. 2118.

Place	Date	Hour	Summary of Events and Information	Remarks and references to Appendices
	Feb.			
ROUSBRUGGE	8th		Moved from ROUSBRUGGE entraining at PROVEN	
SALENCY	9th		Arrived SALENCY via NOYON	
	9-16		General training in gas defence so far as frequent movement of troops would allow. Special attention being paid to horse-respirators, distribution of these within the Division on a scale of 1 respirator to every 3 animals in each unit carried out.	
	17		Moved to BABOEUF	
BABOEUF	18-25		53rd Bde in training at CAILLOUEL area. Lectures & inspections daily. All Machine Gun Coys respirators tested in gas. Lectures to Machine Gun Coys - all ranks on PROJECTOR attacks, how to recognise them &c, & the persistency of gas shell fillings with special reference to Yellow Cross ("mustard gas" or dichlorethyl(sulphide).	
	26		Visited 58th Div Gas officer as preliminary to taking over from him.	
	27		Moved to ROUEZ. Visited 14th Div Gas officer to take over from him. No Strombos horns gas alarms had yet been set up, & protected dugouts were very few. Some dugouts protected with curtains by the FRENCH did not appear to be in an efficient state. 53rd Bde took over 2½ miles of front from 14th Div.	

(A7092). Wt. W12839/M1293. 750,000. 1/17. D. D. & L., Ltd. Forms/C.2118/14.

Instructions regarding War Diaries and Intelligence Summaries are contained in F. S. Regs., Part II. and the Staff Manual respectively. Title pages will be prepared in manuscript.

WAR DIARY
or
INTELLIGENCE SUMMARY.

(*Erase heading not required.*)

18th D Gas Offr.

Army Form C. 2118.

Vol 20

Place	Date	Hour	Summary of Events and Information	Remarks and references to Appendices
	February 1918.		and 53rd Bde 2½ miles of front from 14th Divn. Sufficient alarms &c for this front had already been indented for by 58th & 14th Divns. & it was agreed that they should be handed over in the correct proportion by these Divns. to 18th Divn. on arrival.	
ROUEZ	28		On account of lack of accomodation for gas-store at ROUEZ moved to VILLEQUIER AUMONT.	

[signature] Capt.
18th Divisional Gas Officer

Q 1343

7

Instructions regarding War Diaries and Intelligence Summaries are contained in F. S. Regs., Part II. and the Staff Manual respectively. Title pages will be prepared in manuscript.

WAR DIARY
or
~~INTELLIGENCE SUMMARY.~~
(Erase heading not required.)

18th Div. Anti-Gas School.

Army Form C. 2118.

21

Place	Date	Hour	Summary of Events and Information	Remarks and references to Appendices
ROUEZ	1-3-18		moved, with antigas ordnance store to VILLEQUIER-AUMONT.	
VILLEQUIER AUMONT	1/3/14 3/18		In the sector taken over by 18th Divn from 58th + 14th Divns, from about MOY to just south of VENDEUIL there were a very large number of dugouts - including those in FORT VENDEUIL and FORT LIEZ - which had been constructed by the FRENCH. The gas protection of these was either non-existent or inefficient. The work of making these gas-proof, already begun by 58th + 14th Divns., was therefore pushed on with as rapidly as supplies of material + labour would allow, the protection made consisting of the usual double curtains of blanket or Union Antigas cloth at each entrance.. STROMBOS horn cloud gas alarms had also to be installed; 46 horns were obtained + installed by March 14th, establishing alarm chains of sound from the front line as far back as VILLEQUIER AUMONT. It was expected that the enemy would make extensive use of gas when his impending attack started.	

A7092 Wt. W12839/M1293 750,000. 1/17. D. D & L. Ltd. Forms/C2118/14.

Instructions regarding War Diaries and Intelligence Summaries are contained in F. S. Regs., Part II. and the Staff Manual respectively. Title pages will be prepared in manuscript.

WAR DIARY

or

~~INTELLIGENCE SUMMARY.~~

(Erase heading not required.)

Army Form C. 2118.

Place	Date	Hour	Summary of Events and Information	Remarks and references to Appendices
VILLEQUIER AUMONT	14/3/18		Capt Lord KENNEDY, area gas officer from SCOTLAND arrived for a short period of attachment to D.G.O. to have experience of active service gas defence, & left to be attached to 53rd Infantry Bde. in the line	
VILLEQUIER AUMONT	15 to 19/3/18		Installation of STROMBOS horns + protection of dugouts going forward. About 100 dugouts entrances have so far been protected. Horse respirators were withdrawn from A.S.C. + D.A.C. and distributed among units whose horse lines were in advanced positions likely to be gas shelled. Gas shelling up to this time had been confined to light harassing fire at night on our lines of approach. Many blind shell, fuzes, and samples of earth from gas shell-holes were sent in by gas officers & N.C.Os. of brigades, but no signs of any new enemy gas were discovered. The enemy used PHENYL CARBYLAMINE shell on many occasions. The inspection & testing of respirators in gas chamber was carried on as usual, about 5% of the respirators being condemned for serious faults. The majority of units	

Army Form C. 2118.

WAR DIARY
or
~~INTELLIGENCE SUMMARY.~~
(Erase heading not required.)

Instructions regarding War Diaries and Intelligence Summaries are contained in F. S. Regs., Part II. and the Staff Manual respectively. Title pages will be prepared in manuscript.

Place	Date	Hour	Summary of Events and Information	Remarks and references to Appendices
			frequently practised all ~~at~~ arms in carrying out their duties while wearing respirators, in order to be prepared to carry on under a prolonged enemy gas shell bombardment. HEDGING-GLOVES were issued to artillery personnel to enable them to handle ammunition which might be splashed with YELLOW-CROSS (DICHLORETHYL SULPHIDE) in safety.	
VILLEQUIER AUMONT	19/3/18		Capt KENNEDY returned to D. G. Os. office from 53rd Inf. Bde.	
	21/3/18		The enemy barrage, preparatory for his attack started at about 4.30 am. During the first 2 hours he used a large proportion of green cross (PHOSGENE, CHLORPICRIN &c) + blue cross (DIPHENYL-ARSENIOUS-CHLORIDE) gas shell mixed with High Explosive and shrapnel; during the later stages the proportion of gas shell was small, or nil. Gas shelling was especially heavy on battery positions & villages. REMIGNY was gas shelled very heavily indeed. LY-FONTAINE, FORT	

Instructions regarding War Diaries and Intelligence Summaries are contained in F. S. Regs., Part II. and the Staff Manual respectively. Title pages will be prepared in manuscript.

WAR DIARY
or
~~INTELLIGENCE SUMMARY.~~
(Erase heading not required.)

Army Form C. 2118.

Place	Date	Hour	Summary of Events and Information	Remarks and references to Appendices
			LIEZ and VENDEUIL also received a considerable amount of gas. Movement of troops & the work of batteries in the northern sector seems to have been impeded somewhat owing to the necessity for wearing respirators, but not so much in the southern sector, where however the gas was not so strong. The Division sustained only about 40 gas casualties on this day.	
VILLEQUIER AUMONT	21/3/18	11pm	Moved, with store to UGNY-LE-GAY.	
UGNY-LE-GAY	23/3/18		Moved, with store, to BABOEUF	
BABOEUF	24/3/18		One lorry load of respirators & other stores had to be burned owing to lack of transport to move it. Set out with remainder of stores for THIESCOURT	
	25/3/18		Arrived at rear Divisional Headquarters THIESCOURT. Remainder of stores burnt, as lorry was required for other purposes. Set out for ESTREES-ST DENIS.	
ESTREES-ST DENIS	28/3/18		Left for VILLERS-COTTERETS, with rear Divnl. Hq., to get nearer to Advanced Divnl Hdqs.	
VILLERS COTTERETS	28 to 31/3/18		At VILLERS COTTERETS.	

A R Gregory Capt.
1/4 K Border Regt
D.G.O.

Instructions regarding War Diaries and Intelligence Summaries are contained in F. S. Regs., Part II, and the Staff Manual respectively. Title pages will be prepared in manuscript.

WAR DIARY or ~~INTELLIGENCE SUMMARY.~~ 18th Div. Gas Officer.

(Erase heading not required.)

Army Form C. 2118.

Vol 22

Place	Date	Hour	Summary of Events and Information	Remarks and references to Appendices
VILLERS COTTERETS	1-4-18		left by train for SALEUX	
SALEUX	4-4-18		arrived SALEUX, with rear Divn. Hq., advanced Div. Hq. being at BOVES. Between April 4th + 12th cases of gas shelling by the enemy were investigated. Blue cross (DIPHENYL-CHLOR-ARSINE - 'sneezing gas') + green cross (DIPHOSGENE (CHLORPICRINE) were principally used, together with a lachrymatory gas with very little toxic effect, + very volatile. GENTELLES and BOIS GENTELLES received attention with blue cross particularly.	
AMIENS	12-4-18		moved from SALEUX to AMIENS. Enemy fired a considerable amount of yellow cross (DICHLOR-ETHYL SULPHIDE) into DOMART + the valley in which the town lies. Casualties were caused amongst 18th Divn. Machine gunners + infantry, owing to the dangerous nature of weak fumes not being realised. FRENCH COLONIAL troops also suffered severely, apparently owing to the fact that they found it difficult or impossible to wear respirators for more than a few minutes.	
St FUSCIEN	14-4-18		left AMIENS and joined advanced Divn. Hq at St FUSCIEN, Divn. being then in reserve.	

A7092 Wt. W12-9/M1293 750,000. 1/17. D. D & L. Ltd. Forms/C2118/14.

Army Form C. 2118.

Instructions regarding War Diaries and Intelligence Summaries are contained in F. S. Regs., Part II. and the Staff Manual respectively. Title pages will be prepared in manuscript.

WAR DIARY
or
~~INTELLIGENCE SUMMARY.~~

(Erase heading not required.)

Place	Date	Hour	Summary of Events and Information	Remarks and references to Appendices
ST FUSCIEN	16-4-18		Re-started store of antigas appliances.	
	17+18		VILLERS BRETONNEUX and BOIS L'ABBÉ area was heavily bombarded with yellow cross, by the enemy. This was in the 58th Divn. area, but in view of the possibility of 18th Divn. units being called upon to occupy positions in the area affected, particulars of the bombardment were obtained. About twenty thousand rounds were fired into the area during the 2 days, 58th Divn + AUSTRALIAN troops being affected. Prisoner taken on the first day stated that an enemy gas officer had said that enemy would attack after heavy bombardment of VILLERS BRETONNEUX with yellow cross. By the end of the first day 69 officers + 1016 other ranks were gas casualties, caused chiefly by direct hits on cellars or houses in VILLERS BRETONNEUX, + failure to realize that the faintly smelling vapour given off by the shell liquid lying on the ground after the bombardment had finished was dangerous to live in for many hours on end. All troops were moved out of the town + out of most of the BOIS LABBÉ,	

A7092 Wt. W128.9/M1293 750,000. 1/17. D. D. & L. Ltd. Forms/C2118/14.

Instructions regarding War Diaries and Intelligence Summaries are contained in F. S. Regs., Part II. and the Staff Manual respectively. Title pages will be prepared in manuscript.

WAR DIARY

or

~~INTELLIGENCE SUMMARY.~~

(*Erase heading not required.*)

Army Form C. 2118.

Place	Date	Hour	Summary of Events and Information	Remarks and references to Appendices
			The enemy infantry attack on April 24th. was directed on the flanks of the town; it was reported that enemy troops were ordered not to enter the town, but prisoners were taken whose eyes were inflamed from being in the gas. 8" yellow cross gas shell was used by enemy in this bombardment.	
St FUSCIEN "	19th 24 4/18		Lectures were delivered by Gas officer, to officers & NCOs of all R.E. & infantry units of the Division on the subject of YELLOW-CROSS shell giving an account of its use since March 21st. showing how the gas might be recognised, giving warning of the dangerous nature of the weak vapour from liquid lying about after the bombardment, pointing out that troops must be trained to such a pitch that they can wear their respirators for several hours on end if called upon, for instance to hold a tactically important position which the enemy might try to deny to them by filling it with yellow cross	

A7092 Wt. W1189/M1293 750,000. 1/17. D. D & L. Ltd. Forms/C2118/14.

Instructions regarding War Diaries and Intelligence Summaries are contained in F. S. Regs., Part II. and the Staff Manual respectively. Title pages will be prepared in manuscript.

WAR DIARY
or
~~INTELLIGENCE SUMMARY.~~
(Erase heading not required.)

Army Form C. 2118.

Place	Date	Hour	Summary of Events and Information	Remarks and references to Appendices
ST FUSCIEN	24/4/18		Arrangements were put in hand by the Division Q branch to fit up a special antigas bath at BOVES ~~whose~~ to be used for treating men whose clothes were infected with yellow cross vapour or spray, or who showed signs of incipient blistering. Such men were to discard their infected clothing in the open, & then to bathe in a hot weak solution of BICARBONATE of SODA followed by a shower & wash with soap. They would then be fitted with a complete new outfit of clothing, the yellow cross vapour or spray in the infected clothing being driven off or destroyed by treatment with saturated steam at 100°C in the THRESH clothing disinfector, dried & reissued.	
CAVILLON	27/4/18		moved with store to CAVILLON. Captain H. W. TERRY engineers U.S.R. AMERICAN Expeditionary Force arrived for attachment with a view to training as gas officer to an American Division.	
CAVILLON	27 to 30 4/18		Testing in gas, & inspection of respirators, & drill instruction with various units.	

A7092 Wt. W128.9/M1293 750,000. 1/17. D. D & L. Ltd. Forms/C2118/14.

A.R. Gregory Capt. Gas officer 10th Divn.

(1)

Instructions regarding War Diaries and Intelligence Summaries are contained in F. S. Regs., Part II. and the Staff Manual respectively. Title pages will be prepared in manuscript.

HEAD QUARTERS No. 13/30 19 JUN. 1918 18th DIVISION

WAR DIARY
or
~~INTELLIGENCE SUMMARY.~~
(Erase heading not required.)

D.G.O. 18th DIVISION. No. W.D. 3 Date

Army Form C. 2118.

Vol 23

Place	Date	Hour	Summary of Events and Information	Remarks and references to Appendices
CAVILLON	1.5.18 to 3.5.18		Respirators of various units inspected and tested in gas chamber.	
	4.5.18		In view of the large amount of Yellow cross (DICHLORETHYLSULPHIDE) gas shell used by the enemy in the recent offensive, a short account of its use, properties, & the precautions to be taken was sent to formations through the General Staff of the Division. These notes contained the substance of the lectures delivered to units, as mentioned in War Diary for April 1918.	
BAVELIN-COURT.	5.5.18		moved, with stores, from CAVILLON to BAVELINCOURT.	
BAVELIN-COURT	6.5.18 to 17.5.18		Under 4th Army order, Field & Tunnelling Coys. R.E. were made responsible for fitting double antigas curtains & frames invariably, to every dugout immediately it was completed by them. A large programme of dugout construction had been drawn up for the Divisional area, & each as it was completed was therefore inspected in order to see that it had been made efficiently gas-proof. In all, 24 dugouts were completed & made gas proof, including Brigade, Battn, Battery Hq,	

A7092 Wt. W128.9/M1293 750,000. 1/17. D. D & L. Ltd. Forms/C2118/14.

(2).

Instructions regarding War Diaries and Intelligence Summaries are contained in F. S. Regs., Part II. and the Staff Manual respectively. Title pages will be prepared in manuscript.

WAR DIARY
~~or~~
~~INTELLIGENCE~~ SUMMARY.

(*Erase heading not required.*)

D.G.O.,
18th DIVISION.
No........
Date........

Army Form C. 2118.

Place	Date	Hour	Summary of Events and Information	Remarks and references to Appendices
			signallers and machine-gunners dugouts. — 3 TONS of CHLORIDE of LIME were distributed amongst Brigade, Battn. & Battery headquarters in the line, to be used, if necessary, on yellow cross gas-shell-holes. An ANTIGAS BATH (working on the system mentioned in War diary for April) was instituted at BEHENCOURT.	
BAVELIN-COURT	18.5.18		Capt TERRY - AMERICAN Expeditionary Force, left for attachment to III Corps gas school.	
	19.5.18		41st. SIEGE BATTERY at BRESLE sustained gas casualties to 2 officers and 38 O.R. On investigation it was found that the battery was shelled when in action between midnight and 3 am. with what was taken to be ordinary H.E. shell, but from 10 am. to 4 pm. men were being evacuated with eye, & other, symptoms characteristic of yellow cross. No gas shell was suspected either from the sound of burst or from any smell of gas, the latter being	

(3)

Army Form C. 2118.

D.G.O.
18th DIVISION.
No. ....
Date. ....

Instructions regarding War Diaries and Intelligence Summaries are contained in F. S. Regs., Part II. and the Staff Manual respectively. Title pages will be prepared in manuscript.

~~WAR DIARY~~
~~or~~
INTELLIGENCE SUMMARY.

(Erase heading not required.)

Place	Date	Hour	Summary of Events and Information	Remarks and references to Appendices
			probably masked by fumes of the guns being blown on to the crews by a N.E. wind. It seemed probable that the shell used was that described in a document recently captured from the enemy – viz. one containing a mixed filling of gas & H.E. An account of this shelling, & of the suspected shell was therefore issued to formations through the Divisional General Staff, with a warning that in bombardments which appeared to be H.E. only, a sharp look out must be kept for gas.	
	20.5.16 to 23.5.16		The inspection of gas protection of dugouts as these were completed was continued. Since the Division took over this sector, gas shelling by the enemy took place nearly every night, but never of a severe nature. BRESLE & LAVIEVILLE & Battery positions in the BRESLE valley received a certain amount of gas. The valley running due N. from BUIRE to the AMIENS-ALBERT road was gas shelled	

A7092 Wt. W128 9/M1293 750,000. 1/17. D. D & L. Ltd. Forms/C2118/14.

Instructions regarding War Diaries and Intelligence Summaries are contained in F. S. Regs., Part II. and the Staff Manual respectively. Title pages will be prepared in manuscript.

~~WAR DIARY~~
or
INTELLIGENCE SUMMARY.
(Erase heading not required.)

D.G.O.,
18th DIVISION.
No ....
Date..........

Army Form C. 2118.

(4)

Place	Date	Hour	Summary of Events and Information	Remarks and references to Appendices
			nearly every night, including one bombardment of 200 yellow cross shell – the largest recorded while the Divn. was in this sector. In most cases high explosive shell was mixed with the gas shell. None of the targets engaged by gas shell were occupied at the time, the numerous batteries in the BRESLE valley N.E. of BRESLE (an obvious target for gas shell) had been distributed over a wider area, villages were not occupied by troops, and transport tracks ran across country on high ground, for the most part. Troops of the Division did not sustain more than 6 casualties during the whole time in the sector.	
	24.5.16		A section of a Field Coy R.E. whilst returning from the line was shelled with what appeared to be ordinary 77 m.m. high explosive. After a few hours, however, 2 men showed pronounced yellow cross symptoms. This was further evidence that the enemy was using shell containing a mixed H.E. & gas filling. No specimens of the	

A7092 Wt. W128.9/M1293 750,000. 1/17. D. D & L. Ltd. Forms/C2118/14.

(5)

Army Form C. 2118.

WAR DIARY
or
INTELLIGENCE SUMMARY.
(Erase heading not required.)

Instructions regarding War Diaries and Intelligence Summaries are contained in F. S. Regs., Part II. and the Staff Manual respectively. Title pages will be prepared in manuscript.

Place	Date	Hour	Summary of Events and Information	Remarks and references to Appendices
			new shell were found, though many blind gas shell were found and brought in during the period.	
BAVELIN-COURT	25.5.18		The Division was relieved by 47th Division. Divnl. Hq. moved to MOLLIENS AU-BOIS. Gas officer, with store remained at BAVELINCOURT.	
	29.5.18.		D.G.O. proceeded to III Corps headquarters to act as Chemical Adviser in absence on leave of Capt SLADE. R.E. — Lt. SCAIFE gas officer 53rd. Infantry Bde acted as D.G.O.	
	29 to 31/5/18		D.G.O. carried on with inspections of respirators, & testing of them in gas chamber.	
			A.R. Gregory Capt. Gas officer 18th Division.	
			19-6-18	

A7092 Wt. W128 9/M1293 750,000. 1/17. D. D & L. Ltd. Forms/C2118/14.

Gas Officer. (D.G.O) (1)

Instructions regarding War Diaries and Intelligence Summaries are contained in F. S. Regs., Part II. and the Staff Manual respectively. Title pages will be prepared in manuscript.

WAR DIARY
or
INTELLIGENCE SUMMARY.
(Erase heading not required.)

Army Form C. 2118.

VR 24

Place	Date	Hour	Summary of Events and Information	Remarks and references to Appendices
BAVELIN-COURT	2.6.18		On the Division moving up into the left sector of the Corps front, D.G.O. returned from III Corps to the Division. Office and store moved from BAVELINCOURT to CONTAY.	
CONTAY	3.6.18		On 31st May CONTAY had been bombarded with high velocity long range shell containing YELLOW CROSS. One of these struck the chateau and D.G.O. 58th Divn. had found there a Gr Z 04 fuze. The portion of the chateau which was infected with gas had already been treated with chloride of lime, & doors &c barricaded to prevent access. The use of long range gas shell had already been reported on one occasion viz at RIVERY. With a view to identifying the shell at CONTAY a search was made for fragments by digging up a shell hole. Between 4 + 7 feet below ground fragments of the shell were found, including a false cap, + the	

D. D. & L., London, E.C.
(A10266) Wt W5300/P713 750,000 2/15 Sch. 52 Forms/C2118/16

Army Form C. 2118.

D60 (7)

Instructions regarding War Diaries and Intelligence Summaries are contained in F. S. Regs., Part II. and the Staff Manual respectively. Title pages will be prepared in manuscript.

WAR DIARY
or
INTELLIGENCE SUMMARY.
(Erase heading not required.)

Place	Date	Hour	Summary of Events and Information	Remarks and references to Appendices
			greater part of the shell could be reconstructed by fitting the fragments together. The shell was identified as the new pattern 15. cm. naval shell with false cap, having a range of about 25000 yards.	
CONTAY	4.6.18		A large programme of dugout construction had been prepared for the Corps area. Lists of those already completed, or under construction were therefore prepared from Chief Engineer's (III Corps) list & sent to Artillery, & Infantry Brigade, gas officers so that they might keep in touch with the progress of work, and supervise gas-proofing.	
CONTAY	5 to 7 6/18		Inspection of gas proof dugouts, & testing of respirators of various units in gas chamber.	
	8.6.18		Divnl. Gas N.C.O. at Corps gas school ordered to report to 21st. American Infantry Bde to assist with the fitting of respirators to American troops, and training them in antigas measures.	

D. D. & L., London, E.C.
(A10266) Wt W5300/P713 750,000 2/18 Sch. 52 Forms/C2118/16

(DGO) (3)

Army Form C. 2118.

WAR DIARY
or
INTELLIGENCE SUMMARY.

(Erase heading not required.)

Instructions regarding War Diaries and Intelligence Summaries are contained in F. S. Regs., Part II. and the Staff Manual respectively. Title pages will be prepared in manuscript.

Place	Date	Hour	Summary of Events and Information	Remarks and references to Appendices
CONTAY	9.6.18		LT. ALDOUS Special Bde R.E. arrived for temporary attachment for training as Divisional Gas officer.	
	11.6.18		Information was received from Fourth Army Chemical Adviser, that enemy gas shelling had taken place the day before along the whole Army front, of a fairly heavy nature. The shelling in this Divisional sector was comparatively slight, a total of not more than 200 rounds blue + green cross being received. One casualty was caused from what appeared to be the new YELLOW CROSS 1. Since eye symptoms were shown but the liquid filling of the shell was very volatile compared with ordinary YELLOW CROSS.	
	13.6.18		Artillery gas officer reported an 8 inch "blind" gas shell at a battery position. This was examined in position, confirmed as gas shell with Gr. Z. 92 fuze, & was brought in & description sent to Chemical	

D. D. & L., London, E.C.
(A10266) Wt.W5300/P713 750,000 2/18 Sch. 52 Forms/C2118/16

(D.G.O.) (4)

Army Form C. 2118.

Instructions regarding War Diaries and Intelligence Summaries are contained in F. S. Regs., Part II. and the Staff Manual respectively. Title pages will be prepared in manuscript.

WAR DIARY
or
INTELLIGENCE SUMMARY.
(Erase heading not required.)

Place	Date	Hour	Summary of Events and Information	Remarks and references to Appendices
			Adviser III Corps, by whom it was subsequently collected.	
	17+18 6/18		The whole of the infantry of 54th Bde were examined in respirator drill, their respirators inspected and tested in gas chamber. Short lecture was delivered on the new H.E. shells containing gas, & all ranks warned to be on their guard against gas even during what appeared to be ordinary high explosive bombardment.	
	21 + 22 6/18		The workshop lorry touring in the Corps area to replace the present eyepieces of respirators by TRIPLEX glass eyepieces was set to work on the crews of the Divisional Machine Gun Battn. which were out of the line. About 350 respirators were so fitted and examined.	
	23-6-18		Caves at WARLOY were reconnoitred with a view to reporting on	

D. D. & L., London, E.C.
(A10266) Wt W5300/P713 750,000 2/18 Sch. 52 Forms/C2118/16

D.G.O. (5)

Army Form C. 2118.

Instructions regarding War Diaries and Intelligence Summaries are contained in F. S. Regs., Part II. and the Staff Manual respectively. Title pages will be prepared in manuscript.

WAR DIARY
or
INTELLIGENCE SUMMARY.

(Erase heading not required.)

Place	Date	Hour	Summary of Events and Information	Remarks and references to Appendices
			the most suitable means of making them gas proof.	
	25.6.18		253rd. Tunnelling Coy R.E. tested in respirator drill, respirators examined + tested in gas chamber. Lecture delivered on "Projectors" "Shells containing H.E. + gas" "Gas-proofing of dugouts".	
	26.6.18.		Lt. ALDOUS R.E. left for XIX Corps gas school.	
	28 + 29 6.18.		A permanent gas chamber was fitted up in WARLOY for use of Reserve brigade or other troops.	
			Gas shelling during the month was fairly extensive, but never intense, was confined chiefly to fire on tracks headquarters &c. at night.	
			Gas proofing of dugouts made very good progress. At the end of the month 42 gas proof mined dugouts for headquarters, machine gun emplacements &c were available in the Divnl. area.	A.R. Gregory Capt. 18th D.G.O. 6.7.18

D. D. & L., London, E.C.
(A10266) Wt W5300/P713 750,000 2/18 Sch. 52 Forms/C2118/16

Instructions regarding War Diaries and Intelligence Summaries are contained in F. S. Regs., Part II. and the Staff Manual respectively. Title pages will be prepared in manuscript.

WAR DIARY
or
INTELLIGENCE SUMMARY.
(Erase heading not required.)

Army Form C. 2118.

18 D Gas School

98 25

Place	Date	Hour	Summary of Events and Information	Remarks and references to Appendices
Contay	1-2/7/18		The enemy put down mixed barrage on our front line system during the night – Gas & H.E. 21 Gas Casualties	
"	3-12/7/18		Nothing of importance happened during the period. Strombos Horns established at various points	
Cavillon	13/7/18		Moved to Cavillon after being relieved by 47th (London) Division	
"	14-31/7/18		Units resting and training. Inspections of S.B.Rs carried out and lectures given. Lorry with trained personnel of 1 NCO & 6 ors visited the following units and fitted all S.B.Rs with TRIPLEX glass eyepieces viz/ 18th MG Battn., 18 Divisional Artillery, Signallers, Bde H.Q. and L.T.M. Batteries.	

Basil R Rose
Lieut DGO 18 Div

D. D. & L., London, E.C.
(A10266) Wt W5300/P713 750,000 2/18 Sch. 52 Forms/C2118/16

August 1918

Instructions regarding War Diaries and Intelligence Summaries are contained in F. S. Regs., Part II. and the Staff Manual respectively. Title pages will be prepared in manuscript.

WAR DIARY
or
INTELLIGENCE SUMMARY.
(Erase heading not required.)

D.G.O 18th DIVN Gas

Army Form C. 2118.

Place	Date	Hour	Summary of Events and Information	Remarks and references to Appendices
Cavillon	1/8		Move to St Gratien.	VR 26
St Gratien	2/8 - 4/8		Visits Bdes & Field ambulances re fitting of Glass Eyepieces.	
	5/8		Lt Power handed over duties of DGO to Lt Southam	
	6/8		Heavy Enemy Gas Shelling on Bray Corbie Road	
	7/8		Moved to advanced DHQ Heilly	
	8/8 - 10/8		Visits to units & P.O.W cage re German Respirators	
	11/8		Division out of line owing to converging movements of flank Divisions	
	12/8		Move to Contay	
Contay	12/8		Visit to 55th Infy Brigade BGO re Casualties to Queens.	
			CH Corps Experiment Beaucourt	
	13-21/8		Continuous visits, lectures & training all units	
	22/8		Attack on Albert — visits Albert after attack	
	23/8		Gas Shelling of Albert — visit to Albert	
	24/8		Visit to ADS [illegible] re Gas casualties	

D. D. & L., London, E.C.
(A10266) Wt W5300/P713 750,000 2/18 Sch. 52 Forms/C2118/16

August 1918

Instructions regarding War Diaries and Intelligence Summaries are contained in F. S. Regs., Part II. and the Staff Manual respectively. Title pages will be prepared in manuscript.

WAR DIARY
or
INTELLIGENCE SUMMARY.
(Erase heading not required.)

Army Form C. 2118.

Place	Date	Hour	Summary of Events and Information	Remarks and references to Appendices
Contay	25/8		Visited forward areas Pozières Fricourt Tara Hill &c & all Bdes. Moved to Warloy Baillon	
Warloy Baillon	26/8		Forward areas visited	
	29/8		Moved to Ribemont S/Ancre	
Ribemont S/A	30/31 Aug		Visits to forward areas & all Brigades	
			Edgar [illegible] Lt a/ [illegible] 18th Div	

D. D. & L., London, E.C.
(A10166) Wt W5300/P713 750,000 2/18 Sch. 52 Forms/C2118/16

Instructions regarding War Diaries and Intelligence Summaries are contained in F. S. Regs., Part II. and the Staff Manual respectively. Title pages will be prepared in manuscript.

WAR DIARY
or
INTELLIGENCE SUMMARY.
(Erase heading not required.)

Divl Gas Officer

Army Form C. 2118.

Vol. 28

Place	Date	Hour	Summary of Events and Information	Remarks and references to Appendices
~~Ribemont~~ Bernafay Wood	5/7/18		Capt. F Southam appointed D.G.O. 33 Division and duties taken over by Lieut E. Shannon, East Surrey Regt. pending return of Capt. R.R. Mwer, ~~from leave~~ appointed D.G.O. 18 Division, from leave.	
	5-16.		During period of rest, numerous lectures were delivered to various units on Mustard Gas. Samples prepared and handed over to units with a view to all ranks becoming thoroughly acquainted with the smell of the gas.	
LIERAMONT	17-24		Division moved into the line. Divisional H.Q. being at Lieramont. During this period, casualties from Mustard Gas were relatively small - owing probably to shortage of ammunition of the enemy. Upwards of 500 Bosche respirators were examined as prisoners came in	

D. D. & L., London, E.C.
(A10266) Wt W5300/P713 750,000 2/18 Sch. 52 Forms/C2118/16

Army Form C. 2118.

Instructions regarding War Diaries and Intelligence Summaries are contained in F. S. Regs., Part II. and the Staff Manual respectively. Title pages will be prepared in manuscript.

WAR DIARY
or
INTELLIGENCE SUMMARY.
(Erase heading not required.)

Place	Date	Hour	Summary of Events and Information	Remarks and references to Appendices
			and it was noticed with interest that in some few cases the containers dated back as early as May 1917. As these containers were all in first rate condition, it would seem that the Enemy is short of supplies and was obliged to utilise old stocks. All Brigades and some battalions were visited during this time and some additional lectures given.	
COMBLES	25-27		Move to COMBLES - Short period of rest. Course of lectures continued	
LIERAMONT	28-30		Move back to LIERAMONT - Brigades visited in the line	

HEAD QUARTERS No. 78/57 5-OCT. 1918 18TH DIVISION

Basil R. Power
Capt
D.G.O. 18 Div.

D. D. & L., London, E.C.
(A10266) Wt W5300/P715 750,000 2/18 Sch. 52 Forms/C2118/16

Instructions regarding War Diaries and Intelligence Summaries are contained in F. S. Regs., Part II. and the Staff Manual respectively. Title pages will be prepared in manuscript.

WAR DIARY
or
INTELLIGENCE SUMMARY.
(Erase heading not required.)

Army Form C. 2118.

18 D Gas School
Vol 28

Place	Date	Hour	Summary of Events and Information	Remarks and references to Appendices
BEAUCOURT	1-16 10/18		During this period of rest a series of lectures was arranged and given to (1) Officers & (2) NCOs of Battalions. The object of these lectures was to give a simple explanation of types of gas used by the enemy, particular stress being laid on the properties and effects of Mustard Gas. Samples of Mustard gas were prepared and used at all lectures.	
LE CATEAU	22-30 10/18		On the morning of 23rd line was advanced and captured ground in the neighbourhood of LE FOREST and BOUSIES. Carefully searched for specimens of enemy gas shells. Very little was found. Three rounds of 5.9 cm Green Cross only. During the month casualties from gas have been small.	

[illegible]
Capt DGO 18 Div

D. D. & L., London, E.C.
(A10266) Wt W5300/P713 750,000 2/18 Sch. 52 Forms/C2118/16

Instructions regarding War Diaries and Intelligence Summaries are contained in F. S. Regs., Part II. and the Staff Manual respectively. Title pages will be prepared in manuscript.

WAR DIARY
or
INTELLIGENCE SUMMARY.
(Erase heading not required.)

Army Form C. 2118.

Vol 39

Place	Date	Hour	Summary of Events and Information	Remarks and references to Appendices
LE CATEAU	1-11 11/18		Casualties during this period were negligible and no reports of gas shelling were received. There were some isolated casualties amongst the civilians of LE CATEAU some of whom had continued to live in cellars after bombardment by the Enemy with Yellow Cross shell in the immediate vicinity.	
	11-11-18 to date		There is nothing of interest to report.	
			Basil R. Bower Capt SGO 18 Div	

D. D. & L., London, E.C.
(A10266) Wt W5300/P713 750,000 2/18 Sch. 52 Forms/C2118/16

www.ingramcontent.com/pod-product-compliance
Lightning Source LLC
Chambersburg PA
CBHW080823010526
44111CB00015B/2600